Taking SIDES

Clashing Views on Controversial Issues in Mass Media and Society

Fifth Edition

Taking SIDES

Clashing Views on Controversial Issues in Mass Media and Society

Fifth Edition

Edited, Selected, and with Introductions by

Alison Alexander
University of Georgia

and

Jarice Hanson
University of Massachusetts–Amherst

Dushkin/McGraw-Hill
A Division of The McGraw-Hill Companies

Photo Acknowledgments

Cover image: © 1999 by PhotoDisc, Inc.

Cover Art Acknowledgment

Charles Vitelli

Library of Congress Cataloging-in-Publication Data

Main entry under title:
 Taking sides: clashing views on controversial issues in mass media and society/edited, selected, and with introductions by Alison Alexander and Jarice Hanson.—5th ed.
 Includes bibliographical references and index.
 1. Mass media. 2. Information services. I. Alexander, Alison, *comp.* II. Hanson, Jarice, *comp.*

302.23

0-697-39143-4

 Printed on Recycled Paper

PREFACE

Comprehension without critical evaluation is impossible.

—Friedrich Hegel (1770–1831)
German philosopher

Mass communication is one of the most popular college majors in the country, which perhaps reflects a belief in the importance of communications systems as well as a desire to work within the communications industry. This book, which contains 36 selections presented in a pro and con format, addresses 18 different controversial issues in mass communications and society. The purpose of this volume, and indeed of any course that deals with the social impact of media, is to create a literate consumer of media—someone who can walk the fine line between a naive acceptance of all media and a cynical disregard for any positive benefits that they may offer.

The media today reflect the evolution of a nation that has increasingly seized on the need and desire for more leisure time. Technological developments have increased our range of choices—from the number of broadcast or cable channels we can select to the publications we can read that cater specifically to our individual interests and needs. New and improving technologies allow us to choose when and where to see a film (through the magic of the VCR), to create our preferred acoustical environment (by stereo, CD, or portable headphones), and to communicate over distances instantly (by means of computers and electronic mail). Because these many forms of media extend our capacities to consume media content, the study of mass media and society is the investigation of some of our most common daily activities. Since many of the issues in this volume are often in the news (or even *are* the news!), you may already have opinions on them. We encourage you to read the selections and discuss the issues with an open mind. Even if you do not initially agree with a position or do not even understand how it is possible to make the opposing argument, give it a try. We believe that thinking seriously about mass media is an important goal.

Plan of the book This book is primarily designed for students in an introductory course in mass communication (sometimes called introduction to mass media or introduction to mass media and society). The issues are such that they can be easily incorporated into any media course regardless of how it is organized—thematically, chronologically, or by medium. The 36 selections have been taken from a variety of sources and were chosen because of their usefulness in defending a position and for their accessibility to students.

Each issue in this volume has an issue *introduction,* which sets the stage for the debate as it is argued in the YES and NO selections. Each issue concludes with a *postscript* that makes some final observations about the selections, points the way to other questions related to the issue, and offers suggestions for further reading on the issue. The introductions and postscripts do not preempt what is the reader's own task: to achieve a critical and informed view of the issues at stake. In reading an issue and forming your own opinion you should not feel confined to adopt one or the other of the positions presented. Some readers may see important points on both sides of an issue and may construct for themselves a new and creative approach. Such an approach might incorporate the best of both sides, or it might provide an entirely new vantage point for understanding. Relevant Internet site addresses (URLs) that may prove useful as starting points for further research are provided on the *On the Internet* page that accompanies each part opener. At the back of the book is a listing of all the *contributors to this volume*, which will give you additional information on the communication scholars, practitioners, policymakers, and media critics whose views are debated here.

Changes to this edition   This fifth edition represents a considerable revision. There are 10 completely new issues: *Do Media Drive Foreign Policy?* (Issue 3); *Is Emphasis on Body Image in the Media Harmful to Females Only?* (Issue 4); *Are Newspapers Insensitive to Minorities?* (Issue 5); *Has Coverage of Political Campaigns Improved?* (Issue 9); *Is Advertising Ethical?* (Issue 10); *Do Paparazzi Threaten Privacy and First Amendment Rights?* (Issue 11); *Should Children Be Protected from Internet Pornography?* (Issue 12); *Are V-Chips and Content Ratings Necessary?* (Issue 13); *Media Monopolies: Does Concentration of Ownership Jeopardize Media Content?* (Issue 14); and *Does the Globalization of Media Industries "Homogenize" Media Content?* (Issue 17). In addition, for Issue 1 (*Are American Values Shaped by the Mass Media?*), Issue 7 (*Should Tobacco Advertising Be Restricted?*), and Issue 8 (*Does Media Coverage of Criminal Trials Undermine the Legal Process?*), the issue question has been retained but one or both selections have been replaced to bring a fresh perspective to the debates. In all, there are 24 new readings.

A word to the instructor   An *Instructor's Manual With Test Questions* (multiple-choice and essay) is available through the publisher for the instructor using *Taking Sides* in the classroom. And a general guidebook, *Using Taking Sides in the Classroom,* which discusses methods and techniques for integrating the pro-con approach into any classroom setting, is also available. An online version of *Using Taking Sides in the Classroom* and a correspondence service for Taking Sides adopters can be found at http://www.dushkin.com/usingts/. For students, we offer a field guide to analyzing argumentative essays, *Analyzing Controversy: An Introductory Guide,* with exercises and techniques to help them to decipher genuine controversies.

Taking Sides: Clashing Views on Controversial Issues in Mass Media and Society is only one title in the Taking Sides series. If you are interested in seeing the table of contents for any of the other titles, please visit the Taking Sides Web site at http://www.dushkin.com/takingsides.

Acknowledgments   We wish to acknowledge the encouragement and support given to this project. We are particularly grateful to David Dean, list manager for the Taking Sides series. We are extremely thankful for the care given to the project by all of the staff at Dushkin/McGraw-Hill, and in particular Rose Gleich, administrative assistant, and David Brackley, senior developmental editor. We would also like to extend our appreciation to the many professors who reviewed our fourth edition, and we are grateful for the advice they have provided in the preparation of this edition. To them, and their students, thank you.

Our thanks go to those who responded with specific suggestions for this edition:

Ty Adams
University of Arkansas–
   Monticello

Charles Aust
Kennesaw State University

Janice Barrett
Boston University

Mike Basil
University of Denver

Barbara Burke
University of Minnesota–
   Morris

Gary D. Christenson
Elgin Community College

Robert Finney
California State University–
   Long Beach

Paul Gates
Appalachian State University

Gloria Hurh
Western Illinois University

Barbara Irwin
Canisius College

Cristine Kahn-Egan
Florida State University

Jin Kim
State University of New York
   at Plattsburgh

Mary Loporcaro
St. John Fisher College

Trevy McDonald
North Carolina Central
   University

Harold Moses
Daytona Beach Community
   College

Carol M. Parker
University of Central
   Oklahoma

Jeff Ritter
La Roche College

William J. Ryan
Rockhurst College

Kathryn Segnar
Temple University

Glenda Treadaway
Appalachian State University

Tommy Thomason
Texas Christian University

We also thank Debra Madigan at the University of Massachusetts and Keisha Hoerrner and Cheryl Christopher at the University of Georgia for their valuable assistance. Finally, we would like to thank our families (David, James, Katie, Jaime, and Torie) for their patience and understanding during the period in which we prepared this book.

Alison Alexander
University of Georgia

Jarice Hanson
University of Massachusetts–Amherst

CONTENTS IN BRIEF

CONTENTS

Professor of media studies Neil Postman argues that television promotes triviality by speaking in only one voice—the voice of entertainment. Thus, he maintains television is transforming American culture into show business, to the detriment of rational public discourse. Author Jon Katz maintains that people have to figure out how to live with contemporary media systems without becoming mediaphobes, or people who are frightened and angry at the speed of information and cultural change and are disposed to blame media. Media, Katz affirms, do not create the world—they offer a picture of it.

Author and children's advocate Marie Winn argues that television has a negative influence on children and their families, and she worries that time spent with television displaces other activities, such as family time, reading, and play. Milton Chen, director of the Center for Education and Lifelong Learning at KQED in San Francisco, California, maintains that many of the popular beliefs about television and children are myths. Rather than scapegoating television, he argues, we should learn how to use it wisely.

Patrick O'Heffernan, a senior fellow at the Center for International Strategy, Technology, and Policy at the Georgia Institute of Technology, argues that television plays an increasingly important role in international diplomacy and war. He maintains that it has become the crisis communication system of international relations and is now firmly established as a player in world politics. Television news and government need and use one another, according to O'Heffernan. Warren P. Strobel, the White House correspondent for the *Washington Times*, explores the reality of the "CNN Effect" and finds it to be less than expected. He agrees that television has made a difference, but he argues that shrinking decision-making time and opening up military operations to public scrutiny is not the same as determining policy.

Marketing professors Mary C. Martin and James W. Gentry address the literature dealing with advertising images and the formation of body identity for preadolescent and adolescent females. They report a study to explore how social comparison theory influences young women. *Washington Monthly* editor Michelle Cottle takes the perspective that females are not the only ones influenced by media image. She cites polls and magazine advertising that indicate that males are exposed to images of idealized body type as well, and she argues that these images also have an impact on the male psyche.

Ruth Shalit, a reporter for *The New Republic*, argues that inaccurate coverage of minority news and the treatment of minority news staff at some places are a form of racism. She focuses on the *Washington Post* as an extreme example of this activity. Executive editor Leonard Downie, Jr., and publisher Donald Graham of the *Washington Post* respond to Shalit's charges. They argue that their newspaper has achieved a higher standard of minority reporting and employment than Shalit claims.

President of NBC News Michael Gartner argues that identifying accusers in rape cases will destroy many of society's wrongly held impressions and stereotypes about the crime of rape. Katha Pollitt, journalist and social critic, argues that the decision to reveal victims' identities without their consent cannot be justified.

Doctor Joseph R. DiFranza and his colleagues report a national study that examines the possibility of children being tempted to smoke because of the tobacco industry's use of images that appeal to and are remembered by children. Because of the profound health risks, DiFranza et al. call for restrictions on tobacco ads. Attorney George J. Annas agrees that the tobacco industry has marketed products to children, but he maintains that efforts to restrict advertising are inappropriate, perhaps even illegal. He argues that some of the restrictions that have been placed on tobacco advertisements violate the First Amendment.

Law professor and defense attorney Barry Scheck argues that information uncovered by the press and disclosed to the public before a trial can upset the fairness of the trial process. He references the gag orders provided before the Timothy McVeigh Oklahoma bombing trial and the role of cameras in the O. J.

Simpson murder trial as integral to the outcome of each trial, and he examines how pretrial publicity forced the defense teams to take different approaches. Attorney Bruce W. Sanford chronicles the history of the free press/fair trial debate and maintains that although the precedents exist to control the role of the press in a trial process, some judges, such as Lance Ito in the O. J. Simpson case, "forget" the rules. However, he agrees with the opinions of Supreme Court justices Warren Burger and William Brennan, Jr., that media coverage is essential to public confidence in the criminal justice system.

Kathleen Hall Jamieson, dean of the Annenberg School of Communications at the University of Pennsylvania, writes that negative campaign ads often distort the platforms of the political candidates in an election. She asserts that recent efforts by media outlets to police advertising truthfulness will lead to a better-informed public. S. Robert Lichter and Richard E. Noyes of the Center for Media and Public Affairs (CMPA) assert that journalists' attempts to police political campaigns have turned them into participants, not observers. They argue that journalists' relentless negativism, paired with a lack of substance in the coverage of campaign issues, has undermined public support for all candidates.

John E. Calfee, a former U.S. Trade Commission economist, takes the position that advertising is very useful to people and that the information that advertising imparts helps consumers make better decisions. He maintains that the benefits of advertising far outweigh the negative criticisms. Author Russ Baker focuses on the way in which advertisers seek to control magazine content and, thus, go beyond persuasion and information into the realm of influencing the content of other media.

Investigative reporter Jacqueline Sharkey argues that public outrage over the death of England's Princess Diana may fuel attempts to legally restrict the actions of paparazzi in order to protect individual privacy. Although such restrictions would almost certainly be deemed unconstitutional, she contends that the larger issue is the public's sense of betrayal and declining support for the First Amendment rights of journalists. Photographer Philip Jones Griffiths illuminates the symbiotic relationship between public personalities and their paparazzi: they feed off each other. But invoking privacy rights in public places, argues Griffiths, only scapegoats photographers, harms working journalists, and allows true invaders of privacy such as multinational corporations to persist.

Philip Elmer-Dewitt, a technical issues writer, discusses a Carnegie-Mellon study indicating that the Internet has pornographic pictures and materials that are easily accessible to anyone. He describes efforts to control access to pornography and identifies how and why the issue is of such concern for parents of young children. Author Julia Wilkins refutes studies that purport to demonstrate children's easy access to Internet pornography, and she maintains that such studies contribute to an unwarranted moral panic about pornography.

Senator Joseph Lieberman (D-Connecticut), coauthor of the Parental Empowerment Act, outlines the history of arrogance and unconcern on the part of network and program executives when faced by parents and policymakers. He argues that this history makes legislation necessary in order to bring about responsible reaction to valid social concerns. Media critic Jon Katz rails against the blindness of those who would control children's viewing but will not tackle the real problems of poverty, the breakdown of family structure, and the culture of helplessness. He maintains that the media are not the cause, just the messenger, and that America's real problems lie elsewhere.

Ben H. Bagdikian, a Pulitzer Prize–winning journalist, contends that only 10 corporations control American mass media, with sobering consequences for control of news and loss of citizen access. He argues that the 1996 Telecommunications Act has fostered even more concentration and has aided companies that are intent upon diversifying into every aspect of the media industries. Professors Eli M. Noam and Robert N. Freeman contend there will be more competition among U.S. media markets, not less. Using U.S. Department of Justice procedures for identifying overly concentrated markets, they demonstrate that media industries are only moderately concentrated and advise that such concern should focus on local, not national, media.

Media commentator Amy Waldman asserts that home shopping channels deliver enormous markets for companies selling products and that the isolating features of the television medium make traditional sales tactics such as promising happiness through goods effective. Professor of marketing Roland T. Rust and professor of management Richard W. Oliver argue that traditional advertising agencies are no longer powerful mediators of products in an environment in which companies find more customized ways to reach their potential audiences.

Ted Becker, a writer who specializes in telecommunication issues and who is interested in the success of teledemocratic systems, asserts that online information and communication systems may be very effective for political purposes. Additionally, greater use of the media for democratic purposes ensures greater interest on the part of citizens and more activism. Christopher Georges, who writes frequently on politics and government, looks specifically at "teledemocracy" as practiced and promoted by Ross Perot. Following Perot's use of the media for creating opportunities for dialogue among citizens, Georges warns that even though the process may be popular, it does not necessarily mean that the best candidates are chosen for the job.

Robert W. McChesney, an associate professor of journalism and mass communication, discusses the wave of mergers and acquisitions among media companies in the 1990s and addresses the way content is modified to be palatable to the widest possible audience. He contends that because many of the corporations controlling the media are international, they also seek to develop content for an international market. Georgette Wang, director of the Graduate Institute of Telecommunications at National Chung Cheng University in Taiwan, acknowledges that communication technologies and international media content have changed the amount of information available to other countries, but she asserts that countries have maintained their own cultural integrity in addition to accepting other media fare.

Psychologist Sherry Turkle argues that an individual's behavior changes when he or she interacts with computer networks. She examines how the anonymity of the Internet changes a user's concept of identity and how individuals separate the cybercommunity of online communication from real life. Author Douglas Rushkoff contends that participants in media-saturated environments have adopted the values and techniques necessary to live in what he calls the "datasphere," or "mediaspace." For Rushkoff, it is not the immediate effects that are important but the long-term impact of more media that has conditioned us to change our attitudes and behaviors.

INTRODUCTION

Ways of Thinking About Mass Media and Society

Alison Alexander
Jarice Hanson

The media are often scapegoats for the problems of society. Sometimes the relationships between social issues and media seem too obvious *not* to have some connection. For example, violence in the media may be a reflection of society, or, as some critics claim, violence in the media makes it seem that violence in society is the norm. But, in reality, one important reason that the media are so often blamed for social problems is that the media are so pervasive. Their very ubiquity makes them seem more influential than they actually are. If one were to look at the statistics on violence in the United States, one would see that there are fewer violent acts performed today than in recent history—but the presence of this violence in the media, through reportage or fictional representation, makes it appear more prevalent.

There are many approaches to investigating the relationships that are suggested by media and society. From an organizational perspective, the producers of media must find content and distribution forms that will be profitable. They therefore have a unique outlook on the audience as consumers. From the perspective of the creative artist, the profit motive may be important, but the exploration of the unique communicative power of the media may be paramount. The audience, too, has different use patterns and desires for information or entertainment, and consumers demonstrate a variety of choices in content offered to them as well as what they take from the media. Whether the media reflect society or shape society has a lot to do with the dynamic interaction of many of these different components.

To complicate matters, the "mass" media have changed in recent years. Not long ago, "mass" media referred to messages that were created by large organizations for broad, heterogeneous audiences. This concept no longer suffices for contemporary media environments. While the "mass" media still exist in the forms of radio, television, film, and general interest newspapers and magazines, many media forms today are hybrids of "mass" and "personal" media technologies that open a new realm of understanding about how audiences process the meaning of the messages. Still, most of the new services and forms of media rely, in part, on the major mass media distribution forms and technologies of television, radio, film, and print. The challenge, then, is to understand how individuals in society use media in a variety of formats and contexts and how they make sense of the messages they take from the content of those media forms.

Historically, almost every form of media in the United States was first subject to some type of regulation by the government or by the media industry itself. This has changed over the years; there is now a virtually unregulated media environment in which the responsibility for the content of media no longer rests with higher authorities. We, as consumers, are asked to be critical of the media that we consume. This requires that we be educated consumers, rather than rely on standards and practices of industry or on government intervention into situations involving questionable content. Although this may not seem like a big problem for most adults, the questions become more difficult when we ask who is responsible for explaining questionable content to children or to individuals who are incapable of distinguishing mediated content from reality.

The average American spends over three hours a day viewing television, which is on in the average home for over seven hours a day. Politics has emerged from smoke-filled rooms and is now played out in the media. A proliferation of television channels has resulted from the popularity of cable, but does cable offer anything different from broadcast television? Videocassettes deliver feature-length films to the home, changing the traditional practices of viewing films in a public place. Online computer systems promise to increase access to the channels of information from home, work, and school.

Communications is now a multibillion-dollar industry and the sixth-fastest-growing industry in America. It is clear that the media have changed American society, but our understanding of how and why remains incomplete.

DYNAMICS OF INTERACTION

Communication media are such integral components of our lives that it is easy to take them for granted. *Mass media* is not just a synonym for print, television, radio, or other electronic technologies. Mass media is a particular and special kind of communication that uses sophisticated secondary techniques to extend communication to situations in which face-to-face contact is impossible; that is, mass media provide indirect (or mediated) means by which the primary process of communication is carried out. In an attempt to understand the nature of the mass communication process, we seek to better comprehend both the nature of communication—such as who creates and sends the message, what is communicated, how, and with what result—and the role of the media as agents in the distribution of special types of messages, such as what changes occur as media "comes between" the sender(s) and the receiver(s) of the messages.

The United States today is rich in media technology. Government statistics report that 97.7 percent of American homes have at least one telephone; 98 percent of the homes have access to at least one television set; and 99.2 percent have at least one radio (although the average home has at least five different radio receivers!). In addition to these forms of media that have traditionally been included in types of "mass" distribution technologies, we can consider as well the growth of cable television and the videocassette recorder (VCR) market. Even satellite dishes, computers, the Internet, and cellular phones are increasing in number and augmenting traditional distribution technologies.

Yet many of the questions about media and society remain the same, whatever technology is used. For example: How do audiences use a medium, and what is its influence? To answer that question, we begin by conceiving of groups of "receivers" or "users" as audiences. Audiences are involved in a dual task: receiving messages and producing meaning. The art of receiving is complex, for audiences as receivers of messages do not always perceive or comprehend messages in the exact way that the senders intend them to be received. Also, the audience *produces* meaning, and understanding the role of media in shaping the social reality of audiences (for example, the meanings they produce) is one of the key questions motivating current media research.

Surprisingly, media analysts cannot even agree on what audiences are like. There are a number of dualities in their thinking about audiences: Audiences may be conceived of as active or as passive; they may be seen as having preconceived ideas or as being totally responsive to the information provided by media. They may be seen as homogeneous or as fragmented; they may be seen as too intellectually limited to see that television could be harmful or to recognize the limitations of the medium in some cases (i.e., fantasy is entertainment) but not in others (i.e., believing that news is fact); or, on the other hand, they may be seen as critical and evaluative and not easily persuaded or influenced. You will see all these different characterizations of what audiences are in this volume.

These conceptions of audience are only part of an attempt to analyze the communication experience. We must also address the unique characteristics of how the medium is used to get a better perspective on the social character of the audience experience. For example, television is primarily a domestic medium. Much of television consumption is in the presence of others and is often discussed with others in an informal setting such as the home. In realizing the special considerations of each medium, the environment in which it is used, and the conditions surrounding it, we can better understand how media consumption is integrated with everyday life.

NOTIONS OF MASS MEDIA AND THE INDIVIDUAL

Throughout the years, research on the relationship between media and society has changed. Early in the history of the study of media, it was believed that messages conveyed by media had tremendous power to influence peoples' attitudes and behavior. Researchers have learned that the results of media exposure to a variety of types of content are far more complex than originally felt. Today, the relationship of audiences to the institutions of media suggest that the individual plays a much larger role in determining the meaning of media content. Society at large—including role models, family structure, and social institutions that the individual experiences—all play mediating roles in influencing how and why the individual will relate to the media message.

Another dominant theme in media research has been the *mass society perspective*. This perspective examines not only the nature of the audience as groups of people but also investigates the production of messages that reflect the interests of the dominant elite and provides what senders believe the mass audience will consume or at least tolerate. The mass society perspective has long held a bleak view of large audiences, which are described as acted upon (reactive rather than active) and heterogeneous (large numbers of different people are in the audience) but becoming increasingly homogeneous (in their susceptibility to persuasion). Because of the power of the producers of media messages, the mass society paradigm was developed to understand better the political and economic implications of media that are created by few for the consumption of many. The saying "People only get what they want" is far too simplistic to address the dimensions of what constitutes media content. Decisions about what will be funded, produced, distributed, and marketed call into play a myriad of factors—from morality to economics. If indeed "people only get what they want," if only this one-dimensional agenda prevailed, then there would be no such phenomena as the flop, the sleeper, or the cult media. The relationship of individuals, society, media industries, and time in history all play a part in the acceptance or rejection of media content.

PROGRESS IN MEDIA RESEARCH

Much of media research has been in search of theory. Theory is an organized, commonsense refinement of everyday thinking; it is an attempt to establish a systematic view of a phenomenon in order to better understand that phenomenon. Theory is tested against reality to establish whether or not it is a good explanation. So, for example, a researcher might notice that what is covered by news outlets is very similar to what citizens say are the important issues of the day. From such observation came agenda setting (the notion that media confers importance on the topics it covers, directing public attention to what is considered important).

Much early media research comes from the impact and effect of print media, because it has been around the longest. The ability of newspapers and books to shape and influence public opinion was regarded as necessary to the founding of new forms of governments—including the U.S. government. But the bias of the medium carried certain restrictions with it. Print media was necessarily limited to those individuals who could read. The relationships of information control and the power of these forms of communication to influence readers contributed to the belief that reporting should be objective and fair and that a multiple number of views should be available.

The principles that emerged from this relationship were addressed in an often-quoted statement attributed to Thomas Jefferson, who wrote, "Were it left to me to decide whether we should have a government without newspapers, or newspapers without a government, I should not hesitate a moment to prefer the latter." But the next sentence in Jefferson's statement is equally as important: "But I should mean that every man should receive those papers and be capable of reading them."

Today media research on the relationships of media senders, the channels of communication, and the receivers of messages is not enough. Consumers must realize that "media literacy" is an important concept. People can no longer take for granted that the media exist primarily to provide news, information, and entertainment. They must be more attuned to what media content says about them as individuals and as members of a society. By integrating these various cultural components, the public can better criticize the regulations or lack of regulation that permits media industries to function the way they do. People must realize that individuals may read media content differently.

The use of social science data to explore the effects of media on audiences strongly emphasized psychological schools of thought. It did not take long to move from the "magic bullet theory"—which proposed that media had a major direct effect on the receivers of the message and that the message intended by the senders was indeed injected into the passive receiver—to theories of limited and indirect effects.

Media research has shifted from addressing specifically effects-oriented paradigms to exploring the nature of the institutions of media production themselves as well as the unique characteristics of each form of media as it contributes to what we know and how we use mediated information. Much of this research has provided knowledge about the multidimensional aspects of media that transcends traditional social and behavioral methodologies.

Applying this knowledge to policy and personal decisions has served to integrate other fields of psychology, sociology, and popular culture with the perspectives provided by communication studies.

Other levels of analysis have focused on individual, family, group, social, cultural, and societal interpretations of frames of meaning, as well as economically and structurally derived positions of power, held or exercised by specific individuals within social frameworks. These concepts of power have become increasingly important as media have become more pervasive throughout the world and various societies have experienced inequities in technologies, resources, and production skills.

Today researchers question the notions of past theories and models as well as definitions of *mass* and *society* and now place much of the emphasis of media dynamics in the perspective of global information exchange. A major controversy erupted in the early 1970s when many Third World countries disagreed with principles that sought to reify the industrialized nations' media. The New World Information Order perspective advanced the importance of media in carrying out developmental tasks within nations that have not had the economic and social benefits of industrialized countries, and it noted that emerging nations had different priorities that reflected indigenous cultures, which would sometimes be at odds with Western notions of a free press. The Third World countries' concerns dealt with power as imposed upon a nation from outside, using media as a vehicle for cultural dependency and imperialism.

Today society must also concern itself with the growing numbers of communication channels that have come about through changes in the ways various industries operate. Cable and telephone may well be viewed as the primary means of wired systems of communication. Digital broadcasting and digital information transfer may create yet other hybrids in technological systems and services. The information superhighway has the potential to alter radically the former media industries and the way individuals seek and use media and information.

QUESTIONS FOR CONSIDERATION

In addressing the issues in this book, it is important to consider some recurring questions:

1. Are the media unifying or fragmenting? Does media content help the socialization process, or does it create anxiety or inaccurate portrayals of the world? Do people feel powerless because they have little ability to shape the messages of media?
2. Are the media a unique force for social change, or do they primarily react to social forces? Do the media merely convey information about what other social issues are important? Do the owners and controllers of these messages act in the public interest or do they have other motives? Are audiences primarily reactive to media content or do they psychologically work toward integrating media messages with their own experiences?
3. Whose interests do the media represent? How important is it for the media industries to work for profits, and does this limit the types of content they are willing to produce or the types of audiences they serve?

SUMMARY

We live in a media-rich environment where almost everybody has access to some form of media and some choices in content. As new technologies and services are developed, are they responding to the problems that previous media researchers and the public have detected? Over time, individuals have improved their ability to unravel the complex set of interactions that ties the media and society together, but they need to continue to question past results, new practices and technologies, and their own evaluative measures. When people critically examine the world around them—a world often presented by the media—they can more fully understand and enjoy the way they relate, as individuals, as members of groups, and as members of a society.

On the Internet . . .

http://www.dushkin.com

The Center for Media Education

The Center for Media Education (CME) is a national, non-profit organization dedicated to improving the quality of electronic media, especially on the behalf of children and families. This site discusses such topics as the effect of television violence, online advertising, media images, and new technologies. *http://www.cme.org/*

Communication Studies: General Communication Resources

An encyclopedic resource related to a host of mass communication issues, this site is maintained by the University of Iowa's Department of Communication Studies. It provides excellent links covering advertising, cultural studies, digital media, film, gender issues, and media studies *http://www.uiowa.edu/~commstud/resources/general.html*

Images

Images is a quarterly online journal that publishes articles about a broad range of popular culture artifacts and issues, including movies, television, videos, and other popular visual arts.
http://www.imagesjournal.com/index.html

National Coalition on Television Violence

The National Coalition on Television Violence addresses the issues surrounding what can be done to improve the quality of television, especially for children.
http://www.nctvv.org/

Writers Guild of America

The Writer's Guild of America is the union for media entertainment writers. The nonmember areas of this site offer useful information for aspiring writers. There is also an excellent links section. *http://www.wga.org/*

PART 1

Mass Media's Role in Society

How powerful are the media? Do media merely reflect the social attitudes and concerns of our times, or are they also able to construct, legitimate, and reinforce the social realities, behaviors, attitudes, and images of others? The ways media help us to shape a sense of reality are complex. Should concern be directed toward vulnerable populations such as children? If we truly have a variety of information sources and content to choose from, perhaps we can assume that distorted images are balanced with realistic ones and that common sense prevails. But is this truly the media scenario in which we live? The number of channels received through cable television may seem like many, but is the content really different from channel to channel? How media influences the macrosocial environment cannot be ignored. Is our political and social environment as influenced as our personal and interpersonal one? Questions about the place of media within our technologically reliant society—both as a place for displaying our culture and as a force for cultural change—cannot be ignored.

■ Are American Values Shaped by the Mass Media?

■ Is Television Harmful for Children?

■ Do Media Drive Foreign Policy?

■ Is Emphasis on Body Image in the Media Harmful to Females Only?

■ Are Newspapers Insensitive to Minorities?

ISSUE 1

Are American Values Shaped by the Mass Media?

YES: Neil Postman, from *Amusing Ourselves to Death* (Viking Penguin, 1985)

NO: Jon Katz, from *Virtuous Reality* (Random House, 1997)

ISSUE SUMMARY

YES: Professor of media studies Neil Postman argues that television promotes triviality by speaking in only one voice—the voice of entertainment. Thus, he maintains television is transforming American culture into show business, to the detriment of rational public discourse.

NO: Author Jon Katz maintains that people have to figure out how to live with contemporary media systems without becoming mediaphobes, or people who are frightened and angry at the speed of information and cultural change and are disposed to blame media. Media, Katz affirms, do not create the world —they offer a picture of it.

Can the media fundamentally reshape a culture? Americans are now part of a culture in which information and ideas are disseminated predominantly by television, not by print. This shift from print to electronic media has dramatically and irreversibly altered the content and meaning of public discourse, according to Neil Postman and Jon Katz. Postman, however, strongly believes that the epistemology (the way of knowing) created by television is inferior to that of print for truth telling and rational public discourse. He is not alone in his concern that electronic media are negatively reshaping culture in the United States. Others argue that popular culture is not culture at all and that mass-produced popular culture is destroying the individuality of folk and high arts. Some suggest that the power of the media to shape attitude and opinions, paired with the power of media organizations to craft messages, will inevitably result in homogeneity. This homogenization is the logical consequence of a socialization process whereby values are assaulted year in and year out with consistent and limited messages. These are the conclusions of many who find the benefits of television to be overwhelmed by its attendant perils.

Others, Katz among them, disagree with this view and instead see the individual as a resilient and active respondent in the face of a barrage of media messages who is quite capable of deciphering them. Entertainment can be just that—mere entertainment—depending on what the viewer brings to it; people are not affected uniformly. The individual is complex: an active participant in a culture with a whole host of socializing influences, such as family, school, religious affiliation, and peers. To single out the influence of television in the shaping of the individual may therefore be more difficult than at first it would appear.

The media are so pervasive that it is hard to believe they do not have important effects. Alternatively, many people do not believe that the media have personally influenced them to buy products or have harmed them, nor do they believe that the media hold a place of "prime importance" in shaping their lives. In everyday experience, many people do not consider the media as having an observable impact on them or on those around them. However, to attempt to understand how the media may shape the attitudes of individuals and of society, and how they may shape culture itself, requires that the reader stand back from his or her personal experiences in order to analyze the arguments presented on each side of this debate.

In the following selection, Postman argues that Americans are "amusing [them]selves to death." Americans have become literate in the forms and features of television systems. Because the medium of television has become the dominant factor in the creation of social images, what we know and how we know it comes out of television, rather than print, literacy. The consequences of becoming a show business culture, according to Postman, are dire.

In the second selection, Katz contends that there is an inherent contradiction in American's reaction to media: Americans are avid consumers of television, music, film, and World Wide Web sites who are convinced that this same media is endangering youth and undermining civic and civil discourse. Fears for society are understandable, says Katz, but concern should be focused on problems rather than misdirected to media scapegoats. He concludes that people must take more responsibility for the ethical and moral value systems of their homes and of society in the information age.

YES   Neil Postman

THE AGE OF SHOW BUSINESS

A dedicated graduate student I know returned to his small apartment the night before a major examination only to discover that his solitary lamp was broken beyond repair. After a whiff of panic, he was able to restore both his equanimity and his chances for a satisfactory grade by turning on the television set, turning off the sound, and with his back to the set, using its light to read important passages on which he was to be tested. This is one use of television—as a source of illuminating the printed page....

I bring forward [this] quixotic [use] of television to ridicule the hope harbored by some that television can be used to support the literate tradition. Such a hope represents exactly what Marshall McLuhan used to call "rearview mirror" thinking: the assumption that a new medium is merely an extension or amplification of an older one; that an automobile, for example, is only a fast horse, or an electric light a powerful candle. To make such a mistake in the matter at hand is to misconstrue entirely how television redefines the meaning of public discourse. Television does not extend or amplify literate culture. It attacks it. If television is a continuation of anything, it is of a tradition begun by the telegraph and photograph in the mid-nineteenth century, not by the printing press in the fifteenth.

What is television? What kinds of conversations does it permit? What are the intellectual tendencies it encourages? What sort of culture does it produce?

These are the questions, ... and to approach them with a minimum of confusion, I must begin by making a distinction between a technology and a medium. We might say that a technology is to a medium as the brain is to the mind. Like the brain, a technology is a physical apparatus. Like the mind, a medium is a use to which a physical apparatus is put. A technology becomes a medium as it employs a particular symbolic code, as it finds its place in a particular social setting, as it insinuates itself into economic and political contexts. A technology, in other words, is merely a machine. A medium is the social and intellectual environment a machine creates.

Of course, like the brain itself, every technology has an inherent bias. It has within its physical form a predisposition toward being used in certain ways and not others. Only those who know nothing of the history of technology

From Neil Postman, *Amusing Ourselves to Death* (Viking Penguin, 1985). Copyright © 1985 by Neil Postman. Reprinted by permission of Viking Penguin, a division of Penguin Putnam, Inc. Notes omitted.

believe that a technology is entirely neutral. There is an old joke that mocks that naive belief. Thomas Edison, it goes, would have revealed his discovery of the electric light much sooner than he did except for the fact that every time he turned it on, he held it to his mouth and said, "Hello? Hello?"

Not very likely. Each technology has an agenda of its own. It is, as I have suggested, a metaphor waiting to unfold. The printing press, for example, had a clear bias toward being used as a linguistic medium. It is *conceivable* to use it exclusively for the reproduction of pictures. And, one imagines, the Roman Catholic Church would not have objected to its being so used in the sixteenth century. Had that been the case, the Protestant Reformation might not have occurred, for as Luther contended, with the word of God on every family's kitchen table, Christians do not require the Papacy to interpret it for them. But in fact there never was much chance that the press would be used solely, or even very much, for the duplication of icons. From its beginning in the fifteenth century, the press was perceived as an extraordinary opportunity for the display and mass distribution of written language. Everything about its technical possibilities led in that direction. One might even say it was invented for that purpose.

The technology of television has a bias, as well. It is conceivable to use television as a lamp, a surface for texts, a bookcase, even as radio. But it has not been so used and will not be so used, at least in America. Thus, in answering the question, What is television?, we must understand as a first point that we are not talking about television as a technology but television as a medium.

There are many places in the world where television, though the same technology as it is in America, is an entirely different medium from that which we know. I refer to places where the majority of people do not have television sets, and those who do have only one; where only one station is available; where television does not operate around the clock; where most programs have as their purpose the direct furtherance of government ideology and policy; where commercials are unknown, and "talking heads" are the principal image; where television is mostly used as if it were radio. For these reasons and more television will not have the same meaning or power as it does in America, which is to say, it is possible for a technology to be so used that its potentialities are prevented from developing and its social consequences kept to a minimum.

But in America, this has not been the case. Television has found in liberal democracy and a relatively free market economy a nurturing climate in which its full potentialities as a technology of images could be exploited. One result of this has been that American television programs are in demand all over the world. The total estimate of U.S. television program exports is approximately 100,000 to 200,000 hours, equally divided among Latin America, Asia and Europe. Over the years, programs like "Gunsmoke," "Bonanza," "Mission: Impossible," "Star Trek," "Kojak," and more recently, "Dallas" and "Dynasty" have been as popular in England, Japan, Israel and Norway as in Omaha, Nebraska. I have heard (but not verified) that some years ago the Lapps postponed for several days their annual and, one supposes, essential migratory journey so that they could find out who shot J.R. All of this has occurred simultaneously with the decline of America's moral and political prestige, worldwide. American television programs are in demand not because America is loved but because American television is loved.

We need not be detained too long in figuring out why. In watching American television, one is reminded of George Bernard Shaw's remark on his first seeing the glittering neon signs of Broadway and 42nd Street at night. It must be beautiful, he said, if you cannot read. American television is, indeed, a beautiful spectacle, a visual delight, pouring forth thousands of images on any given day. The average length of a shot on network television is only 3.5 seconds, so that the eye never rests, always has something new to see. Moreover, television offers viewers a variety of subject matter, requires minimal skills to comprehend it, and is largely aimed at emotional gratification. Even commercials, which some regard as an annoyance, are exquisitely crafted, always pleasing to the eye and accompanied by exciting music. There is no question but that the best photography in the world is presently seen on television commercials. American television, in other words, is devoted entirely to supplying its audience with entertainment.

Of course, to say that television is entertaining is merely banal. Such a fact is hardly threatening to a culture, not even worth writing a book about. It may even be a reason for rejoicing. Life, as we like to say, is not a highway strewn with flowers. The sight of a few blossoms here and there may make our journey a trifle more endurable. The Lapps undoubtedly thought so. We may surmise that the ninety million Americans who watch television every night also think so. But what I am claiming here is not that television

is entertaining but that it has made entertainment itself the natural format for the representation of all experience. Our television set keeps us in constant communion with the world, but it does so with a face whose smiling countenance is unalterable. The problem is not that television presents us with entertaining subject matter but that all subject matter is presented as entertaining, which is another issue altogether.

To say it still another way: Entertainment is the supra-ideology of all discourse on television. No matter what is depicted or from what point of view, the overarching presumption is that it is there for our amusement and pleasure. That is why even on news shows which provide us daily with fragments of tragedy and barbarism, we are urged by the newscasters to "join them tomorrow." What for? One would think that several minutes of murder and mayhem would suffice as material for a month of sleepless nights. We accept the newscasters' invitation because we know that the "news" is not to be taken seriously, that it is all in fun, so to say. Everything about a news show tells us this—the good looks and amiability of the cast, their pleasant banter, the exciting music that opens and closes the show, the vivid film footage, the attractive commercials—all these and more suggest that what we have just seen is no cause for weeping. A news show, to put it plainly, is a format for entertainment, not for education, reflection or catharsis. And we must not judge too harshly those who have framed it in this way. They are not assembling the news to be read, or broadcasting it to be heard. They are televising the news to be seen. They must follow where their medium leads. There is no conspiracy here, no lack of intelligence, only a straightforward recognition that "good television" has little to do with what is "good" about exposition or other forms of verbal communication but everything to do with what the pictorial images look like.

... When a television show is in process, it is very nearly impermissible to say, "Let me think about that" or "I don't know" or "What do you mean when you say . . . ?" or "From what sources does your information come?" This type of discourse not only slows down the tempo of the show but creates the impression of uncertainty or lack of finish. It tends to reveal people in the *act of thinking*, which is as disconcerting and boring on television as it is on a Las Vegas stage. Thinking does not play well on television, a fact that television directors discovered long ago. There is not much to *see* in it. It is, in a phrase, not a performing art. . . .

I do not say categorically that it is impossible to use television as a carrier of coherent language or thought in process. William Buckley's own program, "Firing Line," occasionally shows people in the act of thinking but who also happen to have television cameras pointed at them. There are other programs, such as "Meet the Press" or "The Open Mind," which clearly strive to maintain a sense of intellectual decorum and typographic tradition, but they are scheduled so that they do not compete with programs of great visual interest, since otherwise, they will not be watched. After all, it is not unheard of that a format will occasionally go against the bias of its medium. For example, the most popular radio program of the early 1940's featured a ventriloquist, and in those days, I heard more than once the feet of a tap dancer on the "Major Bowes' Amateur Hour." (Indeed, if I am not mistaken, he even once featured a pantomimist.)

But ventriloquism, dancing and mime do not play well on radio, just as sustained, complex talk does not play well on television. It can be made to play tolerably well if only one camera is used and the visual image is kept constant— as when the President gives a speech. But this is not television at its best, and it is not television that most people will choose to watch. The single most important fact about television is that people *watch* it, which is why it is called "tele*vision*." And what they watch, and like to watch, are moving pictures—millions of them, of short duration and dynamic variety. It is in the nature of the medium that it must suppress the content of ideas in order to accommodate the requirements of visual interest; that is to say, to accommodate the values of show business.

Film, records and radio (now that it is an adjunct of the music industry) are, of course, equally devoted to entertaining the culture, and their effects in altering the style of American discourse are not insignificant. But television is different because it encompasses all forms of discourse. No one goes to a movie to find out about government policy or the latest scientific advances. No one buys a record to find out the baseball scores or the weather or the latest murder. No one turns on radio anymore for soap operas or a presidential address (if a television set is at hand). But everyone goes to television for all these things and more, which is why television resonates so powerfully throughout the culture. Television is our culture's principal mode of knowing about itself. Therefore—and this is the critical point—how television stages the world becomes the model for how the world is properly to be staged. It is not merely that on the television screen entertainment is the metaphor for all discourse. It is that off the screen the same metaphor prevails. As typography once dictated the style of conducting politics, religion, business, education, law and other important social matters, television now takes command. In courtrooms, classrooms, operating rooms, board rooms, churches and even airplanes, Americans no longer talk to each other, they entertain each other. They do not exchange ideas; they exchange images. They do not argue with propositions; they argue with good looks, celebrities and commercials. For the message of television as metaphor is not only that all the world is a stage but that the stage is located in Las Vegas, Nevada....

Prior to the 1984 presidential elections, the two candidates [Ronald Reagan and Walter Mondale] confronted each other on television in what were called "debates." These events were not in the least like the Lincoln-Douglas debates or anything else that goes by the name. Each candidate was given five minutes to address such questions as, What is (or would be) your policy in Central America? His opposite number was then given one minute for a rebuttal. In such circumstances, complexity, documentation and logic can play no role, and, indeed, on several occasions syntax itself was abandoned entirely. It is no matter. The men were less concerned with giving arguments than with "giving off" impressions, which is what television does best. Post-debate commentary largely avoided any evaluation of the candidates' ideas, since there were none to evaluate. Instead, the debates were conceived as boxing matches, the relevant question being, Who KO'd whom? The answer was determined by the "style" of the men—how they looked, fixed their gaze, smiled, and delivered one-liners. In the second debate, President Reagan got off a swell one-liner when asked a question about his age. The following day, several newspapers indicated that Ron had KO'd Fritz with his joke. Thus, the leader of the free world is chosen by the people in the Age of Television.

What all of this means is that our culture has moved toward a new way of conducting its business, especially its important business. The nature of its discourse is changing as the demarcation line between what is show business and what is not becomes harder to see with each passing day. Our priests and presidents, our surgeons and lawyers, our educators and newscasters need worry less about satisfying the demands of their discipline than the demands of good showmanship. Had Irving Berlin changed one word in the title of his celebrated song, he would have been as prophetic, albeit more terse, as Aldous Huxley. He need only have written, There's No Business But Show Business.

NO   Jon Katz

VIRTUOUS REALITY

INTRODUCTION

New York Times columnist Bob Herbert was troubled. He'd encountered a poll showing that 60 percent of young Americans were unable to name the president who ordered the nuclear attack on Japan, and that 35 percent didn't know that the first A-bomb was dropped on the Japanese city of Hiroshima. Writing in the familiarly schoolmarmish voice that serious newspapers and broadcasters prefer, Herbert fumed that America has become "a nation of nitwits."

In a different context, insulting and stereotyping an entire country might have provoked outrage. But given current attitudes about media and culture, the idea that we are too stupid to make the "correct" informational choices isn't even controversial. Young people, in particular, are routinely portrayed as ignorant, unacquainted with the basic elements of civilization, unlikely to become good capitalists in the global economy, ill prepared to survive in the adult world. The idea is so often repeated by the news media that it's become a widely accepted article of faith, a central tenet of modern journalism: We represent a superior culture; you'll be sorry for abandoning us. Left to your own devices, you'll read and watch moronic and pointless things and your children will go straight to screen hell.

Intimations of these conflicts go all the way back to the turn of the century, but the start of our cultural civil wars probably dates to 1954, when Dr. Fredric Wertham, a respected psychiatrist, told a congressional committee headed by crime-buster Estes Kefauver that comic books were a major cause of juvenile delinquency, violent crime and deviant sexuality. Wonder Woman promoted lesbianism, warned Wertham, and the relationship between Batman and Robin had "homosexual" overtones. Much worse was just around the corner, had the good doctor but known—the advent of Elvis was mere months away.

A few decades later, we all know the litany: Nobody cares about "real" news anymore. Our standards of literacy, culture and taste have declined past the point of recognition. The tabloids are taking us to hell in an electronic handbasket, obsessed as they are with trashy stories like O.J., Amy Fisher and the Menendez brothers. Our children are mentally deficient, vulnerable to a host of predators lurking out there.

"We are surrounded by a deep and abiding stupidity," Herbert wrote in his op-ed column. . . .

The different ways in which information now travels seem to be sending much of the country into a kind of cultural nervous breakdown. Americans have an extraordinary love-hate relationship with the rich culture they've created. They buy, watch and read it even as they ban, block and condemn it.

That censorship almost never prevails against the new cultural forms it's designed to protect us from seems to escape our collective memory. Take the baby boomers who embraced rock and roll, protested the Vietnam War and led the rebellions of the sixties. Now parents themselves—and on edge after years of media warnings about crib death, child snatching, Lyme disease, sexual molestation and other perils, both real and inflated—they're in a near panic about their children's safety. New forms of media are not exciting opportunities to be explored but simply additional dangers to be added to the list.

It seems they were only kidding about the Revolution. On the whole, they are at least as reflexively disapproving as their own parents were, joining forces with William Bennett and other self-serving blockheads to fuss about how tacky and dangerous popular culture is, clucking endlessly about Bart Simpson and *Melrose Place*.

With the vocal support of consummate boomer Bill Clinton, Congress came up with the now notorious Communications Decency Act (CDA), which was quickly and resoundingly overturned by the federal courts, and a technological fix—the "V" (for "violence") computer chip, to be installed in all American television sets so that parents can block programs they don't want children to see. If parents think programming VCRs is tricky, wait till they set out to program control of the hundreds of thousands of hours of TV programming that now beam into households on schedules that vary weekly. The country's biggest provider of online computer services, America Online, has announced "blocking" software to "empower parents" to control what their children see via the Internet. A number of other high tech firms are marketing software to limit kids' Internet access.

"Americans Despair of Popular Culture," reported a *New York Times* headline in 1995. A survey commissioned by the paper found that far more Americans—21 percent—cited TV as the primary cause of teenage violence than blamed any other factor, including inadequate education, deteriorating family structures or drugs.

Meanwhile, *Time* magazine was publishing the results of a bitterly controversial survey on Internet pornography. *Time*'s cover showed a wild-eyed, terrified child over a "Cyberporn" headline: "A New Study Shows How Pervasive and Wild It Really Is. Can We Protect Our Kids and Free Speech?" The number of broadcasts, articles and books decrying the dangers of new technology and new media must by now be well into the tens of thousands.

The 1990s are the decade of the Mediaphobe.

The Mediaphobe is frightened and angry. His fear transcends traditional social, cultural and political boundaries. You almost have to admire the unity fear can generate: Civil rights activists join forces with right-wing politicians; ex-hippies take up arms alongside Christian evangelists; a liberal boomer president stands shoulder to shoulder with his conservative challengers. A nation bitterly divided on an array of issues from gun control to Medicaid can unite on this: New media, popular culture, modern information technology—all of it endangers our young, corrodes our civic sphere, decivilizes us all. The Mediaphobe defines media narrowly. News comes from a thick, sober daily newspaper, read front to back. Or from an evening newscast, with stories presented in order of descending importance. News does not come from *Inside Edition*, Larry King, Ricki Lake or Snoop Doggy Dogg. MTV News doesn't count. Nor does anything on a computer screen.

Yet for all the clucking by the traditional media, Americans both love and embrace the new cultural machinery. VCRs, computers and CD-ROMs are among the best-selling consumer products in American history, approaching portable phones and microwave ovens as ubiquitous fixtures of middle-class life. The computer culture has swiftly metamorphosed from a fringe countercultural movement little known outside its own techie borders to a mainstream information source used by millions of people, inhabited by the elderly, the pet-loving, the religious and the young, as well as nerds, webheads and some of the world's largest corporations.

Notice the apparent contradiction.

Mediaphobia is exactly what it sounds like—not concern about real problems but an anxiety disorder, an increasingly irrational spiral of often unwarranted fears.

… We need more rational ways of comprehending all these changes and figuring out how to feel about them.

This cultural conflict, the endless nyaaah-nyaaahing about old versus new media, is pointless. Old and new media, perpetually at war, have a kind of reflexive arrogance in common: Each camp sees itself as superior to the other.

There is, of course, no good reason for us to have to choose between old and new media. Both are valid and useful in their way, and neither alternative is going to go away. The emergence of new media and broader definitions of culture doesn't mean that newspapers, book publishing or traditional TV newscasts will or should vanish. But we *are* groping for some sort of coherent response to all of the confusing signals we are, sometimes literally, receiving.…

Reader, beware: I do not believe that media are responsible for violence or the degradation of our culture. I think our culture is diverse and exciting, sometimes brilliant and creative and sometimes adolescent and vulgar. We need to get past these simpleminded cultural characterizations of good and evil.

Though I'm excited by lots of these changes, new media are not a religion for me. They don't reflect a superior civilization, but they do bring us some powerful new political and social ideas, a few bordering on the truly revolutionary. They are a new way to communicate and to create relationships and communities. There are good and bad aspects to all this, possibilities that are extraordinary and liberating and others that are discordant, exclusive, invasive and confusing. A further caveat: I do not believe we are becoming a nation of nitwits, or that our children are in any sense dumber than we were.

The ones I know and meet and e-mail every day are plenty smart, very sophisticated about exploring and manipulating complex machinery, and generally more tolerant, curious and open-minded than their parents. The digital revolution was sparked by, and is still led by, the young, for many of whom it is an integral part of their lives. They are never going to give it up. Accusing them of stupidity and obliviousness says more about us than about them. We, not they, will have to change.

Journalism's long war against the culture of the young has proven destructive for both parties. Decades of attacks on comics, rock, rap, TV, cartoons, computers and video games have left traditional journalism with virtually no young readers or viewers. It's too bad that kids can't benefit from the useful things journalism offers—not only information but analysis, context, criticism. Meanwhile, the press is committing slow suicide, alienating its future, then scratching its head at its dismal demographics.

... It's time for a truce in the media wars. We're simply going to have to live with the fact that we have more information, delivered more rapidly in more diverse forms, than any of us ever imagined, and we're going to have to figure out how to handle it.

Beware, therefore, of windbags and pious souls who presume to know what is moral for you and your family. Stop paying so much attention to the cultural alarmists popping up on talk shows and newspaper op-ed pages. Stay calm. Take a deep breath. This stuff is neither as confusing nor as dangerous as it appears.

Included herein at no extra charge: a media mantra to be recited before your bathroom mirror every morning; to invoke whenever you're horrified by a TV talk-show topic, whenever you're battling with your kids about their latest vitriolic CD or some dopey show on MTV, whenever someone tries to tell you your children are stupider than you were at their age, whenever William Bennet opens his mouth.

The Media Mantra

It's not that complicated. I can figure this out. I can make my own decisions about media, values and morality. I don't have to choose between traditional culture and the new media. I can live a happy and fulfilling life even if I never see the World Wide Web.

Whatever they should or shouldn't watch, however much time they spend online, my children are not dumb and they're not in danger from movies, TV shows, music or computers. Many children—especially underclass children—really are suffering from horrific violence, and they need more and better parenting, better schools, fewer guns and drugs and lots of job opportunities. If I'm so worried about kids, I will help them. If I really want to protect my own children, I will make sure they have more, not less, access to this new cultural and technological world. I won't ever call them stupid for watching things I don't like. I don't have to be at war with them. I can work out a social contract with my children that protects them, guides them through their new culture and brings peace and rationality to our house.

Amen....

ENTER THE MEDIAPHOBE—STAGE RIGHT AND STAGE LEFT

The Mediaphobe is everywhere: in Congress, on campus, at the pediatrician's office and the supermarket checkout counter. Wherever parents gather to watch their kids play soccer or to hold

PTA meetings, there dwells the Mediaphobe.

He's had a couple of great years lately, perhaps his strongest since the early denunciations of rock and roll. He persuaded Congress to pass a law banning indecency on the Internet (promptly overturned) and mandating the V-chip. He got a number of movies and TV shows blamed for acts of copycat violence. He forced a big media conglomerate to sell off its gangsta rap music division. He is responsible for a presidential candidate's fulminations against Hollywood. He pressured advertisers to boycott trashy TV talk shows.

But the mediaphobes are hoping for more. They're still anxious and outraged, still clucking over violent cartoons, rolling their eyes over provocative lyrics and graphic videos. You can hear them swapping their horror stories and survival stratagems: She doesn't read anymore. He ought to be doing his homework first. I won't let them watch all that junk; they just turn into zombies. My phone bill is going through the roof. How do you know what they're doing up there? They could be talking to anybody.

Living rooms, cineplexes and kids' bedrooms have become cultural battlegrounds. Turn off the TV. Get off the computer. We're going to block MTV, drop AOL, cancel the cable.

America Online, more and more aping the behavior of the traditional media organizations it once tried to supplant, proudly announced new blocking software to make it simpler to control the young online as well. Parents can put off-limits any content they fear, disagree with, feel vaguely uncomfortable about. Call it cultural sanitizing. "Parents will be able to block all but Kids Only, the area of the service with content targeted and pro-

grammed specifically for children," an AOL press release proclaimed. The idea, it said, was to "empower parents with the appropriate tools" to restrict access.

Other software manufacturers are developing even more sophisticated software to permit parents to block any Internet topic, discussion or file containing words, language or subjects the parents find offensive.

The Mediaphobe was surely happy to hear the good news about blocking software. Such mechanisms are generally unnecessary and, given the technical skills and ingenuity of the young, highly unlikely to work for very long—but so what? Increasingly flummoxed by all the choices facing his offspring, the Mediaphobe wants to ban more and more things these days. He feels the ground shifting, his fixed points collapsing. Newspapers are in trouble, network TV news has been marginalized, the Washington pundits grow increasingly useless.

The Mediaphobe frequently couches his panic in terms of dangers to others, particularly children. But he's really afraid for himself, of what he doesn't know or is too lazy or intimidated to learn, of the scary new world on the other side of the screen.

No Wonder

You can't blame the Mediaphobe for being afraid. Many of his political representatives and his media outlets are telling him he should be. In its "Cyberporn" cover story published in June 1995, *Time* magazine suggested the Internet was swarming with pornographers and peddlers of bestiality. The FBI raided alleged child pornographers across the country in a sting operation set up via America Online. Senator James

Exon—with the help of Gary Hart's ex-mistress Donna Rice Hughes—pushed a noxious bill through Congress prohibiting "lewd, lascivious, filthy or indecent" imagery in cyberspace. Meanwhile, the press reported that bomb-making tips and hate literature were also being downloaded by teenaged psychotics. Writing in *Newsweek*, an American University professor of literature even predicted the death of the apostrophe, "because reading is dead." Professor Charles R. Larson continued, "Soon, no one will be certain about grammatical usage anyway. Computers will come without an apostrophe key. Why bother about errors on the Internet?"

Books warned that computers were unleashing a whole host of evils. Social historian Kirkpatrick Sale wrote, in *Rebels Against the Future*, that technology was destroying the planet. Technophobe Jeremy Rifkin argued, in *The End of Work*, that within the coming century, technology will render all workers superfluous. Movies like *The Net* and *Virtuosity* suggest a new technoworld that invades our privacy, destroys our freedom or just plain slaughters us. Our country's media and civic intellectuals are in vocal despair.

In fact, new media practitioners *are* often hostile to enormous concentrations of power in few hands. They *do* have little use for conventions like objectivity. They like being able to express their opinions as well as read columnists' and editorialists'.

These enormous differences in values are, as William Kovach of the Nieman Foundation suggests, at the heart of the tension between the new and old information cultures. They help explain why the relentlessly hostile and alarmist coverage of the new information culture and technologies has given rise to epidemic mediaphobia.

Strange Bedfell—Uh—Strange Allies

It's practically an American tradition for certain members of the clergy and community leaders to be at odds with free speech and freewheeling culture, denouncing prostitution, pornography, liquor and tobacco, even forms of singing and dancing.

But mediaphobia is no longer limited to the religious right or to your run-of-the-mill concerned clergy. Nor is it limited to political conservatives, like Bennett and Dole, who use the issue to sell fat hardcovers or rally voter support.

The mediaphobes have assembled a remarkably diverse coalition. To the mix of religious and cultural conservatives have been added the once-rebellious boomers, the children of the sixties whose plunge into parenting has pushed them into the culture wars. Affluent, educated boomers are astonishingly fearful parents. Taking cues—and much of their information—from lazy news media, they have adopted the serious social problems that are far more likely to threaten the poor—crime, AIDS, cripplingly bad education—and transferred their anxiety about them to their own children, who are continually warned about everything from sex to strangers.

These groups agree on little except how dangerous new media are: they share a common desire for ways to control or discourage them. A *New York Times* columnist is as likely to decry new media and culture as a fundamentalist minister; a boomer parent takes the same cultural point of view as censor-happy blockheads like Charlton Heston; a feminist academic may attack music videos as happily as a right-wing Republican.

In Berkeley, a group of college students gathered to kick and smash television sets as an act of "therapy for the victims of technology."

The astonishing breadth of concern suggests that a deeper chord has been touched than worry over violence or explicit sexual imagery can explain. What's at stake appears to be something more basic: the sense that we are in command of our children and our immediate worlds. Mediaphobes mostly fear that they are losing control. And they're probably right.

They seem to think that rather than learning and teaching about the new world, they can stave it off by branding it satanic, sort of like desperately holding up a sprig of wolfsbane—or a V-chip—against a vampire. As anybody who goes to the movies knows, the monster is only briefly deterred; he is too powerful to be so easily vanquished.

Mediaphobes are afraid, though they can't say precisely what they're afraid of. They are quick to denounce censorship but quicker to censor. They pride themselves on their open-mindedness but seem terrified of new ideas and change. They want their children to thrive in the larger world but block access to the very tools and culture they'll need to learn about in order to do that. They either don't know or have forgotten that emerging culture has always seemed dangerous to the entrenched.

The Mediaphobe rarely manages to block the right thing. Instead of getting rid of the guns that kill people, he tries to bump off the cartoons and rap records that don't. Instead of altering the circumstances that generate violence, he wants a V-chip in his TV so he doesn't have to see pictures of it anymore.

History is full of people with similar impulses. If the past tells us anything, it's that the curious and the innovative ultimately prevail. Put your money on the kids. . . .

THE SENSIBLE PERSON

Politicians have been exploiting fears about culture forever. Senator Estes Kefauver did it in the fifties by holding hearings on Wonder Woman and Batman and Robin, a move that led to a self-censoring code adopted by the comics industry. Dan Quayle took on single mother Murphy Brown. Pat Buchanan caws constantly about "the cultural war going on for the soul of the country." Bob Dole tried to make cultural values the heart of his presidential campaign. Newspaper columnists and editorial writers have joined in. Boomer parents, desperate to create brilliant, competitive, "cultured" children, reject many other messages from conservatives like Quayle and Buchanan, but they're enthusiastic about this one.

So the notion that we have two distinct cultural choices has become widely accepted. If you are civilized and literate, you stand for thick biographies, sonatas, oil paintings. Otherwise, you watch *Ren and Stimpy*, listen to degenerate hip-hop, zombie out on MTV videos, or disconnect from the human race with your computer, gradually losing the art of coherent writing or speech.

From any distance, the construct of two such narrow choices seems pointless. Why should media and culture be defined by opportunistic politicians and out-of-touch journalists? Why can't we each make sensible choices that draw from different elements of media and culture, choices that challenge and educate our kids, that fit into our lives?

We can, of course. Sanity begins by ignoring politicians and journalists and relying on individual common sense. Enlightened people will educate themselves about media and culture. They will figure out what they need, drawing from some old and some new sources of news, some old and some new culture, some nearly antiquated technology and some glitzy stuff. Bible-waving conservatives, boomer parents, Chicken Little reporters, censors and intellectuals do not have useful answers for us. Their definitions of decency and culture don't work anymore. Since they cannot guide us, we have to make our own way....

A FINAL WORD

The media were never meant to be repositories of personal or societal values. They are reflections of them. They serve as the arenas in which we make and shape arguments, pressure our government and hold it accountable, attempt to forge a more just, efficient, educated and humane world. Media don't lead, they follow. They don't create our world; they offer us a picture of it.

The media don't render our culture smart or dumb, civilized or raucous, peaceful or violent. They mirror the state of the existing culture. If you watch TV long enough, on enough different channels, you can see as clear a picture of contemporary America as is available from any distinguished reporter anywhere. The O.J. Simpson trial was not, after all, a mere celebrity scandal but a piercing, bitingly truthful, look deep into the heart of contemporary America's soul—its racial morass, its gender wars, its troubled system of justice.

Media, new or old, don't shape the national character. They don't create the economic, racial, social and ethnic divisions of contemporary America. They don't cause poverty, traffic in guns, induce teenage girls to bear children or teenage boys to abandon them. They don't fund schools or make them ineffective or scandalously bad. They don't shape the consciences or values of children. Despite their many pretensions to the contrary, they don't forge our civic or political consciousness either.

Claims to the contrary are as cruel as they are false—they keep us from seeing and treating the problems we really do face, along with their causes.

The media can't bear all this weight. Values, in the final analysis seem to arise elsewhere. They come from spiritual, educational, social—and increasingly, virtual—communities.

Values come from leaders, who set (or don't) a tone of truthfulness, compassion and vision.

They come from education, which prepares (or doesn't) children to live and work in the coming world, not in the past.

And most of all, they come from families, where the patience, care, thoughtfulness and rationality of parents shape the consciences of children, provide them with the means of structuring their own values and teach them, through hundreds of daily examples, how we want children and adults to behave.

We have surrendered public discussion of moral values to opportunistic politicians, cultural conservatives, politically correct ideologues and self-righteous journalists. We have succumbed to the continually repeated notion that our values are being undermined by outside, mostly cultural, forces bombarding us with ugly images, and that if we can just make these powerful images disappear, our "values" will resurface.

What we seem to have lost in the cultural debates is the sense that values come not from them but from us. We are unwilling to take responsibility for the ethical and moral value systems within our homes.

Whatever values we have, impart to our children, pursue in our own lives, are reflected in one form or another in the universe of programs, conferences, publications, broadcasts, movies and Web pages we call media. V-chips won't keep us safe. Blocking software won't protect our children. Only we—and they —can do that.

In the end, America's cultural wars are as pointless as they are unwinnable. We have created the richest cultural life in the world. Some of the things our culture creates are garish and awful, some spectacular and brilliant. We get to decide which varieties we use. We get to introduce our children, carefully and thoughtfully, to a world of once-unimaginable variety, creativity and stimulation.

This seems cause for celebration, not alarm.

POSTSCRIPT

Are American Values Shaped by the Mass Media?

Television is pervasive in American life. Yet the influence of television on society is difficult to ascertain. For example, a number of things have changed drastically since television was introduced in the 1950s: the election process, drug use, crime rates and patterns, civil rights for minorities, and the influx of women into the workforce. Did television cause all that? Probably not, but was it a contributing factor in these changes? How much influence did it have, and, most important, how can one measure television or media influence?

One school of thought argues that television's primary effect is to reinforce the status quo. Does television contribute to the homogenization of society and promote middle-class values? Or can it reveal problems with the status quo and thus encourage constructive public discourse? Although television has certainly become a shared experience for many, its role in maintaining or changing the country's laws or norms remains to be established.

Yet some effects of television have been dramatically illustrated. For example, television is now the primary source of news for most Americans. Television's ability to bring events to millions of viewers may mean that television itself is a factor in determining the events. Television has reshaped American politics, but it may have little influence on how people actually vote. It has also altered the ways in which Americans spend their time, ranking third behind sleep and work. Yet these influences may be only a prelude to larger social changes that will emerge as technology becomes even more pervasive.

Denis McQuail, in *Mass Communication Theory: An Introduction*, 3rd ed. (Sage Publications, 1994), provides an insightful review of mass communication theory, with particular emphasis on the usefulness of theories of society for understanding the influence of mass communication. John Downing, Ali Mohammadi, and Annabelle Srberny-Mohammadi, eds., *Questioning the Media: A Critical Introduction*, 2d ed. (Sage Publications, 1996) provides a readable introduction to critical social issues as they relate to media, particularly media and identity.

For more from Jon Katz, check out *Media Rants: Postpolitics in the Digital Nation* (Hardwired, 1997). A different view on the importance of media in human existence is found in David Marc, *Bonfire of the Humanities: Television, Subliteracy, and Long-Term Memory Loss* (Syracuse University Press, 1995).

ISSUE 2

Is Television Harmful for Children?

YES: Marie Winn, from *Unplugging the Plug-In Drug* (Penguin Books, 1987)

NO: Milton Chen, from *The Smart Parent's Guide to Kids' TV* (KQED Books, 1994)

ISSUE SUMMARY

YES: Author and children's advocate Marie Winn argues that television has a negative influence on children and their families, and she worries that time spent with television displaces other activities, such as family time, reading, and play.

NO: Milton Chen, director of the Center for Education and Lifelong Learning at KQED in San Francisco, California, maintains that many of the popular beliefs about television and children are myths. Rather than scapegoating television, he argues, we should learn how to use it wisely.

From the earliest years of television broadcasting, parents and educators have expressed concerns that television is harmful, particularly to a vulnerable population such as children. These concerns have become important public policy issues. Groups such as Action for Children's Television (ACT) have lobbied the Federal Communications Commission (FCC) for guidelines on appropriate practices for entertaining and advertising to young audiences. The 1990 Children's Television Act was the first congressional act that specifically regulated children's television. It imposed an obligation on broadcasters to serve the educational and informational needs of children. Although no minimum amount of programming was established, some regularly scheduled shows specifically designed to meet these needs are now required along with a compulsory log of such shows to be kept in a public inspection file. All of these efforts point to social concerns about the consequences of television for children, but what do we really know about the effects of television on youth? Has television become a convenient scapegoat for the ills of society, or is it guilty as charged?

Researchers began to study the impact of television on children by asking who watches television, how much, and why. They analyzed what children see on television and what influence that has on their cognitive development, school achievement, family interaction, social behaviors, and general attitudes and opinions. This is a large and complex social issue, so even extensive research has not provided final answers to all the questions that concerned parents, educators, professional mass communicators, and legislators have raised.

Is television a powerful force that can no longer be considered innocuous entertainment? Those who would answer affirmatively might point to the content of children's viewing, arguing that it is a significant part of the socialization process and decrying the stereotypes, violence, and mindlessness of much of television fare. Others might argue that there are negative consequences intrinsic to viewing television: passive children who stare at the screen for hours, shortened attention span, and the displacement of other activities.

For many people, television is a large part of daily life. Yet the amount of time spent on this activity is the primary concern of Marie Winn. In the following selection, she specifically recommends that parents try a TV Turn-Off, and she recounts examples of the personal, educational, and social development of children who have been involved in such programs.

Many say that television is an important part of a child's environment and that, consequently, children and adults should use it for its positive benefits. In the second selection, Milton Chen argues that many of the persistent beliefs about television are myths, and he shows how television can be used to promote learning. Chen does warn that negative consequences can and do occur, but he maintains that they are unlikely if parents are involved in viewing choices. Parental involvement—establishing content and time restrictions as well as coviewing and discussing media messages—establishes the family context within which television can provide a rich source of entertainment and information, according to Chen.

YES

Marie Winn

THE TROUBLE WITH TELEVISION

Of all the wonders of modern technology that have transformed family life during the last century, television stands alone as a universal source of parental anxiety. Few parents worry about how the electric light or the automobile or the telephone might alter their children's development. But most parents do worry about TV.

Parents worry most of all about the programs their children watch. If only these weren't so violent, so sexually explicit, so cynical, so *unsuitable*, if only they were more innocent, more educational, more *worthwhile*.

Imagine what would happen if suddenly, by some miracle, the only programs available on all channels at all hours of day and night were delightful, worthwhile shows that children love and parents wholeheartedly approve. Would this eliminate the nagging anxiety about television that troubles so many parents today?

For most families, the answer is no. After all, if programs were the only problem, there would be an obvious solution: turn the set off. The fact that parents leave the sets on even when they are distressed about programs reveals that television serves a number of purposes that have nothing to do with the programs on the screen.

Great numbers of parents today see television as a way to make child-rearing less burdensome. In the absence of Mother's Helper (a widely used nineteenth-century patent medicine that contained a hefty dose of the narcotic laudanum), there is nothing that keeps children out of trouble as reliably as "plugging them in."

Television serves families in other ways: as a time-filler ("You have nothing to do? Go watch TV"), a tranquilizer ("When the kids come home from school they're so keyed up that they need to watch for a while to simmer down"), a problem solver ("Kids, stop fighting. It's time for your program"), a procrastination device ("I'll just watch one more program before I do my homework"), a punishment ("If you don't stop teasing your little sister, no TV for a week"), and a reward ("If you get an A on your composition you can watch an extra hour of TV"). For parents and children alike it serves as an avoidance mechanism ("I can't discuss that now—I'm watching my program"), a substitute friend ("I need the TV on for company"), and an escape mechanism ("I'll turn on the TV and try to forget my worries").

Most families recognize the wonderful services that television has to offer. Few, however, are aware that there is a heavy price to pay. Here are eight significant ways television wields a negative influence on children and family life:

1. TV Keeps Families from Doing Other Things

> The primary danger of the television screen lies not so much in the behavior it produces—although there is danger there—as in the behavior it prevents: the talks, the games, the family festivities and arguments through which much of the child's learning takes place and through which his character is formed. Turning on the television set can turn off the process that transforms children into people.[1]

Urie Bronfenbrenner's words to a conference of educators almost two decades ago focus on what sociologists call the "reduction effects" of television—its power to preempt and often eliminate a whole range of other activities and experiences. While it is easy to see that for a child who watches 32 hours of television each week, the reduction effects are significant—obviously that child would be spending 32 hours doing *something* else if there were no television available—Bronfenbrenner's view remains an uncommon and even an eccentric one.

Today the prevailing focus remains on improving programs rather than on reducing the amount of time children view. Perhaps parents have come to depend so deeply on television that they are afraid even to contemplate the idea that something might be wrong with their use of television, not merely with the programs on the air.

2. TV Is a Hidden Competitor for All Other Activities

... Almost everybody knows that there are better, more fulfilling things for a family to do than watch television. And yet, if viewing statistics are to be believed, most families spend most of their family time together in front of the flickering screen.

Some social critics believe that television has come to dominate family life because today's parents are too selfish and narcissistic to put in the effort that reading aloud or playing games or even just talking to each other would require. But this harsh judgment doesn't take into consideration the extraordinary power of television. In reality, many parents crave a richer family life and are eager to work at achieving this goal. The trouble is that their children seem to reject all those fine family alternatives in favor of television.

To be sure, the fact that children are likely to choose watching television over having a story read aloud to them, or playing with the stamp collection, or going out for a walk in the park does not mean that watching television is actually more entertaining or gratifying than any of these activities. It does mean, however, that watching television is easier.

In most families, television is always there as an easy and safe competitor. When another activity is proposed, it had better be *really special*; otherwise it is in danger of being rejected. The parents who have unsuccessfully proposed a game or a story end up feeling rejected as well. They are unaware that television is still affecting their children's enjoyment of other activities, even when the set is off.

Reading aloud is a good example of how this competition factor works. Virtually every child expert hails reading aloud as a delightful family pastime. Educators encourage it as an important way for parents to help their children develop a love for reading and improve their reading skills. Too often, however, the fantasy of the happy family gathered around to listen to a story is replaced by a different reality: "Hey kids, I've got a great book to read aloud. How about it?" says the parent "Not now, Dad, we want to watch 'The Cosby Show,' " say the kids.

It is for this reason that one of the most important *Don'ts* suggested by Jim Trelease in his valuable guide *The Read-Aloud Handbook* is the following:

> Don't try to compete with television. If you say, "Which do you want, a story or TV?" they will usually choose the latter. That is like saying to a 9-year-old, "Which do you want, vegetables or a donut?" Since *you* are the adult, *you* choose. "The television goes off at eight-thirty in this house. If you want a story before bed, that's fine. If not, that's fine too. But no television after eight-thirty." But don't let books appear to be responsible for depriving children of viewing time.[2]

3. TV Allows Kids to Grow Up Less Civilized

... It would be a mistake to assume that the basic child-rearing philosophy of parents of the past was stricter than that of parents today. American parents, in fact, have always had a tendency to be more egalitarian in their family life than, say, European parents. For confirmation, one has only to read the accounts of eighteenth- or nineteenth-century Euro-

pean travelers who comment on the freedom and audacity of American children as compared to their European counterparts. Why then do parents today seem far less in control of their children than parents not only of the distant past but even of a mere generation ago? Television has surely played a part in this change.

Today's parents universally use television to keep their children occupied when they have work to do or when they need a break from child care. They can hardly imagine how parents survived before television. Yet parents *did* survive in the years before TV. Without television, they simply had to use different survival strategies to be able to cook dinner, talk on the telephone, clean house, or do whatever work needed to be done in peace.

Most of these strategies fell into the category social scientists refer to as "socialization"—the civilizing process that transforms small creatures intent upon the speedy gratification of their own instinctive needs and desires into successful members of a society in which those individual needs and desires must often be left ungratified, at least temporarily, for the good of the group.

What were these "socialization" strategies parents used to use? Generally, they went something like this: "Mommy's got to cook dinner now (make a phone call, talk to Mrs. Jones, etc.). Here are some blocks (some clay, a pair of blunt scissors and a magazine, etc.). Now you have to be a good girl and play by yourself for a while and not interrupt Mommy." Nothing very complicated.

But in order to succeed, a certain firmness was absolutely necessary, and parents knew it, even if asserting authority was not their preferred way of dealing with children. They knew they had to work steadily at "training" their child to behave in ways that allowed them to do those normal things that needed to be done. Actually, achieving this goal was not terribly difficult. It took a little effort to set up certain patterns—perhaps a few days or a week of patient but firm insistence that the child behave in certain ways at certain times. But parents of the past didn't agonize about whether this was going to be psychologically damaging. They simply had no choice. Certain things simply *had to be done,* and so parents stood their ground against children's natural struggle to gain attention and have their own way.

Obviously it is easier to get a break from child care by setting the child in front of the television set than to teach the child to play alone for certain periods of time. In the first case, the child is immediately amused (or hypnotized) by the program, and the parent has time to pursue other activities. Accustoming children to play alone, on the other hand, requires day-after-day perseverance, and neither parent nor child enjoys the process very much.

But there is an inevitable price to pay when a parent never has to be firm and authoritative, never has to use that "I mean business" tone of voice: socialization, that crucial process so necessary for the child's future as a successful member of a family, a school, a community, and a nation is accomplished less completely. A very different kind of relationship between parent and child is established, one in which the parent has little control over the child's behavior.

The consequences of a large-scale reduction in child socialization are not hard to see in contemporary society: an increased number of parents who feel helpless and out of control of their children's lives and behavior, who haven't established the parental authority that might protect their children from involvement in such dangerous activities as drug experimentation, or from the physical and emotional consequences of precocious sexual relationships.

4. Television Takes the Place of Play

... Once small children become able to concentrate on television and make some sense of it—usually around the end of their second year of life—it's not hard to understand why parents eagerly set their children before the flickering screen: taking care of toddlers is hard! The desperate and tired parent can't imagine *not* taking advantage of this marvelous new way to get a break. In consequence, before they are three years old, the opportunities of active play and exploration are hugely diminished for a great number of children—to be replaced by the hypnotic gratification of television viewing.

Yet many parents overlook an important fact: children who are suddenly able to sustain attention for more than a few minutes on the TV screen have clearly moved into a new stage of cognitive development—their ability to concentrate on TV is a sign of it. There are therefore many other new activities, far more developmentally valuable, that the child is now ready for. These are the simple forms of play that most small children enjoyed in the pre-television era: cutting and pasting, coloring and drawing, building with blocks, playing games of make-believe with toy soldiers or animals or dolls. But the parent who begins to fill in the child's time with television at this point is unlikely to discover these other potential capabilities.

It requires a bit of effort to establish new play routines—more effort, certainly, than plunking a child in front of a television screen, but not really a great deal. It requires a bit of patience to get the child accustomed to a new kind of play—play on his own—but again, not a very great deal. It also demands some firmness and perseverance. And a small amount of equipment (art materials, blocks, etc.), most of it cheap, if not free, and easily available.

But the benefits for both parent and child of *not* taking the easiest way out at this point by using television to ease the inevitable child-care burdens will vastly outweigh the temporary difficulties parents face in filling children's time with less passive activities. For the parent, the need for a bit more firmness leads to an easier, more controlled parent-child relationship. For the child, those play routines established in early childhood will develop into lifelong interests and hobbies, while the skills acquired in the course of play lead to a sense of accomplishment that could never have been achieved if the child had spent those hours "watching" instead of "doing."

5. TV Makes Children Less Resourceful

... Many parents who welcome the idea of turning off the TV and spending more time with the family are still worried that without TV they would constantly be on call as entertainers for their children. Though they *want* to play games and read aloud to their children, the idea of having to replace television minute-for-minute with worthwhile family activities is daunting. They remember thinking up all sorts of things to do when they were kids. But their own kids seem different, less resourceful, somehow. When there's nothing to do, these parents observe regretfully, their kids seem unable to come up with anything to do besides turning on the TV.

One father, for example, says, "When I was a kid, we were always thinking up things to do, projects and games. We certainly never whined to our parents, 'I have nothing to do!' " He compares this with his own children today: "They're simply lazy. If someone doesn't entertain them, they'll happily sit there watching TV all day."

There is one word for this father's disappointment: unfair. It is as if he were disappointed in them for not reading Greek though they have never studied the language. He deplores his children's lack of inventiveness, as if the ability to play were something innate that his children are missing. In fact, while the *tendency* to play is built into the human species, the actual *ability* to play—to imagine, to invent, to elaborate on reality in a playful way—and the ability to gain fulfillment from it, these are skills that have to be learned and developed.

Such disappointment, however, is not only unjust, it is also destructive. Sensing their parents' disappointment, children come to believe that they are, indeed, lacking something, and that this makes them less worthy of admiration and respect. Giving children the opportunity to develop new resources, to enlarge their horizons and discover the pleasures of doing things on their own is, on the other hand, a way to help children develop a confident feeling about themselves as capable and interesting people.

It is, of course, ironic that many parents avoid a TV Turn-Off out of fear that their children won't know what to do with themselves in the absence of television. It is television watching itself that has allowed them to grow up without learning how to be resourceful and television watching that keeps them from developing those skills that would enable them to fill in their empty time enjoyably.

6. TV Has a Negative Effect on Children's Physical Fitness

... Not long ago a study that attracted wide notice in the popular press found a direct relationship between the incidence of obesity in children and time spent viewing television. For the 6–11 age group, "children who watched more television experienced a greater prevalence of obesity, or superobesity, than children watching less television. No significant differences existed between obese, superobese, and nonobese children with respect to the number of friends, their ability to get along with friends, or time spent with friends, alone, listening to the radio, reading, or in leisure time activities," wrote the researchers. As for teenagers, only 10 percent of those teenagers who watched TV an hour or less a day were obese as compared to 20 percent of those who watched more than five hours daily. With most other variables eliminated, why should this be? The researchers provided a commonsense explanation: Dedicated TV watchers are fatter because they eat more and exercise less while glued to the tube.[3]

7. TV Has a Negative Effect on Children's School Achievement

... It is difficult if not impossible to prove that excessive television viewing has a direct negative effect on young children's cognitive development, though by using cautionary phrases such as "TV will turn your brain to mush" parents often express an instinctive belief that this is true.

Nevertheless an impressive number of research studies demonstrate beyond any reasonable doubt that excessive television viewing has an adverse effect on children's achievement in school. One study, for instance, shows that younger children who watch more TV have lower scores in reading and overall achievement tests than those who watch less TV.[4]

Another large-scale study, conducted when television was first introduced as a mass medium in Japan, found that as families acquired television sets children showed a decline in both reading skills and homework time.

But it does not require costly research projects to demonstrate that television viewing affects children's school work adversely. Interviews with teachers who have participated in TV Turn-Offs provide confirmation as well.

Almost without exception, these teachers testify that the quality of homework brought into class during the No-TV period was substantially better. As a fifth grade teacher noted: "There was a real difference in the homework I was getting during No-TV Week. Kids who usually do a good job on homework did a terrific job. Some kids who rarely hand in assignments on time now brought in surprisingly good and thorough work. When I brought this to the class's attention during discussion time they said, 'Well, there was nothing else to do!' "

8. Television Watching May Be a Serious Addiction

... A lot of people who have nothing but bad things to say about TV, calling it the "idiot box" and the "boob tube," nevertheless spend quite a lot of their free time watching television. People are often apologetic, even shamefaced about their television viewing, saying things like, "I only watch the news," or "I only turn the set on for company," or "I only watch when I'm too tired to do anything else" to explain the sizable number of hours they devote to TV.

In addition to anxiety about their own viewing patterns, many parents recognize that their children watch too much television and that it is having an adverse effect on their development and yet they don't take any effective action to change the situation.

Why is there so much confusion, ambivalence, and self-deception connected with television viewing? One explanation is that great numbers of television viewers are to some degree addicted to the *experience* of watching television. The confusion and ambivalence they reveal about television may then be recognized as typical reactions of an addict unwilling to face an addiction or unable to get rid of it.

Most people find it hard to consider television viewing a serious addiction. Addictions to tobacco or alcohol, after all, are known to cause life-threatening diseases—lung cancer or cirrhosis of the liver. Drug addiction leads to dangerous behavioral aberrations—violence and crime. Meanwhile, the worst physiological consequences of television addiction seem to be a possible decline in overall physical fitness, and an increased incidence of obesity.

It is in its psychosocial consequences, especially its effects on relationships and family life, that television watching may be as damaging as chemical addiction. We all know the terrible toll alcoholism or drug addiction takes on the families of addicts. Is it possible that television watching has a similarly destructive potential for family life?

Most of us are at least dimly aware of the addictive power of television through our own experiences with the medium: our compulsive involvement with the tube too often keeps us from talking to each other, from doing things together, from working and learning and getting involved in community affairs. The hours we spend viewing prove to be curiously unfulfilling. We end up feeling depressed, though the program we've been watching was a comedy. And yet we cannot seem to turn the set off, or even *not* turn it on in the first place. Doesn't this sound like an addiction?

NOTES

1. Urie Bronfenbrenner, "Who Cares for America's Children?" Address presented at the Conference of the National Association for the Education of Young Children, 1970.

2. Jim Trelease, *The Read-Aloud Handbook.* Penguin, 1985.

3. W. H. Dietz and S. L. Gortmaker, "Do We Fatten Our Children at the Television Set? Obesity and Television Viewing in Children and Adolescents." *Pediatrics* 75 (1985).

4. S. G. Burton, J. M. Calonico, and D. R. McSeveney, "Effects of Preschool Watching on First-Grade Children." *Journal of Communications* 29:3 (1979).

NO   Milton Chen

SIX MYTHS ABOUT TELEVISION
AND CHILDREN

A curious mythology has grown up around television and its effects on children. Together, these myths would have us believe that TV is single-handedly turning kids into couch potatoes, frying their brains, shortening their attention spans and lowering their academic abilities. Supposedly, TV is a dark and foreboding menace in our children's lives. These myths can be traced to the simplistic, yet persistent, view that TV, as a medium, has effects of its own that transcend any specific content.

Since teachers, parents and the media themselves constantly propagate these myths, it is important to examine them. Although some children who watch TV 30 or 40 hours a week struggle in school, there are deeper reasons why they do besides time spent watching television. Are their parents taking an active role in helping their children learn? Or are these latchkey children who are left to their own devices? Television's effects do depend on how much we watch and, more importantly, on *what* we watch.

None of the following myths is supported by substantive research. In fact, research has often contradicted them. Unfortunately, the propagators of these myths have done a much better job of marketing their opinions than the researchers who have done the studies to debunk them. So here I present, in point-counterpoint fashion, six pervasive myths about TV.

MYTH NO. 1: TV is a passive medium. My child will become a listless couch potato.

FACT NO. 1: Educational TV shows can actively engage your child, physically and intellectually. The activity can and should continue after the show is over.

There are at least two kinds of passivity: physical and intellectual. One of the most common myths about TV viewing is that it is, by definition, a passive activity. Contrary to popular belief, neither physical nor intellectual passivity is an immutable fact of TV viewing, especially for children.

As any parent of a child who watches "Barney & Friends" or "Sesame Street" knows, young viewers are physically engaged, singing, clapping and stretching along with their favorite characters, especially when the shows invite them to do so. Programs such as these also encourage intellectual activity as children learn important concepts, from counting to kindness.

One overlooked and underused feature of television is its ability to prompt viewers to read aloud. Some current children's shows, such as "Ghostwriter" and "Beakman's World," use animation and graphics to highlight key words for viewers to read and pronounce as they are watching.

Many other examples of children's TV demonstrate how young viewers can exercise their cognitive muscles while they watch. A U.S. Department of Education study found that "contrary to popular assertions, children are cognitively active during television viewing in an attempt to form a coherent, connected understanding of television programs."

This activity shouldn't cease after the show is over. The best children's programs provide activities and tips for teachers, child-care providers and parents on related follow-up activities. Whether it's folding origami with Shari Lewis of "Lamb Chop's Play-Along," writing a letter to "Ghostwriter" or borrowing a "Reading Rainbow" book from the library, television can be a creative source of active learning rather than the presumed death of it.

MYTH NO. 2: TV stunts the healthy growth of the brain. It zaps a child's brain waves.

FACT NO. 2: Brain-wave patterns during TV viewing are very similar to brain activity during other activities.

Some educators and commentators, like educational psychologist Dr. Jane Healy, have suggested that TV viewing has a deleterious effect on brain development, that because it is a visual medium, it may overstimulate the right hemisphere (responsible for visual processing) and understimulate the left hemisphere (responsible for language and processing of print). The critique often invokes technical language about "frontal-lobe development," "neural pathways" and "alpha and beta waves," creating both confusion and concern in the minds of many parents.

Does television really interfere with children's brain functioning and zap their synapses? It can seem plausible, especially when such claims are made in jargon with the appearance of medical authority.

A neuropsychologist's authoritative review should put these fears to rest. Dr. Katharine Fite of the Neuroscience and Behavior Program at the University of Massachusetts, Amherst, concluded: "In recent years, a number of claims have appeared in the popular media and press suggesting that television viewing has potentially detrimental effects on human brain development and/or brain activity. An extensive review of the published scientific literature provides no evidence to substantiate such beliefs."

Fite described two major findings from experiments that measured small electrical signals from the scalp, indicating brain activity. These studies found that during TV watching, viewers' brain-wave patterns are "quite similar to those that occur during other waking-state activities. Thus TV viewing should not be characterized as producing a passive or inattentive activity in the brain." She also reported that television is not, as argued, exclusively a right-brain activity.

Parents should rest easier, knowing this alarm about our children's gray matter is only a red herring. Instead, we should devote our own brain waves to the more important questions of what and how much our children are watching.

MYTH NO. 3: TV shortens a child's attention span.

FACT NO. 3: Educational TV shows can actually increase a child's attention and cognitive skills.

Myth No. 3 and its close cousin, Myth No. 2, have been propagated by a small but prolific group of writers and educators who often turn their attack on one specific program. The object of their reproach? Not "Teenage Mutant Ninja Turtles" or the "Mighty Morphin Power Rangers." No, none other than "Sesame Street." The critique is an academic hit-and-run, since these individuals do not stop to conduct any research of their own, nor do they cite the wealth of research that has already been done on the program.

"Sesame Street" is the most widely researched television program in history. In fact, a bibliography published by Children's Television Workshop (CTW) in 1989 lists an astonishing 633 studies on its cognitive and social effects.

Yet some academics and writers insist that "Sesame Street" is a hazard to children's development. As Dr. Daniel Anderson, professor of psychology at the University of Massachusetts, Amherst, explains, these critics believe that the "rapid transitions between scenes... mesmerize children and interfere with their reflection and inference, so that the child is left only with memories of a jumbled, disconnected set of visual images."

But Anderson, who has studied the effect of "Sesame Street" on children's attention spans more thoroughly than anyone else, believes these critics do not give young children enough credit for their purposeful cognitive skills. He summarizes the findings: "The new research showed that the critique was wrong. The child viewer of 'Sesame Street,' rather than being a mesmerized zombie, is selective and intellectually active.... We have evidence that 'Sesame Street' actually enhances attentional and perceptual abilities.... Research on 'Sesame Street' has shown us that young children are far more capable than we previously believed."

Then why is "Sesame Street" so often the target of misguided and uninformed broadsides? Dr. Samuel Ball, who conducted the first evaluations of "Sesame Street," believes that the series was bound to be victimized by some because of its success. In Australia, he observes, "we have what we call the 'tall poppy' syndrome. When you see a tall poppy, you saw off its head, quick smart.... The USA is not barren of this kind of reaction to success, either."

There are precious few genuine educational innovations in our country, and "Sesame Street" is one of them. The series' research record clearly supports its effectiveness: "Sesame Street" boasts votes of approval from the 16 million children who watch the show each week, as well as their parents, who witness their children learning from the Muppets, the music, the animation and the characters treating each other with respect and good humor. Personally, I'd take 100 eager kids watching "Sesame Street" over a few disgruntled academics any day.

MYTH NO. 4: If my child watches TV, she'll be a poor student.

FACT NO. 4: It depends on what and how much she is watching. Students who watch a moderate amount of television, especially educational TV can be excellent students.

The research on this topic will surprise many. Dr. Keith Mielke, senior research fellow at CTW, has examined reviews of research on the relationship of TV viewing to academic achievement.

The studies point out what is commonly touted: Very high levels of TV viewing (35 or more hours per week) negatively correlate with academic achievement. This makes sense, as children who are watching excessive amounts of television do not have time to do much else. But several studies found that academic achievement was positively related to a moderate amount of TV viewing, on the order of 10 to 15 hours a week.

The real issue, Mielke says, is not the sheer number of hours a child watches but what programs she's watching—and how parents and teachers use programs to help maximize learning.

Probably, children who watch 40 hours of TV or more each week are not watching much educational fare. It is also likely that kids who watch a moderate amount receive some strong parental messages about what to watch as well as what to do with the rest of their time, with an educational focus.

MYTH NO. 5: If my child watches TV he won't become a good reader. TV and books are enemies.

FACT NO. 5: Quality children's programs can actually motivate children to read books and lead to a love of reading.

This curious and widespread belief holds that TV viewing is antithetical to book reading and that kids who watch television will not be good readers. I believe this myth is tied to a larger cultural bias: an intellectual snobbery, in favor of books and against TV.

Joan Ganz Cooney, originator of "Sesame Street" and founder of CTW, clarifies the issue: "Thoughtful people would not argue that because children read comic books, they should not therefore do any additional reading in school. Yet they apply a similar argument to the medium of television."

This pro-book, anti-TV bias doesn't stand up against the evidence of specific TV shows, such as "Reading Rainbow," that encourage the reading of books. After viewing this program, children are so excited to get their hands on *Reading Rainbow* than librarians and bookstore owners report dramatically increased circulations and sales. In one study, 86 percent of children's librarians said the series was responsible for increased circulation. Mimi Kayden, director of children's marketing for E. P. Dutton, has said, "Books that would sell 5,000 copies on their own sell 25,000 copies if they're on 'Reading Rainbow.' "

This phenomenon occurs with just about every other popular children's TV show with book and magazine tie-ins. Publishers understand this synergy between TV broadcasts and book sales very well, which explains the many children's books based upon popular characters on children's TV.

A series of *Ghostwriter* books, published just a year ago [1993], has already sold thousands of copies. *Sesame Street* children's books have been best-sellers for more than two decades. *Sesame Street Magazine* is a leading magazine among families with preschoolers and is accompanied by the excellent *Sesame Street Par-*

ent's Guide. Book classics such as *Anne of Green Gables* enjoy renewed sales when their stories are televised.

This phenomenon is certainly not limited to children. Ken Burns' *The Civil War*, Bill Moyers' *Healing and the Mind*, and James Burke's *Connections*, each based on a PBS series, have been best-selling books. After watching a particularly innovative or moving TV show, viewers want to read a book related to it.

MYTH NO. 6: If my child watches TV shows that entertain as well as educate, he'll expect his teachers to sing and dance.

FACT NO. 6: Even young children understand the separate worlds and conventions of TV and the classroom.

One of the strangest myths about children's television is that children who watch Barney and Big Bird will set unrealistic expectations about their teachers' dramatic talents. There is no research to support this notion, nor do teachers report pupils urging them to break out in song or do a little soft-shoe while at the blackboard. Even preschoolers understand what behaviors are appropriate for which situations. I know of no reports in which a child has pointed a make-believe remote at a teacher and attempted to click him off.

Do quality children's programs delude children and their parents into confusing "entertainment" with "education"? Media pundit Neil Postman, in his book *Amusing Ourselves to Death*, contends that this is exactly the problem with educational shows such as "Sesame Street" or "The Voyage of the Mimi," an award-winning series on science and mathematics.

Education, as Postman defines it, is what goes on in the traditional classroom—teacher at the head of the class, students dutifully listening—and entertainment is what television does, using celebrities, music, animation and other cheap thrills. To him, the two are like oil and water.

Education is much more than mere "schooling," but too often we have squeezed the passion and excitement from learning in the classroom. We have disconnected many subjects, such as history, science and art, from the true sense of joy and curiosity that animates the historians, scientists and artists who have made professions out of them. Sadly, we have made learning dull.

* * *

Our job as parents and teachers should be to make learning joyful, stimulating and, as George Leonard says, ecstatic. In our culture, there is a strong belief that learning is serious, hard work.

But the way to get young children interested in embarking on this process is to expose them to the joys of learning early on. If television can help in this regard, so much the better. When we label "Sesame Street" or "Nova" as simple "entertainment," we ignore the ways in which TV programs can use video technology and appealing characters to reveal the compelling nature of a subject.

Instead of condemning television for communicating this revolutionary idea, we should focus on making other educational experiences more lively and engaging. The best children's museums and science centers do this. They are places where kids want to go, where they are learning while they are actively engaged with exhibits, museum staff, teachers, parents and one another.

In the end, learning is a voluntary activity. Whether we're 6 or 60, we can't be forced to learn. TV viewing in the home is also a voluntary activity, something your children do because they want to, for positive as well as not-so-positive reasons. The fact that children like TV is something we can build on. When television is well designed, it can appeal not only to their funny bones but to their hearts and minds as well.

POSTSCRIPT

Is Television Harmful for Children?

Television is frequently castigated for interfering in the education of children. Achievement, intellectual ability, grades, and reading ability have complex relationships with television viewing, as the differing perspectives of Winn and Chen show. Although there is great debate over precisely how television influences attitudes and behavior, there is substantial evidence that television has become very influential as an agent of socialization—that is, as a means by which young children come to know and understand their world.

Yet television as we have traditionally known it is changing dramatically. Cable networks devoted primarily to children, such as Nickelodeon and Disney (as well as cable networks with extensive children's programming like Discovery, Learning Channel, USA, TBS, the Family Channel, and Lifetime), have increased the diversity of children's programming since the 1980s. The 1990s have been influenced by the Children's Television Act and public opinion, and many educational shows have joined the available programming. For example, since 1990 eight of the nine Peabody Awards for children's programs were for informational or educational programs.

Much of what we know comes from the study of children enjoying traditional television, but that knowledge is being challenged by emerging telecommunications technology. Cable, video games, and VCRs have already changed the face of television within the home. Indeed, VCRs have greatly increased the control that parents have over the material to which children are exposed. The Internet, a 500-channel world, increasing international programming ventures, and regulatory changes will change the way children interact with electronic media. What influence that will have on learning from electronic media (notice that simply saying "learning from television" is no longer an adequate descriptor) is very hard to predict.

Robert Liebert and Joyce Sprafkin's *The Early Window: Effects of Television on Children and Youth*, 3rd ed. (Pergamon Press, 1988) is an excellent introduction to the history and issues of media effects. Judith Van Evra offers a view of existing research in *Television and Child Development* (Lawrence Erlbaum, 1990). Nancy Signorelli has produced the useful book *Sourcebook on Children and Television* (Greenwood Press, 1990). And Barrie Gunter and Jill L. McAleer give us a view from the United Kingdom in *Children and Television: The One-Eyed Monster?* (Routledge, 1990).

ISSUE 3

Do Media Drive Foreign Policy?

YES: Patrick O'Heffernan, from "Sobering Thoughts on Sound Bites Seen 'Round the World," in Bradley S. Greenberg and Walter Gantz, eds., *Desert Storm and the Mass Media* (Hampton Press, 1993)

NO: Warren P. Strobel, from "The CNN Effect," *American Journalism Review* (May 1996)

ISSUE SUMMARY

YES: Patrick O'Heffernan, a senior fellow at the Center for International Strategy, Technology, and Policy at the Georgia Institute of Technology, argues that television plays an increasingly important role in international diplomacy and war. He maintains that it has become the crisis communication system of international relations and is now firmly established as a player in world politics. Television news and government need and use one another, according to O'Heffernan.

NO: Warren P. Strobel, the White House correspondent for the *Washington Times*, explores the reality of the "CNN Effect" and finds it to be less than expected. He agrees that television has made a difference, but he argues that shrinking decision-making time and opening up military operations to public scrutiny is not the same as determining policy.

The nature of television news tends to provide the viewer with the most graphic visual images possible. In war, those images can evoke emotions and capitalize on the human dimensions of military actions. Two areas of controversy, however, concern the impact of those images on public opinion and the social responsibility of those who produce and package those images for viewer consumption.

Vietnam was the first military action to be covered live via electronic news gathering (ENG) technologies and satellite distribution. Media critic Michael Arlen was prompted to call Vietnam the first "living room war." His thesis was that American viewers were shocked by the grim reality of war when confronted by real blood and mounting casualty reports. The media coverage, therefore, strongly influenced American sentiment about U.S. involvement. Since then, the notion that media coverage influences public policy has become almost axiomatic. The power of media to frame public opinion, demand instant responses from government officials, and shape foreign policy has become known as the CNN Effect.

There are many examples that seem to support a CNN Effect. In the following selection, Patrick O'Heffernan discusses the importance of television in international diplomacy during the Persian Gulf War of 1991. Next to Vietnam, the 1992 intervention in Somalia may be the most often cited case of media influence on American foreign policy. As political scientist Bernard Cohen notes, "By focusing daily on the starving children in Somalia, a pictorial story tailor-made for television, TV mobilized the conscience of the nation's public institutions, compelling the government into a policy of intervention for humanitarian reasons."

Yet Warren P. Strobel, in the second selection, argues that the issues are much more complex. Using Somalia as an example, he suggests that Somalia was featured on television only after it had generated interest among important foreign policy circles of the U.S. government. Strobel asserts that if television inspired intervention, it did so with the considerable influence of these officials who worked to publicize events in Somalia, interpret them as a unique crisis, and encourage response.

Ironically, this debate occurs in parallel with the shrinking of foreign news. James F. Hoge, Jr., in "Foreign News: Who Gives a Damn?" *Columbia Journalism Review* (November/December 1997), asserts that the coverage of international news by the American media has declined steadily since the late 1970s. One reason is diminished resources for foreign news operations in the belt-tightening of the 1980s. Many foreign news bureaus were closed, which concentrated coverage in major cities and left vast areas with no permanent foreign correspondent. Reliance on local press, occasional stringers, "parachuted-in" foreign correspondents, and wire services has become more prevalent. Lagging public interest is thought to explain the shrinkage as well. To much of the general public, foreign news seems confusing and without sufficient significance to justify working it out, suggests Hoge. If U.S. international relations are left in the hands of an informed few with the consent of an indifferent public, does foreign policy become more susceptible to the CNN Effect?

O'Heffernan raises questions concerning the operation of an electronic press organization that is international in scope and distribution. What is the code of ethics that will inform the crucial decisions that must be made in times of crisis?

YES

Patrick O'Heffernan

SOBERING THOUGHTS ON SOUND BITES SEEN 'ROUND THE WORLD

> Plain old American TV is more powerful than any military weapon. In fact, it should become our avowed way of making war. Call it the thermo-media battlefield: hard news, hard rock, tough talk and Coca-Cola commercials. No bullets, no bloodshed—no way we can lose. (Marash, 1979, p. 17)

The Gulf Crisis was unquestionably a watershed event for television. It crystallized hot new trends in the cool medium that have been growing for as long as 20 years. It forever changed our perception of television in world politics. It generated many firsts in news coverage and stimulated an unprecedented examination and self-examination of the relationship between television and government. In some ways, if the crisis had not occurred, television would have had to invent it.

Media analysts will examine the Gulf War and its coverage for years to come, but it is clear now that the entire Gulf Crisis and its coverage effectively solidified three major developments that have been emerging in television and its role in world politics since the end of the Vietnam War:

- Television has become the crisis communication system of international relations
- Television is now firmly established as a player in world politics
- Television can—under some conditions and in some situations—replace or forestall violence as a tool of national power.

Television and the world political system are linked in a co-evolutionary development process, each stimulating and responding to change in the other. Television's new global political role springs both from changes in the world political structure and from technological and organizational evolution in the medium itself. The globalization of television news has paralleled international interdependence. The decrease in size and cost of electronic news gathering (ENG) equipment has tracked the increased speed of international travel. The spread of cable, direct broadcast satellite (DBS), and other forms of receiving signals from anywhere in the world has preceded, stimulated, and reinforced the growing porosity of national borders. The Gulf Crisis was a key event in this ongoing co-evolutionary dynamic, compressing and highlighting the changes in both television and the global political system. At the same time, it also raised critical long-term questions about the nature of the interdependent and mutually exploitive media-government relationship that is co-evolving on our screens. Before turning to those questions, the trends crystallized in television by the Gulf War deserve examination.

Presidents George Bush and Saddam Hussein raised the sound bite to a worldwide diplomatic art. But unlike secret cables, television broadcasts messages to friend and foe simultaneously, sometimes forcing swift action. The Soviets discovered this when western television flashed satellite photographs of the Chernobyl melt down around the world while Soviet officials were still denying the seriousness of the accident (*New York Times*, 1988).

During the standoff with Saddam Hussein, President Bush ordered a mobile downlink for his political trips in order to be able to watch CNN. President Hussein and his ministers monitored American television both for changes in U.S. positions and intelligence on the U.S. military. The Department of State used television to transmit embassy telephone numbers to Americans hiding in Kuwait, and some of the Americans called CNN to broadcast their description of conditions in Kuwait City.

Television's global crisis communication role has been growing for over a decade. President Carter and Prime Minister Bani Sadr sent coded negotiating messages through radio and television newscasts when no other form of communication was available during the Iran hostage crisis (as told to the author by Jimmy Carter; see O'Heffernan, 1991a, for excerpts from the interview). Lebanese Defense Minister Nabbih Berri used television as a constant negotiating channel on the fate of the TWA 847 hostages. Berri not only communicated on television with U.S. officials, but maintained the negotiating initiative through skillful staging and timing of hostage interviews.[1] While this crisis communications role is not new, the almost hourly exchange of messages, threats, and images on television between the U.S. and Iraq during the Gulf Crisis embedded it in modern diplomacy.

Second, the Gulf Crisis firmly established television as a player in international politics. Television has been a player since the Vietnam War, but largely due to its ability to influence public opinion. With the emergence of live global broadcasts, television now operates in international politics on several different levels:

- It opens the door to private organizations such as Amnesty International and ethnic interest groups to influence foreign policy.[2]
- It speeds up decision making and reduces time for both analysis and delay in policy making.
- It dilutes the secrecy in diplomacy, principally by giving every party in a specific set of talks a way to instantaneously communicate their version of the other side's offers.
- It sometimes adds new, often multinational, issues such as global warming, to a largely bilateral foreign policy agenda. Most importantly, television is a tool routinely used by foreign min-

istries to develop and implement their policies, a use uncharacteristically visible during the Gulf Crisis. In doing so they can often level a diplomatic playing field because television is a tool that can be employed as well by a poor country with skill and cunning as by a rich one with technology and power.

But television is not a neutral player —it has its own agendas. During the Gulf War and other crises, television anchors assumed the mantle of quasi-diplomats, a practice which became embarrassingly obvious when *Nightline* anchor Ted Koppel used "we" several times to refer to the U.S. government.[3] Television discussion shows on CNN, the American broadcast networks, and on many European national news programs took television's quasi-diplomatic role for granted and debated its implications without questioning its existence.

But a diplomatic status of any kind assumes a position or an alignment, an uncomfortable place, it would seem, for American news organizations that pride themselves on "balance" and "objectivity." Unfortunately, balance and objectivity went out the window quickly as American television organizations sensed the opportunities inherent in "supporting our men and women in the desert" and the dangers in looking too closely at the lack of rationale for a popular war promoted by a popular President. The pro-war, pro-America slant of most America news organizations was underscored by the widespread use of former military or diplomatic officers as "experts" brought in to "explain" the war. This practice produced two popular impressions:

• It gave copious air time to men (very few women were used) who were seen as and were in many cases former administration spokesmen, reinforcing the administration's perceived credibility.

• By failing to provide any meaningful time to experts with opposing opinions, it left the impression that all of the facts, knowledge, and expertise lay with the pro-war administration and therefore they must be right.

The result was a clear diplomatic alignment within the American and the global media. Whether or not this kind of diplomatic alignment will exist in the next war or international crisis remains to be seen. But with the major impetus of American television *networks* (not necessarily news organizations) being to deliver audiences to advertisers rather than information to audiences, alignments that assure strong audiences and little controversy will be hard to resist, despite any diplomatic impacts that may result.

Television diplomacy is also not new; Walter Cronkite was instrumental in setting the stage for the Camp David talks in a televised electronic meeting between Sadat and Begin, and many reporters, most visibly Barbara Walters in the 1967 Arab-Israeli war, have served as message carriers between political foes who were not otherwise talking.[4] The Gulf Crisis crystallized the role and made it part of world politics in the post-Cold War era.

This role has diplomatic ramifications. The more television is used for diplomatic communication, the more television can inject its own messages and gatekeep the governmental players. Hussein learned this when CNN broadcast his first hostage encounter with disclaimers, including an interruption by Reid Collins to tell the audience this was Iraqi propaganda. Other Iraqi tapes were broadcast with "bugs" and "crawls," alerting the audience to their official origin and diluting what Hussein undoubtedly hoped would be their impact. Other tapes were simply not run because they were not considered news. Media organizations in the Middle East exercised the same kind of gatekeeper role, depending on their political alignment or the influence that Iraq had cultivated with them in the past. In a number of extreme cases, CNN footage was run by pro-Iraqi stations in the region with voice-overs describing nonexistent cultural or military atrocities by Coalition troops. In most cases, however, the diplomatic role of Middle Eastern news organizations was exercised by the omission of stories on Iraqi misdeeds, or even losses.[5]

American and global television exercised this power in the Gulf Crisis primarily against Iraq. President Bush was generally allowed by television (and to a lesser extent, by the print media) to frame the arguments and set the terms of discourse in the first month of news broadcasts. American television crisis coverage often strayed into jingoism, with generous and unquestioning coverage of U.S. military operations and policy, including a glowing package on *60 Minutes* on Middle East Commander General Schwarzkopf aimed directly at Hussein's officers, in essence saying, "here is the son of a bitch who can destroy you."[6]

While many argue that this is natural in the early stages of a crisis and moreover is appropriate when U.S. troops have been deployed, it carries the danger that policy mistakes will go unchecked by popular complaint and lead to scandals such as the Iran-Contra affair. In fact, the failure of the media to initiate a broad and influential discussion of President Bush's decision not to remove President Hussein or defend the Kurds allowed those decisions to go forward. In retrospect, the wisdom of abandoning the Kurds was dashed with Bush's later decision (forced by media coverage) to assist the Kurds, and the decision to leave President Hussein in power was subject to relentless examination during Bush's campaign for reelection.

Third, television functioned as a surrogate for violence during the early days of the crisis—a new kind of power exercised in a new kind of war. Television enables opposing leaders to compete with one another before a global audience. Rather than territory or other physical spoils of war, the strategic target is world opinion and with it the ability to influence without using force decisions in international organizations and other nations.

The conversion of the cool medium into a substitute for a hot war or a weapon of war may be the most profound impact on television of the Gulf Crisis. This conversion is consonant with other political trends. Harvard political scientist Joseph Nye's concept of "soft power," that is, the ability of one nation to determine the wants and needs of other nations without force, is one such trend (Nye, 1990). In Nye's thesis, soft power is just as important as the "hard power" of economic clout or military force because it rests on a nation's ability to shape the preferences of another nation and to lead rather than force consensus.

This theory argues that nonmilitary influences can either strategically or accidentally change the internal political and cultural dynamics of a nation, regardless of efforts by its leadership. Economic influences such as the penetration of markets by exports and services of another country can concomitantly create a bias in that country toward the exporting nation. Strategic economic pressures purposefully exerted by one country on another can be used to change foreign policy or even internal policy toward another country, without resort to force. Most important, however, may be the pervasive impact of imported media on a nation's culture, economy, and eventually its political system. The spread of American rock-and-roll music through records, cassettes, and now MTV and videos has carried with it the values of capitalism, commercialism, democracy in some forms, and a general admiration for things American. This influence has been reinforced in the past decade by the proliferation of American movies and television in the entertainment industries of virtually all nations. This form of cultural soft power contributed to the fall of the Communist regimes in Germany and Eastern Europe without the firing of a shot.

President Hussein turned to television's soft power because he was stalemated militarily. Television was the weapon of choice in a media blitzkrieg, and President Bush responded in kind. The generals in this war of images were Iraqi Information Minister Nizar Hamdoon, American media guru Roger Ailes, and Hill and Knowlton Public Relations for the Kuwait government in exile. Hussein aimed his television fire at three principal targets: the masses of the Middle East to stimulate a popular Pan-Arabic movement united behind his leadership; the American public to generate sympathy for the hostages and popular pressure to negotiate for their return; and, finally, President Bush in a contest for world opinion.[7] Bush's targets included the people of Iraq and the Middle East, the members of the United Nations whose support he needed for the boycott, the Security Council, and, of course, his American audience.

Television may also delay resorting to violence in a crisis, giving negotiations more time. The media war can distract the belligerents from physical force, and the presence of television may make them reluctant to be the first to shoot before a worldwide audience. This was true for a time while Bush and Hussein hurled press releases and videotapes at each other in the Gulf, with no fighting. While an international entourage of ENG crews and reporters were stationed in Baghdad and Saudi Arabia, and amateur tape trickled in from the Kuwait resistance, both sides held their fire. As Winston Churchill observed, "To talk is better than not to talk. Jaw, jaw is better than war." If he were alive today, he might add that television is also better than war. Unfortunately, as events proved, television's ability to substitute for or delay violence will always be limited by other considerations, and, in some cases, it may actually provide an excuse for violence.

At some point, either diplomacy or violence must resolve the aftermath of the Gulf War. The position of the Kurds in Iraq and Turkey and Iran, the relationship of Iran to Iraq, the United States and the Arab Middle East, the outcome of Shiite resistance to Hussein may all be settled by hard, not soft, power. Surrounding these questions will be the continuing conflict between Israel and the Palestinians over lands they both claim. But regardless of how these issues are resolved, if ever, the television roles and trends crystallized by the crisis force us to ask hard questions about the long-term relationship between media and national governments in world politics.

First is the dilemma of television's responsibility when its broadcasts may be injurious to its home nation's announced or unannounced foreign policy. In a world of global glasnost, television-delivered information may be harmful to some nations, helpful to some, and benign to others. When that information may save lives in one nation but undercut foreign policy objectives in one's own nation, television's responsibility may be divided.

President Bush signaled early in the Gulf Crisis that if the embargo did not work and military force was required to force Hussein out of Kuwait, the hostages could be sacrificed as normal casualties of war. But televised interviews with hostages undercut policy when the TWA hostages being held in Lebanon pleaded with President Reagan on television not to use force to rescue them. As it turned out, the sympathy generated by the television interviews from Baghdad did not generate widespread opposition to the administration's military intentions. But if this situation arises in other hostile events involving Americans trapped abroad, where must television place its loyalty? To whom is it responsible? What has a higher calling —administrative policy or the immediate protection of American lives? What about non-American lives, or even the lives of "enemies"? Can news producers take it upon themselves to organize their broadcasts in such a way that people die because they are the current administration's "enemy"?

Equally difficult will be the question of timing. If television's loyalty is to its nation's policy (setting aside the issue of the media's role of questioning policy decisions), when should it curtail hostage coverage? When the policy is

announced? When the policy seems obvious from diplomatic signals? When the White House asks it to? The questions are not new, but are now more urgent.[8]

Another facet of the question of loyalty and responsibility would have emerged in the Gulf had the embargo been continued in place of military action, causing widespread suffering in Iraq. In that case, Hussein's best media strategy would have been to release pictures of starving hostages and Iraqi citizens, generating popular sympathy in the United States and giving other nations an excuse to break the embargo. The possible scenario of a global rock concert to raise food and medical funds for starving Iraqi mothers and children is not unrealistic in this circumstance, but it would be an embarrassing defeat for the United States. In the event that such a program was produced and distributed by satellite, should U.S. networks take part? What about non-American MTV franchises? Should Americans have been asked on television for money to help civilian Iraqi embargo casualties they saw suffering on their living room screens? Administration officials would likely call such appeals treasonous, but are not "enemy" civilians as human as "friend" civilians? They certainly look that way on television.

The question—"should American news crews in the Middle East have shown the pain caused in Iraq by an extended embargo?"—raises other questions. What about images sent to local U.S. stations by foreign producers, satellite syndicators, and other nation's networks? Should they be banned on U.S. television when they are being seen in other countries? Could they be banned? Who has that power? Should anyone have that kind of prior restraint power?

Does the Supreme Court's decision on the Pentagon Papers apply to broadcast media whose impact may be broader and more immediate? Is there any reason that it should not, television's impact notwithstanding?[9]

Second, what is live television's responsibility in war? Can it report from both sides and not be unpatriotic if its home country is involved? Can it report objectively from both sides during a war in which its home country is a belligerent? Even news organizations that broadcasted only critical reports from North Vietnam were criticized for giving publicity to the enemy. In the Gulf Crisis, the potential for a war starting while American reporters were working in both countries makes this a very unhypothetical question. Live (or tape-delayed) satellite reports from Iraq by American television may be unprecedented, but they are news and are protected morally and legally by the American peoples' right to know. Should Americans report live from the enemy camp or even air reports which have been aired in other nations that may be injurious to American military security or morale? These questions have been asked in the past and frequently answered with the understanding that one's first duty is to one's country. But that was before the existence of global, interconnected, multinational live television with contributors and audiences in dozens of countries. If television has made national borders porous, how long can national loyalty remain impervious?

CNN may have to face this question more immediately than other television organizations because of its position as the global wire service for everyman and the standard setter for world journalism. CNN's audience, employees, contributors, affiliates, constituencies, and influ-ence are truly global. During a crisis, and even on a day-to-day basis, millions of people and governments around the world rely on CNN for immediate and sometimes critical information. Should CNN's loyalty lie with its global viewers during a crisis? If U.S. national interest conflicts with the information needs of its world audience and the work of its non-U.S. contributors, which comes first? The immediate answer is that loyalty is always first to the United States. But as CNN continues to co-evolve with the global political system, that answer may have to be reexamined. If CNN had been operating during the Vietnam war when a majority of our allies and the American people opposed official policy, would it have carried live press conferences by Ho Chi Minh? If other national news organizations ran footage considered unpatriotic by the U.S. government, would CNN have run it? Would CNN's news exchange program World Report have taken stories from China or Vietnam, as it does now?

These are hypothetical questions for the "World's Most Important Network," but scenarios can be developed that pit U.S. foreign policy against CNN's responsibility to its world audience and international contributors. If those scenarios ever materialize, should CNN Center in Atlanta be declared international territory like the United Nations building in New York, and should all of its employees receive world citizenship to operate freely and objectively in the global news environment?[10] While it sounds far-fetched, CNN itself was called far-fetched by virtually everyone in television 10 years ago.

Television news and government need and exploit one another. Government manipulates television news to set political agendas, influence public opinion, and communicate with other governments. Television news takes advantage of government to get low-cost information and access to newsmakers and news events. Moreover, behind the scenes, the television industry wants government to free it from regulation while protecting it from competition. Television's audience —the nation's polity—is also enmeshed in this relationship, receiving a glut of information and emotion, but a dearth of perspective and understanding. The Gulf Crisis has exposed some of the cracks in the love-hate alliance between media and government and forced us all to think about where we are going with it. If we don't, we may get there and realize we don't like what we find.

NOTES

1. Berri conducted intermittent negotiations with Robert McFarland by telephone, while sending messages, setting the agenda, and stimulating public opinion pressure on the White House with television.

2. David Dickson (1990) details the mechanics of ethnic group pressure and media use.

3. ABC produced and ran a promotion spot referring to Koppel as a television statesman, but quickly pulled it when Koppel complained.

4. However, the communications role should not be overstated. In the Gulf Crisis, as in others, the United States communicated with its nemesis through third parties, such as Gorbachev and its Ambassador in Washington. During the TWA hostage crisis, the National Security Advisor

negotiated with Berri by telephone, while Berri used television to keep the initiative.

5. In general, the Middle Eastern print media was more aggressively pro-Iraqi than the electronic media. Part of this was due to years of cultivation by President Hussein through trips to Iraq, gifts of cars or other luxuries to editors and reporters, and the political ideologies of the groups supporting the papers.

6. See Kevin Goldman (1990) for the first of what will undoubtedly be many content studies of Gulf Crisis news coverage on television. His analysis finds that the four news networks (ABC, CBS, CNN, NBC) were far better at resisting Iraq's propaganda than Bush's.

7. Based on the New York Times/CBS News Poll, he lost on this front. The September 8, 1990, poll showed 76% general support for Bush's policies, rising to 84% among those who followed the crisis closely on the news. This level of support is consistent with other polls taken during the crisis period.

8. To not overstate the case, communication is also taking place through intermediaries from the UN, Russia, and other nations.

9. In reality, the answer may now hinge not so much on patriotism or ethics, but on money. There were scattered instances of journalists losing their jobs for not following the popular line of support for war. In one case, an NBC camera crew traveling with Ramsey Clark in Baghdad sent in highly newsworthy exclusive footage of Collation bomb damage, only to see it cut from the evening news by pressure from the business office. When the same footage was sent to another network and edited in for broadcast, the editor was fired in the middle of night and the clips pulled from the show —again, under pressure from the business office that did not want to anger the White House or antagonize audiences that supported the war and did not want to hear that the White House claims of pinpoint bombing on military targets were false. . . .

10. This question applies to other global and regional networks like the BBC.

NO

Warren P. Strobel

THE CNN EFFECT

It's May 31, 1995, there's another flare-up in the long-running Bosnia crisis and the Defense Department spokesman, Kenneth Bacon, is sitting in his office on the Pentagon's policy making E Ring. A clock is ticking over his head. On the wall right outside the door to Bacon's inner office is a television. Aide Brian Cullen glances at it from time to time.

On the bottom of the screen is the familiar CNN logo. Above it is the equally familiar figure of Peter Arnett in flak jacket and helmet, reporting breathlessly from Bosnia, analyzing the latest NATO airstrikes and the Bosnian Serbs' retaliation by taking U.N. peacekeepers hostage. Arnett is answering questions for the host and audience of CNN's interactive "Talk Back Live." Some of that audience is in cyberspace, sending in questions via CompuServe. At the top of the hour, Bacon will escort a "senior Defense Department official" to the podium of the Pentagon briefing room to explain to skeptical reporters why the Clinton administration's latest apparent policy change toward Bosnia is not a change at all.

Here it is, the nexus of media power and foreign policy, where television's instantly transmitted images fire public opinion, demanding instant responses from government officials, shaping and reshaping foreign policy at the whim of electrons. It's known as the CNN Effect.

It's a catchall phrase that has been used to describe a number of different phenomena. Perhaps the best definition, used by Professor Steven Livingston of George Washington University, is a loss of policy control on the part of policy makers because of the power of the media, a power that they can do nothing about.

Or is it the best definition? I'm here to ask Bacon that question. Bacon, a former journalist, is a precise man. He wears a bow tie and wire rim glasses, and looks like he doesn't get ruffled easily. On a day like today, his response is telling. "Policy makers," he says, "are becoming more adept at dealing with the CNN factor."

Bacon's opinion is one heard, in one form or another, over and over in the course of nearly 100 interviews during the last year with secretaries of state, spokespersons and everyone in between. I talked with officials from

From Warren P. Strobel, "The CNN Effect," *American Journalism Review* (May 1996). Copyright © 1996 by *American Journalism Review*. Reprinted by permission.

the Bush and Clinton administrations, the United Nations and relief agencies; military officers who have been in Bosnia, Somalia, Haiti and Rwanda; and journalists who have reported from those places. It is possible, of course, that they are all lying (the officials, that is). After all, who would want to admit that their authority has been usurped, their important jobs made redundant? To paraphrase legendary diplomat George Kennan's almost plaintive diary entry from the day U.S. troops landed in Somalia: If CNN determines foreign policy, why do we need administrators and legislators?

But the closer one looks at those incidents that supposedly prove a CNN Effect, where dramatic and/or real-time images appear to have forced policy makers into making sudden changes, the more the Effect shrinks. It is like a shimmering desert mirage, disappearing as you get closer.

A growing body of academic research is casting doubt on the notion that CNN in particular, or television in general, determines U.S. foreign policy the way it might seem from a quick glance at the live broadcasts from Tiananmen Square in 1989 or the image of the U.S. soldier being dragged through the streets of Mogadishu, Somalia, in October 1993 (see "When Pictures Drive Foreign Policy," December 1993). What officials told me closely parallels the findings of Nik Gowing, diplomatic editor for Britain's Independent Television Network, who interviewed dozens of British and American officials for a Harvard University study. Even many military officers, who might be expected to criticize media performance, have found the CNN Effect to be less than it is billed. But no one is arguing that CNN has had no effect on jour-nalists, government officials, and the way both conduct their business.

* * *

Virtually every official interviewed agrees that the rise of Cable News Network has radically altered the way U.S. foreign policy is conducted. Information is everywhere, not just because of CNN, but through other developments, such as the increasingly sophisticated media systems in developing nations and the explosive growth of the Internet. "It's part and parcel of governing," says Margaret Tutwiler, assistant secretary of state for public affairs under James A. Baker III. During her days at the State Department podium, Tutwiler knew that the most important audience was not the reporters asking the questions, but the array of cameras at the back of the briefing room, which sent her descriptions of U.S. policy to leaders, journalists and the public the globe over.

Baker says CNN has destroyed the concept of a "news cycle." In his days as a political campaign director, the news cycle was much longer, which meant the candidate had more time to respond to an opponent's charges. Now officials must respond almost instantly to developments. Because miniaturized cameras and satellite dishes can go virtually anywhere, policy makers no longer have the luxury of ignoring faraway crises.

These changes also affect modern U.S. military operations, which increasingly involve peacekeeping or humanitarian activities, and in which there is no vital U.S. interest at stake and thus less rationale for controlling the news media. The journalist-military debate over news media pools and other restrictions that date from Grenada and the Persian

Gulf War has been eclipsed by the Somalias and Haitis, where the news media were so pervasive that reporters were often providing information to the military rather than vice versa. U.S. Army Maj. David Stockwell and Col. Barry Willey, the chief military spokesmen in Somalia and Haiti, both described this media presence as alternately helpful and annoying, but in the end an inevitable piece of what the military calls the "operating environment."

But to say that CNN changes governance, shrinks decision making time and opens up military operations to public scrutiny is not the same as saying that it determines policy. Information indeed has become central to international affairs, but whether officials use this or are used by it depends largely on them. The stakes are higher for those who must make policy, but the tools at their command are also more powerful.

* * *

How, then, does the CNN Effect really work? One way to answer that question is to look at some common myths about the network, and at what government officials who must deal with it on a daily basis say really happens.

Myth No. 1

CNN makes life more difficult for foreign policy makers.

For those government officials who know how to use it, Ted Turner's round-the-clock video wire service can in fact be an immense boon. This was seen most vividly during the Persian Gulf War, when the Bush White House, knowing that Iraqi President Saddam Hussein's top aides were reluctant to bring him bad news, got into Saddam's living room

via CNN. And because CNN carried Pentagon briefings in Saudi Arabia and Washington live, officials were talking directly to the American public for hours on end. A study of commentators featured on the network during the gulf war found that the majority of them were retired military officers or other "elites" who by and large supported the administration's view of the crisis. Saddam, of course, used CNN too, as illustrated by the controversy over Peter Arnett's reporting from Iraq. This challenged the administration—but also provided a useful window into what the man in Baghdad was thinking.

It doesn't take a massive confrontation and half a million U.S. troops in the desert for CNN a perform this favor for officials. "Everybody talks about the CNN factor being bad," Pentagon spokesman Bacon says. "But in fact, a lot of it is good." If the Pentagon disagrees with a report by CNN Pentagon correspondent Jamie McIntyre, Defense Secretary William Perry can and will call him to try to put his spin on events. In the good old days of the 6 o'clock evening news, officials would have to wait 24 hours. By then it was usually too late. With CNN, they get many chances throughout the day to try to shape public perceptions.

Because of its speed, CNN also provides a convenient way for administration officials to leak new policies in the hope that they'll define the debate before political opponents do. Many a White House reporter knows that CNN's Wolf Blitzer is a frequent recipient of such leaks. Blitzer is on the White House lawn, repeating to the camera what he's just been told by unnamed officials, while newspaper reporters are still fretting over their leads.

The images of strife and horror abroad that are displayed on CNN and other television outlets also help foreign policy officials explain the need for U.S. intervention. CNN may be the last defense against isolationism. The press "makes the case of the need to be involved sometimes more than we can," says Richard Boucher, State Department spokesman under Baker and former Secretary of State Lawrence Eagleburger.

Myth No. 2

CNN dictates what's on the foreign policy agenda.

Somalia, of course, is the prime example cited. There was equal suffering in southern Sudan in 1992, the common wisdom goes, but the Bush administration was forced to pay attention to Somalia because the TV cameras were there.

While journalists undoubtedly were drawn to the drama of the famine in Somalia, they had a lot of help getting there. Much of this came from international relief agencies that depend on TV images to move governments to respond and the public to open its wallets. "We need the pictures. Always the pictures," says one official who works with the U.N. High Commissioner for Refugees (UNHCR). There isn't anything sinister about this. These private and intergovernmental agencies do good work under dangerous conditions. But for that very reason they are seen by many journalists as lacking the motives that most other sources are assumed to have. In the case of Somalia, these organizations were joined by U.S. government relief agencies and members of Congress interested in Africa in a campaign to generate media attention and government action.

One of the leaders of that campaign was Andrew Natsios, then an assistant administrator of the U.S. Agency for International Development, known for his rapport with reporters. Natsios and his aides gave numerous media interviews and held news conferences in Africa and in Washington in early 1992. "I deliberately used the news media as a medium for educating policy makers in Washington and in Europe" about how to address the crisis, Natsios says. And he says he used the media "to drive policy." Once reporters got to Somalia—sometimes with the UNHCR, the International Committee of the Red Cross and others—they of course sent back graphic reports of the famine that increased the pressure on President Bush to do something.

"It started with government manipulating press," says Herman Cohen, former assistant secretary of state for African affairs, "and then changed to press manipulating the government."

A quick look at the patterns of television reporting on Somalia also raises questions about the media's agenda-setting powers. There were very few television reports on Somalia (15 on the three networks to be exact) prior to Bush's August 1992 decision to begin an airlift. That decision resulted in a burst of reporting. The pattern was repeated later in the year when Bush ordered 25,000 U.S. troops to safeguard humanitarian aid. When they weren't following the actions of relief officials or members of Congress, the cameras were following the troops. CNN, in fact, was less likely than the networks to do independent reporting when Somalia was not on the Washington agenda.

Myth No. 3

*Pictures of suffering force
officials to intervene.*

Televised images of humanitarian suffering do put pressure on the U.S. government to act, as was seen in northern Iraq following the gulf war, in Somalia and in Rwanda. Part of the reason for this, officials say, is because the costs of lending a hand are presumed to be low. (The U.S. foreign policy establishment was disabused of this notion in Somalia, an experience that probably permanently shrunk this facet of the CNN Effect.)

But something interesting happens when the pictures suggest an intervention that is potentially high in costs, especially the cost of American casualties. Images of civil wars, no matter how brutal, simply don't have the same effect as those of lines of refugees or malnourished children at a feeding station.

In the summer and fall of 1992 the Bush administration was under intense pressure from Congress and the U.N. to do something to stop the outrages perpetrated against Bosnia's Muslims. In August, Newsday reported the existence of a string of detention camps where Bosnian Serbs were torturing, raping and killing. Within a few days, Britain's ITN confirmed the worst when it broadcast images of emaciated men trapped behind barbed wire. Yet by this time President Bush and his aides had concluded that intervening in the Bosnian civil war would take thousands of troops who might be mired down for years. CNN and its brethren did not change this calculation.

"It wouldn't have mattered if television was going 24 hours around the clock with Serb atrocities. Bush wasn't going to get in," says Warren Zimmermann, the last U.S. ambassador to Yugoslavia. Former Secretary of State Eagleburger confirmed this, saying: "Through all the time we were there, you have to understand that we had largely made a decision we were not going to get militarily involved. And nothing, including those stories, pushed us into it.... It made us damn uncomfortable. But this was a policy that wasn't going to get changed no matter what the press said."

The pressures that Eagleburger spoke of were very real. But rather than alter firmly held policy, in Bosnia and many other places, officials, in essence, pretended to. They took minimal steps designed to ease the pressure while keeping policy intact. These responses probably account for much of the perception that CNN and television in general change policy. Bush administration concern with the media "only extended to the appearance of maintaining we were behaving responsibly," says Foreign Service officer George Kenney, who resigned publicly to protest the lack of real U.S. action to save Bosnia. Roy Gutman, who won the Pulitzer Prize for his reporting from Bosnia for Newsday, concurs. "What you had is a lot of reaction to reports, but never any policy change."

Images of the brutal slaughter of half a million people in Rwanda in 1994 did not move governments to intervene with force. This was true despite the fact that there was more television coverage of the slaughter than there was of Somalia at any time in 1992 until Bush actually sent the troops. According to officials at the Pentagon and elsewhere, once the slaughter in Rwanda ended and the massive exodus of refugees began, what had seemed like an intervention nightmare became a relatively simple logistical and humanitarian problem that the U.S. military was well-equipped to solve.

Interestingly, the public reacted the same way as the Pentagon did. According to a top relief representative, private relief agencies "got virtually no money whatsoever" from the viewing public when television was broadcasting images of Rwandans who had been hacked to death. Contributions began to pour in when refugees flooded across Rwanda's borders and there were "pictures of women and children... innocents in need."

Myth No. 4

There is nothing officials can do about the CNN Effect.

To the contrary, whether or not the CNN Effect is real depends on the actions of government officials themselves. As ABC News' Ted Koppel puts it, "To the degree... that U.S. foreign policy in a given region has been clearly stated and adequate, accurate information has been provided, the influence of television coverage diminishes proportionately." In other words, the news media fill a vacuum, and CNN, by its reach and speed, can do so powerfully and quickly.

But this gives officials a lot more sway than Kennan thinks they have. The officials I interviewed did not identify a single instance when television reports forced them to alter a strongly held and/or well-communicated policy. Rather, the media seemed to have an impact when policy was weakly held, was already in the process of being changed or was lacking public support.

There is little doubt that the image of a dead U.S. soldier being desecrated in October 1993 forced President Clinton to come up with a rapid response to calls

in Congress for the withdrawal of U.S. troops from Somalia. Often forgotten, however, is that by September 1993 the Clinton administration already was making plans to extract U.S. troops. Just days before the images of the dead soldier were aired, Secretary of State Warren Christopher had told U.N. Secretary General Boutros Boutros-Ghali of Washington's desire to pull out. Congress had withdrawn its approval, and public support for the mission, documented in opinion polls, began falling well before the gruesome video started running on CNN.

What was most important about the imagery, however, was that it could not be explained by U.S. foreign policy makers. The Clinton administration had casually allowed the mission in Somalia to evolve from humanitarian relief to nation-building without explaining to the public and Congress the new costs, risks and goals. The images were the coup de grace. "The message was not handled properly from the administration," says one U.S. military officer who served in Somalia. The images were "a graphic illustration of the futility of what we were doing."

This ability of CNN to alter a policy that is in flux was graphically demonstrated again just a few months later in February 1994 when a mortar shell slammed into a marketplace in Sarajevo, killing 68 people and wounding many more. The images of the "market massacre" caused outrage around the world. The United States abandoned a year-old hands-off policy toward the Balkans and, a few days later, persuaded NATO to declare a zone around Sarajevo free of Bosnian Serb heavy weapons.

But what looks like a simple cause-effect relationship looked different to those making the policy. Here again, just days before, Christopher had presented to his senior government colleagues a plan for more aggressive U.S. action in Bosnia. He and others had become alarmed at the way U.S.-European disputes over Bosnia were debilitating NATO.

A senior State Department official was in a meeting on the new Bosnia policy when the mortaring occurred. He recalls worrying that the new policy would be seen, incorrectly, as a response to the massacre. The images did force the Clinton administration to respond quickly in public and ensured that an internal policy debate that might have lasted for months was telescoped into a few days. But the episode also provides additional evidence that CNN helps officials explain actions they already want to take. The images provided a moment of increased attention to Bosnia that could help justify the administration's policy response. "It was a short window. We took advantage of it. We moved the policy forward. And it was successful," then-White House spokeswoman Dee Dee Myers recalls.

Myth No. 5

The CNN Effect is on the rise.
Sadly, there is at least preliminary evidence that the public and officials are becoming inoculated against pictures of tragedy or brutality coming across their television screens. "We are developing an ability now to see incomprehensible human tragedy on television and understand no matter how horrible it is, we can't get involved in each and every instance," says White House spokesman Michael McCurry. "We are dulling out senses."

When a mortar again struck the Sarajevo marketplace in August 1995, the images were familiar: pools of blood and shredded limbs. For that reason, McCurry says, they had less impact. The policy response—bombing Bosnian Serbs—was driven instead by NATO's pledge a few weeks earlier to use air power to protect remaining U.S.-declared safe areas. NATO knew it had to make good on the pledge if it was to have any credibility left at all. McCurry's point about the dulling of our senses can be heard in what a viewer told an NBC audience researcher: "If I ever see a child with flies swarming around it one more time, I'm not going to watch that show again."

As with any new technology, people are learning over time to adapt to real-time television. While the danger remains that officials will respond to instant reports on CNN that later turn out to be wrong, several current and former spokespeople say that governments are becoming more sophisticated in dealing with time pressures. "As often as not, we buy ourselves time when things happen," Boucher says. "If we think we need the time to decide, we take the time to decide."

Pentagon spokesman Bacon says, "We do not have a big problem with saying, 'Yeah, this looks really awful, but let's find out what the facts really are.'"

On that day last May when I interviewed Bacon, media images had not pushed the United States further into the Balkan tangle. Rather, NATO bombing and the prospect that U.S. troops might go to Bosnia to rescue U.N. peacekeepers had sent journalists scurrying back to Sarajevo. The story was heating up again.

The CNN Effect is narrower and far more complex than the conventional wisdom holds. In a more perfect world, the news media—especially television—would be a more independent force, pointing out problems and helping set the public agenda. In reality, CNN and its brethren follow newsmakers at least as frequently as they push them or make them feel uncomfortable. The struggle between reporters and officials continues as before—just at a faster pace.

POSTSCRIPT

Do Media Drive Foreign Policy?

The American public may not be best served by the notion of a press that presents "just the facts." Journalists must select from a vast array of events and issues and decide what to cover and what to ignore. Sometimes the decisions they make lead to charges of bias. But some selection process is inherent to producing the news. The concepts guiding this selectivity are most frequently described as professional standards of "newsworthiness" and "accuracy." Most research suggests that journalists turn to "official sources" for guidance in deciding what is news. Critics suggest that economic issues are often involved in journalistic decision making, ranging from blatant attempts by advertisers to kill unfavorable stories to the more subtle decisions made by editors not to pursue stories because they are too convoluted to cover easily, too expensive to investigate, too litigious, or not immediately interesting to the public. And, of course, most people share a disdain for the style of electronic journalism frequently referred to as "if it bleeds, it leads." Whatever this selection process, journalists help to create a public agenda. So who sets the agenda? The press? Their corporate owners? The government? The people?

There have been several analyses of the media and war coverage. Gaye Tuchman's *Making News: A Study in the Construction of Reality* (Free Press, 1978) and Edward J. Epstein's *News from Nowhere* (Random House, 1973) are good general overviews. A more recent volume, *Lights, Camera, War: Is Media Technology Driving International Politics?* by Johanna Neuman (St. Martin's Press, 1996), makes the point that effective leaders in each generation have learned how to use new technologies to accomplish their purposes. Jonathan Mermin, in "Television News and American Intervention in Somalia: The Myth of a Media-Driven Foreign Policy," *Political Science Quarterly* (Fall 1997), presents a cogently argued attack on the notion that media drives foreign policy. The volume from which the O'Heffernan selection is taken, *Desert Storm and the Mass Media*, offers a collection of articles that focus on the complexities of mass media journalism when covering a war in the age of electronic news gathering, computers, faxes, and satellites.

Crisis limits options. Whether observing the press or government officials, it is clear that decisions are made without adequate time for analysis and often with inadequate information. Standards of ethical judgment and appropriate action must be learned, but in the heat of crisis, how those standards apply can be ambiguous. This is why case study, hindsight analysis, and hypothetical discussions of possible scenarios are so important in establishing the rules to be followed.

ISSUE 4

Is Emphasis on Body Image in the Media Harmful to Females Only?

YES: Mary C. Martin and James W. Gentry, from "Stuck in the Model Trap: The Effects of Beautiful Models in Ads on Female Pre-Adolescents and Adolescents," *Journal of Advertising* (Summer 1997)

NO: Michelle Cottle, from "Turning Boys into Girls," *The Washington Monthly* (May 1998)

ISSUE SUMMARY

YES: Marketing professors Mary C. Martin and James W. Gentry address the literature dealing with advertising images and the formation of body identity for preadolescent and adolescent females. They report a study to explore how social comparison theory influences young women.

NO: *Washington Monthly* editor Michelle Cottle takes the perspective that females are not the only ones influenced by media image. She cites polls and magazine advertising that indicate that males are exposed to images of idealized body type as well, and she argues that these images also have an impact on the male psyche.

There is plenty of evidence to support the idea that young girls are influenced by the body images of models and actresses they see in the media. In her book *The Beauty Myth* (Anchor Books, 1992), Naomi Wolf writes that the typical model or actress is significantly below what the medical establishment considers a "healthy" body weight. The desire to look like a model or actress has contributed to what could be termed an outbreak in eating disorders among females. Wolf warns that 1 out of 10 college women develop an eating disorder while in college, but the desire to be thin often starts as early as age eight for many girls.

Little attention has been given to the self-images of boys, while the unhealthy aspects of eating disorders and idealized body image has been primarily attributed to girls. In the following selections the authors help us to understand this phenomena on an even broader scale.

Mary C. Martin and James W. Gentry take the position that idealized body image is a female problem, and they attempt to study whether or not social comparison theory (the idea that females compare their own physical attractiveness with models) influences self-esteem. Their studies of fourth-

and sixth-graders help to illuminate differential cognitive levels and the way images influence self-perceptions.

Michelle Cottle adds an interesting dimension to the problem of images and idealized body type. She asserts that men's magazines have also taken the approach to making males feel inadequate through images and stories that work against male vanity. The images and stories she describes raise questions about the content of magazines and the way pictures and stories affect us psychologically.

These issues will undoubtedly spark lively discussions about whether or not images and stories actually do shape the way we think about ourselves in relation to idealized images. The psychological effects of media are difficult to assess, even though the presence of images is pervasive, but it is hard to ignore their potential power. The history of media effects research has much to offer in the way we think about the following selections.

YES

Mary C. Martin and
James W. Gentry

STUCK IN THE MODEL TRAP

A growing concern in our society is the plight of female pre-adolescents and adolescents as they grow up facing many obstacles, including receiving less attention than boys in the classroom, unrealistic expectations of what they can and cannot do, decreasing self-esteem, and being judged by their physical appearance. In particular, girls are generally preoccupied with attempting to become beautiful. As Perry suggests, "Today's specifications call for blonde and thin—no easy task, since most girls get bigger during adolescence. Many become anorexics or bulimics; a few rich ones get liposuction. We make their focus pleasing other people and physical beauty." Further, studies show that self-esteem drops to a much greater extent for female than male pre-adolescents and adolescents, with self-perceptions of physical attractiveness contributing to the drop.

Another growing concern in our society is the role of advertising in contributing to those obstacles. For example, advertising has been accused of unintentionally imposing a "sense of inadequacy" on women's self-concepts. Studies suggest that advertising and the mass media may play a part in creating and reinforcing a preoccupation with physical attractiveness and influence consumer perceptions of what constitutes an acceptable level of physical attractiveness. Further, studies have found that female college students, adolescents, and pre-adolescents compare their physical attractiveness with that of models in ads and that female pre-adolescents and adolescents have desires to be models. An aspiring young model, for example, describes "the model trap":

> Deep down inside, I still want to be a supermodel... As long as they're there, screaming at me from the television, glaring at me from magazines, I'm stuck in the model trap. Hate them first. Then grow to like them. Love them. Emulate them. Die to be them. All the while praying this cycle will come to an end.

Clearly, such findings raise concern about advertising ethics. Jean Kilbourne, for example, addresses how female bodies are depicted in advertising imagery and the potential effects on women's physical and mental health in her videos *Still Killing Us Softly* and *Slim Hopes*. The use of highly attractive models in ads as an "ethical issue" received little or no attention in published research from 1987 to 1993, but the ethics of that practice have begun to be questioned by consumers and advertisers. For example, a consumer movement against advertising has arisen in the United States. The organization Boycott Anorexic Marketing (BAM) is attempting to get consumers to boycott products sold by companies that use extremely thin models in their ads. Such criticisms of advertising are "much too serious to dismiss cavalierly."

Using social comparison theory as a framework, we propose that female pre-adolescents and adolescents compare their physical attractiveness with that of advertising models. As a result, their self-perceptions and self-esteem may be affected. In response to the criticisms, we conducted a study to assess those unintended consequences of advertising. However, unlike previous empirical studies of those effects, ours incorporated the role of a motive for comparison—self-evaluation, self-improvement, or self-enhancement—which may help to explain the inconsistent findings in the advertising/marketing and psychology literature. Specifically, our premise was that changes in self-perceptions and/or self-esteem may be influenced by the type of motive operating at the time of comparison.

PHYSICAL ATTRACTIVENESS AND SELF-ESTEEM IN CHILDREN AND ADOLESCENTS

Cultural norms in the United States dictate the importance of being physically attractive, especially of being thin. The emphasis on being physically attractive begins in infancy and continues throughout childhood and adolescence. How physically attractive a child or adolescent perceives him/herself to be heavily influences his/her self-esteem, particularly beginning in fifth grade. However, the effect of self-perceptions of physical attractiveness on self-esteem differs between girls and boys. For example, Harter, in a cross-sectional study of third through eleventh graders, found that self-perceptions of physical attractiveness and levels of global self-esteem appeared to decline systematically over time in girls but not for boys. Other researchers have documented such decreases throughout adolescence for girls. Boys' self-esteem, in contrast, tends to increase from early through late adolescence.

The nature of physical attractiveness differs for male and female children and adolescents as well. Girls tend to view their bodies as "objects," and their physical beauty determines how they and others judge their overall value. Boys tend to view their bodies as "process," and power and function are more important criteria for evaluating their physical self. For example, Lerner, Orlos, and Knapp found that female adolescents' self-concepts derived primarily from body attractiveness whereas male adolescents' self-concepts were related more strongly to perceptions of physical instrumental effectiveness. The difference in body orientation results in girls paying attention to individual body parts and boys having a holistic body perspective. Because the ideal of attractiveness for girls is more culturally salient, girls have a greater likelihood of being negatively affected by the feminine ideal than boys have of being negatively affected by the masculine ideal.

ADVERTISING AND SOCIAL COMPARISON

Television commercials and magazine advertisements that contribute to the "body-as-object" focus for female pre-adolescents and adolescents, using difficult-to-attain standards of physical attractiveness to market products, are pervasive. For example, in an analysis of *Seventeen*, a magazine with "the potential to influence a substantial proportion of the adolescent female population," Guillen and Barr found that models' body shapes were less curvaceous than those in magazines for adult women and that the hip/waist ratio decreased from 1970 to 1990, meaning that models' bodies had become thinner over time. In addition, nearly half of the space of the most popular magazines for adolescent girls is devoted to advertisements.

Social comparison theory holds that people have a drive to evaluate their opinions and abilities, which can be satisfied by "social" comparisons with other people. With that theory as a framework, recent studies have found that female college students and female pre-adolescents and adolescents do compare their physical attractiveness with that of models in ads. In turn, those comparisons may result in changes in self-perceptions of physical attractiveness or self-perceptions of body image. Given the importance of self-perceptions of physical attractiveness in influencing female self-esteem, the comparisons may result in changes in self-esteem as well. . . .

Using social comparison theory as a basis, Richins found no support for the hypothesis that exposure to advertising with highly attractive models would temporarily lower female college students' self-perceptions of physical attractive-ness. "By late adolescence, however, the sight of extremely attractive models is 'old news' and unlikely to provide new information that might influence self-perception." Martin and Kennedy assessed the effects of highly attractive models in ads on female pre-adolescents and adolescents but found no support for a lowering of self-perceptions. Relying on Festinger's original conception of the theory, those researchers did not account for motive, and appear to have assumed that the motive for comparison was self-evaluation (i.e., girls compare themselves with models in ads to evaluate their own level of physical attractiveness). However, more recent research has shown that social comparisons may occur for other reasons, suggesting that female pre-adolescents and adolescents may compare themselves to models in ads for any one (or a combination) of three motives: self-evaluation, self-improvement, or self-enhancement. For example, Martin and Kennedy found that self-evaluation and self-improvement are common motives when female pre-adolescents and adolescents compare themselves with models in ads. Self-enhancement, in contrast, is not common and does not seem to occur naturally. Similarly, in a series of pretests reported by Martin, self-evaluation and self-improvement were found to be common motives in college students, but self-enhancement was not. Gentry, Martin, and Kennedy, however, found stronger support for self-enhancement in a study using in-depth interviews of first and fifth graders. As girls mature, their motives for comparison apparently vary.

The incorporation of motive may help to clarify the inconsistent findings in the literature. Our subsequent discussion explores possible differential effects of comparisons with advertising models on female pre-adolescents' and adolescents' self-perceptions and self-esteem, depending on whether self-evaluation, self-enhancement, or self-improvement is the primary motive at the time of comparison. We do not examine what motives are occurring naturally, but rather how advertising affects girls when they have a particular motive. Our overriding research question is whether motives make a difference in terms of self-perceptions and self-esteem. Finding differences between motives would clearly encourage consumer educators to stress one motive for social comparison over another. Our hypotheses specify the direction of change for each motive, thus implying response differences between subjects who have a particular comparison motive and subjects in a control group. Finding differences between motives would answer our research question even though differences between a motive group and the control group may not be significant.

Self-Evaluation as a Motive for Comparison

As the motive for comparison, Festinger originally proposed self-evaluation, the judgment of value, worth, or appropriateness of one's abilities, opinions, and personal traits. Information obtained from social comparison is not used for self-evaluation until the age of seven or eight, even though social comparison has been found to occur in children of preschool age. In the context of advertising, given that advertising models represent an ideal image of beauty, we expect comparison to be generally upward. That is, female pre-adolescents and adolescents will generally consider advertising models to be superior in terms of physical attractiveness. Therefore, if self-

evaluation is the primary motive at the time of comparison (a girl is attempting to judge the value or worth of her own physical attractiveness or body image against that of advertising models), comparisons are likely to result in lowered self-perceptions and lowered self-esteem. . . .

METHOD . . .

Subjects

Female pre-adolescents and adolescents in grades four (n = 82; mean age = 9.8 years), six (n = 103; mean age = 11.9 years), and eight (n = 83; mean age = 13.8 years) from a public school system in the Midwest participated in the study (total sample size 268). The public school system is in a county where 98% of the population is white and the median family income is $31,144. Although the sample is not representative of all pre-adolescent and adolescent girls in the United States, it does represent a segment of girls most susceptible to problems linked to physical attractiveness such as eating disorders. As an incentive to participate, the subjects took part in a drawing for two prizes of $50 each. In addition, a $500 donation was made to the public school system.

Fourth, sixth, and eighth graders were chosen for the study because research suggests that the period between the fourth and eighth grades is important in girls' development of positive perceptions of the self. It is a period when female bodies are changing drastically and adult definitions of "beauty" are becoming relevant social norms. We suggest that a girl's transition in this time period is more of a discontinuity than a linear transformation because of the conflicting biological and social processes. For example, Martin and Kennedy found, in an experiment with fourth, eighth, and twelfth grade girls, that self-perceptions of physical attractiveness decreased as the subjects got older. Fourth graders' self-perceptions were significantly higher than those of eighth graders, but eighth graders' self-perceptions were not significantly different from those of twelfth graders. Other evidence suggests that self-perceptions of physical attractiveness start to become particularly important during fifth grade. For example, Krantz, Friedberg, and Andrews found a very high correlation between self-perceived attractiveness and self-esteem in fifth graders.... The strength of the relationship in fifth graders more than tripled the variance accounted for at the third-grade level.

Classroom teachers administered the questionnaires to the subjects at the schools during an hour of class time. To separate the measurement of covariates from the manipulation, two separate booklets were used. The first booklet contained the covariate measures. After subjects completed that booklet, they handed it in and were given a second booklet with a set of ads and dependent variable measures. The assignment to treatments was randomized by giving each classroom a random assortment of the five types of questionnaires with ads. Teachers administered the questionnaires to minimize any source effects caused by having an unfamiliar authority figure collect the data. To facilitate understanding, the teachers administered the questionnaires orally by reading each question aloud and allowing appropriate time for the subjects to mark their responses.

Advertising Stimuli

Full-color ads were created by cutting and pasting stimuli from magazine ads in *Seventeen, Sassy, Teen,* and *YM.* Those magazines were chosen because they are the top four teen magazines in the United States and because they maintain consistency with respect to type of beauty. The stimuli were cut from original ads in a way that eliminated information about the sources. The ads created were for commonly advertised but fictional brand name adornment products: Satin Colors lipstick, Generation Gap jeans, and Hair in Harmony hair care products. The ads appeared to be professionally prepared, were kept very simple, and were realistic as they included partial- and full-body photos of models extracted from actual hair care, jeans, and lipstick ads.

To ensure that the subjects perceived the models in the ads as highly attractive, means of two items that measured the models' perceived attractiveness were calculated for each of the three ads. On 7-point semantic differential scales, subjects were asked to rate the model in the ad from "very overweight and out of shape, fat" to "very fit and in shape, thin" and "very unattractive, ugly" to "very attractive, beautiful" prior to measurement of the dependent variables. The range of mean responses to those items was 5.1 to 6.4, far above the midpoint value of four. Hence, the subjects perceived the models as highly attractive.

Manipulation of Motives

Motives were manipulated through instructions given prior to exposure to a set of ads, advertising headlines and copy, and a listing exercise. The manipulations were based on the following operational definitions of each motive.

1. Self-evaluation—a girl's explicit comparison of her physical attractiveness with that of models in ads to determine whether she is as pretty as or prettier than the models on specific dimensions such as hair, eyes, and body.
2. Self-improvement—a girl's explicit comparison of her physical attractiveness with that of models in ads to seek ways of improving her own attractiveness on specific dimensions such as hairstyle and makeup.
3. Self-enhancement 1—a girl's explicit comparison of her physical attractiveness with that of models in ads in an attempt to enhance her self-esteem by finding ways in which she is prettier than the model on specific dimensions (inducement of a downward comparison).
4. Self-enhancement 2—a girl's discounting of the beauty of models in ads and, in turn, the avoidance of an explicit comparison of her own physical attractiveness with that of the models in an attempt to protect/maintain her self-esteem.

Prior to exposure to a set of ads, the subjects were given instructions in which they were shown a drawing of "Amy looking at an advertisement in a magazine" and were told a story about Amy comparing herself with a model in an ad for a particular motive. Then the subjects were asked to look at the ads on the following pages and view the ads as Amy had viewed them.

As consistency in ad design across experimental groups was essential, the headline and copy were the only components manipulated in the four sets of ads designed to induce particular mo-tives. Minor deviations from the ad design were necessary for the control group because their ads did not include a model. The instructions, headlines, and copy were developed from "stories" written by female adolescents in projective tests in previous studies. . . .

The subjects also completed a listing exercise after viewing each ad. They looked at each ad and listed specific ways in which the manipulated motive may have occurred. For example, in the self-improvement condition, subjects were asked to look at the model and "list ideas you get on how to improve your looks." The intent of the study was not to measure naturally occurring motives for social comparison, but rather to investigate how the use of various motives changes cognitive and affective reactions to stimuli showing physically attractive models.

If a subject successfully completed the listing exercises, the manipulation was considered successful. One author analyzed the responses to each listing exercise, coding for the subject's success or failure in completing it. Criteria for a successful response were specific references to aspects of physical attractiveness that were compared in the ad and no indication that another motive was present. For example, for a successful manipulation of self-improvement, one respondent listed the following ideas she got from looking at the model in the ad: "Use the product. Get a perm. Wear lots of make-up and have as pretty of a face as she does."

A response failed if it indicated that no motive or another motive was present. The failed responses were discarded, resulting in seven subjects being dropped (three subjects from the self-evaluation condition, one subject from the self-improvement condition, and three subjects from the self-enhancement 2 condition). For example, one subject in the self-evaluation condition was dropped because, when asked to list "ways in which your hair, face, and body look compared to the model's hair, face, and body," she wrote, "She looks different because I am a different person. I don't really compare to her." One subject in the self-improvement condition was dropped because, when asked to "list the ideas you get from the model on how you could improve the way you look," she wrote, "I could never look like her and will not try. I know that she has to be willing to work to look like she does. I don't worry about the way I look, it's just not at all that important to me." . . .

DISCUSSION

In general, our results suggest that motives do play an important role in the study context as we found differential effects for changes in self-perceptions of physical attractiveness, self-perceptions of body image, and self-esteem. Consistent with predictions of social comparison theory, female pre-adolescents' and adolescents' self-perceptions and self-esteem can be detrimentally affected, particularly when self-evaluation occurs: self-perceptions of physical attractiveness were lowered in all subjects. . . . In sixth graders, self-perceptions of body image were lowered (i.e., body was perceived as larger) in subjects who self-evaluated. . . .

On a positive note, the inclusion of motives shows that detrimental effects do not always occur. That is, positive temporary effects occur when either self-improvement or self-enhancement is the motive for comparison: self-perceptions of physical attractiveness were raised

in subjects who self-improved or self-enhanced through downward comparisons. . . . Self-perceptions and self-esteem were unaffected in most cases in subjects who self-enhanced by discounting the beauty of models. . . . The only exception occurred when sixth graders' self-perceptions of body image were raised (i.e., body was perceived as skinnier). . . .

Social comparison theory, as it currently stands, cannot explain all of our results. In particular, how the processes may change over the course of one's lifetime is not articulated theoretically or empirically. A closer examination of the results and some speculation may help to explain the inconsistent and contradictory support for the hypotheses. Though no statistically significant differences were detected, the findings for the fourth graders are interesting and offer some food for thought. Their self-evaluations produced the lowest self-perceptions of physical attractiveness and the highest (i.e., most skinny) self-perceptions of body image in comparison with the other motives. Perhaps in childhood girls (like boys) desire to grow up and "get bigger." Hence, if the fourth graders in our study desired to "get bigger," a skinnier body image would actually represent a "lowering" of self-perceptions. In that case, low self-perceptions of physical attractiveness and skinny self-perceptions of body image after self-evaluation would be consistent, supporting the notion that self-evaluation through comparisons with models in ads has detrimental effects on female pre-adolescents and adolescents.

In comparison with the fourth graders, the sixth graders produced somewhat different results. Sixth graders' self-evaluations produced the lowest self-perceptions of physical attractiveness and the lowest (i.e., the least skinny) self-perceptions of body image in comparison with the other motives. For sixth graders, unlike fourth graders, the direction of changes in self-perceptions of physical attractiveness and body image were consistent. Perhaps a transition occurs between the fourth and sixth grade, from "bigger is better" to "skinnier is better."

In self-esteem, only fourth graders were affected after self-enhancement. Self-esteem was raised in fourth graders who self-enhanced through downward comparisons.... However, self-esteem was lowered in fourth graders who self-enhanced by discounting the beauty of the models.... Martin and Kennedy found that fourth graders aspire to be models more than older adolescents, and perhaps fourth graders are discounting their own future when they discount the beauty of models. Further, fourth graders may be young enough not to realize that not all will grow up to be as beautiful as advertising models. The lack of effects of self-enhancement on sixth and eighth graders' self-esteem may be due to their reluctance to accept that they can look better than advertising models... or that they can discount the beauty of models....

IMPLICATIONS AND DIRECTIONS FOR FUTURE RESEARCH

Our results have implications for advertisers and educators. Educators can use the framework of social comparison theory to instruct children and adolescents about how (i.e., which motives to use) and when (i.e., in what circumstances and with whom) to use others for comparison. With respect to advertising models, children and adolescents may be able to use the processes of self-improvement and self-enhancement to their advantage, as both led to temporary increases in self-perceptions (in comparison with the control group or girls in another manipulated condition). As Martin and Kennedy found, however, self-enhancement is not a naturally occurring motive when female pre-adolescents and adolescents compare themselves with models in ads. Hence, the involvement of educators would be crucial. Not only would emphasis on self-enhancement be advantageous in terms of self-perceptions, but advertisers could benefit as well, as research suggests that making consumers feel physically attractive encourages sales of cosmetic and other adornment products. That possibility is encouraging, but must be viewed with caution until further research has been conducted. Our results suggest that the relationships between motives and self-perceptions and self-esteem are not straightforward and that there are particular times in childhood and adolescence when efforts to instruct young people in how to view ads may be most appropriate. Simply beginning education at a very early age is not the answer. For example, self-enhancement by discounting the beauty of models essentially did not work for fourth graders, as it caused their self-esteem to decrease. Discounting the beauty of models appears to have led fourth graders to discount their own futures in terms of physical attractiveness. In addition, if fourth graders believe "bigger is better," they may not have enough intellectual maturity to realize that "bigger is better" conflicts with the beauty and slenderness of advertising models.

Sixth and eighth graders, in contrast, may be reluctant to accept the notion of discounting models' beauty, hence the lack of effect on their self-esteem. That reluctance might be due partly to their having developed a more sophisticated level of advertising skepticism, as "adolescents have the confidence to rely on their own judgment and the discernment necessary to separate advertising truth from advertising hype." Boush and his coauthors found that self-esteem is related directly to mistrust of advertiser motives and disbelief of advertising claims. Hence, education before sixth grade may be critical to get female pre-adolescents and adolescents to accept the notion of discounting the beauty of advertising models.

The period between the fourth and eighth grades appears to be a critical one on which future research would be beneficial to assess further what role each of the motives has and for what ages. Other issues also warrant attention. For example, in our study, the models in the ads were in their late teens or early adulthood. Future research might address the effects of younger models, as well as more ordinary-looking models, in ads. Another need is to assess whether the type of physical attractiveness is important. . . . Further, future research should incorporate the role of "esteem relevance" and "perceived control" to determine whether and to what extent those variables account for natural tendencies to have one motive rather than another. In addition, differential levels of esteem relevance and perceived control may lead to different types and levels of responses. For example, cognitive responses (e.g., self-perceptions) may differ from affective responses (e.g., self-esteem) after comparisons with models in ads, which may help to explain the inconsistent results found here and in similar studies.

Finally, some researchers have acknowledged that the minimal effects or lack of effects found in studies assessing temporary changes in self-perceptions or self-esteem may differ from what may be found in the long term. Thornton and Moore concluded that "with long-term comparisons such as this, particularly with the pervasive presence of idealized media images in our culture and the continued, and perhaps increasing, emphasis placed on physical appearance, there exists the potential for bringing about more significant and lasting changes in the self-concept." The motive of self-improvement, however, represents a unique situation in that temporary changes may differ from the long-term changes. When one commonly compares oneself to advertising models for self-improvement, one may eventually realize that the ideal is not as attainable as originally believed. . . .

Given the criticisms of advertising based on its cultural and social consequences, a better understanding of the role of comparison motives and the other issues mentioned here is needed. Such understanding may lead to a unified effort by educators to help prevent detrimental effects on female pre-adolescents and adolescents. However, a unified effort by educators may not be enough, and a call for legislation to control the use of models in advertising may arise in response to consumer movements such as Boycott Anorexic Marketing (BAM). Advertising researchers must respond with studies to determine more clearly the unintended consequences of advertising.

NO

Michelle Cottle

TURNING BOYS INTO GIRLS

I love *Men's Health* Magazine. There. I'm out of the closet, and I'm not ashamed. Sure, I know what some of you are thinking: What self-respecting '90s woman could embrace a publication that runs such enlightened articles as "Turn Your Good Girl Bad" and "How to Wake Up Next to a One-Night Stand"? Or maybe you'll smile and wink knowingly: What red-blooded hetero chick *wouldn't* love all those glossy photo spreads of buff young beefcake in various states of undress, ripped abs and glutes flexed so tightly you could bounce a check on them? Either way you've got the wrong idea. My affection for *Men's Health* is driven by pure gender politics—by the realization that this magazine, and a handful of others like it, are leveling the playing field in a way that *Ms.* can only dream of. With page after page of bulging biceps and Gillette jaws, robust hairlines and silken skin, *Men's Health* is peddling a standard of male beauty as unforgiving and unrealistic as the female version sold by those dewy-eyed pre-teen waifs draped across the covers of *Glamour* and *Elle.* And with a variety of helpful features on "Foods That Fight Fat," "Banish Your Potbelly," and "Save Your Hair (Before it's Too Late)," *Men's Health* is well on its way to making the male species as insane, insecure, and irrational about physical appearance as any *Cosmo* girl.

Don't you see, ladies? We've been going about this equality business all wrong. Instead of battling to get society fixated on something besides our breast size, we should have been fighting spandex with spandex. Bra burning was a nice gesture, but the greater justice is in convincing our male counterparts that the key to their happiness lies in a pair of made-for-him Super Shaper Briefs with the optional "fly front endowment pad" (as advertised in *Men's Journal,* $29.95 plus shipping and handling). Make the men as neurotic about the circumference of their waists and the whiteness of their smiles as the women, and at least the burden of vanity and self-loathing will be shared by all.

This is precisely what lads' mags like *Men's Health* are accomplishing. The rugged John-Wayne days when men scrubbed their faces with deodorant soap and viewed gray hair and wrinkles as a badge of honor are fading. Last year, international market analyst Euromonitor placed the U.S. men's toiletries market—hair color, skin moisturizer, tooth whiteners, etc.—at $3.5 billion. According to a survey conducted by DYG researchers for *Men's Health* in November 1996, approximately 20 percent of American men get manicures or pedicures, 18 percent use skin treatments such as masks or mud packs, and 10 percent enjoy professional facials. That same month, *Psychology Today* reported that a poll by Roper Starch Worldwide showed that "6 percent of men nationwide actually use such traditionally female products as bronzers and foundation to create the illusion of a youthful appearance."

What men are putting *on* their bodies, however, is nothing compared to what they're doing *to* their bodies: While in the 1980s only an estimated one in 10 plastic surgery patients were men, as of 1996, that ratio had shrunk to one in five. The American Academy of Cosmetic Surgery estimates that nationwide more than 690,000 men had cosmetic procedures performed in '96, the most recent year for which figures are available. And we're not just talking "hair restoration" here, though such procedures do command the lion's share of the male market. We're also seeing an increasing number of men shelling out mucho dinero for face peels, liposuction, collagen injections, eyelid lifts, chin tucks, and, of course, the real man's answer to breast implants: penile enlargements (now available to increase both length and diameter).

Granted, *Men's Health* and its journalistic cousins (*Men's Journal, Details, GQ,* etc.) cannot take all the credit for this breakthrough in gender parity. The fashion and glamour industries have perfected the art of creating consumer "needs," and with the women's market pretty much saturated, men have become the obvious target for the purveyors of everything from lip balm to lycra. Meanwhile, advances in medical science have made cosmetic surgery a quicker, cleaner option for busy executives (just as the tight fiscal leash of managed care is driving more and more doctors toward this cash-based specialty). Don't have several weeks to recover from a full-blown facelift? No problem. For a few hundred bucks you can get a micro-dermabrasion face peel on your lunch hour.

Then there are the underlying social factors. With women growing ever more financially independent, aspiring suitors are discovering that they must bring more to the table than a well-endowed wallet if they expect to win (and keep) the fair maiden. Nor should we overlook the increased market power of the gay population—in general a more image-conscious lot than straight guys. But perhaps most significant is the ongoing, ungraceful descent into middle age by legions of narcissistic baby boomers. Gone are the days when the elder statesmen of this demographic bulge could see themselves in the relatively youthful faces of those insipid yuppies on "Thirtysomething." Increasingly, boomers are finding they have more in common with the *parents* of today's TV, movie, and sports stars. Everywhere they turn some upstart Gen Xer is flaunting his youthful vitality, threatening boomer dominance on both the social and professional fronts. (Don't think even Hollywood didn't shudder when the Oscar for best original screenplay this year went to a couple of guys barely old enough to shave.) With whippersnappers looking to steal everything from their jobs to their women, post-pubescent men have at long last discovered the terror of losing their springtime radiance.

Whatever combo of factors is feeding the frenzy of male vanity, magazines such as *Men's Health* provide the ideal meeting place for men's insecurities and marketers' greed. Like its more established female counterparts, *Men's Health* is an affordable, efficient delivery vehicle for the message that physical imperfection, age, and an underdeveloped fashion sense are potentially crippling disabilities. And as with women's mags, this cycle of insanity is self-perpetuating: The more men obsess about growing old or unattractive, the more marketers will exploit and expand that fear; the more marketers bombard men with messages about the need to be beautiful, the more they will obsess. Younger and younger men will be sucked into the vortex of self-doubt. Since 1990, *Men's Health* has seen its paid circulation rise from 250,000 to more than 1.5 million; the magazine estimates that half of its 5.3 million readers are under age 35 and 46 percent are married. And while most major magazines have suffered sluggish growth or even a decline in circulation in recent years, during the first half of 1997, *Men's Health* saw its paid circulation increase 14 percent over its '96 figures. (Likewise, its smaller, more outdoorsy relative, Wenner Media's *Men's Journal,* enjoyed an even bigger jump of 26.5 percent.) At this rate, one day soon, that farcical TV commercial featuring men hanging out in bars, whining about having inherited their mothers' thighs will be a reality. Now *that's* progress.

VANITY, THY NAME IS MAN

Everyone wants to be considered attractive and desirable. And most of us are aware that, no matter how guilty and shallow we feel about it, there are certain broad cultural norms that define at-

tractive. Not surprisingly, both men's and women's magazines have argued that, far from playing on human insecurities, they are merely helping readers be all that they can be—a kind of training camp for the image impaired. In recent years, such publications have embraced the tenets of "evolutionary biology," which argue that, no matter how often we're told that beauty is only skin deep, men and women are hard-wired to prefer the Jack Kennedys and Sharon Stones to the Rodney Dangerfields and Janet Renos. Continuation of the species demands that specimens with shiny coats, bright eyes, even features, and other visible signs of ruddy good health and fertility automatically kick-start our most basic instinct. Of course, the glamour mags' editors have yet to explain why, in evolutionary terms, we would ever desire adult women to stand 5'10" and weigh 100 pounds. Stories abound of women starving themselves to the point that their bodies shut down and they stop menstruating—hardly conducive to reproduction—yet Kate Moss remains the dish du jour and millions of Moss wannabes still struggle to subsist on a diet of Dexatrim and Perrier.

Similarly, despite its title, *Men's Health* is hawking far more than general fitness or a healthful lifestyle. For every half page of advice on how to cut your stress level, there are a dozen pages on how to build your biceps. For every update on the dangers of cholesterol, there are multiple warnings on the horrors of flabby abs. Now, without question, gorging on Cheetos and Budweiser while your rump takes root on the sofa is no way to treat your body if you plan on living past 50. But chugging protein drinks, agonizing over fat grams, and counting the minutes until your next Stairmaster session is equally unbalanced. The line between taking pride in one's physical appearance and being obsessed by it is a fine one—and one that disappeared for many women long ago.

Now with lads' mags taking men in that direction as well, in many cases it's almost impossible to tell whether you're reading a copy of *Men's Health* or of *Mademoiselle:* "April 8. To commemorate Buddha's birthday, hit a Japanese restaurant. Stick to low-fat selections. Choose foods described as *yakimono,* which means "grilled," advised the monthly "to do list" in the April *Men's Health.* (Why readers should go Japanese in honor of the most famous religious leader in *India's* history remains unclear.) The January/February list was equally thought provoking: "January 28. It's Chinese New Year, so make a resolution to custom-order your next takeout. Ask that they substitute wonton soup broth for oil. Try the soba noodles instead of plain noodles. They're richer in nutrients and contain much less fat." The issue also featured a "Total Body Workout Poster" and one of those handy little "substitution" charts (loathed by women everywhere), showing men how to slash their calorie intake by making a few minor dietary substitutions: mustard for mayo, popcorn for peanuts, seltzer water for soda, pretzels for potato chips. . . .

As in women's magazines, fast results with minimum inconvenience is a central theme. Among *Men's Health's* March highlights were a guide to "Bigger Biceps in 2 Weeks," and "20 Fast Fixes" for a bad diet; April offered "A Better Body in Half the Time," along with a colorful four-page spread on "50 Snacks That Won't Make You Fat." And you can forget carrot sticks—this think-thin eating guide celebrated the wonders of

Reduced Fat Cheez-its, Munch 'Ems, Fiddle Faddle, Oreos, Teddy Grahams, Milky Ways, Bugles, Starburst Fruit Twists, and Klondike's Fat Free Big Bear Ice Cream Sandwiches. Better nutrition is not the primary issue. A better butt is. To this end, also found in the pages of *Men's Health* is the occasional, tasteful ad for liposuction—just in case nature doesn't cooperate.

But a blueprint to rock-hard buns is only part of what makes *Men's Health* the preeminent "men's lifestyle" magazine. Nice teeth, nice skin, nice hair, and a red-hot wardrobe are now required to round out the ultimate alpha male package, and *Men's Health* is there to help on all fronts. In recent months it has run articles on how to select, among other items, the perfect necktie and belt, the hippest wallet, the chicest running gear, the best "hair-thickening" shampoo, and the cutest golfing apparel. It has also offered advice on how to retard baldness, how to keep your footwear looking sharp, how to achieve different "looks" with a patterned blazer, even how to keep your lips from chapping at the dentist's office: "[B]efore you start all that 'rinse and spit' business, apply some moisturizer to your face and some lip balm to your lips. Your face and lips won't have that stretched-out dry feeling . . . Plus, you'll look positively radiant!"

While a desire to look good for their hygienists may be enough to spur some men to heed the magazine's advice (and keep 'em coming back for more), fear and insecurity about the alternatives are generally more effective motivators. For those who don't get with the *Men's Health* program, there must be the threat of ridicule. By far the least subtle example of this is the free subscriptions for "guys who need our help" periodically announced in the front section of the magazine. April's dubious honoree was actor Christopher Walken:

> Chris, we love the way you've perfected that psycho persona. But now you're taking your role in "Things to Do in Denver When You're Dead" way too seriously with that ghostly pale face, the "where's the funeral?" black clothes, and a haircut that looks like the work of a hasty undertaker.... Dab on a little Murad Murasun Self-Tanner ($21) ... For those creases in your face, try Ortho Dermatologicals' Renova, a prescription anti-wrinkle cream that contains tretinoin, a form of vitamin A. Then, find a barber.

Or how about the March "winner," basketball coach Bobby Knight: "Bob, your trademark red sweater is just a billboard for your potbelly. A darker solid color would make you look slimmer. Also, see 'The Tale of Two Bellies' in our February 1998 issue, and try to drop a few pounds. Then the next time you throw a sideline tantrum, at least people won't say, 'look at the crazy *fat* man.'"

Just as intense as the obsession with appearance that men's (and women's) magazines breed are the sexual neuroses they feed. And if one of the ostensible goals of women's mags is to help women drive men wild, what is the obvious corollary objective for men's magazines? To get guys laid—well and often. As if men needed any encouragement to fixate on the subject, *Men's Health* is chock full of helpful "how-tos" such as, "Have Great Sex Every Day Until You Die" and "What I Learned From My Sex Coach," as well as more cursory explorations of why men with larger testicles have more sex ("Why Big Boys Don't Cry"), how to maintain orgasm intensity as you age ("Be one of the geysers"), and how to achieve

stronger erections by eating certain foods ("Bean counters make better lovers"). And for those having trouble even getting to the starting line, last month's issue offered readers a chance to "Win free love lessons."

THE HIGH PRICE OF PERFECTION

Having elevated men's physical and sexual insecurities to the level of grand paranoia, lads' mags can then get down to what really matters: moving merchandise. On the cover of *Men's Health* each month, in small type just above the magazine's title, appears the phrase "Tons of useful stuff." Thumbing through an issue or two, however, one quickly realizes that a more accurate description would read: "Tons of expensive stuff." They're all there: Ralph Lauren, Tommy Hilfiger, Paul Mitchell, Calvin Klein, Clinique, Armani, Versace, Burberrys, Nautica, Nike, Omega, Rogaine, The Better Sex Video Series.... The magazine even has those annoying little perfume strips guaranteed to make your nose run and to alienate everyone within a five-mile radius of you.

Masters of psychology, marketers wheel out their sexiest pitches and hottest male models to tempt/intimidate the readership of *Men's Health*. Not since the last casting call for "Baywatch" has a more impressive display of firm, tanned, young flesh appeared in one spot. And just like in women's magazines, the articles themselves are designed to sell stuff. All those helpful tips on choosing blazers, ties, and belts come complete with info on the who, where, and how much. The strategy is brilliant: Make men understand exactly how far short of the ideal they fall, and they too become vulnerable to the lure of high-priced underwear, cologne, running shoes, workout gear, hair dye, hair strengthener, skin softener, body-fat monitors, suits, boots, energy bars, and sex aids. As Mark Jannot, the grooming and health editor for *Men's Journal*, told "Today" show host Matt Lauer in January, "This is a huge, booming market. I mean, the marketers have found a group of people that are ripe for the picking. Men are finally learning that aging is a disease." Considering how effectively *Men's Health* fosters this belief, it's hardly surprising that the magazine has seen its ad pages grow 510 percent since 1991 and has made it onto *Adweek's* 10 Hottest Magazines list three of the last five years.

To make all this "girly" image obsession palatable to their audience, lads' mags employ all their creative energies to transform appearance issues into "a guy thing." *Men's Health* tries to cultivate a joking, macho tone throughout ("Eat Like Brando and Look Like Rambo" or "Is my tallywhacker shrinking?") and tosses in a handful of Y-chromosome teasers such as "How to Stay Out of Jail," "How to Clean Your Whole Apartment in One Hour or Less," and my personal favorite, "Let's Play Squash," an illustrated guide to identifying the bug-splat patterns on your windshield. Instead of a regular advice columnist, which would smack too much of chicks' magazines, *Men's Health* recently introduced "Jimmy the Bartender," a monthly column on "women, sex, and other stuff that screws up men's lives."

It appears that, no matter how much clarifying lotion and hair gel you're trying to sell them, men must never suspect that you think they share women's insecurities. If you want a man to buy wrinkle cream, marketers have learned, you better pitch it as part of a comfortingly macho shaving regimen. Aramis,

for example, assures men that its popular Lift Off! Moisture Formula with alpha hydroxy will help cut their shave time by one-third. "The biggest challenge for products started for women is how to transfer them to men," explained George Schaeffer, the president of OPI cosmetics, in the November issue of *Soap-Cosmetics-Chemical Specialties*. Schaeffer's Los Angeles-based company is the maker of Matte Nail Envy, and unobtrusive nail polish that's proved a hit with men. And for the more adventuresome shopper, last year Hard Candy cosmetics introduced a line of men's nail enamel, called Candy Man, that targets guys with such studly colors as Gigolo (metallic black) and Testosterone (gunmetal silver).

On a larger scale, positioning a makeover or trip to the liposuction clinic as a smart career move seems to help men rationalize their image obsession. "Whatever a man's cosmetic shortcoming, it's apt to be a career liability," noted Alan Farnham in a September 1996 issue of *Fortune*. "The business world is prejudiced against the ugly." Or how about *Forbes'* sad attempt to differentiate between male and female vanity in its Dec. 1 piece on cosmetic surgery: "Plastic surgery is more of a cosmetic thing for women. They have a thing about aging. For men it's an investment that pays a pretty good dividend." Whatever you say, guys.

The irony is rich and bittersweet. Gender equity is at last headed our way—not in the form of women being less obsessed with looking like Calvin Klein models, but of men becoming hysterical over the first signs of crows feet. Gradually, guys are no longer pumping up and primping simply to get babes, but because they feel it's something everyone expects them to do.

Women, after all, do not spend $400 on Dolce & Gabbana sandals to impress their boyfriends, most of whom don't know Dolce & Gabbana from Beavis & Butthead (yet). They buy them to impress other women—and because that's what society says they should want to do. Most guys haven't yet achieved this level of insanity, but with grown men catcalling the skin tone and wardrobe of other grown men (Christopher Walken, Bobby Knight) for a readership of still more grown men, can the gender's complete surrender to the vanity industry be far behind?

The ad for *Men's Health* web site says it all: "Don't click here unless you want to look a decade younger... lose that beer belly... be a better lover... and more! Men's Health Online: The Internet site For Regular Guys." Of course, between the magazine's covers there's not a "regular guy" to be found, save for the occasional snapshot of one of the publication's writers or editors—usually taken from a respectable distance. The moist young bucks in the Gap jeans ads and the electric-eyed Armani models have exactly as much in common with the average American man as Tyra Banks does with the average American woman. Which would be fine, if everyone seemed to understand this distinction. Until they do, however, I guess my consolation will have to be the image of thousands of once-proud men, having long scorned women's insecurities, lining up for their laser peels and trying to squeeze their middle-aged asses into a snug set of Super Shaper Briefs—with the optional fly front endowment pad, naturally.

POSTSCRIPT

Is Emphasis on Body Image in the Media Harmful to Females Only?

The selections by Martin and Gentry and by Cottle contain negative criticism about advertising, but they also suggest that age affects how susceptible people are to different aspects of advertising images. While one selection focuses on girls at a time in their lives when their bodies are changing, the second selection indicates that adult males, too, can be highly influenced by the images they see and by what seems to be a preoccupation with youth.

These selections also raise questions about the magazine industry and the hypersegmentation by market. If people's tastes and choices of media are being met by a wider variety of specialized publications (or even lifestyle TV channels, such as ESPN or Lifetime), perhaps there is a shift in the idea of a "mass audience." This concept has traditionally meant that the audience was characterized by homogeneity. Perhaps now the audience is less characterized by a sameness, but the content of the media may suggest a "homogenized" ideal for the different groups that make up the audience.

Standards of beauty and success are culturally defined. It is often interesting to pick up magazines or newspapers from other countries or ethnic groups and examine the images in ads to see if specific cultural differences are apparent.

There are many excellent references on the topics raised by this issue. John Tebbel and Mary Ellen Zuckerman have produced a history of magazines entitled *The Magazine in America, 1741–1990* (Oxford University Press, 1991). Books like Naomi Wolf's *The Beauty Myth* (Anchor Books, 1992) and Julia T. Wood's *Gendered Lives: Communication, Gender, and Culture* (Wadsworth, 1994) are particularly insightful regarding the images of women and minorities.

Some videotapes are also available for extended discussion, such as Jeanne Kilbourne's *Still Killing Us Softly* and *Slim Hopes* (Media Education Foundation).

ISSUE 5

Are Newspapers Insensitive to Minorities?

YES: Ruth Shalit, from "Race in the Newsroom," *The New Republic* (October 2, 1995)

NO: Leonard Downie, Jr., and Donald Graham, from "Race in the Newsroom: An Exchange," *The New Republic* (October 16, 1995)

ISSUE SUMMARY

YES: Ruth Shalit, a reporter for *The New Republic,* argues that inaccurate coverage of minority news and the treatment of minority news staff at some places are a form of racism. She focuses on the *Washington Post* as an extreme example of this activity.

NO: Executive editor Leonard Downie, Jr., and publisher Donald Graham of the *Washington Post* respond to Shalit's charges. They argue that their newspaper has achieved a higher standard of minority reporting and employment than Shalit claims.

As you will see by the following selections, minority representation in employment and the type of coverage a major newspaper provides for its readers present a controversial and problematic issue. Ruth Shalit makes several claims that seem to reflect poorly on the management of the *Washington Post,* but Leonard Downie, Jr., and Donald Graham's response shows that there are clashing views on the realities of minority representation within an organization. Similarly, because the *Washington Post* serves a community largely populated by minorities, one might expect to see some sensitivity reflected in its local news reporting. Shalit's original report elicited a response from Downie and Graham that points to the different realities presented by the conflict.

This subject is an important one because it asks us to consider the effectiveness of affirmative action, including what the term *diversity* means and how it might best be realized. As you read the selections, ask yourself whether the authors are demonstrating a bias or whether the "facts" speak for themselves. How does one know when an action is taken in bad faith or when a well-intentioned action has unintended negative consequences for someone?

The topics raised in this issue are relevant to almost any large organization that is attempting to reflect the interests of minority groups that more accurately represent the demographics of a community or of the nation. Media organizations have been highly criticized over the years for not responding to the needs of minorities, and the actions they have taken have provided high-profile examples of leadership in some cases and insensitivity in others. Because so many of these cases are presented to the public by other forms of media (in this case, the liberal *Washington Post* newspaper, critiqued by a reporter from the conservative *New Republic* magazine), some ideological posturing may also be present. Should these types of critiques also be treated objectively and without bias, or is it possible to maintain such a position under such circumstances?

You will probably find many aspects of organizational and social issues to explore as you read these selections. You may wish to explore other case studies in media ownership and the images with regard to different social groups. While some of the specific cases reflect changing demographics, an emphasis on different forms of media, or regulatory measures that have affected minority ownership and/or representation, all present constant struggles in the media landscape.

YES
Ruth Shalit

RACE IN THE NEWSROOM

If any organization could justify racial preferences as restitution for past sins, it would be *The Washington Post*. As the monopoly daily in a majority-black city, the paper had compelling reason to diversify what had been an overwhelmingly white newsroom. Twenty-five years ago, the *Post*—like most newspapers—was a largely white, middle-class bastion. There were no black assignment editors, no black foreign correspondents, no black reporters on the National staff: And its paternalism toward the black community was legendary. In 1950, for example, Publisher Philip Graham famously agreed to suppress news of a race riot in exchange for a promise by authorities to integrate the city's swimming pools.

In 1972, a contingent of black reporters, including the pathbreaking journalists Herbert Denton and Leon Dash, filed a complaint with the EEOC [Equal Employment Opportunity Commission] alleging they were victims of a racially discriminatory glass ceiling. Under an informal agreement, the paper grudgingly stepped up minority hiring, installing a black reporter on its National desk and bringing aboard several black sportswriters. If the *Post* was at first reluctant in its embrace of diversity, it soon got with the program. In the mid-'80s, the paper redoubled its affirmative action efforts following the publication of several internal reports lamenting the slow pace of integration. By 1986, the *Post* had hired its first full-time minority recruiter and set new, more aggressive affirmative action goals: one out of every four hires had to be a minority, and one out of every two a woman.

Over the years, these diversity efforts have been propelled by a peculiar series of racial psychodramas. On September 28, 1980, the paper ran the now-notorious story of "Jimmy," an 8-year-old heroin addict. Although written by a 26-year-old black reporter, Janet Cooke, the piece dripped with racial innuendo. Heroin, Jimmy supposedly told Cooke, "be real different from herb. That's baby s—. Don't nobody here hardly ever smoke no herb. You can't hardly get none right now anyway." The accompanying drawing featured a dazed-looking young man, his scrawny arm gripped by a giant fist as a needle is inserted. Black readers, including Mayor Marion Barry, immediately denounced the Pulitzer Prize-winning story as racist and preposterous; but the *Post* defended it almost to the end. When it was exposed as a hoax, the paper was mortified.

Then there was the infamous magazine incident. In 1986, the *Post* endured a prolonged black boycott after the debut issue of its Sunday magazine featured a cover story about a black murder suspect, along with a column by Richard Cohen about white jewelry-store owners who, fearing robbery, refused to buzz young black men into their stores. Hundreds of black protesters, led by talk-show host Cathy Hughes, dumped thousands of copies of the magazine, some in flames, on the steps of the *Post*'s building on 15th Street. They repeated the ceremony every Sunday for thirteen weeks, stopping only after *Post* Publisher Donald Graham apologized and agreed to a series of appearances on Hughes's talk show.

The Cooke and magazine incidents, says Managing Editor Robert Kaiser, were "the product of a different newspaper." And, indeed, there's no question that the *Post* has, over the years, benefited greatly from its enhanced racial and sexual representativeness. "When all of our staff came from the same background, we missed what was going on," says Downie, who argues persuasively that a diverse staff is necessary to covering a diverse community.

Yet it is also true that, after a decade of determined diversity hiring, something at newspapers in general, and the *Post* in particular, has gone wrong. According to advocacy groups such as the National Association of Black Journalists (NABJ), a rising tide of racial prejudice is washing over America's newsrooms. In *Muted Voices*, the NABJ's 1994 Print Task Force report, the authors write that their findings are "indicative of despair.... Black journalists are strangling with their

pain." Much of this pain, however, seems to be caused less by old-fashioned bigotry than by a sort of post-affirmative action racism. "[T]he idea that an African-American has been hired because of a political agenda of management or external pressure [is] still alive," the report laments.

To hear *Muted Voices* tell it, black reporters and their (mostly white) bosses are living in different worlds. While two-thirds of black journalists surveyed by NABJ said newsroom managers are not committed to retaining and promoting blacks, 94 percent of managers say they are. Ninety-two percent of the managers say promotion standards are the same for blacks and whites; 59 percent of black journalists say they think blacks have to meet *higher* standards.

At the *Post*, tensions are running particularly high. "A great deal of babbling goes on here about diversity," says National reporter John Goshko. "Nobody is happy. Many of the older white males feel that they are being discriminated against. Many minorities, particularly blacks, feel discriminated against. Each side will give you chapter and verse." White reporters, especially white middle-aged males, have become increasingly hostile to racial preferences. "We used to say: 'Let's go out and get the best guy in the world,'" says columnist Richard Harwood, the *Post*'s former deputy managing editor. "'Let's get the best, without regard to anything else.' If there is, over time, a policy of giving considerable preference on the basis of color, your standards change. And I think that's the problem we're facing."

Not surprisingly, the *Post*'s minority journalists see things quite differently. Far from coddling them, they say, the *Post* has ensured that for reporters of color the path of upward mobility is treacherous. Like Alice and the Red Queen, they must run twice as hard merely to stay in place. "You see a glass ceiling slowly turning into lead," says Metro reporter Ruben Castaneda. "You realize there's no future." "Everyone in management has good intentions," says Gary Lee, a black reporter on the *Post*'s National staff. "But there's an entrenched newsroom culture that doesn't change." Even the Asian Americans are grumpy and radicalized. "Some [Asian reporters] think it's not a very welcoming atmosphere," says Metro reporter Spencer Hsu. "There are issues of mentoring and racial typing that can have a significant impact on our careers.

"It is a paradox," muses Assistant Managing Editor David Ignatius, "that this liberal institution that professes to care deeply about the community has a bad reputation in the African American community and has had some very unhappy African American staffers." In the past five years alone, fifteen black reporters have quit the paper. Some of the departed have written biting accounts of their time at the *Post*. In her 1993 memoir, *Volunteer Slavery*, former *Post* reporter Jill Nelson argues that racial insensitivity at the paper shattered her self-esteem and stymied her career....

* * *

These portrayals of the *Post* as a hotbed of racial iniquity have devastated the paper's top executives—Executive Editor Downie, Managing Editor Kaiser and Deputy Managing Editor Michael Getler. Children of the '60s all, they feel impelled to diversify not only because of legal and political pressures but because of personal inclination and social conscience.

"There is a moral dimension to this," says Kaiser. "We've learned a lot, we white guys, in the last twenty or twenty-five years or so."...

In 1993, the *Post* commissioned an internal task force on newsroom life, headed by Getler, then the paper's assistant managing editor for Foreign News. For five months, Getler roamed the newsroom, trying to find out why, as one reporter he spoke to put it, "Very few people appear to be happy, most seem afraid." At the end of his labors he issued a ninety-page study, henceforth referred to as the Getler report.

The report, Getler wrote in the introduction, was "a growl from the belly of the *Post*." What people growled about mostly was race. Black staffers accused the *Post* of harboring a bias against them:

> Racial and ethnic minority staffers say the *Post* is not doing what it can, and should, by them.... Many African-Americans complained that, to be given good stories or challenging beats, they must work harder than whites at the same experience level....

At the same time, white staffers said they felt threatened by the *Post*'s rigid hiring targets. "One editor offered a common reaction," wrote Getler. " 'When you start to push for more black editors and more women, and maybe a few gays, the middle-aged straight white male is the last one you're going to worry about.' "

Getler and the other members of the *Post*'s diversity task force concluded the report by calling for the appointment of a deputy managing editor to oversee diversity issues. "Our group feels strongly," Getler wrote, "that the new person must be the third-ranking editor in the newsroom, with authority from the executive editor and the managing editor to make things happen." The job went to Getler. "I was surprised," he says modestly.

A friendly, approachable man who spent many years as a reporter and editor before becoming the *Post*'s diversity czar, Getler now spends his days patrolling the newsroom, blasting stereotypes and preaching inclusion. "There is racism, whether it's conscious or unconscious," he explains. "Most people say, 'Me? I'm not a racist. I'm a nice guy.' But you can have attitudes that you're not even aware of." Getler has set about remedying those attitudes. "The *Post*," he says, "is a very candid place. It's not defensive about itself. It's a place where you can say anything you want.... It's a place that lays open its warts in order to fix them." ...

* * *

Kevin Merida, a lanky and dashing black reporter with a soft voice and easygoing manner, laughs out loud at the suggestion that minority journalists are being hired and promoted ahead of schedule. "The biggest myth in journalism," he calls it. To the contrary, he says, the newspaper business brutally limits the aspirations of African Americans. "A little light is always going on in your head," he says. "There's a general sense of feeling, somehow, that your value, your worth, is not completely taken into account." He says, "There's a sense that you're not valued as you would like to be valued."

Merida's consternation is puzzling to white reporters. The *Post*'s National staff is tiny, the waiting list, endless. But Merida didn't have to slug it out at the bottom in Metro with everybody else. After being lured away from *The Dallas Morning News,* where he was an assistant managing editor, he was immediately dispatched to the National desk. He's got what would seem a plum job, covering Congress and the '96 campaign. Moreover, he has the latitude and standing to pursue stories of special interest to him. "I'm a black man," he says. "The black experience is part of who I am. And I try to incorporate that in my coverage." Merida cites three recent examples: a sympathetic profile of embattled senator Carol Moseley-Braun; a story criticizing the art in the Capitol as colonialist and lacking in racial diversity; and a story about how the Senate had condemned Khalid Muhammad for his statements about Jews, yet seemed to be holding Senator Ernest Hollings, who disparaged "African potentates," to a different standard.

Merida's insecurity about his position in the newsroom may, more than anything else, be a function of the tokenist assumption—the suspicion that he got his job because he was black. At *The Dallas Morning News,* Merida advanced from reporter to AME [Assistant Managing Editor] in one fell swoop, a precipitous promotion that has dogged him all the way to Washington. "Have you ever heard of that happening in the entire history of the news business?" asks one white *Post* reporter. "There's supposed to be a very clear path. It's like being a private, and suddenly you're a general." It's the classic plight of the affirmative-action baby, whose genuine accomplishments are tainted by a preferential system beyond his control.

* * *

The *Post*'s diversity goals have spawned a burgeoning bureaucracy administered by Jeanne Fox-Alston, director of hiring and recruiting. In 1986, she was plucked off the *Post*'s graphics desk and instructed to revamp the paper's personnel office so that, in her words, it "focused more on women and minorities." These days, one of her tasks is to winnow out white males, some of whom she regards as having an overly developed sense of entitlement. "Some of them have had some really good stories," she says. Fox-Alston is a small, reedy woman in her early 40s, with a gray topknot and the tight, pursed mouth you see on the assistant principal. "They've put their years in. Maybe they've even won awards. And they see people being hired who perhaps don't have as much experience as they do. Why?" Mockingly, Fox-Alston's voice keens into the upper register. " 'It must be because I'm a white male,' " she whines. "Well, there's more to it than that." Fox-Alston elaborates. "There's one guy from a New Orleans paper who's been trying to get hired here for quite a while. And he wrote the deputy managing editor a letter, saying, 'Friends at the *Post* tell me the only reason I haven't been hired is because I'm a white man.' Now, in talking to the deputy managing editor about this particular candidate, I said, 'Well, it's true that on his résumé he has some good experience and stuff like that. But you know, he's terribly annoying, and he's not as good as he thinks.' " Fox-Alston leans back in satisfaction. "He didn't get hired." ...

* * *

... [D]iversity training may not be sufficient to stem the current white backlash against affirmative action, which sometimes bubbles over into pure racial animosity. In my discussions with white reporters and editors, I was surprised to hear many of them question, in the coarsest terms, the ability of their minority colleagues. "She can't write a lick," for example, or "He's dumb as a post." Or worse: "When she files, you literally don't understand what she's saying. And you have to go back to her again and again and ask: What are you trying to say?"

The ugliness of these sentiments suggests that covert racism may be simply inflamed by the push for diversity. But at the *Post*, the explosive interaction of aggressive hiring with instinctive white anxiety has given such feelings a pretext. Even President Clinton acknowledges that federal law requires that minorities be hired from the relevant pool of qualified applicants, not in proportion to their population in society at large. In other words, the *Post*'s goal —to reproduce in its building the precise ethnic makeup of its community— is not only irrational but arguably illegal. "The concept of diversity begins with the idea that a newspaper's staff and coverage should reflect the racial, gender and ethnic makeup of its market," concludes the Getler report. But to comply with the Supreme Court's standards, the *Post* should instead be tailoring its goals to the pool of qualified aspiring journalists. According to *The Chronicle of Higher Education*, blacks and Hispanics compose 10.6 percent of the available pool of college graduates; within that group, the pool of students expressing an interest in communications is a mere 13 percent. Even without making allowances for the *Post*'s attempt to skim off the best people from the best schools, the attempt to mirror the 32.3 percent of blacks and Hispanics in metropolitan Washington itself seems flamboyantly unrealistic.

In 1994, the paper made thirty-eight new hires. Of those thirty-eight, ten were members of minority groups. "Our goal for about the past eight years has been that at least a quarter of our hires be people of color," says Fox-Alston. In pursuing this goal in spite of a minuscule pool, the *Post* has committed itself to a course of quite extraordinary affirmative action; and so the complaints about compromising standards, while undoubtedly overstated by aggrieved white reporters, are corroborated by the stark numerical reality.…

Many reporters, meanwhile, resent being viewed as walking monuments to the paper's virtue. "I worked the night police," says Carlos Sanchez, who left the paper in 1994 and is now working at *The Fort Worth Star-Telegram*. "I had nothing to do with the Hispanic community unless they were killed. One evening I show up for work. And [Metro Editor] Milton Coleman is there, conveying his apologies for not informing me prior to that evening that I needed to attend a formal dinner with him. I wasn't dressed for dinner. I was extremely uncomfortable.… But I went." To Sanchez's chagrin, the dinner turned out to be a love-in with local Hispanic community leaders at a Salvadoran restaurant. "I found myself kinda being showcased," he says. "That bothered me."

… Consider the case of Leon Dash—a driven, brilliant journalist who has long concentrated his reporting on the least attractive features of black Washington. In 1986, his exceptional *Post* series on the teenage pregnancy epidemic among inner-city black youths punctured the conventional liberal wisdom that the crisis of black teenage parents was simply one of ignorance about birth control. Dash was one of the first reporters to note that for underclass pubescent girls, "a child was a tangible achievement in otherwise dreary and empty lives."

In October of 1994, the *Post* devoted eight days to Dash's "Rosa Lee" series, which probed the intertwined pathologies of a three-generational family of black, welfare-dependent petty criminals. The riveting series examined the intractability of underclass poverty, crime and drug use across generations. It won Dash a Pulitzer. Many black *Post* reporters, however, read the series with dismay. "I didn't like the Rosa Lee stories," says Kevin Merida. "We spend too much time in journalism chronicling failure and despair. Is this what we have to do to win a prize? Write about black pathology? I just don't know what good a series like that does."

Black reporters' complaints about the series prompted an anguished round of brown-bag lunches and assemblies, in which top *Post* editors defended themselves against the charge of conspiring to besmirch the black community. Downie issued a flurry of penitent memos, promising to redouble his efforts to publish "solutions stories." Dash, meanwhile, has been made a newsroom pariah. "Since the series came out, black people at the *Post* have shunned me," he says. "They are still shunning me." Dash says the brown-bag lunches were unpleasant experiences for him. "People kept asking me, why didn't I focus on Rhodes scholars and college graduates? Why didn't I focus on people who have overcome these situations? Well, because those people aren't part of the generation that is trapped in this permanent underclass."

Unfortunately, reporters like Leon Dash may be a dying breed, given the climate of victimism and aggrievement that prevails in today's newsrooms. For a glimpse of the paper of the future, consider the fifty-eight-page instruction book on "Content Audits," published by the American Society of Newspaper Editors. The brochure instructs editors to map their coverage out on a grid and compute "total number items," "total minority items," "percent minority"; and to rate stories "P" for positive ("Shows minorities smiling [unless text contradicts smile], achieving, in respected role, etc."), "N for Negative" ("the old arrest shot or other negative roles") or just "Neutral." ("Daily life. Not bad or good.") To "reap the rewards of the audit," papers are urged to "develop a pool of senior-level minority editors who can sit in on news editorial meetings and flag insensitive stories or narrowly focused pictures."

At the *Post*, the commandment to avoid offense at all costs dovetails conveniently with a long history of timorousness about racial matters. Over the years, for example, the paper has taken many hits for its tortured coverage of Mayor Marion Barry. Though the *Post* pleaded Barry's case in three glowing editorial endorsements—in '78, '82 and '86—Barry continues to pillory the paper as part of a white conspiracy to harass him. Then, of course, there's the '86 magazine boycott, the impact of which should not be underestimated. "I've come across a number of stories in my career where that incident was mentioned," says one *Post* reporter. " 'Change this, tone this down, do this, do that.' There is a feeling that if we say anything more complex than 'The sun rises in the East,' we step in shit."

In a memo circulated in December to the paper's editors, Joann Byrd, the *Post*'s ombudsman, elaborated on this theme. "The distance between the paper and many in the black community is an enormous and difficult challenge for the *Post*," she wrote. "It is the prism through which a huge segment of the population sees all the paper's reporting —and judges it to be indifferent or racist." Byrd's concerns were reflected in the Getler report, which concluded that one of the best ways to ensure responsible minority coverage was "to have minority editors to help steer us in a positive direction in our coverage of issues involving minorities." ...

* * *

After encountering the racial strife at *The Washington Post*, it's tempting to despair that major American institutions will ever achieve both racial integration and racial harmony. If the *Post*, which tries so hard and means so well, is failing so dramatically to achieve its goals, what hope is there for the rest of us?

"When racial things come up in this newsroom, we should talk about them," says Len Downie. "We should not run away from them. We ought to talk about them." In fact, the more everyone talks, the worse everyone feels. "It's a truism in this world of diversity training that things get worse before they get better," says David Ignatius hopefully. "And maybe that's what we're seeing. When people are talking about issues that are really painful, you're not going to hear violins start playing."

By focusing obsessively on the ideals and the instruments of diversity, by exhorting its staff to reflect endlessly on their own resentments, the *Post* is ensuring that the resentments will never be transcended.

NO

Leonard Downie, Jr., and Donald Graham

RACE IN THE NEWSROOM: AN EXCHANGE

LEONARD DOWNIE JR., EXECUTIVE EDITOR

To the editors:

In her polemic against diversity at *The Washington Post*, Ruth Shalit purports to be concerned that our efforts to diversify our newsroom staff may compromise our journalistic standards. In fact, Shalit's article demonstrates a shameful absence of journalistic standards on the part of *The New Republic* and Shalit herself.

She uses the maddening technique of big-lie propaganda to misrepresent how we work in our newsroom and how we cover the news. Fact, falsehood, rumor and quotes wrested out of context are laced together with the author's ideological preconceptions. This presents a misleadingly distorted, single-dimensional view of our complex, competitive, free-wheeling, outspoken newsroom.

Shalit herself signals her own controlling bias when she asserts that "if editors refuse to adjust their traditional hiring standards, they will end up with a nearly all-white staff"—presumably more like that of the magazine for which she works. Her assertion is as unfounded as it is ugly. We have not adjusted standards in any way in our hiring of dozens of talented journalists of color who do distinguished work, and we know we will continue to attract many more of their caliber. Shalit's racial McCarthyism will not deter our efforts to diversify the staff of *The Washington Post* so we can report intelligently on an increasingly diverse community and nation.

The Washington Post has no "goal to reproduce in its building the precise ethnic makeup of its community." Shalit repeatedly uses this straw man to feed the idea that our hiring is being dictated by the numbers, forcing a compromising of standards.

Our stated goal for many years has been to try to have our new hires be 50 percent women and 25 percent minorities, consistent with filling every vacancy with the best-qualified person possible. This has never meant turning away any journalist because he was a white man nor lowering our standards to hire any woman or minority journalist. Our nationally recognized newsroom recruiter, Jeanne Fox-Alston, who was portrayed in a particularly cruel, false light by Shalit, has definitely not been "winnowing out white males," as can be seen from our publicly available newsroom statistics. In the nine years since establishing this goal, we have hired ninety-eight minority staff members in our newsroom, forty-five of them women; at the same time, we have hired 232 whites, 109 of them women.

We emphatically have not "been forced to hire inappropriate people, reporters who lack the skills to do daily newspaper work competently." Many new hires are risky at a newspaper as demanding as *The Washington Post*; the eventual wash-out rate has been no different for minority hires than for whites.

Shalit displays an amateurish inability to get her facts straight. Revealingly, many of these errors could have been corrected if—during her extensive interviews with senior editors of the *Post*—she had asked us or anyone with firsthand knowledge about various unfounded rumors she passed off as facts. Shalit also omitted from her article a large number of interviews with reporters and editors here that conflicted with her point of view. And she juxtaposed quotes from other interviews with statements of her own that were quite different from the questions she asked to obtain the quotes.

Some of her most egregious errors are maliciously hurtful to fine people such as Milton Coleman, who has been our Assistant Managing Editor [AME] in charge of Metropolitan News for nearly ten years. Shalit asserts that Ben Bradlee and I had "settled on Kevin Klose" for this job in 1986 (Shalit misdescribes Klose, who was then our Chicago correspondent, as an editor on the National staff). Shalit says Don Graham, the publisher of the *Post*, then intervened to force Ben and me to select Coleman instead. This account is pure fiction. Kevin Klose was never our choice for the job, and the purported conversation with Don Graham that she describes never took place. In fact, in the eleven years since I became managing editor in 1984, Don Graham has never dictated a single newsroom personnel decision (or news coverage decision, for that matter). Ben Bradlee and I selected Milton Coleman ourselves, and remain proud that we did so.

Shalit also slurs Eugene Robinson, our Foreign editor, by suggesting that he was our second choice for the job and implying that we sought him for the position primarily because of his race. She asserts that the Foreign editorship was first offered to our former Cairo correspondent, Caryle Murphy. This is false. No one here ever discussed the job of Foreign editor with Murphy. Gene Robinson—a former city editor here and a distinguished foreign correspondent in Latin America and in London—quickly emerged as the best-prepared person for the job, regardless of race. He was the only person to whom the job was offered.

Shalit has considerable sport at the expense of Doug Farah, our Central American correspondent. She invents from whole cloth a purported meeting where senior editors were described by her as being surprised to discover that Farah was not an Hispanic. No such meeting ever occurred. Here the number of errors is quite breathtaking. Shalit says Farah was born in Bolivia; he was born in Massachusetts. She reports that his family is from Kansas, also incorrect. She claims that the idea of hiring him onto a Metro staff Hispanic-coverage task force was nixed because Farah himself was not Hispanic; in fact, he was hired as our full-time Central American correspondent (after spending several years there as our stringer) one year before the Hispanic task force was even created. She invents a "protracted battle" over whether or not to hire Farah: there was never any question that we would put Farah on the staff after his distinguished service as our stringer in Central America.

Shalit slurs National reporter Kevin Merida, suggesting that he was hired directly onto the National staff because he is black. She describes the National staff as "tiny," but it has nearly fifty reporters. She conjures up a long "waiting list" for membership on the staff; there is no such list. She writes that Merida was jumped ahead of this imaginary queue without being asked to "slug it out at the bottom in Metro"; in fact, we have hired a number of reporters directly from other newspapers onto our National staff. We had been talking to Kevin Merida about joining the National staff since the mid-1980s, while he built a fine reputation as a political reporter for *The Dallas Morning News*, where he covered the White House and national politics before becoming an assistant managing editor in Dallas.

Who is Ruth Shalit and what qualifies her to pass judgment on these fine journalists? The record shows that, in the relatively short time she has been on your staff, she has twice been caught committing plagiarism in the pages of *The New Republic* and that a number of her earlier articles have drawn critical letters complaining about numerous inaccuracies.

Shalit's cavalier disregard for facts is really quite astounding—as is *The New Republic's* willingness to print a story that contains so many errors. Among the many others are: Shalit claims that the National staff is reserving a race-relations reporting job for an African American, when the job was last held by Peter Perl, a white man. She claims applicants were rejected for a job writing about culture in Style because they were the "wrong color," but the only applicant for that position who was actually turned down after extensive interviews was black. She writes that the late Herb Denton joined an EEOC complaint filed by some *Post* reporters in 1972; Denton did not. She writes that there were no black reporters on our Foreign or National staffs "twenty-five years ago"; there were.

Shalit argues in her article that a preoccupation with racial sensitivity here has led us to abandon aggressive reporting on local problems and officials, particularly Washington's mayor, Marion Barry, as though it were some other newspaper that revealed Barry's drug use at a downtown hotel, or some other newspaper that showed how he was manipulating the city's campaign finance laws during the last mayoral election, or some other newspaper that detailed how Barry's Washington home was handsomely remodeled by friends and city contractors, or some other newspaper whose tough coverage (and reporters, many of them black) is currently being attacked at most of their public appearances by both the Mayor and Mrs. Barry.

In particular, Shalit chose to demonize Milton Coleman by accusing him of stopping, stalling or watering down local investigative reporting for racial reasons. This is a preposterous slur against one of our most courageous journalists and effective editors. I have been deeply involved in the editing of most investigative projects here during the time Milton Coleman has been AME for Metropolitan News, and I have seen no evidence of racial attitudes involved in our joint decisions to send various projects back for more reporting and rewriting. We have demanding standards of accuracy, completeness, fairness, clarity and impact that stories must meet before they are published in *The Washington Post* (if only *The New Republic* had similar standards), and we have accordingly delayed or abandoned countless stories, regardless of subject, over the years.

Shalit falsely accuses us of adhering to a "commandment to avoid offense at all costs" in any coverage touching on race. Could she be referring to the same newspaper that published Leon Dash's distinguished series on Rosa Lee Cunningham, which both won the Pulitzer Prize and caused very strong emotional responses, both negative and positive, among our black and white readers? Aggressive accountability reporting in all areas is perhaps the single most important part of the mission of this newspaper.

We remain committed to increasing the diversity of our newsroom staff and to publishing the best possible newspaper we can every day. This is not always easy to do under the pressure of daily deadlines in a very competitive atmosphere, which can exacerbate the workplace tensions, racial and other kinds, found in most large offices these day. Reporting on and writing about this challenging situation in a thoughtful, well-informed fashion would be a real contribution to all of our understanding of the dynamics of diversity in American media. It is unfortunate, to say the least, that *The New Republic* and Ruth Shalit have instead made the water much muddier.

DONALD GRAHAM, PUBLISHER

To the editors:

I am very sorry that so many *Washington Post* writers and editors do not meet Ruth Shalit's standards. They do meet mine.

Ms. Shalit makes a series of assertions backed up by a string of blind quotes, to the effect that affirmative action has led the *Post* to compromise its hiring standards and to pull its punches in news coverage. Her evidence is that some journalists in our newsroom are willing to grouse about the subject.

Since she works at *The New Republic*, the last practitioner of de facto segregation since Mississippi changed, Ms. Shalit has little or no experience in working with black colleagues. But she knows that newsroom second-guessing of any and all editors' decisions is as newsworthy as dog-bites-man. Ms. Shalit even prints a mean attack on our director of hiring and recruiting by people the *Post* has chosen not to hire.

Is the *Post*'s minority staff lacking in talent? Ms. Shalit does not mention that the Pulitzer Prize has been awarded to two African American *Post* staffers in the last two years or that two others were finalists; does not mention the three Polk Awards, an ASNE award for writing, the Livingston award or the White House press photographers awards won by other *Post* minority staffers. Our journalists appear to meet the standards of those award panels. But not Ms. Shalit's.

I have spent a fair amount of time with Len Downie worrying about recent attempts to hire minority *Post* staffers by *The New York Times, The Wall Street Journal, The Dallas Morning News,* Knight-Ridder ABC, *The New Yorker* and *Sports Illustrated,* among many others (not, of course, *The New Republic,* which I am told has never had a full-time black staffer). Our staffers seem to meet the standards of those publications. But not Ms. Shalit's.

I've watched *Post* editors hire reporters for a few years now. There are more truly outstanding reporters on the *Post* today, both sexes, all races, than there ever have been in the history of the paper. The *Post* does try hard to find minority reporters and editors. It tries to hire only excellent reporters, succeeds in many cases, and fails about as often with whites as with blacks, Hispanics and Asians.

Evaluations of individual reporters are necessarily subjective. But when it comes to news coverage, Ms. Shalit can be examined. She finds our coverage of Marion Barry since his release from prison "more uncritical than before." Really, Ms. Shalit? Did you see the ten to twelve editorials opposing his reelection? Did you see Colbert King's op-ed page columns, since the election? Did you see the *Post* editorials with headlines like "MAYOR BARRY'S RECKLESS THREATS," " 'WHAT CRISIS IN D.C.,' HE ASKS," "VICTORY FOR THE LAW OF THE STREETS" and "MELTDOWN"? Did you see the piece that launched the current grand jury investigation? Or the pieces from our city staff with headlines like "AUTHORITIES SEIZE FILES ON BARRY," "BARRY BRUSHES ASIDE QUESTIONS; MAYOR WALKS OUT WHEN ASKED ABOUT TIES TO BUSINESSMEN," "BARRY'S SECURITY COSTS ANGER D.C. COUNCIL," "RESIDENTS TRASH TRIP BY BARRY," "BARRY DENIES STEEP DISCOUNT ON HOTEL SUITE WAS ILLEGAL GIFT" and on and on.

Among honest people, evaluations of the same set of facts will differ. A reporter who claims to evaluate the *Post*'s Barry coverage and leaves out all the articles I have mentioned is not an honest reporter.

I am mentioned in Ms. Shalit's piece only briefly: she alleges that I over-ruled Ben Bradlee and Len Downie to make Milton Coleman the Assistant Managing Editor for Metropolitan News. This is fantasy. I wasn't asked for my opinion and didn't give it. I would be proud if I had selected Milton Coleman, who has put together what I consider an outstanding Metro staff by (yes) particularly careful hiring. Ms. Shalit accuses Mr. Coleman of pulling his punches in coverage of black leaders, including Louis Farrakhan. The reason Ms. Shalit has heard Mr. Farrakhan's name is that he became nationally famous for threatening Milton Coleman's life over Coleman's coverage of the Jesse Jackson campaign of 1984. As I learned in 1984, Milton Coleman is one of the bravest people I've ever met. A choice between his standards and Ms. Shalit's would be my easiest call, any day of the week.

Ms. Shalit describes a place where blacks and whites watch each other closely, where race becomes an excuse for some and a flashpoint for others. Sounds like America in 1995. Except, of course, for *The New Republic.* (Motto: Looking for a qualified black since 1914.)

The Washington Post will go on trying to hire the best reporters we can, and will go on trying to identify and hire outstanding minority journalists. When Ms. Shalit alleges low standards, my answer is: J. A. Adande, Louis Aguilar, David Aldridge, John Anderson, Marie Arana-Ward, Juana Arias, Nora Boustany, Donna Britt, Dudley Brooks, Warren Brown, DeNeen Brown, Stephen Buckley, Ruben Castaneda, Rajiv Chandrasekaran, Deirdre Childress, Kenneth Cooper, Leon Dash, Marcia Davis, Lynne Duke, Gabriel Escobar, Louis Estrada, Anthony Faiola, Michael Fletcher, John Fountain, Lisa Frazier, Mary Ann French, Patrice Gaines, Dorothy Gilliam, Robin Givhan, Malcolm Gladwell, Hamil Harris, Craig Herndon, Spencer Hsu, Desson Howe, Keith Jenkins, Jon Jeter, Colbert King, Athelia Knight, Gary Lee, Nathan McCall, Kevin Merida, Courtland Milloy, David Nakamura, Ellen Nakashima, Terry Neal, David Nicholson, Lan Nguyen, Lonnae O'Neal Parker, Peter Pae, Phillip Pan, Robert Pierre, Carol Porter, Rudy Pyatt, William Raspberry, Keith Richburg, Michelle Singletary, Marcia Slacum-Greene, Lena Sun, Pierre Thomas, Avis Thomas-Lester, Jacqueline Trescott, Eric Wee, Michael Wilbon, Daniel Williams, Juan Williams, Yolanda Woodlee and John Yang. I cite only reporters, columnists, photographers and artists because readers may judge their work for themselves. I am proud to have *The Washington Post* judged by their work.

POSTSCRIPT

Are Newspapers Insensitive to Minorities?

Media organizations have long been criticized for being resistant to change and for supporting the status quo. In the case of publishing houses for newspapers, magazines, or books, the specific parameters have been drawn to address each medium's need to reflect the community it serves. One might expect newspapers in locations that serve minorities to do a better job at representing minority interests, both in hiring and in the treatment of news, than publishers that serve broader constituencies. But how much change is enough?

Because the selections by Shalit and by Downie and Graham specifically deal with the efforts and practices of the *Washington Post*, some very specific actions are discussed. It might be interesting for you to consider how well your own community's media reflect the population they serve. What about your school newspaper, radio station, or arts organization? How well do they reflect the demographics of the community they serve?

There are many studies dealing with the topic of race and media. One of the best short essays on the subject is Michael Parenti's article "Cover Story: The Myth of a Liberal Media," *The Humanist* (January/February 1995). Also see James Fallows, *Breaking the News: How the Media Undermine American Democracy* (Pantheon Books, 1996). A recent book that takes a look at the organizational issues within business is Anthony Stith's *Breaking the Glass Ceiling: Racism and Sexism in Corporate America* (Warwick, 1998).

On the Internet . . .

http://www.dushkin.com

The Centre for Cultural and Media Studies
The Centre for Cultural and Media Studies (CCMS) is the
South African region's premier graduate research and educational unit in media studies. The staff, research, and publications of the CCMS are internationally renowned and read,
and its leading staff members have been visiting professors
in a variety of universities all over the world.
http://www.und.ac.za/und/ccms/index.html

Freedom Forum
The Freedom Forum is a nonpartisan, international foundation dedicated to free press, free speech, and free
spirit for all people. Its mission is to help the public and
the news media understand one another better. The
press watch area of this site is very intriguing.
http://www.freedomforum.org/

Fairness and Accuracy in Reporting
Fairness and Accuracy in Reporting (FAIR) is a national
media watch group that offers well-documented criticism
of media bias and censorship. FAIR seeks to invigorate
the First Amendment by advocating for greater diversity
in the press. FAIR scrutinizes media practices that marginalize public interest, minority, and dissenting viewpoints.
http://www.fair.org/

United States House of Representatives
This page of the House of Representatives leads to information about current and past House members and agendas, the legislative process, and more. You can learn
about events on the House floor as they happen.
http://www.house.gov/

Society of Professional Journalists
At this site you will find the Electronic Journalist, the online service for the Society of Professional Journalists.
This site links you to articles on media ethics, accuracy
in media, media leaders, and other media topics.
http://www.spj.org/

Television News Archive, Vanderbilt University
Since August 5, 1968, the Television News Archive has systematically recorded, abstracted, and indexed national television newscasts. This database is the guide to the Vanderbilt
University collection of network television news programs.
http://tvnews.vanderbilt.edu/

PART 2

Media Ethics

Media ethics concerns the delicate balance between society's interests and the interests of individuals, groups, and institutions such as the press and the government. Questions of ethics are, by definition, issues of right and wrong. But they are among the most difficult issues we face because they require decisions of us, even in the face of articulate and intelligent opposition. What is the appropriate balance between responsibility and liberty? Who should decide where the lines between right and wrong are to be drawn, and on what values should these decisions be made? Are all decisions relative to the individual case, or are there larger, overriding principles to which we should all pledge our allegiance? Most important, to whom should we entrust the power to make and implement ethical choices? In this section, the reader must grapple with the questions ethics ask of us and critically examine the purposes and actions of some of the most fundamental institutions we know.

■ Should the Names of Rape Victims Be Reported?

■ Should Tobacco Advertising Be Restricted?

■ Does Media Coverage of Criminal Trials Undermine the Legal Process?

■ Has Coverage of Political Campaigns Improved?

■ Is Advertising Ethical?

■ Do Paparazzi Threaten Privacy and First Amendment Rights?

ISSUE 6

Should the Names of Rape Victims Be Reported?

YES: Michael Gartner, from "Naming the Victim," *Columbia Journalism Review* (July/August 1991)

NO: Katha Pollitt, from "Naming and Blaming: Media Goes Wilding in Palm Beach," *The Nation* (June 24, 1991)

ISSUE SUMMARY

YES: President of NBC News Michael Gartner justifies his decision to name the accuser in the William Kennedy Smith rape case, claiming that names add credibility to a story. He further argues that a policy of identifying accusers in rape cases will destroy many of society's wrongly held impressions and stereotypes about the crime of rape.

NO: Using examples from the William Kennedy Smith case, journalist and social critic Katha Pollitt identifies six reasons commonly cited by proponents of naming alleged rape victims and argues that not one of them justifies the decision to reveal victims' identities without their consent.

In 1991 a woman claimed she was raped at the Kennedy compound in Palm Beach, Florida, one night during the Easter weekend. After an investigation by the local police, William Kennedy Smith, nephew of Senator Edward M. Kennedy (D-Massachusetts), was charged with the assault. The subsequent trial later that same year resulted in an acquittal for Smith. The case received widespread media coverage, in part because it involved a Kennedy, and in part because the circumstances of the case tapped into the ongoing national debate over so-called acquaintance rape, or date rape. On the night of the incident, Smith and the woman met at an exclusive club, they spent some time drinking and partying, and the woman later drove Smith home and accepted his invitation to take a walk on the beach. According to the woman, the police, and the local prosecutor, what eventually took place that night was rape. Smith, his supporters, and the jury, however, saw it as consensual sex. In addition to raising the question of date rape, the case also provoked controversy because of how various news organizations handled the issue of whether or not to reveal the woman's identity.

Shielding the names and identities of victims of rape has long been a press tradition. But when the William Kennedy Smith story first broke, both the NBC television network and the *New York Times* reported the woman's name;

furthermore, the *New York Times* ran a story that gave details on her personal background. These actions sparked controversy among the public and among journalists and media critics.

Who should control the decision to use the names of victims when the media reports rape cases? Should it be only the victims? Considering that the names of other crime victims are generally not withheld, does concealing identities in news coverage of rape perpetuate stereotypes about rape? What rights does the alleged rapist have? What, in short, are the legitimate privacy interests of those involved? How can those interests be balanced with the public interest and the press's responsibility to fully report a story?

These are difficult ethical questions for journalists. In making a decision, how does a journalist balance competing demands, such as the common good versus the rights of an individual, or absolute freedom of the press versus the right to privacy? Does one value predominate over another?

Michael Gartner, president of NBC News, decided to break with journalistic tradition and broadcast the name of the alleged victim of the incident at the Kennedy compound without her consent. In the following memo to his staff dated April 24, 1991, Gartner outlines his reasons for making the controversial decision. Some NBC affiliates complained, and even among his own staff the decision was not unanimously supported, but Gartner maintains that it is usually journalistically responsible to reveal the names of rape victims. Katha Pollitt, in opposition, argues that society's attitudes toward rape justify privacy for rape victims. Naming names is media exploitation, she asserts, and it does not serve a good purpose.

YES   Michael Gartner

NAMING THE VICTIM

This past April [1991]—following a woman's allegations that she had been raped by Senator Edward Kennedy's nephew William Kennedy Smith—NBC News broke ranks with a tradition honored by other mainstream news organizations by reporting the name of the alleged victim without her consent. The following day *The New York Times* published the woman's name, asserting that the NBC disclosure had already made her name public knowledge. These decisions set off a great deal of internal discussion at both organizations and in the press at large. In this memo to his staff, Michael Gartner, president of NBC News, justifies his decision.

To the staff:

Why did NBC News name the woman who says she was raped at the Kennedy compound in Florida over the Easter weekend? How was that decision made?

For years, the issue has been debated by journalists and feminists: should the names of rape victims or alleged rape victims be made public? Among journalists, there is no agreement; among feminists, there is no agreement.

At NBC, we debated the journalistic arguments.

Some background: I have been deeply interested in this subject for years, discussing it and debating it. Years ago, I concluded that journalistically it is usually right to name rape victims. Usually, but not always.

Here is my reasoning:

First, we are in the business of disseminating news, not suppressing it. Names and facts are news. They add credibility, they round out the story, they give the viewer or reader information he or she needs to understand issues, to make up his or her own mind about what's going on. So my prejudice is always toward telling the viewer all the germane facts that we know.

Second, producers and editors and news directors should make editorial decisions; editorial decisions should not be made in courtrooms, or legislatures, or briefing rooms—or by persons involved in the news. That is why I oppose military censorship, legislative mandate, and the general belief that we should only print the names of rape victims who volunteer their names.

In no other category of news do we give the newsmaker the option of being named. Those are decisions that should be made in newsrooms—one way or another.

Third, by not naming rape victims we are part of a conspiracy of silence, and that silence is bad for viewers and readers. It reinforces the idea that somehow there is something shameful about being raped. Rape is a crime of violence, a horrible crime of violence. Rapists are horrible people; rape victims are not. One role of the press is to inform, and one way of informing is to destroy incorrect impressions and stereotypes.

Fourth, and finally, there is an issue of fairness. I heard no debate in our newsroom and heard of no debate in other newsrooms on whether we should name the suspect, William Smith. He has not been charged with anything. Yet we dragged his name and his reputation into this without thought, without regard to what might happen to him should he not be guilty—indeed, should he not even be charged. Rapists are vile human beings; but a suspect isn't necessarily a rapist. Were we fair? Probably, yes, because he was thrust into the news, rightly or wrongly. But so was Patricia Bowman, and we should treat her the same way journalistically. We are reporters; we don't take sides, we don't pass judgment.

Those are the points made in our internal debates. At NBC News, I first raised the issue when the woman was raped in Central Park. We had one story on Nightly News, and after that I told some colleagues that if that were to become a continuing national story we should debate the question of naming the woman. As it turned out, it did not become a continuing national story, and we did not have the debate at that time.

Two weeks ago, I began debating in my own mind the issue of the Florida case. I joined in the debate with some colleagues from outside NBC News last week. On Monday of this week, I raised the issue with three colleagues within NBC News. We discussed it at some length. Should we do this, and if we did it how should we frame it?

On Tuesday, the discussions continued. They were passionate and spirited, but not mean-spirited. By the end of the day, the debate probably encompassed 30 persons, men and women of all views. There was no unanimity; if a vote had been taken, it probably would have been not to print the name. But I decided, for the reasons listed here, to air the name. The fact that her identity was known to many in her community was another factor—but not a controlling one—in my decision.

There were those—including some involved in the preparation, production and presentation of the piece—who disagreed intellectually. But no one asked to be removed from the story, and everyone did a thorough job. The story was clear and fair and accurate; it was not sensational, and—for those who think it was done for the ratings or the like—it was not hyped or promoted. It was presented as just another very interesting story in a Nightly News broadcast that, that night, was full of especially compelling stories.

At 5:00 P.M., we did send an advisory to affiliates that we were naming the woman, for our Florida affiliates, especially, needed to be told in advance. In the time since, six of our 209 affiliates have complained to us about the decision; at least one, WBZ in Boston, bleeped out the woman's name and covered her picture. Several affiliates said we ran counter to their own policies, but just as we respect their views they respected ours and ran the story. Several other affiliates called to say they agreed with our decision. Most said nothing.

I am particularly proud of the process we went through in reaching our conclusion; in fact, the process was more important than the conclusion. There was vigorous and free debate about an issue of journalism; all sides were discussed. The story was shaped and reshaped as a result of that debate. When we ultimately decided to air the name, everyone involved at least understood the reasons, and everyone then did the usual first-rate work.

Our decision engendered a national debate. Much of the debate has been focused on the wrong issues, but much of it has been focused on the right issue: the crime of rape. The debate itself has raised the awareness of the horribleness of the crime, the innocence of victims, the vileness of rapists. That has been a beneficial side-effect.

Rape is rarely a national story. If another rape becomes a big story, we will have the same debate again. The position at NBC News is this: we will consider the naming of rape victims or alleged rape victims on a case-by-case basis.

NO

Katha Pollitt

MEDIA GOES WILDING IN PALM BEACH

I drink, I swear, I flirt, I tell dirty jokes. I have also, at various times, watched pornographic videos, had premarital sex, hitchhiked, and sunbathed topless in violation of local ordinances. True, I don't have any speeding tickets, but I don't have a driver's license either. Perhaps I'm subconsciously afraid of my "drives"? There are other things, too, and if I should ever bring rape charges against a rich, famous, powerful politician's relative, *The New York Times* will probably tell you all about them—along with, perhaps, my name. Suitably adorned with anonymous quotes, these revelations will enable you, the public, to form your own opinion: Was I asking for trouble, or did I just make the whole thing up?

In April the media free-for-all surrounding the alleged rape of a Palm Beach woman by William Smith, Senator Ted Kennedy's nephew, took a vicious turn as the *Times*—following NBC, following the *Globe* (supermarket, not Boston, edition), following a British scandal sheet, following *another* British scandal sheet—went public with the woman's name, and a lot more: her traffic violations, her mediocre high school grades, her "little wild streak," her single motherhood, her mother's divorce and upwardly mobile remarriage. Pretty small potatoes, really; she sounds like half my high school classmates. But it did make a picture: bad girl, loose woman, floozy.

Or did it? In a meeting with more than 300 outraged staff members, national editor Soma Golden said that the *Times* could not be held responsible for "every weird mind that reads [the paper]." NBC News chief Michael Gartner was more direct: "Who she is, is material in this.... You try to give viewers as many facts as you can and let them make up their minds." Forget that almost none of these "facts" will be admissible in court, where a jury will nonetheless be expected to render a verdict.

In the ensuing furor, just about every advocate for rape victims has spoken out in favor of preserving the longstanding media custom of anonymity, and in large part the public seems to agree. But the media,[1] acting in its capacity as the guardian of public interest, has decided that naming the victim is an issue up for grabs. And so we are having one of these endless, muddled, two-sides-to-every-question debates that, by ignoring as many facts as possible

From Katha Pollitt, "Naming and Blaming: Media Goes Wilding in Palm Beach," *The Nation* (June 24, 1991). Copyright © 1991 by The Nation Company, L.P. Reprinted by permission of *The Nation* magazine.

and by weighing all arguments equally, gives us that warm American feeling that truth must lie somewhere in the middle. Anna Quindlen, meet Alan Dershowitz. Thank you very much, but our time is just about up.

Sometimes, of course, the truth does lie somewhere in the middle. But not this time. There is no good reason to publish the names of rape complainants without their consent, and many compelling reasons not to. The arguments advanced in favor of publicity reveal fundamental misconceptions about both the nature of the media and the nature of rape.

Let's take a look at what proponents of naming are saying.

The media has a duty to report what it knows. Where have you been? The media keeps information secret all the time. Sometimes it does so on the ground of "taste," a waffle-word that means whatever an editorial board wants it to mean. Thus, we hear about (some of) the sexual high jinks of heterosexual celebrities but not about those of socially equivalent closet-dwellers, whose opposite-sex escorts are portrayed, with knowing untruthfulness, as genuine romantic interests. We are spared—or deprived of, depending on your point of view—the gruesome and salacious details of many murders. (Of all the New York dailies, only *Newsday* reported that notorious Wall Street wife-killer Joseph Pikul was wearing women's underwear when arrested. Not fit to print? I was *riveted*.) Sometimes it fudges the truth to protect third parties from embarrassment, which is why the obituaries would have us believe that eminent young bachelors are dying in large numbers only from pneumonia.

And of course sometimes it censors itself in "the national interest." The claim that the media constitutes a fourth estate, a permanent watchdog, if not outright adversary, of the government, has always been a self-serving myth. Watergate occurred almost twenty years ago and has functioned ever since as a kind of sentimental talisman. Like Charles Foster Kane's Rosebud sled. As we saw during the gulf war, the media can live, when it chooses, quite comfortably with government-imposed restrictions. Neither NBC nor *The New York Times*, so quick to supply their audiences with the inside scoop on the Palm Beach woman, felt any such urgency about Operation Desert Storm.

Anonymous charges are contrary to the American way. Anonymous charges are contrary to American *jurisprudence*. The Palm Beach woman has not made an anonymous accusation. Her name is known to the accused and his attorney, and if the case comes to trial, she will have to appear publicly in court, confront the defendant, give testimony and be cross-examined. But the media is not a court, as the many lawyers who have made this argument—most prominently Alan Dershowitz and Isabelle Pinzler of the American Civil Liberties Union's Women's Rights Project—ought to know.

The media itself argues in favor of anonymity when that serves its own purposes. Reporters go to jail rather than reveal their sources, even when secrecy means protecting a dangerous criminal, impeding the process of justice or denying a public figure the ability to confront his or her accusers. People wouldn't talk to reporters, the press claims, if their privacy couldn't be guaranteed—the same greater-social-good argument it finds unpersuasive when made about rape victims and their reluctance to talk, unprotected, to the police. The media's selective interest in concealment, moreover, undermines its vaunted mission on behalf of the public's right to know. Might not the identity of an anonymous informant (one of those "sources close to the White House" or "highly placed observers," for instance) help the public "make up its mind" about the reliability of the statements? I don't want to digress here into the complex issue of protecting sources, but there can be little question that the practice allows powerful people, in and out of government, to manipulate information for their own ends. Interestingly, the *Times* story on the Palm Beach woman concealed (thirteen times!) the names of those spreading malicious gossip about her, despite the *Times*'s own custom of not using anonymous pejoratives. That custom was resuscitated in time for the paper's circumspect profile of William Smith, which did not detail the accusations against him of prior acquaintance rapes that have been published by *The National Enquirer* and the gossip columnist Taki, and which referred only vaguely to "rumors" of "a pattern of aggressiveness toward women in private." (These, the *Times* said, it could not confirm—unlike the accuser's "little wild streak.")

How *did* the *Times* manage to amass such a wealth of dirt about the Palm Beach woman so quickly? It's hard to picture the reporter, distinguished China hand Fox Butterfield, peeking into the window of her house to see what books were on the toddler's shelf. Could some of his information or some of his leads have come, directly or circuitously, from the detectives hired by the Kennedy family to investigate the woman and her

friends—detectives who, let's not forget, have been the subject of complaints of witness intimidation? The *Times* denies it, but rumors persist. One could argue that, in this particular case, *how* the *Times* got the story was indeed part of the story —perhaps the most important part.

That anonymity is held to be essential to the public good in a wide variety of cases but is damned as a form of censorship in the Palm Beach case shows that what the media is concerned with is not the free flow of information *or* the public good. What is at stake is the media's status, power and ability to define and control information in accordance with the views of those who run the media.

Consider, for example, the case of men convicted of soliciting prostitutes. Except for the occasional athlete, such men receive virtual anonymity in the press. Remember the flap in 1979 when Manhattan D.A. Robert Morgenthau released a list of recently convicted johns and the *Daily News* and two local radio stations went public with it? Universal outrage! Never mind that solicitation is a crime, that convictions are a matter of public record, that the wives and girlfriends of these men might find knowledge of such arrests extremely useful or that society has a declared interest in deterring prostitution. Alan Dershowitz, who in his syndicated column has defended both the content of the *Times* profile and its use of the woman's name, vigorously supported privacy for johns, and in fact made some of the same arguments that he now dismisses. Reporting, he said, was vindictive, subjected ordinary people to the glaring light of publicity for a peccadillo, could destroy the johns' marriages and reputations, and stigmatized otherwise decent people. Dershowitz did not, however, think privacy for johns meant privacy for prostitutes: They, he argued, have no reputation to lose. Although solicitation is a two-person crime, Dershowitz thinks the participants have unequal rights to privacy. With rape, he treats the rapist and his victim as *equally* placed with regard to privacy, even though rape is a one-person crime.

But here the woman's identity was already widely known. Well, I didn't know it. I did, however, know the name of the Central Park jogger—like virtually every other journalist in the country, the entire readership of *The Amsterdam News* (50,000) and the listening audience of WLIB-radio (45,000). Anna Quindlen, in her courageous column dissenting from the *Times's* profile naming the Palm Beach woman, speculated that roughly equivalent large numbers of people knew the identity of the jogger as knew that of William Smith's alleged victim before NBC and the *Times* got into the act. Yet the media went to extraordinary lengths to protect the remaining shreds of the jogger's privacy—film clips were blipped, quotes censored.

What separates the jogger from the Palm Beach woman? You don't have to be the Rev. Al Sharpton to suspect that protecting the jogger's identity was more than a chivalrous gesture. Remember that she too was originally blamed for her assault: What was she doing in the park so late? Who did she think she was? It's all feminism's fault for deluding women into thinking that their safety could, or should, be everywhere guaranteed. But partly as a result of the severity of her injuries, the jogger quickly became the epitome of the innocent victim, the symbol, as Joan Didion pointed out in *The New York Review of Books*, for New York

City itself (white, prosperous, plucky) endangered by the black underclass. A white Wellesley graduate with a Wall Street job attacked out of nowhere by a band of violent black strangers and, because of her comatose state, unable even to bring a rape complaint—this, to the media, is "real rape." The Palm Beach woman, on the other hand, is of working-class origins, a single mother, a frequenter of bars, who went voluntarily to her alleged attacker's house (as who, in our star-struck society, would not?). The jogger could have been the daughter of the men who kept her name out of the news. But William Smith could have been their son.

Rape is like other crimes and should be treated like other crimes. Isn't that what you feminists are always saying? As the coverage of the Palm Beach case proves, rape isn't treated like other crimes. There is no other crime in which the character, behavior and past of the complainant are seen as central elements in determining whether a crime has occurred. There are lots of crimes that could not take place without carelessness, naïveté, ignorance or bad judgment on the part of the victims: mail fraud ("Make $100,000 at home in your spare time!"), confidence games and many violent crimes as well. But when my father was burglarized after forgetting to lock the cellar door, the police did not tell him he had been asking for it. And when an elderly lady (to cite Amy Pagnozzi's example in the *New York Post*) is defrauded of her life savings by a con artist, the con artist is just as much a thief as if he'd broken into his victim's safe-deposit box. "The complainant showed incredibly bad judgment, Your Honor," is not a legal defense.

Why is rape different? Because lots of people, too often including the ones in the jury box, think women really do want to be forced into sex, or by acting or dressing or drinking in a certain way, give up the right to say no, or are the sort of people (i.e., not nuns) who gave up the right to say no to one man by saying yes to another, or are by nature scheming, irrational and crazy. They also think men cannot be expected to control themselves, are entitled to take by force what they cannot get by persuasion and are led on by women who, because they are scheming, irrational and crazy, change their minds in mid-sex. My files bulge with stories that show how widespread these beliefs are: The Wisconsin judge who put a child molester on probation because he felt the 3-year-old female victim had acted provocatively; the Florida jury that exonerated a rapist because his victim was wearing disco attire; and so on.

In a bizarre column defending Ted Kennedy's role on the night in question, William Safire took aim at the Palm Beach woman, who was "apparently" not "taught that drinking all night and going to a man's house at 3:30 A.M. places one in what used to be called an occasion of sin." (All her mother's fault, as usual.) The other woman present in the Kennedy mansion that night, a waitress named Michelle Cassone, has made herself a mini-celebrity by telling any reporter who will pay for her time that she too believes that women who drink and date, including herself, are "fair game."

By shifting the debate to the question of merely naming victims, the media preempts a discussion of the way it reports all crimes with a real or imaginary sexual component. But as the *Times* profile shows, naming cannot be divorced from blaming. When the victim is young and attractive (and in the tabloids *all* female victims are attractive), the sexual element in the crime is always made its central feature—even when, as in the case of Marla Hanson, the model who was slashed by hired thugs and whose character was savaged in *New York*, there is no sexual element. I mean no belittlement of rape to suggest it was one of the lesser outrages visited on the Central Park jogger. She was also beaten so furiously she lost 80 percent of her blood and suffered permanent physical, neurological and cognitive damage. Yet, paradoxically, it was the rape that seized the imagination of the media, and that became the focus of the crime both for her defenders and for those who defended her attackers.

Naming rape victims will remove the stigma against rape. Of all the arguments in favor of naming victims, this is the silliest, and the most insincere. Sure, NBC's Michael Gartner told *Newsweek*, the consequences will be "extraordinarily difficult for this generation, but it may perhaps help their daughters and granddaughters." How selfish of women to balk at offering themselves on the altar of little girls yet unborn! If Gartner wishes to make a better world for my descendants, he is amply well placed to get cracking. He could demand nonsensationalized reporting of sex crimes; he could hire more female reporters and producers; he could use NBC News to dispel false notions about rape—for example, the idea that "who the woman is, is material." Throughout the country there are dozens of speakouts against rape at which victims publicly tell of their experiences. Every year there are Take Back the Night marches in Manhattan. Where are the cameras and the reporters on these occasions? Adding misery to hundreds of thousands of women a year and—as just about every expert in the field believes—dramatically lowering the already abysmal incidence of rape reporting (one in ten) will not help my granddaughter; it will only make it more likely that her grandmother, her mother and she herself will be raped by men who have not been brought to justice.

This argument is, furthermore, based on a questionable assumption. Why would society blame rape victims less if it knew who they were? Perhaps its censure would simply be amplified. Instead of thinking, If ordinary, decent, conventional women get raped in large numbers it *can't* be their fault, people might well think, Goodness, there are a lot more women asking for it than we thought. After the invasion of Kuwait, in which scores of women were raped by Iraqi soldiers, there was no dispensation from the traditional harsh treatment of rape victims, some of whom, pregnant and in disgrace, had attempted suicide, gone into hiding or fled the country. One woman told *USA Today* that she wished she were dead. America is not Kuwait, but here, too, many believe that a woman can't be raped against her will and that damaged goods are damaged goods. (Curious how publicity is supposed to lessen the stigma against rape victims but only adds to the suffering of johns.)

One also has to wonder about the urgency with which Gartner and the other male proponents of the anti-stigma theory, with no history of public concern for women, declare themselves the best judge of women's interests and advocate a policy that they themselves will never have to bear the consequences of. Gartner cited, as did many others, the *Des Moines Register* profile of a named rape victim but neglected to mention that the victim, Nancy Ziegenmeyer, volunteered the use of her name, seven months after reporting the crime—in other words, after she had had a chance to come to terms with her experience and to inform her family and friends in a way she found suitable. (Ziegenmeyer, by the way, opposes involuntary naming.) Why is it that, where women are concerned, the difference between choice and coercion eludes so many? Rapists, too, persuade themselves that they know what women really want and need.

William Smith's name has been dragged through the mud. Why should his accuser be protected? Actually, William Smith has been portrayed rather favorably in the media. No anonymous pejoratives for him: He is "one of the least spoiled and least arrogant of the young Kennedys" (*Time*); an "unlikely villain" (*Newsweek*); "a man of gentleness and humor," "the un-Kennedy," "a good listener" (*The New York Times*); from a "wounded," "tragic" family (*passim*). Certainly he has been subjected to a great deal of unpleasant media attention, and even if he is eventually found innocent, some people will always suspect that he is guilty. But no one forced the media to sensationalize the story; that was a conscious editorial decision, not an act of God. Instead of heaping slurs on the Palm Beach woman in order to even things up, the media should be asking itself why it did not adopt a more circumspect attitude toward the case from the outset.

The tit-for-tat view of rape reporting appeals to many people because of its apparent impartiality. Feminists of the pure equal-treatment school like it because it looks gender neutral (as if rape were a gender-neutral crime). And nonfeminist men like it because, while looking gender neutral, it would, in practice, advantage men. "Should the press be in the business of protecting certain groups but not others—," wrote *Washington Post* columnist Richard Cohen, "alleged victims (females), but not the accused (males)? My answer is no." Cohen, like Michael Gartner, presents himself as having women's best interests at heart: "If rape's indelible stigma is ever to fade, the press has to stop being complicitous in perpetuating the sexist aura that surrounds it." Thus, by some mysterious alchemy, the media, which is perhaps the single biggest promoter of the sexist aura surrounding crimes of violence against women, can redeem itself by jettisoning the only policy it has that eases, rather than augments, the victim's anguish.

Behind the tit-for-tat argument lies a particular vision of rape in which the odds are even that the alleged victim is really the victimizer—a seductress, blackmailer, hysteric, who is bringing a false charge. That was the early word on the Palm Beach woman, and it's hard not to conclude that publicizing her identity was punitive: She's caused all this trouble, is visiting yet more "tragedy" on America's royal family, and had better be telling the truth. In fact, the appeal of naming the victim seems to rest not in the hope that it "may perhaps" someday make rape reporting less painful but in the certainty that right now it makes such reporting *more* painful, thereby inhibiting false accusations. Although studies have repeatedly shown that fabricated rape charges are extremely rare, recent years have seen a number of cases: Tawana Brawley, for example, and Cathleen Crowell Webb, who recanted her testimony after finding Jesus and then hugged her newly freed, no-longer-alleged-assailant on the *Donahue* show. A year ago a Nebraska woman who admitted filing a false charge was ordered by a judge to purchase newspaper ads and radio spots apologizing to the man she had accused. (She was also sentenced to six months in jail.) It is not unknown for other criminal charges to be fabricated, but has anyone ever been forced into a public apology in those cases? The tenor of the equal-publicity argument is captured perfectly by the (female) letter writer to *Time* who suggested that newspapers publish both names and both photos too. Why not bring back trial by ordeal and make the two of them grasp bars of red-hot iron?

* * *

Fundamentally, the arguments about naming rape victims center around two contested areas: acquaintance rape and privacy. While the women's movement has had some success in expanding the definition of rape to include sexual violation by persons known to the victim —as I write, *The New York Times* is running an excellent series on such rape, containing interviews with women named or anonymous by their choice (atonement?) —there is also a lot of backlash.

The all-male editorial board of the *New York Post*, which rather ostentatiously refused to print the Palm Beach woman's name, has actually proposed a change in the law to distinguish between "real rape" (what the jogger suffered) and acquaintance rape, confusedly described as a "sexual encounter, forced or not," that "has been preceded by a series of consensual activities." *Forced or not?*

At the other end of the literary social scale, there's Camille (No Means Yes) Paglia, academia's answer to Phyllis

Schlafly, repackaging hoary myths about rape as a bold dissent from feminist orthodoxy and "political correctness." Indeed, an attack on the concept of acquaintance rape figures prominently in the many diatribes against current intellectual trends on campus. It's as though the notion of consensual sex were some incomprehensible French literary theory that threatened the very foundations of Western Civ. And, come to think of it, maybe it does.

Finally, there is the issue of privacy. Supporters of naming like to say that anonymity implies that rape is something to be ashamed of. But must this be its meaning? It says a great deal about the impoverishment of privacy as a value in our time that many intelligent people can find no justification for it but shame, guilt, cowardice and prudishness. As the tabloidization of the media proceeds apace, as the boundaries between the public and the personal waver and fade away, good citizenship has come to require of more and more people that they put themselves forward, regardless of the cost, as exhibit A in a national civics lesson. In this sense, rape victims are in the same position as homosexuals threatened with "outing" for the good of other gays, or witnesses forced to give painful and embarrassing testimony in televised courtrooms so that the couch potatoes at home can appreciate the beauty of the legal process.

But there are lots of reasons a rape victim might not want her name in the paper that have nothing to do with shame. She might not want her mother to know, or her children, or her children's evil little classmates, or obscene phone callers, or other rapists. Every person reading this article probably has his or her secrets, things that aren't necessarily shameful (or things that are) but are liable to misconstructions, false sympathy and stupid questions from the tactless and ignorant. Things that are just plain nobody's business unless you want them to be.

Instead of denying privacy to rape victims, we should take a good hard look at our national passion for thrusting unwanted publicity on people who are not accused of wrong-doing but find themselves willy-nilly in the news. ("How did it *feel* to watch your child being torn to pieces by wild animals?" "It felt terrible, Maury, terrible.") I've argued here that society's attitudes toward rape justify privacy for rape complainants, and that indeed those attitudes lurk behind the arguments for publicity. But something else lurks there as well: a desensitization to the lurid and prurient way in which the media exploits the sufferings of any ordinary person touched by a noteworthy crime or tragedy. Most of the people who have spoken out against anonymity are journalists, celebrity lawyers, media executives and politicos—people who put themselves forward in the press and on television as a matter of course and who are used to taking their knocks as the price of national attention. It must be hard for such people to sympathize with someone who doesn't want to play the media game—especially if it's in a "good cause."

I'm not at all sure there is a good cause here. Titillation, not education, seems the likely reason for the glare on the Palm Beach case. But even if I'm unduly cynical and the media sincerely wishes to conduct a teach-in on rape, the interests of the public can be served without humiliating the complainant. Doctors educate one another with case histories in which patients are identified only by initials and in which other nonrelevant identifying details are changed. Lawyers file cases on behalf of Jane Doe and John Roe and expect the Supreme Court to "make up its mind" nonetheless.

If the media wants to educate the public about rape, it can do so without names. What the coverage of the Palm Beach case shows is that it needs to educate itself first.

NOTES

1. I use "media" in the singular (rather than the strictly grammatical plural) because I am talking about the communications industry as a social institution that, while hardly monolithic (as the debate over naming shows), transcends the different means—"media" plural—by which the news is conveyed.

POSTSCRIPT

Should the Names of Rape Victims Be Reported?

During the extensive televised coverage of the William Kennedy Smith trial, a dot was used to cover the woman's face. After the trial's conclusion, the woman herself went public and gave a handful of print and broadcast interviews.

With regard to rape and other sex crimes, the media must answer questions beyond whether or not to name the victims. Do common news practices, for example, yield biases that perpetuate myths and injustice? Helen Benedict, in *Virgin or Vamp: How the Press Covers Sex Crimes* (Oxford University Press, 1992), harshly critiques the manner in which newspapers have handled sex crimes.

Ethical guidelines require journalists to make specific choices as they balance freedom and responsibility in their day-to-day reporting. In making decisions, journalists are most often guided by the practices of the profession, their education, their on-the-job socialization, and the written codes of the organizations for which they work. Debates such as the one presented here are inevitable when traditional practices come under scrutiny.

The history of journalism has borne witness to many styles of approaching a story. In his book *Goodbye Gutenberg: The Newspaper Revolution of the 1980s* (Oxford University Press, 1980), Anthony Smith says, "Investigation has become the most highly praised and highly prized form of journalism, taking the place of opinion leadership, the historic purpose of the press." He suggests that the investigative reporter typically finds him- or herself in the position of both judge and jury—the authority to whom the public turns to get the whole story.

Ethical issues are not easily resolved: We should always struggle to discuss them, think about them, and let them guide our consciences. Only when we cease thinking about them is it too late to do anything about them.

There are many books on different styles of journalism, and the biographies of such people as Horace Greeley, William Randolph Hearst, Joseph Pulitzer, and even Rupert Murdoch show how each individual shaped a special time in journalism history. Other sources that describe journalistic themes and public reaction include Ben H. Bagdikian's *The Information Machines: Their Impact on Men and the Media* (Harper & Row, 1971); the Roper Organization's *Trends in Public Attitudes Toward Television and Other Media, 1969–1974* (Television Information Office, 1975); and John P. Robinson's *Daily News Habits of the American Public*, ANPA New Research Center Study No. 15 (September 22, 1978). Also, among the periodicals that cover journalistic styles and practices are *Columbia Journalism Review, Editor and Publisher,* and *American Society of Newspaper Editors (ASNE) Newsletter.*

Further readings on ethics and the media include Everette Dennis, Donald Gillmore, and Theodore Glasser, eds., *Media Freedom and Accountability* (Greenwood Press, 1989) and Bruce Swain, *Reporters' Ethics* (Iowa State University Press, 1978), which examine a number of issues that reporters must face. More recent books include *Ethical Issues in Journalism and the Media* edited by Andres Beasly and Ruth Chadwick (Routledge, Chapman & Hall, 1992) and *Good News: Social Ethics and the Press* by Clifford G. Christians, John P. Ferre, and Mark Fackler (Oxford University Press, 1993).

ISSUE 7

Should Tobacco Advertising Be Restricted?

YES: Joseph R. DiFranza et al., from "RJR Nabisco's Cartoon Camel Promotes Camel Cigarettes to Children," *Journal of the American Medical Association* (December 11, 1991)

NO: George J. Annas, from "Cowboys, Camels, and the First Amendment— The FDA's Restrictions on Tobacco Advertising," *The New England Journal of Medicine* (December 5, 1996)

ISSUE SUMMARY

YES: Doctor Joseph R. DiFranza and his colleagues report a national study that examines the possibility of children being tempted to smoke because of the tobacco industry's use of images that appeal to and are remembered by children. Because of the profound health risks, DiFranza et al. call for restrictions on tobacco ads.

NO: Attorney George J. Annas agrees that the tobacco industry has marketed products to children, but he maintains that efforts to restrict advertising are inappropriate, perhaps even illegal. He argues that some of the restrictions that have been placed on tobacco advertisements violate the First Amendment.

The marketing of tobacco products has been controversial for some time, but discussions have become more heated in recent years as the extent of the tobacco industry's knowledge of nicotine as an addictive drug and the long-term effects of smoking on a person's health has come into question. Court cases and public scrutiny of the tobacco industry have led to legal sanctions and restrictions on the marketing of tobacco products, most specifically with regard to tobacco ads that appeal to children. Although tobacco industry officials claim that they do not try to induce children to smoke, evidence indicates that advertising strategies do, indeed, target a potential audience of young people. Research shows that most long-term smokers begin smoking at the age of 12 or 13 and become hooked for life.

In the following selections, Joseph R. DiFranza and his colleagues raise ethical concerns about the effects of the tobacco industry's using appeals that may tempt children to start smoking, and they explain how advertising effectively reaches consumers. Arguing from a legal position, George J. Annas examines the Federal Drug Administration's current efforts to restrict advertising, particularly to the youth market. Citing several precedents regarding the restriction of advertising, he draws the conclusion that current governmental efforts to curb ads will remain ineffective and may violate the advertisers' First Amendment right to free speech.

This issue brings up several topics for discussion. One important question is whether or not children should be protected from activities and behaviors that may have long-term negative effects. Also, should advertisers exercise standards regarding the products they promote? Should the tobacco industry divulge all of their research regarding the hazards of smoking? Do ethical standards change when appeals are made to children as potential consumers?

Annas raises another important ethical dimension: How far can the First Amendment be used in defending free speech? Since the Bill of Rights was written—over 200 years ago—the type of "speech" that Americans engage in has changed dramatically. Does the right of free speech extend to advertising?

Advertising has traditionally been classified as "commercial" speech, which gives greater license to its use. Should commercial speech also be subject to a more stringent interpretation when the rights of children are involved? If so, should other products be given special consideration? At what point does censorship enter into the picture? Also, if tobacco advertising can be restricted, what about advertising for other potentially harmful products?

Issues involving tobacco advertising are timely and important. Many states have enacted laws to encourage counteradvertising to promote the health benefits of not smoking. In Britain, the figures of Joe Camel and the Marlboro Man have been banned from all advertising. A range of data suggests that antismoking campaigns have different levels of effects. In many ways, antismoking campaigns use many of the same tools and techniques to get the public's attention as do the advertisers of tobacco products. What can be learned from these campaigns about strategies for instituting long-term behavior change?

YES

Joseph R. DiFranza et al.

RJR NABISCO'S CARTOON CAMEL PROMOTES CAMEL CIGARETTES TO CHILDREN

With the number of US smokers declining by about 1 million each year, the tobacco industry's viability is critically dependent on its ability to recruit replacement smokers. Since children and teenagers constitute 90% of all new smokers, their importance to the industry is obvious. Many experts are convinced that the industry is actively promoting nicotine addiction among youth.

Spokespersons for the tobacco industry assert that they do not advertise to people under 21 years of age, the sole purpose of their advertising being to promote brand switching and brand loyalty among adult smokers. However, industry advertising expenditures cannot be economically justified on this basis alone. This study was therefore undertaken to determine the relative impact of tobacco advertising on children and adults.

There is abundant evidence that tobacco advertising influences children's images of smoking. In Britain, the proportion of children who gave "looks tough" as a reason for smoking declined after tough images were banned from cigarette advertisements. Children as young as the age of 6 years can reliably recall tobacco advertisements and match personality sketches with the brands using that imagery. In fact, cigarette advertising establishes such imagery among children who are cognitively too immature to understand the purpose of advertising. Subsequently, children who are most attuned to cigarette advertising have the most positive attitudes toward smoking, whether or not they already smoke. Children who are more aware of, or who approve of, cigarette advertisements are more likely to smoke, and those who do smoke buy the most heavily advertised brands.

Historically, one brand that children have not bought is Camel. In seven surveys, involving 3400 smokers in the seventh through 12th grades, conducted between 1976 and 1988 in Georgia, Louisiana, and Minnesota, Camel was given as the preferred brand by less than 0.5%. In 1986, Camels were most popular with smokers over the age of 65 years, of whom 4.4% chose

From Joseph R. DiFranza, John W. Richards, Jr., Paul M. Paulman, Nancy Wolf-Gillespie, Christopher Fletcher, Robert D. Jaffe, and David Murray, "RJR Nabisco's Cartoon Camel Promotes Camel Cigarettes to Children," *Journal of the American Medical Association*, vol. 266, no. 22 (December 11, 1991), pp. 3149–3152. Copyright © 1991 by The American Medical Association. Reprinted by permission. References omitted.

Camels, and least popular among those 17 to 24 years of age, of whom only 2.7% preferred Camels.

In 1988, RJR Nabisco launched the "smooth character" advertising campaign, featuring Old Joe, a cartoon camel modeled after James Bond and Don Johnson of "Miami Vice." Many industry analysts believe that the goal of this campaign is to reposition Camel to compete with Philip Morris' Marlboro brand for the illegal children's market segment. To determine the relative impact of Camel's Old Joe cartoon advertising on children and adults, we used four standard marketing measures.

1. Recognition. We compared the proportions of teenagers and adults aged 21 years and over who recognize Camel's Old Joe cartoon character.
2. Recall. We compared the ability of teenagers and adults to recall from a masked Old Joe advertisement the type of product being advertised and the brand name.
3. Appeal. We compared how interesting and appealing a series of Old Joe cartoon character advertisements were to teenagers and adults.
4. Brand preference. We compared brand preferences of teenaged smokers prior to the Old Joe cartoon character campaign with those 3 years into the campaign to determine if the campaign had been more effective with children or with adults, and to determine if Camel had been repositioned as a children's brand.

METHODS

Subjects
Since adolescent brand preferences may vary from one geographic location to another, we selected children from Georgia, Massachusetts, Nebraska, New Mexico, and Washington, representing five regions. One school in each state was selected based on its administration's willingness to participate. Schools with a smoking prevention program focused on tobacco advertising were excluded.

A target of 60 students in each grade, 9 through 12, from each school was set. In large schools, classes were selected to obtain a sample representative of all levels of academic ability. Students were told that the study concerned advertising and were invited to participate anonymously.

Since adult brand preferences are available from national surveys, adult subjects were recruited only at the Massachusetts site. All drivers, regardless of age, who were renewing their licenses at the Registry of Motor Vehicles on the days of the study during the 1990–1991 school year were asked to participate. Since licenses must be renewed in person, this is a heterogeneous population.

Materials
Seven Camel Old Joe cartoon character advertisements were obtained from popular magazines during the 3 years prior to the study. One ad was masked to hide all clues (except Old Joe) as to the product and brand being advertised.

The survey instrument collected demographic information and information on past and present use of tobacco, including brand preference. Children were considered to be smokers if they had smoked one or more cigarettes during the previous week. Previously validated questions were used to determine children's intentions regarding smoking in the next month and year and their attitudes toward the advertised social benefits of smoking.

Subjects rated the ads as "cool or stupid" and "interesting or boring." Subjects were asked if they thought Old Joe was "cool" and if they would like to be friends with him. Each positive response to these four questions was scored as a one, a negative response as a zero. The "appeal score" was the arithmetic sum of the responses to these four questions, with the lowest possible score per respondent being a zero and the highest a four.

Procedure

Subjects were first shown the masked ad and asked if they had seen the Old Joe character before. They were then asked to identify the product being advertised and the brand name of the product. Subjects who could not answer these questions were required to respond "Don't know" so they would not be able to write in the correct answer when the unmasked advertisements were shown. The subjects were then shown, one at a time, the six unmasked advertisements and asked to rate how the advertisements and the Old Joe cartoon character appealed to them. Subjects then completed the remainder of the survey instrument.

Adolescent brand preference data from this study were compared with the data obtained by seven surveys completed prior to the kickoff of Camel's Old Joe cartoon character campaign early in 1988.

Tests of significance were made using the Two-tailed Student's t Test for continuous data and the χ^2 and Fisher's Exact Test for discrete data. A P value of less than .05 was used to define statistical significance.

The study was conducted during the 1990–1991 school year.

RESULTS

A total of 1060 students and 491 subjects from the Registry of Motor Vehicles were asked to participate. Usable surveys were obtained from 1055 students (99%) and 415 license renewal applicants (84.5%). Seventy drivers were under 21 years of age, leaving 345 adults aged 21 years or older. Students ranged in age from 12 to 19 years (mean, 15.99 years) and adults from 21 to 87 years (mean, 40.47 years). Females represented 51.0% of the students and 54.8% of the adults.

Children were much more likely than adults to recognize Camel's Old Joe cartoon character (97.7% vs 72.2%). It is not plausible that the children were simply saying they had seen Old Joe when they had not, since they also demonstrated a greater familiarity with the advertisement on the two objective measures.

When shown the masked advertisement, the children were much more successful than the adults in identifying the product being advertised (97.5% vs 67.0%) and the Camel brand name (93.6% vs 57.7%). Even when the analysis was limited to those subjects who were familiar with the Old Joe cartoon character, children were still more likely than adults to remember the product (98.6% vs 89.6%) and the Camel brand name (95.0% vs 79.1%). This confirms that Old Joe cartoon advertisements are more effective at communicating product and brand name information to children than to adults.

Because Massachusetts adults may not be representative of adults in the other four states where children were surveyed, the above analyses were repeated comparing only Massachusetts children and adults. In all cases the differences between adults and children were significant and of even greater magnitude, excluding the possibility that the above findings were due to a lighter level of advertising exposure in the Massachusetts area.

On all four measures, the children found the Camel cartoon advertisements more appealing than did the adults. Children were more likely to think the advertisements looked "cool" (58.0% vs 39.9%) or "interesting" (73.6% vs 55.1%). More of the children thought Old Joe was "cool" (43.0% vs 25.7%) and wanted to be friends with him (35.0% vs 14.4%).

The brand preference data revealed a dramatic reversal in the market segment pattern that existed prior to Camel's Old Joe cartoon character campaign. Camel was given as the preferred brand by 32.8% of children up to the age of 18 years who smoked, 23.1% of Massachusetts adult smokers aged 19 and 20 years, and 8.7% of those 21 years of age and over. The figures for the Massachusetts adults were significantly higher than the national market share for Camel, 4.4%, suggesting that Massachusetts adults may be more familiar with the Old Joe Camel campaign than adults in general. Camel cigarettes are now most popular with children and progressively less popular with older smokers.

About equal proportions of adults (28.2%) and children (29.0%) reported some current cigarette use, making it unlikely that this factor influenced any of the above findings. Although there were some statistically significant differences in the responses of children from different regions, these were not the focus of this study.

When compared with nonsmokers, children who were currently smoking gave higher approval ratings to the advertisements. Approving attitudes to-ward cigarette advertisements seem to precede actual smoking. Among the non-smoking children, those who either were ambivalent about their future smoking intentions or expressed a definite intention to smoke were more approving of the advertisements than those children who intended not to smoke.

Children were more likely to smoke if they believed that smoking is pleasurable and that it makes a person more popular, all common themes in cigarette advertising. Among nonsmoking children, those who believed that smoking would make them more attractive were eight times more likely to express an intention to smoke in the next year.

COMMENT

Our data demonstrate that in just 3 years Camel's Old Joe cartoon character had an astounding influence on children's smoking behavior. The proportion of smokers under 18 years of age who choose Camels has risen from 0.5% to 32.8%. Given that children under 18 years account for 3.3% of all cigarette sales, and given a national market share of 4.4% for Camel, we compute that Camel's adult market share is actually 3.4%. Given a current average price of 153.3 cents per pack, the illegal sale of Camel cigarettes to children under 18 years of age is estimated to have risen from $6 million per year prior to the cartoon advertisements to $476 million per year now, accounting for one quarter of all Camel sales.

From both a legal and moral perspective, it is important to determine if the tobacco industry is actively promoting nicotine addiction among youngsters. However, from a public health perspective it is irrelevant whether the effects of tobacco advertising on children are intentional. If tobacco advertising is a proximate cause of disease, it must be addressed accordingly. In the following discussion we will examine the evidence produced by this study, the marketing practices of the tobacco industry as a whole as revealed in industry documents, and the marketing practices used by RJR Nabisco, in particular, to promote Camel cigarettes. The quotations cited below are from tobacco industry personnel and from documents obtained during litigation over Canada's ban of tobacco advertising.

Our data show that children are much more familiar with Camel's Old Joe cartoon character than are adults. This may be because children have more exposure to these advertisements, or because the advertisements are inherently more appealing to youngsters. The tobacco industry has long followed a policy of preferentially placing selected advertisements where children are most likely to see them. For example, print advertisements are placed in magazines "specifically designed to reach young people." Paid cigarette brand promotions appear in dozens of teen movies. Camels are featured in the Walt Disney movies *Who Framed Roger Rabbit?* and *Honey I Shrunk the Kids.*

The industry targets poster advertisements for "key youth locations/meeting places in the proximity of theaters, records [sic] stores, video arcades, etc." It is common to see Old Joe poster advertisements in malls, an obvious gathering spot for young teens. Billboards, T-shirts, baseball caps, posters, candy cigarettes, and the sponsorship of televised sporting events and entertainment events such as the Camel "Mud and Monster" series are all used to promote Camels. All are

effective marketing techniques for reaching children.

The fact that children are much more attracted to the themes used in the Old Joe cartoon character advertisements may also explain why they are more familiar with them. The themes used in tobacco advertising that is targeted at children are the result of extensive research on children conducted by the tobacco industry to "learn everything there was to learn about how smoking begins." Their research identifies the major psychological vulnerabilities of children, which can then be exploited by advertising to foster and maintain nicotine addiction.

The marketing plan for "Export A" cigarettes describes their "psychological benefits"; "Export smokers will be perceived as... characterized by their self-confidence, strength of character and individuality which makes them popular and admired by their peers."

Consider a child's vulnerability to peer pressure. According to one industry study, "The goading and taunting that exists at the age of 11 or 12 to get nonsmokers to start smoking is virtually gone from the peer group circles by 16 or 17." If peer influence is virtually gone by the age of 16 years, who is the intended target group for RJR-MacDonald's Tempo brand, described as individuals who are "[e]xtremely influenced by their peer group"? (RJR-MacDonald is a wholly owned subsidiary of RJR Nabisco.) The recommended strategy for promoting this brand is the "[m]ajor usage of imagery which portrays the positive social appeal of peer group acceptance." In one Camel advertisement, a cowboy (a Marlboro smoker?) is being denied admission to a party because "only smooth characters [ie, Camel smokers] need apply". It appears that Camel advertisements are also targeted at individuals who are influenced by their peer group.

Children use tobacco, quite simply, because they believe the benefits outweigh the risks. To the insecure child, the benefits are the "psychological benefits" promised in tobacco advertisements: confidence, an improved image, and popularity. Children who believe that smoking will make them more popular or more attractive are up to 4.7 times more likely to smoke.

Previous research makes it clear that children derive some of their positive images of smoking from advertising. Children who are aware of tobacco advertising, and those who approve of it, are also more likely to be smokers. Children's favorable attitudes toward smoking and advertising precede actual tobacco use and correlate with the child's intention to smoke, suggesting that the images children derive from advertising encourage them to smoke. Our data confirm these earlier findings. Among nonsmoking children, those who were more approving of the Old Joe advertisements were more likely either to be ambivalent about their smoking intentions or to express a definite intention to smoke. Nonsmoking children who believed that smoking would make them more popular were eight times more likely to express an intention to smoke in the future.

Since a child's intention to smoke is considered to be a good predictor of future smoking behavior, it seems reasonable to conclude that a belief in the psychological benefits of smoking, derived from advertising, precedes, and contributes to, the adoption of smoking.

There are other lines of evidence indicating that tobacco advertising increases the number of children who use tobacco. In countries where advertising has been totally banned or severely restricted, the percentage of young people who smoke has decreased more rapidly than in countries where tobacco promotion has been less restricted. After a 24-year decline in smokeless tobacco sales, an aggressive youth-oriented marketing campaign has been followed by what has been termed "an epidemic" of smokeless tobacco use among children, with the *average* age for new users being 10 years.

Many of the tobacco industry documents cited above provide abundant evidence that one purpose of tobacco advertising is to addict children to tobacco. In the words of one advertising consultant, "Where I worked we were trying very hard to influence kids who were 14 to start to smoke." Two marketing strategy documents for Export A also reveal that it is the youngest children they are after. "Whose behavior are we trying to affect?: new users." The goal is "[o]ptimizing product and user imagery of Export 'A' against young starter smokers." The average age for starter smokers is 13 years.

The industry also researches the best ways of keeping children from quitting once they are "hooked on smoking." The purpose of one tobacco industry study was to assess the feasibility of marketing low-tar brands to teens as an alternative to quitting. The study found that for boys, "[t]he single most commonly voiced reason for quitting among those who had done so ... was sports." The tobacco industry's sponsorship of sporting events, such as the Camel Supercross motorcycle race, should be seen in relation to its need to discourage teenage boys from quitting. Similarly, its emphasis on slimness serves as a constant reinforcement of teenage girls' fears of gaining weight as a result of quitting.

Our study provides further evidence that tobacco advertising promotes and maintains nicotine addiction among children and adolescents. A total ban of tobacco advertising and promotions, as part of an effort to protect children from the dangers of tobacco, can be based on sound scientific reasoning.

NO

George J. Annas

COWBOYS, CAMELS, AND
THE FIRST AMENDMENT

The Marlboro Man and Joe Camel have become public health enemies number one and two, and removing their familiar faces from the gaze of young people has become a goal of President Bill Clinton and his health care officials.[1] The strategy of limiting the exposure of children to tobacco advertisements is based on the fact that almost all regular smokers begin smoking in their teens. This approach is politically possible because most Americans believe that tobacco companies should be prohibited from targeting children in their advertising.

Shortly before the 1996 Democratic National Convention, the President announced that he had approved regulations drafted by the Food and Drug Administration (FDA) to restrict the advertising of tobacco products to children. At the convention, Vice-President Al Gore told the delegates, "Until I draw my last breath, I will pour my heart and soul into the cause of protecting our children from the dangers of smoking."[2] In a press conference at the White House immediately following the announcement, Health and Human Services Secretary Donna Shalala said, "This is the most important public health initiative in a generation. It ranks with everything from polio to penicillin. I mean, this is huge in terms of its impact."[3]

No one doubts that a substantial reduction in the number of teenage smokers would mean a substantial reduction in the number of adult smokers when these teenagers grow up, and this reduction would have a major effect on health and longevity. Since almost 50 million Americans smoke, the result of reducing the number of young smokers substantially would indeed be "huge in terms of its impact." The real question is not whether the goal is appropriate but whether the means proposed to reach it are likely to be effective. In this regard, the FDA regulations may be unsuccessful for either of two related reasons: the implementation of the regulations may not reduce the number of teenagers who start smoking, or some of the regulations may be found to violate the First Amendment.

From George J. Annas, "Cowboys, Camels, and the First Amendment—The FDA's Restrictions on Tobacco Advertising," *The New England Journal of Medicine*, vol. 335, no. 23 (December 5, 1996). Copyright © 1996 by The Massachusetts Medical Society. Reprinted by permission.

THE REGULATIONS

The FDA's new regulations are designed to reduce the demand for tobacco products among teenagers, which is consistent with the goal of the Healthy People 2000 program to reduce by half (to 15 percent) the proportion of children who use tobacco products.[1,4] The FDA has somewhat modified the time line: the goal of its regulations is to cut underage smoking by half in seven years. Although the FDA has never before asserted jurisdiction over cigarettes or smokeless tobacco, the agency bases its claim to jurisdiction over these two types of products on its authority to regulate medical devices, defining cigarettes as a "drug-delivery device." Of course, this means that the FDA also defines nicotine as a drug. The regulations apply to sellers, distributors, and manufacturers of tobacco products. Sellers may not sell cigarettes or smokeless tobacco to anyone under the age of 18 years and must verify the age of purchasers under 26 by checking a form of identification bearing a photograph, in a "direct, face-to-face exchange." Exceptions are sales through mail orders and vending machines located in facilities that persons under the age of 18 years are not permitted to enter at any time. The distribution of free samples is also outlawed, as is the sale of cigarettes in packs of fewer than 20 (so-called kiddie packs). All cigarettes and smokeless tobacco products must bear the following statement: "Nicotine delivery devices for persons 18 or older."[1]

The most controversial portions of the regulations deal with advertising. One section outlaws all outdoor advertising within 1000 feet of public playgrounds and elementary and secondary schools. Advertising is restricted to "black text on a white background."[1] This restriction applies to all billboards but not to "adult publications." Such publications are defined by the regulations as "any newspaper, magazine, periodical or other publication... whose readers younger than 18 years of age constitute 15 percent or less of the total readership as measured by competent and reliable survey evidence; and that is read by fewer than 2 million persons younger than 18 years of age."[1] Tobacco manufacturers and distributors are prohibited from marketing any item (other than cigarettes or smokeless tobacco) that bears a brand name used for cigarettes or smokeless tobacco and are prohibited from offering any gift to a person purchasing cigarettes or smokeless tobacco products.[1] Finally, "no manufacturer, distributor, or retailer may sponsor or cause to be sponsored any athletic, musical, artistic, or other social or cultural event, or any entry or team in any event, [under] the brand name [of a tobacco product] (alone or in conjunction with any other words)."[1] Such events, may, however, be sponsored under the name of the corporation that manufactures the tobacco product, provided that the corporate name existed before 1995 and does not include a brand name.

THE LEGAL CHALLENGE

Tobacco companies have already filed suit to enjoin enforcement of the regulations. According to FDA Commissioner David Kessler, the FDA decided to assert its jurisdiction over cigarettes when the scientific community determined that the nicotine in tobacco products is addictive, and when the FDA concluded that the tobacco companies were probably manipulating the levels of nicotine to maintain their market of addicted users.[5] Under the legislation that gives the FDA its authority, a drug is any product "intended to affect the structure or any function of the body." The FDA contends that cigarettes and smokeless tobacco can be properly viewed as devices for delivering the drug nicotine, because they meet all three independent criteria for determining whether a product is a drug-delivery device: "a reasonable manufacturer would foresee that the product will be used for pharmacologic purposes [or] that consumers actually use it for such purposes [or] the manufacturer experts or designs the product to be used in such a manner."[5]

The primary argument of the tobacco companies is that Congress has consistently refused to give the FDA jurisdiction over tobacco products, and until now, the FDA itself has consistently said that it has no jurisdiction over such products. Moreover, the companies assert that if the FDA had jurisdiction over cigarettes as a drug or drug-delivery device, the FDA would have to ban them as not being "safe," which Congress has repeatedly refused to do or permit.

The second argument used by the tobacco companies, which is the focus of this article, is that the regulations violate the First Amendment of the U.S. Constitution by restricting the right to free speech in advertising. Congress could vote to give the FDA authority over tobacco but could not, of course, change the First Amendment.

THE FIRST AMENDMENT AND ADVERTISING

The basic test used to determine whether the government can ban advertising is set out in the Supreme Court's 1980 opinion in *Central Hudson Gas & Electric Corpo-*ration v. *Public Service Commission of New York.*[6] This case involved a regulation that prohibited electric utilities from advertising to promote the use of electricity. The court adopted a four-part test to determine whether this regulation was constitutional: (1) to be protected by the First Amendment, the advertising must concern a lawful activity and not be misleading, (2) for the ban to be valid, the state's interest in banning the advertising must be "substantial," (3) the ban must "directly advance" the state's interest, and (4) it must be no more extensive than necessary to further the state's interest.[6] In *Central Hudson*, the Supreme Court concluded that although the state had a substantial interest in energy conservation that was advanced by the ban on advertising, the ban nonetheless failed the fourth part of the test. The ban failed that part because it was overly broad, prohibiting the promotion of potentially energy-saving electric services, and there was no proof that a more limited restriction of advertising could not have achieved the same goal. The court suggested, as an example, that a narrower regulation could have required "that the advertisements include information about the relative efficiency and expense of the offered services."

In 1986, in *Posadas de Puerto Rico Associates* v. *Tourism Company of Puerto Rico,* the Supreme Court upheld a ban on advertisements for casino gambling in Puerto Rico.[7] The court held that this ban met the four parts of the test in *Central Hudson.* Adding that the government could ban advertising for any activity that it could outlaw, the court said it would be "a strange constitutional doctrine which would concede to the legislature the authority to totally ban a product or activity, but deny to the legislature the authority to forbid the stimulation of demand for the product or activity through advertising."[7] The court gave a number of other examples of "vice" products or activities, including cigarettes, alcohol beverages, and prostitution, which struck many in the public health community as warranting restricted advertising. Of course, fashions change, and many states now promote and advertise gambling, in the form of lotteries and casinos, as good for the financial health of the government. Nonetheless, in the wake of the May 1996 decision in *44 Liquormart* v. *Rhode Island*,[8] the most recent and comprehensive case involving free speech in advertising, it is unlikely that *Posadas* will continue to be invoked. Moreover, the four-part test in *Central Hudson* will be more strictly applied in the future.

THE *44 LIQUORMART* CASE

In *44 Liquormart v. Rhode Island*, a liquor retailer challenged the Rhode Island laws that banned all advertisements of retail liquor prices, except at the place of sale, and prohibited the media from publishing any such advertisements, even in other states. 44 Liquormart had published an advertisement identifying various brands of liquor that included the word "wow" in large letters next to pictures of vodka and rum bottles. An enforcement action against the company resulted in a $400 fine. After paying the fine, 44 Liquormart appealed, seeking a declaratory judgment that the two statutes and the implementing regulations promulgated under them violated the First Amendment.

The U.S. District Court declared the ban on price advertising unconstitutional because it did not "directly advance" the state's interest in reducing alcohol consumption and was "more extensive than necessary to serve that interest."[9] The Court of Appeals reversed the decision, finding "inherent merit" in the state's argument that competitive price advertising would lower prices and that lower prices would induce more sales.[10] In reviewing these decisions, the Supreme Court unanimously found that the state laws violated the First Amendment, but no rationale for this opinion gained more than four votes. Justice John Paul Stevens (who wrote the principal opinion) began his discussion by quoting from an earlier case involving advertisements of prices for prescription drugs:

> Advertising, however tasteless and excessive it sometimes may seem, is nonetheless dissemination of information as to who is producing and selling what product, for what reason, and at what price. So long as we preserve a predominantly free enterprise economy, the allocation of our resources in large measure will be made through numerous private economic decisions. It is a matter of public interest that those decisions, in the aggregate, be intelligent and well informed. To this end, the free flow of commercial information is indispensable.[8]

Justice Stevens went on to note that "complete speech bans, unlike content-neutral restrictions on the time, place, or manner of expression... are particularly dangerous because they all but foreclose alternative means of disseminating certain information."[8] Bans unrelated to consumer protection, Stevens noted further, should be treated with special skepticism when they "seek to keep people in the dark for what the government perceives to be their own good." Stevens moved on to apply *Central Hudson's* four-point test. He concluded that "there is no question that Rhode Island's price advertising ban constitutes a blanket prohibition against truthful, nonmisleading speech about a lawful product." Stevens also agreed that the state has a substantial interest in "promoting temperance."

But can the state meet part three of the test, by showing that the ban is effective in advancing this interest? Four justices defined the third part of the test as requiring the state to "bear the burden of showing not merely that its regulation will advance its interest but also that it will do so 'to a material degree.' "[8] This requirement is necessary because of the "drastic nature" of the state's ban: "the wholesale suppression of truthful, nonmisleading information." Justice Stevens concluded that Rhode Island did not meet this requirement and could not do so without "any findings of fact" or other evidence. The common-sense notion that prohibitions against price advertising will lead to higher prices and thus lower consumption (an assumption made in *Central Hudson*) was found insufficient to support a finding that the restriction of advertising would "significantly reduce market-wide consumption."[8] "Speculation or conjecture" does not suffice.[9]

As for the fourth part of the test, Justice Stevens concluded that the ban also failed because Rhode Island did not show that alternative forms of regulation that do not limit speech, such as limiting per capita purchases or using educational campaigns that address the problem of excessive drinking, could not be equally or more effective in reducing consumption. All nine members of the Supreme Court agreed with this conclusion. Finally, Justice Stevens (again on behalf of four justices) argued that in *Posadas* the

court had wrongly concluded that since the state could ban a product or activity, it could ban advertising about it. He argued that the First Amendment was much stronger than that decision implied, noting "We think it quite clear that banning speech may sometimes prove far more intrusive than banning conduct," and thus it is not true that "the power to prohibit an activity is necessarily 'greater' than the power to suppress speech about it.... The text of the First Amendment makes clear that the Constitution presumes that attempts to regulate speech are more dangerous than attempts to regulate conduct."[8] Stevens also rejected the idea that "vice" activities have less protection from the First Amendment than other commercial activities, noting that the distinction would be "difficult, if not impossible, to define."

FREE SPEECH AND THE FDA REGULATIONS

Selling cigarettes and smokeless tobacco to persons under the age of 18 is illegal is all states, so advertising to this age group is not protected by the First Amendment. Nor does outlawing vending machines that children have access to pose a problem with respect to the First Amendment. Because the FDA regulations are intended to apply only to children and do not foreclose alternative sources of information, it is impossible to predict with certainty how the Supreme Court will respond to a First Amendment challenge (assuming the court finds that the FDA has authority in this area). Nonetheless, the areas of primary concern can be identified.

Bans will be subject to a higher standard of review than restrictions. Forms of advertising that are banned include the distribution of products (other than cigarettes and smokeless tobacco) with the tobacco brand name or insignia on them, the placement of billboards within 1000 feet of playgrounds and elementary and secondary schools, and the use of brand names for sporting and cultural events. If the court adopts the strict version of the third part of the test in *Central Hudson*, the FDA will have to present evidence that these bans will reduce underage smoking to a material degree. Moreover, to meet the fourth part of the test, which the court unanimously found was not met in *44 Liquormart*, the FDA must also show that no other, less restrictive method, such as antismoking advertising or better enforcement of existing laws, would work as well. This will be difficult, especially since the FDA commissioner has already said he believes that antismoking advertising is effective in helping young people understand the risks of smoking and that, after the publication of its rules, the agency plans "to notify the major cigarette and smokeless-tobacco companies that it will begin discussing a requirement that they fund an education program in the mass media."[5] The court could decide that a nonspeech ban should have been tried first.

Restrictions on advertising may be easier to uphold, but even they are not obviously permissible. The tobacco companies spend $6 billion a year in advertising and promotion, about $700 million of which is spent on magazine advertisements.[11] The core antiadvertising regulation requires that advertisements on all billboards and in publications that do not qualify as adult publications be limited to black text on a white background.[1] This is a restriction (not a ban) and does not prohibit the inclusion of factual information (such as the price of liquor, which was at issue in *44 Liquormart*). The rationale for these rules is that images in bright colors, of which Joe Camel is the primary example, entice children to start smoking or continue to smoke. Since no objective information is being banned or restricted, the court may find that such a restriction need meet only a common-sense test.[12] If, however, the court takes a more sophisticated view of advertising —which is largely focused on image rather than text—it may well hold that the same rules apply and that therefore the burden of proof is on the FDA to demonstrate that such a restriction would reduce underage smoking to a material degree. No study has yet been able to show evidence of this effect. Consistent with the view that "pop art" should be protected at least as much as text is the view that advertising images are forms designed to elicit certain responses and as such are entitled to at least as much protection from the First Amendment as objective information.

Drastic restrictions on advertising may also be ineffective or even counterproductive. In Britain, for example, where both Joe Camel and the Marlboro Man are outlawed and tobacco advertisers are prohibited from using anything that suggests health, fresh air, or beauty, creative advertisers have found other ways to promote tobacco products. Advertisements for Silk Cut cigarettes feature various images of silk being cut (e.g., scissors dancing a cancan in purple silk skirts and a rhinoceroses whose horn pierces a purple silk cap), and Marlboro advertisements portray bleak and forbidding western U.S. landscapes with the words, "Welcome to Marlboro Country." It has been suggested that by using such surreal images, tobacco advertisers may be appealing to fantasies of death and sexual violence that have a powerful (if unconscious) appeal to consumers.[13] Such imagery may actually have greater appeal for teenagers than Joe Camel. U.S. advertising agencies have already experimented with black-and-white, text-only advertisements. One agency proposed that the required phrase, "a nicotine-delivery device," can be used in conjunction with the phrase ".cyber cigarettes" on one line, under the phrase (in larger type) "pleasure.com" and a sideways smiling face, formed by a colon, a hyphen, and a closed parenthesis[:-)], to suggest that nicotine is a pleasure of the cyberspace age.[14]

The FDA knows it has a First Amendment problem here. In its comments accompanying the regulations, the agency argues that it is not required to "conclusively prove by rigorous empirical studies that advertising causes initial consumption of cigarettes and smokeless tobacco."[1] In fact, the FDA says it is impossible to prove this. Instead, the agency argues it need only demonstrate that there is "more than adequate evidence" that "tobacco advertising has an effect on young people's tobacco use behavior if it affects initiation, maintenance, or attempts at quitting."[1] The FDA's position follows from the conclusion of the Institute of Medicine:

Portraying a deadly addiction as a healthful and sensual experience tugs against the nation's efforts to promote a tobacco-free norm and to discourage tobacco use by children and youths. This warrants legislation restricting the features of advertising and promotion that make tobacco use attractive to youths. The question is not, "Are advertising and promotion the causes of youth initiation?" but rather, "Does the preponderance of evidence suggest that features of advertising and promotion tend to encourage youths to smoke?" The answer is yes and this is a sufficient basis for action, even in the absence of a precise and definitive causal chain.[13]

The Surgeon General has reached a similar conclusion:

Cigarette advertising uses images rather than information to portray the attractiveness and function of smoking. Human models and cartoon characters in cigarette advertising convey independence, healthfulness, adventure-seeking, and youthful activities—themes correlated with psychosocial factors that appeal to young people.[15]

The Supreme Court may make an exception for tobacco advertisements because of the clear health hazards and the use of restrictions instead of bans, but the extent of the restrictions will have to be justified. In this regard, the 15 percent young-readership rule for publications is difficult to justify as either not arbitrary or not more restrictive than necessary. The FDA admits, for example, that its rule would require the following magazines to use black-and-white, text-only advertisements: *Sports Illustrated* (18 percent of its readers are under the age of 18), *Car and Driver* (18 percent), *Motor Trend* (22 percent), *Road and Track* (21 percent), *Rolling Stone* (18 percent), *Vogue* (18 percent), *Mademoiselle* (20 percent), and *Glamour* (17 percent).[1] The FDA seems particularly offended by "a cardboard Joe Camel pop-out" holding concert tickets in the center of *Rolling Stone*.[5] (Some Americans might wish to censor the photograph of a naked Brooke Shields on the cover of the October 1996 issue as well, although that image is clearly protected by the First Amendment.) A 25 percent rule, for example, would exempt all these magazines.

The FDA justifies the 15 percent rule by arguing that young people between the ages of 5 and 17 years constitute approximately 15 percent of the U.S. population and that "if the percentage of young readers of a publication is greater than the percentage of young people in the general population, the publication can be viewed as having particular appeal to young readers."[1] A similar argument can, of course, be made with regard to sporting and cultural events—some of which may have very few young people in attendance.[15] On the other hand, the billboard restrictions seem to have a more solid justification.

Tobacco companies profit handsomely by selling products that cause serious health problems and contribute to the deaths of millions of Americans. There is also little doubt that nicotine is physically addictive and that it is in the interest of tobacco companies to get children addicted early, since very few people take up smoking after the age of 18 years. The FDA admits, however, that it cannot prove that cigarette advertising causes children to begin to smoke, and the agency has not tried alternative measures, such as strictly enforcing current laws that prohibit sales to minors and engaging in a broad-based educational campaign against smoking, to reduce the number of children who smoke. Until the FDA either proves that cigarette advertising causes children to start smoking or uses methods of discouraging smoking that stay clear of the First Amendment, bans and restrictions on advertising will raise enough problems with the First Amendment to ensure that they will be tied up in court for years. This does not mean, however, that no immediate legal actions can be taken against tobacco companies. In a future article, I will discuss current trends in litigation against these companies and assess the likely impact of antismoking lawsuits on the tobacco companies.

REFERENCES

1. Food and Drug Administration, Department of Health and Human Services. Regulations restricting the sale and distribution of cigarettes and smokeless tobacco to protect children and adolescents. Fed Regist 1996;61 (168):44, 396–618.
2. Gore speech: "America is strong. Bill Clinton's leadership paying off." New York Times, August 29, 1996: B12.
3. Press Briefing by Secretary of HHS Donna Shalala, FDA Commissioner David Kessler, and Assistant Secretary Phil Lee. White House, Office of Press Secretary, August 23, 1996.
4. Trends in smoking initiation among adolescents and young adults—United States, 1980–1989. MMWR Morb Mortal Wkly Rep 1995;44:521–5.
5. Kessler DA, Witt AM, Barnett PS, et al. The Food and Drug Administration's regulation of tobacco products. N Engl J Med 1996; 335:988–94.
6. Central Hudson Gas & Electric Corp. v. Public Service Commission of New York, 447 U.S. 557 (1980).
7. Posadas du Puerto Rico Associates v. Tourism Company of Puerto Rico, 478 U.S. 328 (1986).
8. 44 Liquormart, Inc. v. Rhode Island, 116 S. Ct. 1495 (1996).
9. 44 Liquor Mart, Inc. v. Racine, 829 F. Supp. 543 (R.I. 1993).
10. 44 Liquor Mart, Inc. v. Rhode Island, 39 F. 3d 5 (1st Cir. 1994).
11. Committee on Preventing Nicotine Addiction in Children and Youths. Institute of Medicine. Growing up tobacco free: preventing nicotine addiction in children and youths. Washington, D.C.: National Academy Press, 1994:131.
12. Glantz L. Regulating tobacco advertising: the FDA regulations and the First Amendment. Am J Public Health (in press).
13. Parker-Pope T. Tough tobacco-ad rules light creative fires. Wall Street Journal. October 9, 1996:B1.
14. Brownlee L. How agency teams might cope with U.S. ad restraints. Wall Street Journal. October 9, 1996:B1.
15. Department of Health and Human Services. Preventing tobacco use among young people: a report of the Surgeon General. Washington, D.C.: Government Printing Office, 1994:195.

POSTSCRIPT

Should Tobacco Advertising Be Restricted?

There are several resources available with which to further examine this issue. The government report on the Hearing Before the Committee on Labor and Human Resources of the United States Senate, 101st Congress, Second Session, on the Tobacco Product Education and Health Protection Act of 1990 (Senate Hearing 101-707, available in most government repository libraries on microfiche) is one of the first fully documented sources on the tobacco industry's disclosure of addictive agents in cigarettes.

Simon Chapman has written a book on the techniques and marketing tools used for cigarette advertising entitled *Great Expectorations: Advertising and the Tobacco Industry* (Comedia Publishing Group, 1986). Bruce Maxwell and Michael Jacobson have examined appeals to certain target audiences in their book *Marketing Disease to Hispanics: The Selling of Alcohol, Tobacco, and Junk Foods* (Center for Science in the Public Interest, 1989).

There are a number of good, general references on advertising, including Roland Marchand's *Advertising the American Dream* (University of California Press, 1985) and Robert Goldman's *Reading Ads Socially* (Routledge, 1992).

Among books that are critical of the advertising industry in general, a recent text lends itself to the discussion of the potential for the regulation of the advertising industry: Matthew P. McAllister's *The Commercialization of American Culture: New Advertising, Control and Democracy* (Sage Publications, 1995).

ISSUE 8

Does Media Coverage of Criminal Trials Undermine the Legal Process?

YES: Barry Scheck, from "Feeding the Ravenous Appetite of the Press," *Media Studies Journal* (Winter 1998)

NO: Bruce W. Sanford, from "No Contest," *Media Studies Journal* (Winter 1998)

ISSUE SUMMARY

YES: Law professor and defense attorney Barry Scheck argues that information uncovered by the press and disclosed to the public before a trial can upset the fairness of the trial process. He references the gag orders provided before the Timothy McVeigh Oklahoma bombing trial and the role of cameras in the O. J. Simpson murder trial as integral to the outcome of each trial, and he examines how pretrial publicity forced the defense teams to take different approaches.

NO: Attorney Bruce W. Sanford chronicles the history of the free press/fair trial debate and maintains that although the precedents exist to control the role of the press in a trial process, some judges, such as Lance Ito in the O. J. Simpson case, "forget" the rules. However, he agrees with the opinions of Supreme Court justices Warren Burger and William Brennan, Jr., that media coverage is essential to public confidence in the criminal justice system.

It seems that whenever there is a high-profile criminal court case, like those of O. J. Simpson, Timothy McVeigh, and Louise Woodward (the "au pair" case), the press becomes an important mediator between the courtroom and the public. A fundamental question arises: Does pretrial publicity, or the influence of public opinion as the trial proceeds, affect the right of the defendant to a fair trial? At these times, critics of the system debate both the First Amendment to the Constitution (including freedom of the press) and the Sixth Amendment (the right of the accused to a fair trial).

It is interesting to note that the authors of the following selections do not question whether or not media should be allowed to cover high-profile cases at all; they take the presence of media as inevitable. They do, however, offer different perspectives on how and why the media contribute to the shaping of the audience's sense of what constitutes news and on how much the media can influence the outcome of a criminal case. Both perspectives indicate that the judge hearing a criminal case bears some responsibility for controlling how and what the media knows.

In the first selection, Barry Scheck acknowledges that a reporter has a right to investigate a case, but he says that any privileged information must not be disclosed if the defendant is going to have a fair trial. He feels that if a reporter uncovers privileged information before it is revealed in court, the reporter may run the risk of being jailed for theft of information. Similarly, Scheck feels that cameras in the courtroom may put greater pressure on the judge because the public viewing the court procedures may begin to second-guess the judge's actions. This could ultimately affect the judge's decisions.

In the second selection, Bruce W. Sanford reinforces Supreme Court chief justice Warren Burger's belief that the question of free press versus fair trial is "almost as old as the Republic." Sanford, however, believes that history's lessons have made the criminal legal system better, fairer, and more responsible to the public as well as to the participants in the courtroom. He contrasts the actions of Judge Ito in the O. J. Simpson case and Judge Richard Matsch, who presided over the trial of Timothy McVeigh, as examples of judges' creating different environments that controlled the actions of the press. The use of gag orders and jury privacy were used differently by the two judges in their respective trials and therefore influenced the way the press operated in informing the public of the courtroom events.

Judge Matsch has been widely praised for allowing the press to cover the McVeigh trial while controlling the courtroom procedures. Judge Ito, on the other hand, has been criticized for allowing the media to control the court proceedings. The two trials raise other questions as well. Because Simpson was a celebrity, was his life more "public" than McVeigh's? Did the earlier Simpson trial "prime" Judge Matsch to exert more control over his court?

These questions and many others arise during high-profile cases, and future trials will undoubtedly continue to force us to consider the many consequences of media coverage of court procedures and to debate the free press/fair trial issue.

YES

Barry Scheck

FEEDING THE RAVENOUS
APPETITE OF THE PRESS

MSJ: *Most reporters would say that by searching out the facts of a case and being the eyes and ears of the public, they help ensure a fair trial. As a law professor and a defense attorney, does it look that way to you?*

BARRY SCHECK: I have no quarrel with the reporter trying to find out everything that he or she can about a case and reporting it accurately, trying to find out whether a defendant is guilty or innocent or to make a vigorous inquiry into any aspect of a case.

However, the perennial tension that lies at the heart of the fair trial/free press controversy concerns the desire of people in the press to know privileged information that should not be disclosed if you're going to have a fair trial.

I'm talking here not just about information that is privileged because it is the statement of the defendant or it's part of the confidential information of the defense camp, but also information that is secret and privileged from the point of view of the prosecution, and certainly, the privileged decision-making process of the courts themselves.

When you disclose this kind of information prior to the trial, and the information comes out in a fashion that is not orderly and not within the trial process itself, you will skew the process and make it unfair.

And from the point of view, not just of the defense but of the prosecution and the court, what we see now in high-profile cases is a ravenous appetite on the part of the press to obtain information that they have no legal right to get. And when they get it and disclose it, it undermines the fairness of our trial processes.

No better example exists than the disclosure of information prior to the selection of the jury in the Oklahoma City bombing case, the trial of Timothy McVeigh.

McVeigh's lawyers are saying, as I've seen them quoted in the press, that the reporter for the *Dallas Morning News* obtained from a computer thousands of files on the case that contained privileged information, conversations between McVeigh and his lawyers; reports by defense investigators; reports from the

From Barry Scheck, "Feeding the Ravenous Appetite of the Press," *Media Studies Journal*, vol. 12, no. 1 (Winter 1998). Copyright © 1998 by *Media Studies Journal*. Reprinted by permission.

prosecution itself that they were obligated by discovery to turn over. But they're not public documents.

It may be from the point of view of the reporter a great story. But it seems to me, if you think that that's such a great story—to get this information in advance, before it's revealed in court in the natural and orderly processes of a trial—fine, print it. That's your First Amendment right once you get it.

But it's also the obligation of government to put you in jail because, as far as I'm concerned, that's theft. It's the kind of thing that we ordinarily overlook in the way the news is obtained from other governmental sources because leaking is part of the business of government and it's part of the business of the press.

I'm not saying that there's necessarily going to be a prior restraint, but I think that if you think that's such a great story, then you ought to be willing to go to jail if that's the means by which you got it. That's the distinction that's been overlooked. And I'm really curious to see what, if anything, is done, subsequent to the McVeigh case, about what was reported to be these kinds of wholesale leaks.

* * *

MSJ: *Do you think some of the gag orders around the McVeigh case in Denver, some of the restrictions on what you can do, were onerous?*
BARRY SCHECK: There was a big untold story about the McVeigh case.

Judge Matsch did a number of things, which I think everybody agrees were very good. For example, he allowed the lawyers to talk until the eve of jury selection. Then he gagged them. That seemed reasonable, pursuant to Rule 3.6 and the *Gentile* case and the nature of

that proceeding [3.6 is a section of the American Bar Association's rules for the lawyers' conduct; in the *Gentile* case, the U.S. Supreme Court set limits on what a lawyer could say to the press]. And I was not particularly bothered by the wall he put up so that journalists couldn't see the jurors.

But I didn't think enough attention was paid to the extraordinary restrictions that he imposed upon arguments. Most of the important legal motions in the McVeigh cases were argued in camera [in private, or in a judge's chambers], early in the morning, under seal.

Some of these restrictions one can understand to the extent that Judge Matsch was trying to prevent disclosures that could poison the jury pool for purposes of the upcoming Nichols case.

But it did seem to me that some of these restrictions probably couldn't be justified on those grounds and were part of his well-known views that were somewhat antagonistic to legal commentators and extensive press coverage.

MSJ: *Why do you think the press missed this?*
BARRY SCHECK: Lawyers for the press did appeal these restrictions, but when the appellate courts literally sat on those appeals, the press stopped complaining.

They began to accept it, primarily because they suddenly seized upon this trial as the anti-Simpson example. And I was troubled by that. I thought that was a failure of good journalism. They sort of picked the angle that they decided to have in that story and anything Judge Matsch (for whom, incidentally, I have a tremendous amount of respect) did was going to be right.

They just began to take what the court was offering, without a full understanding of all the secret rulings that were truly dictating the kind of proceeding that they were seeing.

* * *

MSJ: *In your experience, are the police and the prosecution more likely to leak to reporters?*
BARRY SCHECK: Everybody leaks, to the extent that they see that it is going to be to their advantage. In that respect, criminal trials are supposedly no different than any other kind of political event or news event that reporters commonly cover.

In fact, right now, the rules of professional responsibility recognize this reality. Criminal defense lawyers are now allowed to make statements to level the playing field if law enforcement officials issue prejudicial leaks at the beginning of a criminal investigation. But you are limited in your response to clearing up the prejudicial publicity.

* * *

MSJ: *Writing in* Media Studies Journal *a few years back, William Kunstler said: "The responsibility for seeking and finding press outlets for defendants with 'newsworthy' cases falls squarely on the shoulders of their defense counsel. Whenever and wherever practicable, fire must be met with fire, and it is often only lawyers who have any chance of igniting a flame friendly to their clients." Do you work that way?*
BARRY SCHECK: Yeah. I'll give you a pretty simple example. Here [at Cardozo Law School of Yeshiva University] we are involved in this work at the Innocence Project.

We're using DNA technology to overturn these wrongful convictions, and the impact that these cases have had upon the criminal justice system in the various different jurisdictions has been absolutely enormous.

When you get involved in a high-profile case, it's your responsibility to try to use it to good ends. I made a deal with NBC that they would do four shows on "Dateline" about cases of individuals that have been falsely accused and wrongly convicted—as it turns out, not any case that I was working on as counsel. And that we would also take those four shows, and in the terms of the trade, we'd repurpose them for a cable show on MSNBC where we were able to deal with the issue in some greater depth.

They readily agreed to that deal, and it's been a win/win situation for everybody because the stories that they're looking at are all good stories that they probably would have covered anyhow.

It's just that I was in a position to bring those stories to their attention, and they applied ordinary journalistic standards, standards that I take very seriously about all these kinds of cases.

* * *

MSJ: *Do you think that most reporters who write about DNA evidence understand it enough to adequately assess the strategy that you used, the way you interpret DNA?*
BARRY SCHECK: No. It is always remarkable to me, with the tremendous resources available to the press, that most reporters don't really go out and attempt to educate themselves seriously about DNA testing. And there are always oversimplifications of what it means to the criminal justice system.

In the Innocence Project at Cardozo, we have assisted or represented 34 individuals who have been able to demonstrate that they were wrongly convicted of a crime, through the use of DNA evidence.

And overall, there are now 45 such individuals in this country. Many of them death-penalty cases. We're using DNA evidence on the old samples. We will always have the tests replicated by prosecution laboratories. We do everything we can to ensure that there is no contamination of samples, that the testing is done correctly, in accordance with the highest scientific standards.

So Peter Neufeld and I have always viewed our work in this area as a matter of law reform to move forensic science, and the use of DNA testing in particular in forensic science, forward—for law enforcement, for defendants, for the sake of the system as a whole. And since the Simpson case, we were able to pass model legislation in the state of New York and set up what's known as a Forensic Science Review Board, which regulates all the crime laboratories in the state of New York, including the DNA laboratories.

Peter and I have been appointed by the chief judge of the New York Court of Appeals and the speaker of the assembly to serve on that commission, and we have for the last two years. And we're doing a lot to create DNA data banks, making sure all the laboratories in New York state area are accredited.

Oddly enough, the Simpson case actually helped in this effort, because whether people believed O.J. Simpson was guilty or innocent, the entire forensic community, I believe, has recognized that the conduct of the Los Angeles Police Department Crime Lab, their DNA laboratories and the Medical Examiner's Office was deplorable. It's not the way to handle a major case.

And as a consequence, laboratories all across the country have been seeking accreditation and seeking to reform their practices. As for the Simpson case, that's the only silver lining I've ever seen in it—it has really helped advance the cause of raising the standards of forensic science. And we think we've been a part of that, and we'll continue to be.

* * *

MSJ: *Part of the Simpson case that got a lot of notoriety during the criminal trial was the use of cameras in the courts. How do you think the presence of cameras affects the trial?*

BARRY SCHECK: I can think of a lot of good aspects to the way behavior is sometimes changed by cameras in the courtroom. Sometimes judges and lawyers on either side strive to be on their very best behavior. Similarly, there are benefits that occur when witnesses are seen on television and people call in with facts about the case.

On the other hand, television has this feedback effect that influences the behavior of participants in a very negative way. I saw a lot of that, frankly, in the Simpson case and in other trials.

Judges take a lot of heat with viewers second-guessing their decisions every day. And the lawyers, in terms of their demeanor, and everything they do, are subject to a different kind of criticism when the trial is televised than when it isn't. It does affect their behavior.

And when you get into a situation like Simpson, where all of a sudden the tabloidization of the trial begins to occur and everything devolves to the lowest common denominator in terms of coverage, it gets really hard to handle. But even more important than that, I think it profoundly affects witnesses. We saw it in the William Kennedy Smith case, for example, where all of a sudden, the tabloids began paying witnesses $25,000, $50,000 for their testimony, which fatally undermines the witness.

If you had C-SPAN-type coverage, where people see it every day, it would be much better. And if the coverage were better, then the experiment of cameras in the courtroom, I think, would work out better.

I'd love to see the franchise on televising trials in a particular jurisdiction bid upon by public interest entities. The C-SPAN-type court channel would get the first day of coverage. You would be able to see the trial from beginning to end.

Then, if you gave that particular channel the exclusive right to broadcast the pictures for that day and the regular news could get it a day later, I think that would be an interesting experiment. Because then at least the public would be drawn to the best and least-editorialized version of the events of the trial.

You wouldn't be totally restricting the press from having access to the witnesses' testimony, but there would at least be one good shot in terms of having people focus on the full events of the trial that day.

* * *

MSJ: *A lot of the pieces that I've read about you mention your roots in the '60s and all the work that you did in legal aid law. In the '90s, are reporters less likely to respect those characteristics than they were, say, 30 years ago?*

BARRY SCHECK: It's very peculiar. Basically, I've been either a public defender or a law professor for my entire career, representing almost predominantly the indigent. I work with DNA and the Innocence Project and virtually all the work we've done has been pro bono work.

But the O.J. Simpson case sort of skewed everything. People had their responses to that and nothing is going to alter them. And I don't think that the coverage was particularly sophisticated in that regard.

It was very odd to me that people wouldn't even focus on the fact that our clinic had represented Hedda Nussbaum and a lot of battered women before it was fashionable to take up the cause of battered women.

So there's not a lot of room for nuance when you get involved in these kinds of cases, and one learns that the hard way. But it goes with the territory, I suppose. Of course, I had no idea what the Simpson case would eventually become.

I suppose we could have dropped out of it, although that presents certain duty-of-loyalty problems. Once we saw how absolutely enormous it was going to become, we had obligations as lawyers and we went through with them. I don't regret it for a second.

* * *

MSJ: *From your perspective, do reporters tend to favor either the prosecution or the defense?*

BARRY SCHECK: I don't think that there's any typical bias one way or the other. What reporters are generally interested in is a good story. And the more they tend towards writing for tabloid publications, they're interested in the best tabloid story.

They like people that are good copy. That give them good stories. It tends to be, however, that there are more law enforcement sources from which to get information. In a criminal case, what ordinarily happens is that the initial rush of publicity is always in favor of the prosecution. After all, there's an arrest, there's the crime, and the defense is literally on the defensive in most instances.

* * *

MSJ: *Are there particular reporters whose work you admire that you think is worth emulating in their coverage of the courts?*

BARRY SCHECK: Sure. I've always thought that lawyers generally owe a debt of gratitude to Steve Brill. I think that *American Lawyer* magazine and the in-depth coverage it gave to all kinds of issues involved in the practice of law, and the kind of coverage that you could expect from those journalists was always a cut above everyone else.

I should say, by way of disclosure, that Steve and I went to college together and we're friends for a long time.

* * *

MSJ: *You've said that there should be a code of ethics for lawyers who serve as commentators in the news media.*

BARRY SCHECK: Lawyers bear a lot of responsibility for the nature of coverage and commentary when we're called upon as experts by the media to talk about what's going on in legal cases. And some of these aspirational standards may sound almost silly but they're pretty simple.

For example, it's the job of a commentator to be informed, to be prepared. What's happened to many lawyers is that, during the course of the Simpson case and thereafter, for example, the local news show producers would call them in and say, Hey, here's your gig: Tell us what you think of what happened today.

And they would not have read the transcripts. They would not have been following the case on a day-to-day basis. They were earning a living. No problem with that. But they really weren't informed, and therefore they would be confining their comments to style points and spin and things that they thought they could comment on.

Much of my critique here, incidentally, is very similar to what James Fallows has written in *Breaking the News* about political commentary.

Another standard would be to disclose conflicts of interest. A lot of commentators on the air have entangling conflicts. Some may be disabling, but those should be disclosed.

We, as a profession, have to resist those people in the media that want us to come on when we don't know what we're talking about, or ask us for glib opinions that we shouldn't be giving. To be gratuitously critical or gratuitously knowledgeable, or pretend to be knowledgeable, is really dangerous.

And I think that it's bad journalism, but even more importantly, it's ethically questionable for a lawyer to do that. After all, you're being brought on as an expert who's giving some additional insight to the public, and it's a lawyer's responsibility to know what he or she is talking about.

You shouldn't be pigeonholed. You shouldn't create conflict where there isn't any. Very often people call you up and say, We will only put you on if you'll say X viewpoint, because that's what they say is good television or good journalism.

Say no. Or go on and say what you think. We have a certain responsibility to try to raise the level of commentary about the courts. And in turn, maybe we will have some effect on news producers and the powers that be in the medium to raise their standards as well.

NO

Bruce W. Sanford

NO CONTEST

When the phrases "free press" and "fair trial" roll off the tongue, the word *versus* is usually sandwiched between them.

The two Anglo-American ideals are presented as if they were inherently at odds with each other, as if they were mutually exclusive. Rarely are we offered the possibility of enjoying both.

But this is one trumped-up "conflict" that we can't blame on television. As Chief Justice Warren Burger wrote more than 20 years ago, the problems created by the collision between the First and the Sixth amendments are "almost as old as the Republic." Aaron Burr's 1807 prosecution for treason, he noted, provoked so much courtroom drama, and accompanying publicity, that commentators fretted about whether incendiary newspaper coverage would incinerate the possibility for a fair trial. Chief Justice John Marshall rejected Burr's argument.

The evolution of a body of law to govern these clashes took more than a century and a half to unfold, however. And when the Supreme Court finally started to face the tough questions surrounding press freedom and the right to a fair trial in the 1960s and '70s, it was in the midst of aggressively expanding the boundaries of both: Journalists *and* criminal defendants have been among the great winners in modern constitutional law. Indeed, if one overarching theme is discernible from the High Court's pronouncements of the past 40 years, it is, quite simply, that judges need a vigorous, probing, enterprising media to ensure both a criminal defendant's rights and public confidence in our system of justice.

Since the mid-1980s, however, the Court's voice has gone quiet. For more than a decade, not one decision has addressed the media's First Amendment rights to cover the courts. The silence undoubtedly reflects a judicial attitude toward the ubiquitous media that, like the rest of the country's, borders on contempt. The silence suggests that future activity in this corner of the law will likely occur at the margins rather than through bold new pronouncements. And in recent years the privacy interests of jurors and witnesses have become a paramount consideration in the courtroom, adding a new dimension to judges' efforts to balance the rights of the media and the rights of the accused.

* * *

When the free press/fair trial issue arrived at the Supreme Court in the 1960s, it was clothed as a Sixth Amendment matter rather than a First Amendment one. In that decade, the justices, well launched on their odyssey to revolutionize criminal procedure, struck down a number of convictions based on unfair publicity.

In *Estes v. Texas*, decided in 1965, the Court reviewed the prosecution of Billy Sol Estes, a buccaneer financier, for fraud. Both a pretrial hearing, as well as parts of the trial itself, were broadcast on television. The pretrial hearing in particular was marked by massive disruption from camera crews—an ironic footnote given that it was called to decide whether to permit television coverage during the trial.

The Court said that Estes was so thoroughly harmed by these events that it would depart from its normal rule and reverse his conviction without looking for particular ways in which he was actually prejudiced. (The opinion amounted to an early indictment of televised trials that left a constitutional odor for more than 15 years, until the Court in 1981 said that broadcasting trials does not intrinsically violate the Sixth Amendment.) But while criticizing television's impact on the trial, the Court in *Estes* did not say much about how to control coverage without obliterating it. The First Amendment side of the equation, in other words, was not brought into play.

The Court began to pay more serious attention to the free press/fair trial issue a year later when it was confronted with the egregious excesses of the Sam Sheppard murder trial. Here was a courtroom "circus" out of control. Trial Judge Edward Blythin, a former mayor of Cleveland, gave daily interviews, reporters roamed the courtroom like proprietary floorwalkers and the Supreme Court—normally restrained in its descriptions—conjured up Fellini images by labeling it a "Roman holiday." To hardly anyone's surprise, except, perhaps, *Cleveland Press* editor Louis Seltzer, who hounded the philandering physician with avenging coverage, Dr. Sam's conviction for the gory slaying of his pregnant wife was reversed. "Let's get a grip," the High Court seemed to say. "And, for God's sake (or justice's), let's have some decorum. Let's keep these, ahem, journalists in their place before they spoil everything."

* * *

In overturning Sheppard's conviction, justices went a bit further than they had in *Estes*—this time, they laid out some suggestions to trial judges for managing press coverage.

For starters, the Court endorsed limiting the number of reporters in the courtroom. It also proposed insulating witnesses from the media and issuing gag orders to prevent lawyers from granting out-of-court interviews. Additionally, the Court said that news organizations could be warned about publishing information not introduced into evidence. Other strategies put forward were to sequester juries, transfer cases to far-away venues and postpone trials....

In the wake of *Sheppard*, reporters found themselves increasingly hobbled in their court coverage by gag orders issued against the press itself. These prior restraints were virtually wiped out by *Nebraska Press* in a majority opinion written, ironically, by Anglophile Warren Burger, which said we would be different from England—we would not muzzle court coverage. In that case, lower courts in Nebraska had directed news organizations not to disseminate accounts of confessions made by an accused murderer, nor to publish other facts that were "strongly implicative" of his guilt. This time, when the free press/fair trial issue · arrived at the Supreme Court, it was dressed in First Amendment clothes because the gag order had been challenged by several state press and broadcast associations.

The Court said for the first time that such gag orders were presumptively unconstitutional. Chief Justice Burger analyzed the issue within the long line of precedent frowning on prior restraints, which he called the "most serious" and "least tolerable" of infringements on speech rights. For a Court that had given a green light to the *New York Times* and the *Washington Post* five years earlier to print the Pentagon Papers despite the cries of harm to national security, it did not seem a great leap to allow the publication of material relating to a murder trial in Nebraska.

While the Court in *Sheppard* had listed strategies for combating unfair publicity with little regard for how those measures might affect the functioning of the media, in *Nebraska Press* it went over the same ground with an eye for using techniques that would not directly interfere with what journalists could write or broadcast, such as the careful screening of jurors during the voir dire process. From 1966 to 1976, the Court's emphasis had shifted seismically.

* * *

If the clear message of *Nebraska Press* was that the media must be free to publish what it can find out, it did not prevent judges from hindering coverage of trials through indirect means—by choking off

sources of information. The Supreme Court indicated that the standards for limiting what attorneys can say to the press are less exacting than for limiting what the press can say to the public. Consequently, the placing of gag orders on lawyers continues to be a common practice in high-stakes criminal proceedings.

Another indirect means to curtail publication of bothersome information is simply to close the courthouse door to the press and public. In 1979, the Supreme Court seemed to approve of just such a tactic in *Gannett v. DePasquale*. In *Gannett*, two persons on trial for murder requested the closure of a pretrial suppression hearing. The prosecution did not oppose the defendants' motion, and the trial judge agreed.

When the Court reviewed the judge's decision, the question was presented as a Sixth Amendment one—to whom does the constitutional guarantee of a "public trial" belong? The answer, according to the Court, was that it belongs to the defendant—and neither the public nor the press can use the Sixth Amendment to compel open proceedings if the accused does not want it. The Court completely ducked the First Amendment side of the issue, saying only that the trial judge had given "all appropriate deference" to these considerations before closing the suppression hearing.

"All appropriate deference?" That sounds like a First Amendment executioner's song. Justice William Rehnquist, in a concurring opinion, sang the last verse. He wrote that once the parties agree to exclude the public from a trial, the judge does not have to make any further inquiry. And he also took up the free speech implications that the Court itself avoided and made a severe conclusion:

The public and the press do not have any right to attend judicial proceedings under the First Amendment.

Gannett closed the decade of the 1970s on a depressing, one-sided and perhaps even predictable note. Earlier in the 1970s, news organizations had argued that "the public's right to know" could be leveraged to secure journalists special privileges to visit prisons and obtain government-controlled information. The press had also asked to be exempt from obligations that compromised its news-gathering capabilities, such as testifying at grand jury hearings about confidential sources. The Supreme Court, however, roundly rejected any version of the "right to know" each time the media brought it forward.

But something about *Gannett*, and its implications for the public, as well as the press, rattled a common nerve. As detailed by Lucas Powe Jr. in *The Fourth Estate and the Constitution*, angry criticism and protests erupted after America's newspaper publishers erected a huge cardboard, seven-layer cake dedicated to the imperiled First Amendment in the lobby of the Waldorf-Astoria Hotel. The sagging monster looked as if it might march on Washington. Meeting in New York, several justices, in unusual public comments, hastily retreated from the case —including Chief Justice Burger, who said that the opinion's holding only applied to pretrial proceedings and had been misread by lower courts. In the year after *Gannett* was decided, 272 motions were filed nationwide to close criminal proceedings, according to Powe, and 33 trials were closed outright. Clearly, the Court had goofed, overemphasizing Sixth Amendment interests and overlooking the First Amendment values that contribute to a fair trial.

* * *

It didn't take long for the Court to reverse course, and when it did, it created a brand new First Amendment right out of whole cloth.

A year later, in *Richmond Newspapers v. Virginia*, a state judge had closed the murder trial of John Paul Stevenson with a simple one-sentence order, citing *Gannett*. In a previous stage of the case, the judge had declared a mistrial when a prospective juror had apparently informed others of a news article reporting that Stevenson's earlier conviction for the crime had been thrown out on appeal.

When the Supreme Court took up the case, the First Amendment access question this time was squarely before it. And while the Court by no means spoke with a single voice (there were six opinions for the seven justices in the majority), it delivered a remarkably important message: Trials such as Stevenson's are presumed to be open to the press and public, although the words of the Constitution nowhere commanded it. Not since *New York Times v. Sullivan* had the Court taken such a breathtaking constitutional step in the free speech area.

Chief Justice Burger justified the Court's action as a matter of tradition, finding strong support in his beloved Anglo-American jurisprudence for open trials. To this historical consideration, Justice William Brennan Jr.'s concurring opinion added another doctrinal point: Access should be favored when it contributes to the functioning of the judicial process in question.

Brennan's theoretical framework has been the driving force behind the extension of *Richmond Newspapers'* presumption of openness to other aspects of the criminal justice system. There have been only three other High Court decisions developing this new First Amendment right of access of the public (and its "surrogate," the press) to attend criminal proceedings. All followed quickly on the heels of *Richmond Newspapers.*

In 1982, in *Globe Newspaper v. Superior Court,* the Court struck down a Massachusetts statute that required judges to exclude the public from proceedings at which juvenile victims of sex offenses were scheduled to testify. State statutes needed to confer discretion and flexibility on judges, not automatic orders. Two years later in California, in *Press-Enterprise v. Riverside County,* the Court held that only on rare occasions could judges conduct voir dire behind closed doors, such as when intense privacy interests of potential jurors are at stake. And in 1986, in another case involving the *Press-Enterprise,* the Court said that since preliminary hearings function essentially in the place of trials, they too are held to a rule of presumptive openness.

* * *

No two justices wrote more of the key opinions in the free press/fair trial field than Burr and Brennan. In their decisions, however, one finds strikingly different conceptions of the role of the media. In *Nebraska Press,* Burger looks back at the *Sheppard* case and concludes: "Beyond doubt the press had shown no responsible concern for the constitutional guarantee of a fair trial." Later in that opinion, he observes that the First Amendment places something akin to a fiduciary duty on the press—"a jury widely acknowledged but not always observed by editors and publishers." For Burger, therefore, the equation seems to be "fair trial *despite* free press."

Yet Brennan, the most influential intellectual force of the Court during the last half of the 20th century, believed the presence of the press in the courthouse gallery did not diminish the Sixth Amendment rights of the accused but actually enhanced them. "Public access," he wrote in *Richmond Newspapers,* "acts as an important check, akin in purpose to the other checks and balances that infuse our system of government." And in *Globe Newspaper,* he further explained his structural conception of the First Amendment, arguing that open trials ensure that a "constitutionally-protected discussion of government affairs is an informed one." For him, fair trials existed *because* of free press.

The Supreme Court has ignored the *Richmond Newspapers* thread for more than 10 years now, suggesting that it has gone as far as it intends to go in opening up the judicial system and the wealth of information that is filed in documents and testimony in both criminal and civil cases. No one expects the Court to uncloak the secrecy of grand jury proceedings, for example. Such a move would not be supported by historical tradition, nor would it appear to enhance the functioning of the investigative task that grand juries are called to perform.

In lower courts, nevertheless, the accumulated Supreme Court wisdom of the 1960s, '70s and '80s requires judges to use carefully tailored means whenever they try to exclude the press from the courtroom. Instinct or outrage is not enough—they must find a substantial probability that the defendant's right to a fair hearing is endangered, that closing the proceedings would avert this threat and that no reasonable alternatives to closure exist. Like all multi-pronged tests in constitutional law, this standard gives judges some flexibility and enables them to meet the day-to-day crises that pop up in criminal trials.

* * *

In celebrated cases, some judges can forget these rules. Lance Ito impulsively closed off all the O.J. Simpson jury voir dire despite the irony that it was a similar closure in his own state court system that had triggered the 1984 *Press-Enterprise* case a mere decade earlier. Ito's mistake was righted quickly enough, but it revealed the need (even after clear-cut Supreme Court decisions) for the press to have lawyers ready on short notice to prevent judges from drifting back to a pre-*Richmond Newspapers* mindset.

In contrast to Judge Ito, Richard Matsch, the well-respected judge who presided over the trial of Timothy McVeigh for the Oklahoma City bombing, used carefully calibrated means of controlling press access to certain sources of information and proceedings. To be sure, he heard a din of media objections along the way, but he has been widely credited with pulling off a serious and successful trial.

Matsch issued two gag orders over lawyers involved in the case, the second of which was put in effect during jury selection and was so far-reaching that it prohibited all out-of-court statements. He also showed extraordinary concern for the privacy of the jury, a solicitude first sanctioned in *Press-Enterprise:* The court did not release jurors' names, scrambled the identification numbers by which potential panel members were known during the screening process and conducted so-called for cause challenges to particular jurors outside of public view. Matsch even ordered the construction of a wall between the jury box and the gallery. In all of these actions, he showed how he could work within the existing free press/fair trial framework and still respond to the practicalities of the situation in Denver.

The press tried—unsuccessfully—to use the trial to extend the *Richmond Newspapers* precedent to an unresolved area—does a First Amendment right of access attach to court documents? A coalition of media representatives, organized with little or no consultation with their individual counsel, challenged Judge Matsch's decision to redact several key motions, such as those filed by McVeigh and co-defendant Terry Lynn Nichols, seeking separate trials. The U.S. Court of Appeals for the 10th Circuit, however, affirmed Matsch without deciding whether a right of access applied. The media initiative was probably doomed from the outset and certainly not orchestrated or timed cleverly to enhance the likelihood of success.

Unluckily for the media initiative, Judge Matsch was no oaf or bogeyman. He did not try to interfere unnecessarily with news gathering. Early in the case, he declined to conduct an investigation of alleged leaks of material exchanged between the parties during discovery. And after the *Dallas Morning News* published its account of McVeigh's alleged confession, the judge denied a defense motion to dismiss the case. Instead of brow-beating the media for creating a possible disruption of the trial process—a criticism that many in the press itself were willing to make—Matsch reaffirmed free press principles.

"Crimes are prosecuted publicly," he wrote in a March 17, 1997, opinion. "The Constitution commands it. A free and unfettered press is essential to the proper functioning of all democratic institutions, including the people's courts."

Some may think that Matsch was merely playing lip service to the constructive role of the media, given the restrictions he set up in his own courtroom. But even if that were the case, his language returns us to the unifying theme that Chief Justice Burger and Justice Brennan could agree on: that media coverage of trials— even at times messy, chaotic coverage— ultimately is as responsible as anything for public confidence in the criminal justice system. It would be constructive to hear the Supreme Court say so again— and soon.

POSTSCRIPT

Does Media Coverage of Criminal Trials Undermine the Legal Process?

It seems that almost every new high-profile case has some distinctive features that lead us back to the fundamental question of whether or not media coverage of criminal trials undermines the legal process. In addition to gag orders, jury privacy, and prior restraint, some court cases are moved to other counties (such as the 1992 trial of the four Los Angeles, California, police officers who were charged with assaulting black motorist Rodney King) or other states (like the Oklahoma bomber trials conducted in Denver, Colorado). These moves are attempts to find jurors who may have been less influenced by public opinion formation from the press.

Different states often have different protocols on how and when cameras and reporters are allowed into courtrooms, but few have any restrictions on how the media frame a story outside of the courtroom. Should there be federal mandates on court procedures? Should coverage be limited to the remarks of attorneys or judges? Should tabloid media be allowed to buy stories from jurors or witnesses?

We have entered an era in which the public may expect to have greater access to the inner workings of courts. Court TV has become popular, and it even boasts a cult audience following. Geraldo Rivera has a nationally syndicated television show that often analyzes high-profile cases for months after the trials have been concluded. High-profile defense attorneys like Johnnie Cochran are parodied on *Seinfeld* and *The Simpsons*. Does this make people more critical of the judicial system or, perhaps, more cynical?

Many additional references about this topic come from specific cases and are often written from the point of view of one of the members of the legal team. Some of the most well known attorneys in high-profile cases have written their own opinions of their cases and of the legal system. Alan Dershowitz, F. Lee Bailey, Gerry Spence, and Robert Shapiro have written memoirs as well as accounts of many of their cases. One best-selling book by an attorney is Christopher A. Darden's account of the O. J. Simpson case, coauthored with Jess Walter, entitled *In Contempt* (Regan Books, 1996).

ISSUE 9

Has Coverage of Political Campaigns Improved?

YES: Kathleen Hall Jamieson, from *Packaging the Presidency: A History and Criticism of Presidential Campaign Advertising,* 3rd ed. (Oxford University Press, 1996)

NO: S. Robert Lichter and Richard E. Noyes, from *Good Intentions Make Bad News: Why Americans Hate Campaign Journalism* (Rowman & Littlefield, 1995)

ISSUE SUMMARY

YES: Kathleen Hall Jamieson, dean of the Annenberg School of Communications at the University of Pennsylvania, writes that negative campaign ads often distort the platforms of the political candidates in an election. She asserts that recent efforts by media outlets to police advertising truthfulness will lead to a better-informed public.

NO: S. Robert Lichter and Richard E. Noyes of the Center for Media and Public Affairs (CMPA) assert that journalists' attempts to police political campaigns have turned them into participants, not observers. They argue that journalists' relentless negativism, paired with a lack of substance in the coverage of campaign issues, has undermined public support for all candidates.

Probably nothing has so transformed the American political process as the emergence of television as a force in elections. Today many more people see candidates on television than hear them in person. Candidates appear in a variety of media formats—television and radio talk shows, late-night entertainment, morning news and information programs, online, and even MTV. Spin doctors, advertising wizards, and media consultants assume ever more important places on the campaign planning committees of candidates. Never before have candidates used the power of the media to such a comprehensive extent to reach potential voters.

In principle, public opinion is the basis of democracy. Yet how is public opinion formed, and how stable is it in the face of the media's power to alter it? Can carefully cultivated images sway voters? And can voters be "conned" by attack ads, which manipulate the truth about another candidate's record?

In the following selection, Kathleen Hall Jamieson cites improvements in elections since 1988, a presidential campaign that is notorious for its negativity. Since then, she says, journalists have made a concerted effort to analyze ads for their truthfulness and for manipulation of facts or images. Political advertising is now the major means by which candidates for the presidency communicate their messages to voters. And when ads lie, according to Jamieson, the vigilance of the press and opponents can protect the public.

In the second selection, S. Robert Lichter and Richard E. Noyes sound a warning: Despite their good intentions, journalistic endeavors to police the accuracy of campaign advertising have had significant negative consequences. Journalists continued to focus on the "horse-race" aspects of the campaign at the cost of focus on the issues. A relentless negativism, which was unintentionally enhanced by the criticism of ad campaigns, led to a public perception that the race was much more negative than political observers thought. Journalistic balance also suffered. According to Lichter and Noyes, as journalists pushed politicians aside, the public turned to alternate sources of media, particularly the talk show. The home page of the CMPA expands upon the views of Lichter and Noyes. See http://www.cmpa.com/index.htm.

In the fast-moving world of American campaign politics, the public may never know just how much influence an advertising campaign has on a particular election. Certainly candidates believe that these campaigns are essential, and they almost certainly will continue to spend large portions of their campaign funds to reach the American people through political advertising. The media may be able to shape public discourse. If the media set the agenda for public discussion, whether intentionally or unintentionally, the candidate who can shape the mediated political discourse—who can control the issues of the campaign through careful media manipulation—can gain an important edge in the campaign.

YES

Kathleen Hall Jamieson

PACKAGING THE PRESIDENCY

INTRODUCTION

Never before in a presidential campaign have televised ads sponsored by a major party candidate lied so blatantly as in the campaign of 1988.

Television ads of previous presidential contenders have, to be sure, seized upon votes cast by the opposition candidate and sundered them from context, resurrected political positions from the distant past and interpreted legislative moves as sweeping endorsements of unpopular positions. And, in eras gone by, the penny press, which didn't even feign political neutrality, published scurrilous assaults on would-be presidents—albeit to far more limited audiences than those reached by televised broadcasts. But in the era of mass visual communication, major party candidates, until 1988, assumed that outright lying in an ad would create an outcry from the press, a devastating counter-assault from the other side and a backlash from an incensed electorate.

... The best available defense seems to be the vigilance of the opposing candidate and party....

[B]ut there is also the real risk that a counter-attack may simply legitimize false claims and magnify their impact. It can also reduce the campaign to a shouting match in which each candidate calls the other a liar, leaving the electorate disillusioned and confused. That was where the campaign of 1988 wound up. It's also where future campaigns are likely to be headed unless this country can discover among the ranks of its politicians a pair of candidates self-assured enough to campaign on the facts.

By most available accounts, the presidential campaign of 1992 was helpful to the electorate and an improvement over that of 1988. A survey conducted by The Times Mirror Center for the People and the Press found 77% of respondents saying that "they had learned enough during the campaign to make an informed choice among President George Bush, Governor Bill Clinton, and Independent candidate Ross Perot." Where in 1988 48% found debates helpful, in 1992 that percentage had risen to 70%.

From Kathleen Hall Jamieson, *Packaging the Presidency: A History and Criticism of Presidential Campaign Advertising*, 3rd ed. (Oxford University Press, 1996). Copyright © 1984, 1992, 1996 by Kathleen Hall Jamieson. Reprinted by permission of Oxford University Press, Inc. Notes omitted.

The public was less pleased with the performance of the press: 36% gave campaign coverage an A or B grade, up slightly from 30% in 1988. Of particular note is that 35% thought the press was unfair in its coverage of Bush....

Although exit polls reported that talk shows were second only to debates in the help they provided voters, "nearly one in five voters could not evaluate their conduct in this campaign." Talk shows are important because they allow voters to interact with candidates. Inclusion of voters in the second presidential debate was a similarly empowering move.

If the 1992 campaign marked the demise of the public speech to a national audience in prime time, and with it an absence of broadcast policy argument, it also signaled the rise of new forms of exposition. The venues in which candidates appeared multiplied with the access created by cable. All three candidates made appearances on MTV, and were seen or heard on the Nashville Network; Clinton also took questions from four religious congregations on VISN....

By contrast to 1988 when it was difficult to secure a network interview with George Bush until the closing weeks of the campaign, the candidates appeared early and often in 1992. Indeed on some days one could not watch a morning show without facing a candidate. The *New York Times* responded by creating a box that forecast the candidates' TV appearances.

The questions that were answered well in the 1992 audience participation formats (including call shows on radio) were "What will you do in office?" "What have you done in the office you hold?" And "What fault do you find with the record and performance of your opponent?" What was asked less often, and answered even less than it was asked, was "Why are your proposals more likely to accomplish your shared goals than your opponents'?"

In 1992 more so than 1988 voters received helpful, accurate information from the press on the candidates' charges and countercharges about their own and their opponents' records. By arbitrating, the press helped the public evaluate the evidence being offered on both sides. This does not necessarily mean that the electorate rejected ads containing false information, but that its ability to assess the claims in the ads was enhanced.

Reporters policed the fairness and accuracy of accusations at the Republican and Democratic conventions and did a better job at the Republican convention. So, for example, when Republicans claimed that Hillary Clinton had compared marriage to slavery, reporters defanged that claim by citing the historical context Ms. Clinton had referred to. They did the same for the assertion that Ms. Clinton wanted children who were unhappy over their allowance to be able to sue their parents. Likewise, reporters and columnists went after the Bush claim that Clinton had raised taxes 128 times during his 11 years as governor. Using the Republican criteria, noted the journalists, the Bush-Reagan years had produced more tax increases than the Clinton years.

In at least one instance reporters also moved to correct a misstatement on talk radio. When Bush alleged on Rush Limbaugh's national radio show that Clinton said he loathed the military, print and broadcast reporters rushed an accurate statement from the source— Clinton's letter—to the attention of the public.

In 1992, for the first time the advertising of a presidential campaign was "policed" by both print and broadcast reporters. The most systematic and highest quality analysis was done by Brooks Jackson of CNN. On NPR Andy Bowers led analyses of radio, an important move since the most serious campaign distortions were found in the final weeks on local radio. Eric Engberg of CBS and Jackson of CNN critiqued the key radio ads on television.

It was in the adwatches that one learned that Democratic radio ads were falsely accusing Bush of wanting to "virtually eliminate all compensation for over one million disabled veterans." The watches also pointed out sins of omission. As a Clinton ad claimed, George Bush did "sign the second biggest tax increase in American history." Unacknowledged, observed the adwatches, was the complicity of the Democratic Congress. And yes, as a Clinton ad averred, 17,000 Arkansans had moved "from welfare to work" since July 1989. But during that time, noted the reporters, the welfare rolls actually increased as new recipients of Aid to Families with Dependent Children and food stamps replaced the beneficiaries of the Clinton jobs program.

Reporters also informed their audiences how the campaigns arrived at their claims. Both camps, said the journalists, eagerly worked up economic models showing that disaster loomed if the other was elected. Republican plans to cap entitlements at the rate of inflation became "slashing benefits for nearly 30 million older Americans..." in a Democratic radio ad. And the Bush ad populated with ordinary working folk about to be taxed into the Democratic poorhouse assumed that when Clinton said he would raise taxes on those making over $200,000, he actually meant everyone earning over $36,000. The funny figures on both sides were calculated, said the adwatches, by assuming anemic economic growth, costly and unproductive stimulus packages, and a dissembling opponent. The process was aided by the fact that neither side had offered enough detail to let anyone determine where the money would come from and where it would go. Hence, reasoned the Democratic aspirants to the post of Secretary of the Treasury, George Bush can't reduce taxes 1% across the board, implement his capital gains cut, and not slash Medicare and veteran's benefits. And so, calculated the Republicans hoping to retire in their cabinet and subcabinet posts, Clinton will have to increase the taxes on steamfitters and realtors to pay for his proposals.

The real utility of the adwatches was not in their warnings to the readers and viewers of news—numbers that are necessarily small. Their value came instead in the ability of the other side to use the news corrections in counter-advertising.

The press and political-insiders thought the adwatches made a difference in the conduct of the campaign. Reporters applauded news coverage of ads. Seventy-seven percent of those surveyed approved of these policing efforts. One television newsperson told Times Mirror that the debunking of the ads "is the primary reason why no Willie Horton ads or their cousins have appeared in this campaign. Our coverage is keeping the bastards honest." "We'll need a Teddy White to come along later to see if those who planned commercials really sat around worrying about whether we'd criticize them or not," another editor told the surveyors.

The election debriefings provided an answer. "It was a terrible feeling when I used to open the [New York] Times and they used to take my commercial apart, or watch CNN and watch them take it apart.... I think these reality checks made our commercials less effective," observed Bush-Quayle adman Harold Kaplan at The Annenberg School debriefing."...

CONCLUSION

Political advertising is now the major means by which candidates for the presidency communicate their messages to voters. As a conduit of this advertising, television attracts both more candidate dollars and more audience attention than radio or print. Unsurprisingly, the spot ad is the most used and the most viewed of all available forms of advertising. By 1980 the half-hour broadcast speech—the norm in 1952—had been replaced by the 60-second spot.

Ads enable candidates to build name recognition, frame the questions they view as central to the election, expose their temperaments, talents, and agendas for the future in a favorable light, and attack what they perceive as their opponent's fatal flaws. In part because more voters attend to spot ads than to network news and in part because reporters are fixated with who's winning and losing instead of what the candidates are proposing, some scholars believe that ads provide the electorate with more information than network news. Still, ads more often successfully reinforce existing dispositions than create new ones.

By personalizing issues, ads also assert their relevance to our lives. In the 1950s the public at large did not find political matters salient to it. From the late 1950s to the early 1970s our perception of the rele-vance of political matters to one's day-to-day life increased at all educational levels. Citizens saw a greater connection between what occurred in the political world and what occurred at home and work. Television ads' ability to personalize and the tendency of TV news to reduce issues to personal impact have, in my judgment, facilitated that change. Democratic ads argued in 1964, for example, that a vote against nonproliferation could increase the Strontium 90 in children's ice cream.

As the salience of political issues increased so too did the consistency of the beliefs of individual voters. Dissonant views are less likely to be simultaneously held now than before. This tendency is also reinforced by political advertising, for politicians have increasingly argued the interconnection of issues of importance to them. In 1980 Reagan predicated a strong defense on a strong economy. In 1968 Nixon tied crime, lawlessness, and the war in Vietnam into a single bundle and laid it on Humphrey's doorstep.

Ads also define the nature of the presidency by stipulating the attributes a president should have. In the process they legitimize certain occupations. Ike polished the assumption that being a general was a suitable qualification. Carter argued that being an outsider as well as an engineer, a farmer, a businessman but not a lawyer qualified him. Reagan contended that being the governor of a large state and a union leader were stronger qualifications than being an incumbent president. Clinton made the same case for being the governor of a small state. In their bids for second terms Eisenhower, Nixon, Johnson, Ford, and Carter argued that being the incumbent qualified one for the presidency.

... [V]arious styles of leadership [are] reflected in the candidates' treatment of their advertisers and advertising. Where Nixon maintained tight control over advertising decisions in 1960, Kennedy delegated all responsibility for advertising to others. At the same time, ad campaigns that lurched uncertainly from one message to another and from one set of strategists to another (as did Ford's, Mondale's, Dukakis's, and Bush's in 1992) suggested perhaps that the candidate and his advisors were unable to provide a clear sense of the direction in which they wanted to take the country, an observation consistent with the failure of these campaigns to forecast their candidates' visions of the future....

When the acceptance speech and the election eve telecasts are taken as the brackets bounding advertising, a focus on paid messages can reveal a campaign's fundamental coherence or incoherence. In a coherent campaign, the acceptance speech at the convention synopsizes and polishes the message the candidate has communicated in the primaries as a means of forecasting both the themes of the general election campaign and this person's presidency. The message is then systematically developed in the advertising of the general election and placed in its final form on election eve where the candidate tries on the presidency by indicating for the country his vision of the next four years under his leadership. From the first campaign advertising of January through the last on election eve in November, when candidates offer consistent, coherent messages about themselves and the future as they envision it, they both minimize the likelihood that their record or plans will be distorted effectively by opponents and create a clear set of expectations to govern their conduct in office. However, these same expectations may haunt them when they seek reelection. So, for example, Bush's 1988 "Read my lips. No new taxes" pledge was recycled as an indictment by Pat Buchanan in the 1992 New Hampshire primary.

Viewing campaign advertising as an extended message instead of a series of individual ones also enables us to see how a candidate's response to attacks in the primaries can either strengthen or strangle the candidate's chances in the general election. When attacks are raised in the primaries and effectively neutralized, as were questions about Kennedy's age and religion in 1960, the issue can be effectively dispatched in the general election. Kennedy's widely aired speech to the Houston ministers builds on a structure of beliefs first cemented in Kennedy's speeches and ads in the West Virginia primary. And the thorough discussion of Clinton's draft record in the 1992 primaries made the charges less damaging when broadcast in Bush ads in the general election.

Preventing candidates from using advertising to create a sense of themselves discrepant from who they are and what they have done is the vigilant presence of opponents and the potentially vigilant presence of the press. Throughout we have seen instances in which candidates' words and actions in settings they did not control undermined the crafted images of their ads. So, for example, the image of the sweating, gaunt, pale Nixon of the first debate in 1960 clashed with the polished presence in his ads.

When ads lie, the vigilance of press and opponents can, but does not necessarily, protect the public. When NBC and

CNN joined the *Atlanta Constitution* in exposing false inferences invited by an anti-Bush ad aired by Buchanan in the 1992 Georgia primary, a CNN survey showed a public backlash against the criticized ad. And a study... confirmed that the analysis did minimize the power of the offending ad.

In many ways televised political advertising is the direct descendant of the advertised messages carried in song and on banners, torches, bandannas, and broadsides. Ads continue to ally the candidate with the people, only now that takes the form of showing the candidate pressing the flesh or answering questions from groups of citizens. Candidates continue to digest their messages into slogans, yet these now appear at the end of broadcast ads rather than on banners and torches. Candidates continue to overstate their accomplishments and understate their failures. So, for example, as governor despite his claims to the contrary, Ronald Reagan did not increase welfare benefits 43%, although he did increase them just as, contrary to his advertising, Andy Jackson had served in one, not two wars.

What differentiates the claims of Jackson's time from those aired today is the role the press has now assumed as monitor of presidential advertising. While the partisan papers controlled by his opponent revealed Jackson's actual war record and noted that this was not the hand that guided the plow, those papers were not a credible source of information for Jackson's likely supporters. By contrast, in the 1992 presidential race, articles and news stories—bearing the imprint of neither party—publicly scrutinized the adequacy of candidates' claims. The difficulty in relying on news to correct distortions in advertising is, of course, that comparatively few people consume news while many are exposed to ads. The impact of adwatches is not lost on consultants, however, who justifiably fear that their content will appear in opponents' ads.

One of the argumentative ploys born in the political and product advertising of the nineteenth century was refined by politicians in the age of television and then shunted aside by Watergate. By visually associating the favored candidate with pictures of well-fed cattle, happy families, large bundles of grain, and bulging factories, banners and broadsides argued to literate and illiterate alike that this candidate stood for prosperity. The opponent, on the other hand, was visually tied to drawings of starving cattle, poverty-ravished families, empty grain bins, and deserted factories. Some of these associations obviously had no direct bearing on what sort of president the candidate would make.

Political argument by visual association flowered for the same reason it appeared in product advertising. Initially, advertising for products simply identified the existence, cost, function, and way to obtain the product. As success bred success, products performing the same function proliferated. Distinguishing attributes—some real, some fictional —were sought to persuade customers that one product rather than its twin should be purchased. Van Buren and Harrison were parity products, differentiated by the associations sculpted by their respective campaigns. Since the advertising of the early nineteenth century relied on drawings rather than photographs, the range of possible associations was limited only by the artist's imagination.

The wizardry of videotape and film editing did not change the nature of argument from visual association—it simply increased its subtlety. In the process, the evidentiary burden that candidates should assume dropped. So, for example, Goldwater's ads juxtaposed a picture of Billie Sol Estes with scenes of street riots and intercut a picture of Bobby Baker. Goldwater then appeared on screen to indict the Democrats for their disregard of law, order, and morality. Estes' relation to Baker, the relation of either to the street riots, or the relation among the three and Lyndon Johnson are not explicitly argued.

In 1968 this type of argument reached a new level of complexity in the Republican ad that intercut scenes from the Vietnam War and from the riots outside the Democratic convention with pictures of Hubert Humphrey, including one in which he appears to be smiling. The juxtaposition of highly evocative images invites the audience to impute causality.

The form of argument embodied in this ad is as powerful as it is irrational. It solicits a visceral, not an intellectual response. As a vehicle of attack this type of ad was vanquished by Watergate, which forced politicians and the public to consider what is and is not fair attack in a political campaign. Lurking in the McGovern campaign of 1972 and Bush campaign of 1988 are the forms of attack that replace it: the personal witness, neutral reporter, and pseudo-documentary ads. These mimic some features of actual news. The personal testimony ads consist of real individuals reporting their opinions of the opposing candidate's performance. They resemble person-in-the-street interviews and pose as a report of a survey; the opinions expressed are not scripted—indeed, their ungrammatical nature underscores their spontaneity. They do not appear to be unfair because, first, we are taught that everyone is entitled to express his or her opinion and, second, these people are voicing opinions that the electorate presumably is disposed to share. In 1976 Ford pioneered this form against Carter. Carter used it less successfully against Reagan. Bush used it against Dukakis in 1988 and Clinton in 1992.

In the neutral reporter spot, an announcer whose delivery is deliberately low key details facts about the opponent. The ad itself rarely draws any conclusion from the data. That task is left to the audience. Ford did this in a 1976 ad comparing Carter's statements in the campaign with his actual record as governor of Georgia. An ad by Carter did the same to Reagan in 1980. And the neutral reporter form—recapping optimistic statements made by Bush about the economy—was the stock-in-trade of Democratic ads in the 1992 general election.

Pseudo-documentary ads dramatize supposedly real conditions. . . .

By replacing attack ads that use visual, not verbal, means to prompt sweeping inferences with attack ads that verbally and visually invite judgments based on verifiable facts, Watergate temporarily transformed a form of presidential attack advertising from an exercise in the prompting of false inferences to an exercise in traditional argument. In 1988, invitations to false inference were back with a vengeance.

The widespread perception that being able to present broadcast messages persuasively to a mass public would emerge as a criterion governing selection of presidential candidates is not convincingly confirmed from 1952 to 1992. Of the candidates to receive their party's nomination since 1952, Kennedy, Bush, and Dukakis were adequate speakers, Goldwater and Nixon often excellent, and only

Reagan a master. While Clinton's extemporaneous delivery rivals Reagan's for its sense of personal conviction, his scripted delivery is considerably less compelling. In short, the ability to deliver televised messages artfully, while certainly an asset for those who possess it, has not become so central a qualification for the presidency that it has exiled candidates who lack it.

Another misconception about political advertising holds that spots and paid programming are somehow alien to the political speech, a thing apart, a bad dream, an aberration. An analysis of both the stock campaign speeches and the acceptance addresses of the presidential candidates suggests instead that the advertising is rarely anything but a digest of the speeches being delivered throughout the country. Occasionally, but not often, the candidate will say something important in a stump speech that does not appear in the paid broadcasting. But these things are usually strategic blunders such as Carter's assertion in 1980 that Reagan would rend the country North from South.

. . . [T]he convention acceptance speeches are a reliable predictor of the content of the candidate's ads in the general election. Indeed in both 1988 and 1992 sections of Bush's acceptance speeches reappeared in his ads. For those who read the campaign's position papers, examine its brochures, and listen to its stump speeches, the ads function as reinforcement. Those who ignore the other campaign-produced materials receive a digest of them in the ads. This is true both of the advertising against the opponent and that supporting the candidate.

The cost of reaching voters through broadcast advertising poses other problems. Since spot advertising is both costly and often the most cost-efficient means of reaching a mass of voters, the contemporary reliance on spots means that those who cannot afford to purchase them, with rare exceptions, are denied the ability to have their ideas either heard or taken seriously in presidential primaries.

For these and related reasons public concern over the nature and influence of political advertising has been rising. Responding to this escalating public concern, legislators drafted or considered drafting bills that can be grouped into three broad categories. The first would have either the public or the radio and TV stations assume the burden of financing some or all of candidate advertising; the second would give candidates attacked by PACs free response time or—regardless of the origin of attack—would give the attacked candidate free response time; the third would promote changes in the form by offering free time to those agreeing to certain formats (e.g., talking head ads) or lengths (e.g., a minimum length or free time in no less than five-minute and half-hour blocks).

Underlying the debate over these and similar proposals is widening consensus that the electoral process would benefit if the candidates' cost of reaching a mass audience could be reduced; if all bona-fide candidates could be provided with sufficient access to communicate their basic ideas; if politicians made greater use of longer forms of communication and the electorate as a whole attended more readily to such forms; if candidates assumed or could be enticed to assume the obligation of being viewed by the public in forms that they do not control such as debates; if the advantage PACs can bring to a presidential candidate could be countered or muted.

Still, if political advertising did not exist, we would have to invent it. Political advertising legitimizes our political institutions by affirming that change is possible within the political system, that the president can effect change, that votes can make a difference. As a result, like campaigns in general, advertising channels discontent into the avenues provided by the government and acts as a safety valve for pressures that otherwise turn against the system to demand its substantial modification or overthrow.

Political advertising does this, in part, by underscoring the power of the ballot. Your vote makes a difference, it says, at the same time as its carefully targeted messages imply that the votes that would go to the opponent are best left uncast.

Political ads affirm that the country is great, has a future, is respected. The contest they reflect is over who should be elected, not over whether there should be an election. The very existence of the contest suggests that there is a choice, that the voters' selection of one candidate over the other will make a difference.

NO

S. Robert Lichter and
Richard E. Noyes

GOOD INTENTIONS MAKE BAD NEWS

THE COST OF GOOD INTENTIONS

Can't we just cut this stuff out and get back to grown-up journalism?

——John Leo, *U.S. News & World Report*, 1995

Media bashing has joined the mainstream. Press criticism was once the prerogative of the political right and the academic left; today the catcalls come from all quarters. The profession that prizes its role as the public's tribune is facing a vote of no confidence. Opinion analyst Andrew Kohut puts the case succinctly: "The public is saying the national media is part of the problem."

Even more notable is the rising chorus of mea culpas from journalists themselves: The *Columbia Journalism Review* deplores "a generation of vipers." A National Press Club symposium is plaintively titled, "Why Do They Hate Us?" CBS's Mike Wallace not only confesses to committing journalistic "malpractice," he calls for awarding booby prizes to "censure practices that diminish the public trust in us."

Ironically, the volume of criticism has risen in the wake of a coordinated effort to upgrade the profession's performance by acting more aggressively as the public's surrogate. During the 1992 presidential elections, the national news media's leading lights set out to improve the electoral system by policing the campaign and forcing the candidates to be on their best behavior.

To accomplish this they made virtues out of press practices that were once widely considered to be vices. Journalists were called upon to become participants rather than observers, to take over the campaign agenda from the politicians, and to tell the "truth" rather than just the facts, even if this helped some candidates and hurt others. This [selection] examines the cost of their good intentions to their own profession and to the political system.

There seemed to be good reasons for making these changes. After the 1988 presidential campaign, traditional journalism was widely criticized for triviality and cowardice in its political reporting. The conventional wisdom held that the candidates—especially George Bush—ran superficial and negative campaigns that year. Critics charged that reporters not only failed to challenge such conduct, but that old-style campaign coverage, punctuated by new-style feeding frenzies, just made things worse. In advance of 1992, leading academics and journalists devised new ways for news organizations to do a better job. Reporters would produce more meaningful coverage by ignoring photo opportunities and cynically crafted sound bites. Instead, they would impose a strict diet of substantive issues on the candidates. They would enforce fair campaign practices by supervising the candidates' speeches and advertisements and calling voters' attention to misleading claims or outright falsehoods.

This high-minded approach was supposed to produce serious, substantive, and even-handed oversight that would redeem both the media and the political system for their past sins against the public interest. But our systematic inquiry into the actual coverage suggests otherwise. In their efforts to cure what ailed the electoral process, they broke the cardinal rule of medicine: First, do no harm.

Not only did the news continue to feature negativism, "horse-racism," and tabloid titillation, but it became less balanced and even more intrusive. In many respects, the candidates and the often-derided talk shows performed better than the mainstream media did during Campaign '92. Moreover, the media have remained in their new campaign mode ever since, creating new impediments to rational public debate and policy making....

The coverage was indeed somewhat more oriented toward policy issues in 1992 than it was in 1988. But not by much —a large majority of news stories still contained little or no substantive infor-mation about the candidates' records and proposals. Most references were limited to brief and superficial throw-away lines in discussions of campaign strategy or tactics. Fewer than one in ten mentions of the candidates' policies described their details and implications.

And what of the media's effort to inject more substance into the campaign debate by forcing the candidates to dance to their tune? As it turned out, they struck a sour note. The candidates' own speeches actually discussed policy issues far more frequently and in considerably greater detail than did either print or broadcast reports.

The candidates also ran more positive campaigns than voters might have guessed, since news reports consistently emphasized their most negative rhetoric. In general, the media told people how policy issues were relevant to the horse race; the candidates told people why issues were relevant to their lives.

The negative tone of the coverage extended beyond evaluations of the candidates to the campaign itself. On the major networks alone, nearly 300 on-air sources complained about the quality of the fall campaign, the paid political ads, and the choice of candidates. On-air critics outnumbered defenders of the process by a margin of twenty to one.

By contrast, post-election polls showed that three in five voters were satisfied with the choice of candidates, three in four said they learned enough from the campaign to make an informed choice, and two in five even rated the much-criticized campaign commercials as helpful. You wouldn't know any of that from watching TV news. Such relentless negativism does not simply reflect public alienation, it intensifies it.

We even found instances of network correspondents criticizing the candidates for "not talking about" issues that they had in fact addressed, as texts of the speeches they delivered earlier that same day prove. Their real crime lay in not discussing these issues in a fashion that journalists would have found newsworthy. Unfortunately, the viewers couldn't have known that. Nonetheless, any absence of substance in Campaign '92 was due more to the choices made by journalists than the failure of politicians to address the issues.

The media fared even worse on the fairness issue. After 1988, many journalists felt that a fetish for artificial "balance" had kept them from telling the truth about the men who would be president. In 1992, they resolved to call it the way they saw it. The news went boldly where only editorials had gone before, and news organizations instituted "Ad Watches" and "reality checks" to keep the candidates honest. The result was some of the least balanced, most negative, and most opinionated coverage in the era of mediated elections.

Many journalists regard the "Ad Watches" as their profession's proudest achievement of the campaign. But this innovation seems far more problematic in retrospect. Despite the false sense of certainty they conveyed, these pieces rarely corrected factual misrepresentations. All too frequently, they simply replaced the campaigns' interpretations of ambiguous facts with their own. Further, they had the unintended effect of portraying the candidates' overall advertising campaigns as more negative than they really were....

Even as journalists were moving aggressively to wrest the campaign agenda from the politicians, voters began moving in the opposite direction, toward more direct and less mediated communication with the candidates....

While mainstream journalists chafed against competition from the likes of Larry King and Phil Donahue, so many citizens voted with their remote controls to endorse the talk show campaign that the networks were forced to join the bandwagon. Our analysis reveals one good reason for the new format's popularity: The talk shows provided more substantive information and a more positive and balanced portrait of the candidates than the "establishment" media did. The most popular campaign news reform in 1992 was not directed by the national media; it was directed against them.

The media's reform agenda for elections was undermined by the very feature that made it so appealing to journalists in the first place—it accelerated the trend toward placing them at center stage and pushing the politicians to the sidelines. Journalists could convince themselves that this was needed because they identified their perspectives and interests with those of the public. Clearly, the public didn't agree. Polls show continued concern over media negativism and intrusiveness, along with rising anger over sensationalism and partisanship.

Why did the skein of good intentions unravel so rapidly? Because the follies of '92 were preordained by the structure and culture of contemporary campaign journalism, which the in-house reformers took for granted. By trying to bring the entire election process into accord with media interests, they undermined the professional norms that had served to check media foibles and excesses. These standards have long been under siege within journalism, but the ramparts were finally breached in 1992.

[M]ainstream journalists need to go back to the future. If they are to recover their public mandate, they must rediscover the values and practices that set their trade apart from punditry, propaganda, and melodrama. Above all, they should aim at providing an accurate account of the battle of ideas and values, rather than trying to settle it. . . .

Journalists largely ignored the wake-up call they got from voters in 1992. If they do the same thing in [the future], they may find the audience refusing to take *their* calls. Despite their self-image as the public's surrogate, growing perceptions of self-serving and out of touch reporting are creating a popular revolt. The audience has begun to demand information *without* representation from the media insiders whose claim to speak for "the people" looks increasingly shaky. Incumbents beware! . . .

The Media: Focus on the Home Front

Citizens and their elected leaders have a communications problem, but the media are hurting, not helping, the situation. After 1988, voters *were* dissatisfied with the media and the campaign. The Barone Center was on target when it charged that "the public is losing its grip on the democratic process. Elections, the litmus tests of democracy, are becoming mud-wrestling contests that are irrelevant to the realities that face the candidates once elected." David Broder, a Pulitzer Prize-winning journalist and television commentator, and others were absolutely right to believe that the process, including the media, had to undergo reform so that the public would again feel invited to participate rather than just observe.

Sadly, voters did not renew their faith in journalism during the 1992 campaign.

By arousing such suspicions about their own impartiality and seriousness, journalists' efforts to assume a greater voice in the campaign created a public backlash.

Polls found that nine out of ten Americans thought that newspapers "would rather take cheap shots at candidates' personal lives than help voters understand the issues." Nearly three in four felt the national media have gotten out of touch with what most Americans really think. And almost two-thirds agreed that the media "favor some candidates over others." Voters had lost faith in news media that had lost sight of them.

The reformers correctly perceived the disconnect between the public and the nation's politics, and the need for systemic reform. The problem was that the solutions they proffered were ill-suited to reconnecting citizens and candidates. Taken as a whole, their prescriptions demanded a more intrusive and aggressive role for journalists—more *mediation*, at a time when the public desired more *direct* communication with their elected leaders. Voters felt shut out of a process that seemed to talk about them, and claimed to speak for them, but rarely spoke *to* them.

Further, by becoming "partisans in behalf of the process," journalists became as responsible as the candidates, consultants, and pundits for the tone and shortcomings of the campaign. Instead of changing the system, they became more closely identified with it. In 1992, as they stopped to criticize the candidates' ads and campaign conduct, reporters took that much more time away from the issues, and added that much more negativity to the process. You cannot stay clean after joining in a mud fight.

In spite of voter dismay, the newfound aggressiveness adopted by leading news organizations has persisted since 1992. Unlike his predecessors, President Clinton enjoyed no media "honeymoon." He faced mostly bad press from the start of his term. During his first two years in office, our studies show, he has been subjected to three times as much criticism as praise on the network evening news shows. Only a small fraction of the criticism has focused on the president's lingering character problem—most news reports rebuked specific administration policies or the president's general leadership ability.

The national media's coverage of the 1994 midterm election campaigns was even more superficial than in 1992. Applying the same criteria to evening news coverage as we had in presidential races, we found that barely one out of five assessments of the candidates focused on the substance of their records or proposals. The majority concerned the campaign horse race— this despite the Republicans' much-publicized "Contract with America," which detailed a substantive legislative platform signed by most G.O.P. House candidates.

Republicans and Democrats engaged in a vigorous debate over the "Contract" in 1994, while television news focused on polls, projections, and their latest round of "Ad Watches." For a media dogged by perceptions that it is part of an entrenched establishment, it is perhaps no coincidence that the most positive national news coverage went to three beleaguered incumbents—New York Governor Mario Cuomo, Texas Governor Ann Richards, and Massachusetts Senator Edward Kennedy.

Finally, just as President Clinton was denied a media honeymoon, the ambitious 100-day agenda of the Republican 104th Congress received heavily negative media coverage. Both the broadcast networks (71% negative evaluations) and leading newspapers (70% negative from the *New York Times*, 65% negative from the *Washington Post*) focused on complaints and criticism in their coverage. The hostile newspaper coverage was mirrored by an even more negative editorial line. The skew against the G.O.P., commented Ellen Hume, shows that reporters are "really out of touch with the resurgent conservative mood in the country."

As these figures illustrate, the national news media continue to embrace their role as a major player in the game of politics, albeit one without governing responsibility or a guiding philosophy, beyond that of challenging all comers. Their aggressive attitude toward political leaders has been reflected in mostly bad press for successive administrations and Congresses controlled by both political parties. In the current media environment, writes *Roll Call* editor Morton Kondracke, "negativism trumps ideology every time."

The media's persistent negativism and superficiality have not gone unnoticed. The public's disapproval has persisted, and in some cases deepened, since the last presidential election. In 1993, barely a quarter of the public (26%) thought that "the press looks out for ordinary people" while 65% thought the press "looks out for mainly powerful people."

A 1994 Times Mirror survey showed that about two-thirds of the public thought television and newspaper coverage of political issues frequently favors one side over another. A 1995 CNN poll found that 60% say the news media are generally "out of touch with average Americans." Nearly three in five Americans (57%) report their belief that "the news media gets in the way of society solving its problems," while only a third (33%) believe the media "helps society." ...

Everyone loses if political leaders must communicate with citizens via information media that much of the public doesn't trust. For better or for worse, the news media are still our eyes and ears on public life. When people doubt the essential fairness and accuracy of the information they receive, they are rendered deaf and blind, hence unable to make informed judgments.

The doubt stems from concerns that the media's own institutional values and interests—not the public's concerns—drive much of the coverage. The public has repeatedly told pollsters that the media are too cynical, too adversarial, and too focused on the misdeeds and personal failings of public officials. Instead of diminishing longstanding public concern over media negativism and intrusiveness, recent trends in journalism have increased the concern over sensationalism and partisanship. As a result, trust in the media is being replaced by skepticism about its understanding of everyday life.

Yet many journalists are still reluctant to acknowledge these problems. When Times Mirror recently asked national media journalists why they think the public is angry with the press, most pointed their fingers elsewhere: 27% replied that tabloids have given the mainstream media a bad name, 22% said the public was blaming the messenger, and 13% said the public was just angry with all institutions. When asked whether the public's disaffection was justified, more national journalists gave an unequivocal no (29%) than an unqualified yes (22%).

Journalists cannot expect to redeem the political process when their own reputations are so frayed. Large segments of the public believe the media are incapable of serving society in a neutral role, let alone a constructive one. Each time reporters adopt a more aggressive posture, their stock drops among the public. As crusading news organizations overreach in their posture of principled negativism, their ability to provide the public with trustworthy information is diminished.

As the reformers proved, media coverage can be changed by rational persuasion and exhortation. Three suggestions that might help journalism rebuild its public standing:

Step One: Lose the Attitude News organizations need to stop confusing a sharp tongue with serious oversight. The natural instinct of journalists is to question and challenge authority. This is to the good: politicians need to be questioned and challenged. But at the end of the day, when the stories are written, the focus should be more on hard news, and less on soft-core commentary.

The media's skepticism about a second Bush term didn't just ensure that reporters asked the president and his staff tougher questions; it seeped into the tone of their finished stories. They invited the public to share their skepticism and unfairly prejudiced the political environment. They were so skeptical of Bush that they *weren't skeptical* about the Democrats' claims of a failing economy. Hewing more closely to the facts, and reducing the role of speculation and commentary (which is often mislabeled as "analysis") would protect journalists against making these sort of errors in the future.

One consequence of such reportage is that the public increasingly sees the press as just another political player. Ordinary citizens think that journalists get up each morning hoping to add to their scalp collection. The profession would generally benefit from a reduction in the negative posturing that dominates so much of journalism's political writing.

This is not to suggest that reporters should abandon their watchdog role or stop asking tough questions of politicians. But the watchdog role is undermined by overuse—a steady diet of adversarial coverage can leave voters too numb to respond to serious vices or genuine virtue in public life. It also leaves them aggrieved at the messengers as well as the miscreants.

For example, "Ad Watches" put journalists in the position of acting as truthtellers. But their version of the truth proved as open to debate as anyone else's interpretation. A better policy might be to establish a forum—either within the media or outside it—where candidates could be assured of a public hearing if they have a charge to make against an opponent. The opponent would have a right to respond with supporting evidence— and a public debate would begin.

The notion behind "Ad Watches" was that, in such shouting matches, voters wouldn't be able to recognize the truth unless reporters added their own voices to the melee. A better starting point would be to assume that voters are able to analyze the facts and the arguments, and to separate truth from fiction—as long as they have all the facts in front of them. A full debate, like *MacNeil-Lehrer's* "Fact or Fiction," works far better than the bottom-line "Ad Watches." And a

debate spares reporters the need to risk their impartiality by directly criticizing the candidates.

We are not advocating a policy of witless "good news" reporting. Rampant "positivism" offers as many dangers as unchecked negativism, including flackery and favoritism. Journalists need to rediscover the virtue of neutrality in their reports and to edge back out of their own spotlight. Viewers and readers suspect that the media are becoming advocates of their own agenda. Shifting the attention back onto the politicians would not only put the focus where it belongs —it would also give journalism a sorely needed chance to repair its own credibility.

Step Two: Adopt the Voters' Agenda The best thing about the 1992 campaign was that we saw, via the talk shows, how voters would conduct the campaign. The reformers were right about one thing— the voters' agenda has been ignored by traditional media coverage, and this is a source of conflict between the people and the press. But the problem isn't only that candidates talk about flags and furloughs; it's also that reporters talk ceaselessly about the polls and the process. They view the campaign from the inside, while voters are left without guidance or information about the issues that matter to them.

Instead of just assuming that they speak for the public, reporters need to adopt the voters' agenda, *as the voters themselves define it*. When voters had their chance on the talk shows, they asked about substantive matters, trying to fathom what the next four years would be like under each candidate. They kept coming back to the basics— What is your health care plan? What would you do about the economy? How would you help fight crime? Voters didn't betray a fascination with the process; those who had a chance to question the candidates were absorbed by the stakes and substance of the campaign.

Voters wanted to know about the candidates' stances on the issues, their priorities, and what they would do as president. Reporters asked questions about the candidates' strategies, tactics, and the latest flare-up on the campaign trail. Those are the questions that inform their daily judgment about whether anything "newsworthy" happened on the trail. Reporters want to know *who* will win and *how* they do it. Voters want to know *why* each candidate should win—preferably, in the candidate's own words. . . .

The media's policy stories need to begin with the candidates themselves. Their speeches, we found, were three times as likely as traditional news to stress the substance of the campaign. Reporters would serve the public better if their ears pricked up at each policy proposal a candidate made at speeches or rallies, rather than each negative sound bite uttered. It is hardly fair for journalists to criticize the candidates for shirking substance when most of their coverage does the same. And, it is arrogant for news organizations to offer their own issue agenda until they cover the issues the candidates are running on.

Step Three: Cover the Campaign   Nowhere has the coverage of presidential campaigns lapsed more than during the nominating conventions. In 1992 CBS skipped the second night of the Democratic National Convention entirely, in order to broadcast the All-Star Game. That same night, ABC and NBC offered one-hour specials filled with their own commentary and interviews, and showing almost none of the floor action. Only CNN and C-SPAN offered full coverage of the 1992 conventions. . . .

Nothing better illustrates the disconnect between the voters and the media. While exposure to daily doses of television campaign news does not correlate with increases in voter information, voters do learn about the candidates and their platforms from the conventions. They similarly learn from the debates and other live events. The responsibility of the networks is not merely to assess and criticize the campaign—it is also to show it to voters, letting them witness its main events and draw their own conclusions.

The networks' retreat from the conventions is coincident with their increased reluctance to cover day-to-day campaign events. Disdaining "staged" events, the coverage now subordinates the candidates' daily activities and focuses on journalists' own judgment of what is (or is not) important.

But journalists' analyses cannot be properly evaluated by voters unless they share some of the external context of the campaign. Coverage that merely analyzes campaign events, without first offering an impartial recounting of the event, offers voters a take-it-or-leave-it proposition that diminishes their ability to evaluate the candidates.

There is another good reason for journalists to get back on the campaign trail—to protect their own role. Ross Perot showed how, the campaign trail can be bypassed as a primary means of communicating with citizens. The principal value of rallies and speeches lies in the media's coverage of them, which greatly multiplies the audience for each event. If news organizations continue to reject this role, the candidates will continue to seek out new ways to bypass the middleman and take their messages directly to the people.

This would also encourage the candidates not to let the campaign trail languish as a forum for conducting the ongoing campaign debate. Routinely offering lengthier excerpts of their speeches would give the candidates more incentive to use their speeches as a forum for debating major issues. By dismissing campaign trail events as "staged," journalists simply encourage candidates to spend more time off the trail, talking directly to citizens, through interactive media formats. Clearly, reporters have a crucial job to do every four years. They are the watchdogs who most carefully scrutinize each of the candidates. They challenge them with tough questions, and they issue daily reports. But their role is but one part of a much larger electoral process, and citizens need more views of the campaign than those of journalists. Voters need to witness the campaign more directly, so that they can make up their own minds, based on their own values and priorities.

When news organizations become blind to voters' information needs, they only add to public grievances with the media. Reporters can't get so swept up in their adversarial relationship with the candidates that they lose sight of the voters' need to experience the campaign without commentary, to hear the candidates' words without constant reporter rebuttal, and to begin accumulating the basic information that journalists already possess....

Incentives to Change

Chronic voter dissatisfaction with the campaign process is a symptom of a se-rious and systemic political disorder. We have witnessed increasing public disapproval of presidential candidates, which corresponds closely to increased media influence over elections, and increasingly sensationalized negative images of them. By fixating on the flaws and failings of candidates, political journalism undermines public support for candidates of all parties and ideological persuasions. By exaggerating conflict, the media vastly complicate the processes of coalition-building and governance that are vital to a healthy political structure.

In 1992, journalism professor Jay Rosen argued that the role of the press in public life was compromised by journalists' lack of vision. While their influence was considerable, it was not grounded in a disciplined view of their role in politics.

> "All we own is our credibility," say many in the profession, and they interpret this to mean that the press cannot afford to be caught with an agenda. At the same time, however, they agree that it is the journalists' mission to be "tough" on politicians and a persistent check on government power. The consequences of holding these two beliefs—no to an explicit agenda, yes to a tough, critical stance—have been severe. The journalist's critical method is degenerating into madness as "gotcha" becomes the battle cry of a hardened and increasingly purposeless press.

After 1988, the media tried to develop a new sense of purpose by developing an aggressive agenda to repair campaigns. The consequence was to drive the candidates and voters away from the mainstream media, and to further erode the public's faith in journalism's impartiality. In 1992, the media continued to structure their campaign coverage in a way that left citizens informationally malnourished. The coverage focused on the inside story of campaigns for an audience of political insiders. But ordinary citizens follow politics more sporadically and from a very different perspective. As a result, citizens increasingly felt abandoned by journalists, and they walked away in increasing numbers.

In 1992, Jonathan Alter, senior editor of *Newsweek* speculated that if the public's flight continues apace, the national media may cease to be a popular force:

> In the future, the national media may increasingly become an elite media shaping elite opinion—with the *Washington Post*, the *CBS Evening News*, and *Newsweek* all going for the same few million people who run the country. A lot of journalists will make perfectly fine livings doing this (and certain elite advertisers will love it), but the big guns will have ceded the mass market altogether. And they will thus have ceded their connection, however tenuous, to the majority of people who live—and vote—in America.

The experience of 1992 shows that the public, when given a chance, will seek out alternatives to the current brand of campaign coverage. The warm reception voters gave the talk shows and other forms of political communication shows that they are prepared to replace the "incumbent" news media with one more to their liking. Unless traditional journalism responds to voter displeasure, it risks becoming an increasingly marginal feature of a diverse media landscape.

Change is coming. The dominant media of the next century will give voters more control over the information they receive, and thus more autonomy over the decisions they make. The question for 1996 and beyond is whether or not traditional news can adapt to this new media environment.

This is not a trivial concern, for failure will have consequences that reverberate far beyond the news industry. While the media's recent track record is dismal in many respects, the health of American democracy requires an institution with many of the traits embodied by traditional journalism— valuable qualities that would be at risk in the transition to a new order.

POSTSCRIPT

Has Coverage of Political Campaigns Improved?

Press management of campaign advertising is only one topic in the debate over the practices of campaign journalism. A 1996 Freedom Forum poll found that three-quarters of American voters believe that the press has a negative impact on U.S. presidential campaigns (with 83 percent agreeing that campaign coverage leads candidates to perform for the cameras rather than focus on issues), detracts from a discussion of the issues, gives undue advantage to front-running candidates, is often confusing and unclear, and even discourages good people from running for president. This would come as no surprise to James Fallows, who argues that the media's self-aggrandizement gets in the way of solving America's real problems in *Breaking the News: How the Media Undermine American Democracy* (Pantheon Books, 1996). Although Americans are becoming increasingly concerned with the immediate and long-term impact of political decisions, many say that the media couch coverage in terms of the struggle between candidates, ignoring the relevance of issues.

Yet these same critics rely heavily on journalists to provide the information they need to make up their minds. They turn to journalists for more information about the candidates, particularly their issue positions, and for more information about how election outcomes will affect voters (but seek less information on who is ahead and on the personal lives of candidates).

The implications of these arguments for the understanding of the political process are important. It seems clear that people are unhappy with current political campaigns. As reflected in the Freedom Forum poll, people want even more coverage, especially young people. Political Web sites are proliferating, with over 1,500 identified in late 1995. Yet even these sites suffer from the familiar problem of too much trivia and too little debate. It remains to be seen whether or not the advent of new technology will be able to fulfill its promise of creating dialogue between voters and candidates.

A number of books try to analyze the linkage of politics and media. Two of these are *The Interplay of Influence: News, Advertising, Politics, and the Mass Media* by Kathleen Hall Jamieson and Karlyn Kohrs Campbell (Wadsworth, 1996) and *Is Anyone Responsible: How Television Frames Political Issues* by Shanto Iyengar (University of Chicago Press, 1991). Several recent books have specifically tackled the history and problems of campaign advertising, such as *Air Wars: Television Advertising in Election Campaigns, 1952–1996* by Darrell M. West (Congressional Quarterly Books, 1997) and *Going Negative: How Attack Ads Shrink and Polarize the Electorate* by Stephen Ansolabehere and Shanto Iyengar (Free Press, 1997).

ISSUE 10

Is Advertising Ethical?

YES: John E. Calfee, from "How Advertising Informs to Our Benefit," *Consumers' Research* (April 1998)

NO: Russ Baker, from "The Squeeze," *Columbia Journalism Review* (September/October 1997)

ISSUE SUMMARY

YES: John E. Calfee, a former U.S. Trade Commission economist, takes the position that advertising is very useful to people and that the information that advertising imparts helps consumers make better decisions. He maintains that the benefits of advertising far outweigh the negative criticisms.

NO: Author Russ Baker focuses on the way in which advertisers seek to control magazine content and, thus, go beyond persuasion and information into the realm of influencing the content of other media.

Professor Dallas Smythe first described commercial media as a system for delivering audiences to advertisers. This perception of the viewing public as a "market" for products as well as an audience for advertising—a main source of media revenue—reflects the economic orientation of the current media system in America. The unplanned side effects of advertising, however, concern many critics. For example, socialization into consumption, consumerism, materialism, and high expectations are one set of concerns. Many of these questions have often been asked: Is advertising deceptive? Does it create or perpetuate stereotypes? Does it create conformity? Does it create insecurity in order to sell goods? Does it cause people to buy things that they do not really need?

John E. Calfee addresses some of these questions in the following selection, but he focuses on how the information in ads benefits consumers. He takes the position that advertising is in the public interest and that even controversies about ads may be beneficial because they can result in competitive pricing for consumers. Citing some specific cases, he claims that individuals can learn about important issues (such as health) through ads. He even considers what he calls "less bad" ads, which give consumers important negative information that can be useful to their well-being.

In the second selection, Russ Baker provides many different examples to show that the advertising industry has become too large and too powerful. He maintains that by giving corporations too much say in magazine and newspaper copy, advertisers may ultimately distort free press and free inquiry. When publishers bow to corporate control over material that is not advertising, they may lose focus and become mere extensions of advertisers.

These two selections raise concerns about the ethical nature of ads. Calfee focuses only on the good that advertising does, while Baker addresses the ethical nature of the control that corporations and advertising have in influencing media content. Both authors examine important concepts of fairness, honesty, and integrity in the world of advertising.

YES

John E. Calfee

HOW ADVERTISING INFORMS
TO OUR BENEFIT

A great truth about advertising is that it is a tool for communicating information and shaping markets. It is one of the forces that compel sellers to cater to the desires of consumers. Almost everyone knows this because consumers use advertising every day, and they miss advertising when they cannot get it. This fact does not keep politicians and opinion leaders from routinely dismissing the value of advertising. But the truth is that people find advertising very useful indeed.

Of course, advertising primarily seeks to persuade and everyone knows this, too. The typical ad tries to induce a consumer to do one particular thing—usually, buy a product—instead of a thousand other things. There is nothing obscure about this purpose or what it means for buyers. Decades of data and centuries of intuition reveal that all consumers everywhere are deeply suspicious of what advertisers say and why they say it. This skepticism is in fact the driving force that makes advertising so effective. The persuasive purpose of advertising and the skepticism with which it is met are two sides of a single process. Persuasion and skepticism work in tandem so advertising can do its job in competitive markets. Hence, ads represent the seller's self interest, consumers know this, and sellers know that consumers know it.

By understanding this process more fully, we can sort out much of the popular confusion surrounding advertising and how it benefits consumers.

How Useful Is Advertising?   Just how useful is the connection between advertising and information? At first blush, the process sounds rather limited. Volvo ads tell consumers that Volvos have side-impact air bags, people learn a little about the importance of air bags, and Volvo sells a few more cars. This seems to help hardly anyone except Volvo and its customers.

But advertising does much more. It routinely provides immense amounts of information that benefits primarily parties other than the advertiser. This may sound odd, but it is a logical result of market forces and the nature of information itself.

The ability to use information to sell products is an incentive to create new information through research. Whether the topic is nutrition, safety, or more mundane matters like how to measure amplifier power, the necessity of achieving credibility with consumers and critics requires much of this research to be placed in the public domain, and that it rest upon some academic credentials. That kind of research typically produces results that apply to more than just the brands sold by the firm sponsoring the research. The lack of property rights to such "pure" information ensures that this extra information is available at no charge. Both consumers and competitors may borrow the new information for their own purposes.

Advertising also elicits additional information from other sources. Claims that are striking, original, forceful or even merely obnoxious will generate news stories about the claims, the controversies they cause, the reactions of competitors (A price war? A splurge of comparison ads?), the reactions of consumers and the remarks of governments and independent authorities.

Probably the most concrete, pervasive, and persistent example of competitive advertising that works for the public good is price advertising. Its effect is invariably to heighten competition and reduce prices, even the prices of firms that assiduously avoid mentioning prices in their own advertising.

There is another area where the public benefits of advertising are less obvious but equally important. The unremitting nature of consumer interest in health, and the eagerness of sellers to cater to consumer desires, guarantee that advertising related to health will provide a storehouse of telling observations on the ways in which the benefits of advertising extend beyond the interests of advertisers to include the interests of the public at large.

A Cascade of Information. Here is probably the best documented example of why advertising is necessary for consumer welfare. In the 1970s, public health experts described compelling evidence that people who eat more fiber are less likely to get cancer, especially cancer of the colon, which happens to be the second leading cause of deaths from cancer in the United States. By 1979, the U.S. Surgeon General was recommending that people eat more fiber in order to prevent cancer.

Consumers appeared to take little notice of these recommendations, however. The National Cancer Institute decided that more action was needed. NCI's cancer prevention division undertook to communicate the new information about fiber and cancer to the general public. Their goal was to change consumer diets and reduce the risk of cancer, but they had little hope of success given the tiny advertising budgets of federal agencies like NCI.

Their prospects unexpectedly brightened in 1984. NCI received a call from the Kellogg Corporation, whose All-Bran cereal held a commanding market share of the high-fiber segment. Kellogg proposed to use All-Bran advertising as a vehicle for NCI's public service messages. NCI thought that was an excellent idea. Soon, an agreement was reached in which NCI would review Kellogg's ads and labels for accuracy and value before Kellogg began running their fiber-cancer ads.

The new Kellogg All-Bran campaign opened in October 1984. A typical ad began with the headline, "At last some news about cancer you can live with." The ad continued: "The National Cancer

Institute believes a high fiber, low fat diet may reduce your risk of some kinds of cancer. The National Cancer Institute reports some very good health news. There is growing evidence that may link a high fiber, low fat diet to lower incidence of some kinds of cancer. That's why one of their strongest recommendations is to eat high-fiber foods. If you compare, you'll find Kellogg's All-Bran has nine grams of fiber per serving. No other cereal has more. So start your day with a bowl of Kellogg's All-Bran or mix it with your regular cereal."

The campaign quickly achieved two things. One was to create a regulatory crisis between two agencies. The Food and Drug Administration thought that if a food was advertised as a way to prevent cancer, it was being marketed as a drug. Then the FDA's regulations for drug labeling would kick in. The food would be reclassified as a drug and would be removed from the market until the seller either stopped making the health claims or put the product through the clinical testing necessary to obtain formal approval as a drug.

But food advertising is regulated by the Federal Trade Commission, not the FDA. The FTC thought Kellogg's ads were nondeceptive and were therefore perfectly legal. In fact, it thought the ads should be encouraged. The Director of the FTC's Bureau of Consumer Protection declared that "the [Kellogg] ad has presented important public health recommendations in an accurate, useful, and substantiated way. It informs the members of the public that there is a body of data suggesting certain relationships between cancer and diet that they may find important." The FTC won this political battle, and the ads continued.

The second instant effect of the All-Bran campaign was to unleash a flood of health claims. Vegetable oil manufacturers advertised that cholesterol was associated with coronary heart disease, and that vegetable oil does not contain cholesterol. Margarine ads did the same, and added that vitamin A is essential for good vision. Ads for calcium products (such as certain antacids) provided vivid demonstrations of the effects of osteoporosis (which weakens bones in old age), and recounted the advice of experts to increase dietary calcium as a way to prevent osteoporosis. Kellogg's competitors joined in citing the National Cancer Institute dietary recommendations.

Nor did things stop there. In the face of consumer demand for better and fuller information, health claims quickly evolved from a blunt tool to a surprisingly refined mechanism. Cereals were advertised as high in fiber and low in sugar or fat or sodium. Ads for an upscale brand of bread noted: "Well, most high-fiber bran cereals may be high in fiber, but often only one kind: insoluble. It's this kind of fiber that helps promote regularity. But there's also a kind of fiber known as soluble, which most high-fiber bran cereals have in very small amounts, if at all. Yet diets high in this kind of fiber may actually lower your serum cholesterol, a risk factor for some heart diseases." Cereal boxes became convenient sources for a summary of what made for a good diet.

Increased Independent Information. The ads also brought powerful secondary effects. These may have been even more useful than the information that actually appeared in the ads themselves.

One effect was an increase in media coverage of diet and health. *Consumer Re-*

ports, a venerable and hugely influential magazine that carries no advertising, revamped its reports on cereals to emphasize fiber and other ingredients (rather than testing the foods to see how well they did at providing a complete diet for laboratory rats). The health-claims phenomenon generated its own press coverage, with articles like "What Has All-Bran Wrought?" and "The Fiber Furor." These stories recounted the ads and scientific information that prompted the ads; and articles on food and health proliferated. Anyone who lived through these years in the United States can probably remember the unending media attention to health claims and to diet and health generally.

Much of the information on diet and health was new. This was no coincidence. Firms were sponsoring research on their products in the hope of finding results that could provide a basis for persuasive advertising claims. Oat bran manufacturers, for example, funded research on the impact of soluble fiber on blood cholesterol. When the results came out "wrong," as they did in a 1990 study published with great fanfare in *The New England Journal of Medicine*, the headline in *Advertising Age* was "Oat Bran Popularity Hitting the Skids," and it did indeed tumble. The manufacturers kept at the research, however, and eventually the best research supported the efficacy of oat bran in reducing cholesterol (even to the satisfaction of the FDA). Thus did pure advertising claims spill over to benefit the information environment at large.

The shift to higher fiber cereals encompassed brands that had never undertaken the effort necessary to construct believable ads about fiber and disease. Two consumer researchers at the FDA reviewed these data and concluded they were "consistent with the successful ed-ucational impact of the Kellogg diet and health campaign: consumers seemed to be making an apparently thoughtful discrimination between high- and low-fiber cereals," and that the increased market shares for high-fiber non-advertised products represented "the clearest evidence of a successful consumer education campaign."

Perhaps most dramatic were the changes in consumer awareness of diet and health. An FTC analysis of government surveys showed that when consumers were asked about how they could prevent cancer through their diet, the percentage who mentioned fiber increased from 4% before the 1979 Surgeon General's report to 8.5% in 1984 (after the report but before the All-Bran campaign) to 32% in 1986 after a year and a half or so of health claims (the figure in 1988 was 28%). By far the greatest increases in awareness were among women (who do most of the grocery shopping) and the less educated: up from 0% for women without a high school education in 1984 to 31% for the same group in 1986. For women with incomes of less than $15,000, the increase was from 6% to 28%.

The health-claims advertising phenomenon achieved what years of effort by government agencies had failed to achieve. With its mastery of the art of brevity, its ability to command attention, and its use of television, brand advertising touched precisely the people the public health community was most desperate to reach. The health claims expanded consumer information along a broad front. The benefits clearly extended far beyond the interests of the relatively few manufacturers who made vigorous use of health claims in advertising.

A Pervasive Phenomenon. Health claims for foods are only one example, however, of a pervasive phenomenon —the use of advertising to provide essential health information with benefits extending beyond the interests of the advertisers themselves.

Advertising for soap and detergents, for example, once improved private hygiene and therefore, public health (hygiene being one of the under-appreciated triumphs in twentieth century public health). Toothpaste advertising helped to do the same for teeth. When mass advertising for toothpaste and tooth powder began early in this century, tooth brushing was rare. It was common by the 1930s, after which toothpaste sales leveled off even though the advertising, of course, continued. When fluoride toothpastes became available, advertising generated interest in better teeth and professional dental care. Later, a "plaque reduction war" (which first involved mouthwashes, and later toothpastes) brought a new awareness of gum disease and how to prevent it. The financial gains to the toothpaste industry were surely dwarfed by the benefits to consumers in the form of fewer cavities and fewer lost teeth.

Health claims induced changes in foods, in non-foods such as toothpaste, in publications ranging from university health letters to mainstream newspapers and magazines, and of course, consumer knowledge of diet and health.

These rippling effects from health claims in ads demonstrated the most basic propositions in the economics of information. Useful information initially failed to reach people who needed it because information producers could not charge a price to cover the costs of creating and disseminating pure information. And this problem was alleviated by advertising, sometimes in a most vivid manner.

Other examples of spillover benefits from advertising are far more common than most people realize. Even the much-maligned promotion of expensive new drugs can bring profound health benefits to patients and families, far exceeding what is actually charged for the products themselves.

The market processes that produce these benefits bear all the classic features of competitive advertising. We are not analyzing public service announcements here, but old-fashioned profit-seeking brand advertising. Sellers focused on the information that favored their own products. They advertised it in ways that provided a close link with their own brand. It was a purely competitive enterprise, and the benefits to consumers arose from the imperatives of the competitive process.

One might see all this as simply an extended example of the economics of information and greed. And indeed it is, if by greed one means the effort to earn a profit by providing what people are willing to pay for, even if what they want most is information rather than a tangible product. The point is that there is overwhelming evidence that unregulated economic forces dictate that much useful information will be provided by brand advertising, and *only* by brand advertising.

Of course, there is much more to the story. There is the question of how competition does the good I have described without doing even more harm elsewhere. After all, firms want to tell people only what is good about their brands, and people often want to know what is wrong with the brands. It turns out that competition takes care of this problem, too.

Advertising and Context. It is often said that most advertising does not contain very much information. In a way, this is true. Research on the contents of advertising typically finds just a few pieces of concrete information per ad. That's an average, of course. Some ads obviously contain a great deal of information. Still, a lot of ads are mainly images and pleasant talk, with little in the way of what most people would consider hard information. On the whole, information in advertising comes in tiny bits and pieces.

Cost is only one reason. To be sure, cramming more information into ads is expensive. But more to the point is the fact that advertising plays off the information available from outside sources. Hardly anything about advertising is more important than the interplay between what the ad contains and what surrounds it. Sometimes this interplay is a burden for the advertiser because it is beyond his control. But the interchange between advertising and environment is also an invaluable tool for sellers. Ads that work in collaboration with outside information can communicate far more than they ever could on their own.

The upshot is advertising's astonishing ability to communicate a great deal of information in a few words. Economy and vividness of expression almost always rely upon what is in the information environment. The famously concise "Think Small" and "Lemon" ads for the VW "Beetle" in the 1960s and 1970s were highly effective with buyers concerned about fuel economy, repair costs, and extravagant styling in American cars. This was a case where the less said, the better.

The ads were more powerful when consumers were free to bring their own ideas about the issues to bear.

The same process is repeated over again for all sorts of products. Ads for computer modems once explained what they could be used for. Now a simple reference to the Internet is sufficient to conjure an elaborate mix of equipment and applications. These matters are better left vague so each potential customer can bring to the ad his own idea of what the Internet is really for.

Leaning on information from other sources is also a way to enhance credibility, without which advertising must fail. Much of the most important information in advertising—think of cholesterol and heart disease, antilock brakes and automobile safety—acquires its force from highly credible sources *other* than the advertiser. To build up this kind of credibility through material actually contained in ads would be cumbersome and inefficient. Far more effective, and far more economical, is the technique of making challenges, raising questions and otherwise making it perfectly clear to the audience that the seller invites comparisons and welcomes the tough questions. Hence the classic slogan, "If you can find a better whisky, buy it."

Finally, there is the most important point of all. Informational sparseness facilitates competition. It is easier to challenge a competitor through pungent slogans—"Where's the beef?", "Where's the big saving?"—than through a step-by-step recapitulation of what has gone on before. The bits-and-pieces approach makes for quick, unerring attacks and equally quick responses, all under the watchful eye of the consumer over whom the battle is being fought. This is an ideal recipe for competition.

It also brings the competitive market's fabled self-correcting forces into play. Sellers are less likely to stretch the truth, whether it involves prices or subtleties about safety and performance, when they know they may arouse a merciless response from injured competitors. That is one reason the FTC once worked to get comparative ads on television, and has sought for decades to dismantle government or voluntary bans on comparative ads.

'Less-Bad' Advertising.   There is a troubling possibility, however. Is it not possible that in their selective and carefully calculated use of outside information, advertisers have the power to focus consumer attention exclusively on the positive, i.e., on what is good about the brand or even the entire product class? Won't automobile ads talk up style, comfort, and extra safety, while food ads do taste and convenience, cigarette ads do flavor and lifestyle, and airlines do comfort and frequency of departure, all the while leaving consumers to search through other sources to find all the things that are wrong with products?

In fact, this is not at all what happens. Here is why: Everything for sale has something wrong with it, if only the fact that you have to pay for it. Some products, of course, are notable for their faults. The most obvious examples involve tobacco and health, but there are also food and heart disease, drugs and side effects, vacations and bad weather, automobiles and accidents, airlines and delay, among others.

Products and their problems bring into play one of the most important ways in which the competitive market induces sellers to serve the interests of buyers. No matter what the product, there are usually a few brands that are "less bad" than the others. The natural impulse is to advertise that advantage—"less cholesterol," "less fat," "less dangerous," and so on. Such provocative claims tend to have an immediate impact. The targets often retaliate; maybe their brands are less bad in a different respect (less salt?). The ensuing struggle brings better information, more informed choices, and improved products.

Perhaps the most riveting episode of "less-bad" advertising ever seen occurred, amazingly enough, in the industry that most people assume is the master of avoiding saying anything bad about its product.

Less-Bad Cigarette Ads.   Cigarette advertising was once very different from what it is today. Cigarettes first became popular around the time of World War I, and they came to dominate the tobacco market in the 1920s. Steady and often dramatic sales increases continued into the 1950s, always with vigorous support from advertising. Tobacco advertising was duly celebrated as an outstanding example of the power and creativity of advertising. Yet amazingly, much of the advertising focused on what was wrong with smoking, rather than what people liked about smoking.

The very first ad for the very first mass-marketed American cigarette brand (Camel, the same brand recently under attack for its use of a cartoon character) said, "Camel Cigarettes will not sting the tongue and will not parch the throat." When Old Gold broke into the market in the mid-1920s, it did so with an ad campaign about coughs and throats and harsh cigarette smoke. It settled on the slogan, "Not a cough in a carload."

Competitors responded in kind. Soon, advertising left no doubt about what was wrong with smoking. Lucky Strike ads said, "No Throat Irritation—No Cough... we... removed... harmful corrosive acids," and later on, "Do you inhale? What's there to be afraid of?... famous purifying process removes certain impurities." Camel's famous tag line, "more doctors smoke Camels than any other brand," carried a punch precisely because many authorities thought smoking was unhealthy (cigarettes were called "coffin nails" back then), and smokers were eager for reassurance in the form of smoking by doctors themselves. This particular ad, which was based on surveys of physicians, ran in one form or another from 1933 to 1955. It achieved prominence partly because physicians practically never endorsed non-therapeutic products.

Things really got interesting in the early 1950s, when the first persuasive medical reports on smoking and lung cancer reached the public. These reports created a phenomenal stir among smokers and the public generally. People who do not understand how advertising works would probably assume that cigarette manufacturers used advertising to divert attention away from the cancer reports. In fact, they did the opposite.

Small brands could not resist the temptation to use advertising to scare smokers into switching brands. They inaugurated several spectacular years of "fear advertising" that sought to gain competitive advantage by exploiting smokers' new fear of cancer. Lorillard, the beleaguered seller of Old Gold, introduced Kent, a new filter brand supported by ad claims like these: "Sensitive smokers get real health protection with new Kent," "Do you love a good smoke but not what the smoke does to you?" and "Takes out more nicotine and tars than any other leading cigarette—*the difference in protection is priceless*," illustrated by television ads showing the black tar trapped by Kent's filters.

Other manufacturers came out with their own filter brands, and raised the stakes with claims like, "Nose, throat, and accessory organs not adversely affected by smoking Chesterfields. First such report ever published about any cigarette," "Takes the fear out of smoking," and "Stop worrying... Philip Morris and only Philip Morris is entirely free of irritation used [sic] in all other leading cigarettes."

These ads threatened to demolish the industry. Cigarette sales plummeted by 3% in 1953 and a remarkable 6% in 1954. Never again, not even in the face of the most impassioned anti-smoking publicity by the Surgeon General or the FDA, would cigarette consumption decline as rapidly as it did during these years of entirely market-driven anti-smoking ad claims by the cigarette industry itself.

Thus advertising traveled full circle. Devised to bolster brands, it denigrated the product so much that overall market demand actually declined. Everyone understood what was happening, but the fear ads continued because they helped the brands that used them. The new filter brands (all from smaller manufacturers) gained a foothold even as their ads amplified the medical reports on the dangers of smoking. It was only after the FTC stopped the fear ads in 1955 (on the grounds that the implied health claims had no proof) that sales resumed their customary annual increases.

Fear advertising has never quite left the tobacco market despite the regulatory straight jacket that governs cigarette advertising. In 1957, when leading cancer experts advised smokers to ingest less tar, the industry responded by cutting tar and citing tar content figures compiled by independent sources. A stunning "tar derby" reduced the tar and nicotine content of cigarettes by 40% in four years, a far more rapid decline than would be achieved by years of government urging in later decades. This episode, too, was halted by the FTC. In February 1960 the FTC engineered a "voluntary" ban on tar and nicotine claims.

Further episodes continue to this day. In 1993, for example, Liggett planned an advertising campaign to emphasize that its Chesterfield brand did not use the stems and less desirable parts of the tobacco plant. This continuing saga, extending through eight decades, is perhaps the best documented case of how "less-bad" advertising completely offsets any desires by sellers to accentuate the positive while ignoring the negative. *Consumer Reports* magazine's 1955 assessment of the new fear of smoking still rings true:

> *"... companies themselves are largely to blame. Long before the current medical attacks, the companies were building up suspicion in the consumer by the discredited 'health claims' in their ads.... Such medicine-show claims may have given the smoker temporary confidence in one brand, but they also implied that cigarettes in general were distasteful, probably harmful, and certainly a 'problem.' When the scientists came along with their charges against cigarettes, the smoker was ready to accept them."*

And that is how information works in competitive advertising.

Less-bad can be found wherever competitive advertising is allowed. I already described the health-claims-for-foods saga, which featured fat and cholesterol and the dangers of cancer and heart disease. Price advertising is another example. Prices are the most stubbornly negative product feature of all, because they represent the simple fact that the buyer must give up something else. There is no riper target for comparative advertising. When sellers advertise lower prices, competitors reduce their prices and advertise that, and soon a price war is in the works. This process so strongly favors consumers over the industry that one of the first things competitors do when they form a trade group is to propose an agreement to restrict or ban price advertising (if not ban all advertising). When that fails, they try to get advertising regulators to stop price ads, an attempt that unfortunately often succeeds.

Someone is always trying to scare customers into switching brands out of fear of the product itself. The usual effect is to impress upon consumers what they do not like about the product. In 1991, when Americans were worried about insurance companies going broke, a few insurance firms advertised that they were more solvent than their competitors. In May 1997, United Airlines began a new ad campaign that started out by reminding fliers of all the inconveniences that seem to crop up during air travel.

Health information is a fixture in "less-bad" advertising. Ads for sleeping aids sometimes focus on the issue of whether they are habit-forming. In March 1996, a medical journal reported that the pain reliever acetaminophen, the active ingredient in Tylenol, can cause liver damage in heavy drinkers. This fact immediately became the focus of ads for Advil, a competing product. A public debate ensued, conducted through advertising, talk shows, news reports and pronouncements from medical authorities. The result: consumers learned a lot more than they had known before about the fact that all drugs have side effects. The press noted that this dispute may have helped consumers, but it hurt the pain reliever industry. Similar examples abound.

We have, then, a general rule: sellers will use comparative advertising when permitted to do so, even if it means spreading bad information about a product instead of favorable information. The mechanism usually takes the form of less-bad claims. One can hardly imagine a strategy more likely to give consumers the upper hand in the give and take of the marketplace. Less-bad claims are a primary means by which advertising serves markets and consumers rather than sellers. They completely refute the naive idea that competitive advertising will emphasize only the sellers' virtues while obscuring their problems.

NO

Russ Baker

THE SQUEEZE

In an effort to avoid potential conflicts, it is required that Chrysler Corporation be alerted in advance of any and all editorial content that encompasses sexual, political, social issues or any editorial that might be construed as provocative or offensive. Each and every issue that carries Chrysler advertising requires a written summary outlining major theme/articles appearing in upcoming issues. These summaries are to be forwarded to PentaCom prior to closing in order to give Chrysler ample time to review and reschedule if desired. . . . As acknowledgment of this letter we ask that you or a representative from the publication sign below and return to us no later than February 15.

—from a letter sent by Chrysler's ad agency, PentaCom, a division of BBDO North America, to at least fifty magazines

Is there any doubt that advertisers mumble and sometimes roar about reporting that can hurt them? That the auto giants don't like pieces that, say, point to auto safety problems? Or that Big Tobacco hates to see its glamorous, cheerful ads juxtaposed with articles mentioning their best customers' grim way of death? When advertisers disapprove of an editorial climate, they can —and sometimes do—take a hike.

But for Chrysler to push beyond its parochial economic interests—by demanding summaries of upcoming articles while implicitly asking editors to think twice about running "sexual, political, social issues"—crosses a sharply defined line. "This is new," says Milton Glaser, the *New York* magazine cofounder and celebrated designer. "It will have a devastating effect on the idea of a free press and of free inquiry."

Glaser is among those in the press who are vocally urging editors and publishers to resist. "If Chrysler achieves this," he says, "there is no reason to hope that other advertisers won't ask for the same privilege. You will have thirty or forty advertisers checking through the pages. They will send notes to publishers. I don't see how any good citizen doesn't rise to this occasion and say this development is un-American and a threat to freedom."

Hyperbole? Maybe not. Just about any editor will tell you: the ad/edit chemistry is changing for the worse. Corporations and their ad agencies have clearly turned up the heat on editors and publishers, and some magazines are capitulating, unwilling to risk even a single ad. This makes it tougher for those who do fight to maintain the ad-edit wall and put the interests of their readers first. Consider:

- A major advertiser recently approached all three newsweeklies—*Time, Newsweek,* and *U.S. News*—and told them it would be closely monitoring editorial content. So says a high newsweekly executive who was given the warning (but who would not name the advertiser). For the next quarter, the advertiser warned the magazines' publishing sides it would keep track of how the company's industry was portrayed in news columns. At the end of that period, the advertiser would select one—and only one—of the magazines and award all of its newsweekly advertising to it.

- An auto manufacturer—not Chrysler—decided recently to play art director at a major glossy, and the magazine played along. After the magazine scheduled a photo spread that would feature more bare skin than usual, it engaged in a back-and-forth negotiation with that advertiser over exactly how much skin would be shown. CJR's source says the feature had nothing to do with the advertiser's product.

- Kimberly-Clark makes Huggies diapers and advertises them in a number of magazines, including *Child, American Baby, Parenting, Parents, Baby Talk,* and *Sesame Street Parents.* Kimberly-Clark demands—in writing in its ad insertion orders—that these ads be placed only "adjacent to black and white happy baby editorial," which would definitely not include stories about, say Sudden Infant Death Syndrome or Down's syndrome. "Sometimes we have to create editorial that is satisfactory to them," a top editor says. That, of course, means something else is likely lost, and the mix of the magazine is altered.

- Former Cosmo Girl Helen Gurley Brown disclosed to *Newsday* that a Detroit auto company representative (the paper didn't say which company) asked for—and received—an advance copy of the table of contents for her bon voyage issue, then threatened to pull a whole series of ads unless the representative was permitted to see an article titled "How to Be Very Good in Bed." Result? "A senior editor and the client's ad agency pulled a few things from the piece," a dispirited Brown recalled, "but enough was left" to salvage the article.

Cosmo is hardly the only magazine that has bowed to the new winds. Kurt Andersen, the former *New York* magazine editor—whose 1996 firing by parent company, K-III was widely perceived to be a result of stories that angered associates of K-III's founder, Henry R. Kravis—nonetheless says that he always kept advertisers' sensibilities in mind when editing the magazine. "Because I worked closely and happily with the publisher at *New York,* I was aware who the big advertisers were," he says. "My antennae were turned on, and I read copy thinking, 'Is this going to cause Calvin Klein or Bergdorf big problems?'"

National Review put a reverse spin on the early-warning-for-advertisers discussion recently, as *The Washington Post* revealed, when its advertising director sent an advance copy of a piece about utilities deregulation to an energy supplier mentioned in the story, as a way of luring it into buying space.

And Chrysler is hardly the only company that is aggressive about its editorial environment. Manufacturers of packaged goods, from toothpaste to toilet paper, aggressively declare their love for plain-vanilla. Colgate-Palmolive, for example, won't allow ads in a "media context" containing "offensive" sexual content or material it deems "antisocial or in bad taste"—which it leaves undefined in its policy statement sent to magazines. In the statement, the company says that it "charges its advertising agencies and their media buying services with the responsibility of pre-screening any questionable media content or context."

Procter & Gamble, the second-largest advertising spender last year ($1.5 billion), has a reputation as being very touchy. Two publishing executives told Gloria Steinem, for her book *Moving Beyond Words*, that the company doesn't want its ads near anything about "gun control, abortion, the occult, cults, or the disparagement of religion." Even nonsensational and sober pieces dealing with sex and drugs are no-go.

Kmart and Revlon are among those that editors list as the most demanding. "IBM is a stickler—they don't like any kind of controversial articles," says Robyn Mathews, formerly of *Entertainment Weekly* and now *Time*'s chief of makeup. She negotiates with advertisers about placement, making sure that their products are not put near material that is directly critical. AT&T, Mathews says, is another company that prefers a soft climate. She says she often has to tell advertisers, "We're a *news* magazine. I try to get them to be realistic."

Still, the auto companies apparently lead the pack in complaining about content. And the automakers are so powerful—the Big Three pumped $3.6 billion into U.S. advertising last year—that most major magazines have sales offices in Detroit.

After *The New Yorker*, in its issue of June 12, 1995, ran a Talk of the Town piece that quoted some violent, misogynist rap and rock lyrics—along with illustrative four-letter words—opposite a Mercury ad, Ford Motor Company withdrew from the magazine, reportedly for six months. The author, Ken Auletta, learned about it only this year. "I actually admire *The New Yorker* for not telling me about it," he says. Yet afterwards, according to *The Wall Street Journal*, the magazine quietly adopted a system of warning about fifty companies on a "sensitive advertiser list" whenever potentially offensive articles are scheduled.

* * *

It is the Chrysler case, though, that has made the drums beat, partly because of Chrysler's heft and partly because the revelation about the automaker's practice came neatly packaged with a crystalline example of just what that practice can do to a magazine.

In the advertising jungle Chrysler is an 800-pound gorilla—the nation's fourth-largest advertiser and fifth-largest magazine advertiser (it spent some $270 million at more than 100 magazines last year, behind General Motors, Philip Morris, Procter & Gamble, and Ford). Where it leads, other advertisers may be tempted to follow.

The automaker's letter was mailed to magazines in January 1996, but did not come to light until G. Bruce Knecht of *The Wall Street Journal* unearthed it this April in the aftermath of an incident at *Esquire*. The *Journal* reported that *Esquire* had planned a sixteen-page layout for a 20,000-word fiction piece by accomplished author David Leavitt. Already in page proofs and scheduled for the April '97 issue, it was to be one of the longest short stories *Esquire* had ever run, and it had a gay theme and some raw language. But publisher Valerie Salembier, the *Journal* reported, met with then editor-in-chief Edward Kosner and other editors and voiced her concerns: she would have to notify Chrysler about the story, and she expected that when she did so Chrysler would pull its ads. The automaker had bought four pages, the *Journal* noted—just enough to enable the troubled magazine to show its first year-to-year ad-page improvement since the previous September.

* * *

Kosner then killed the piece, maintaining he had editorial reasons for doing so. Will Blythe, the magazine's literary editor, promptly quit. "I simply can't stomach the David Leavitt story being pulled," he said in his letter of resignation. "That act signals a terrible narrowing of the field available to strong, adventuresome, risk-taking work, fiction and nonfiction alike. I know that editorial and advertising staffs have battled—sometimes affably, other times savagely—for years to define and protect their respective turfs. But events of the last few weeks signal that the balance is out of whack now—that, in effect, we're taking marching orders (albeit, indirectly) from advertisers."

The Chrysler letter's public exposure is a rough reminder that sometimes the biggest problems are the most clichéd:

as financial concerns become increasingly paramount it gets harder to assert editorial independence.

After the article about *Esquire* in the *Journal*, the American Society of Magazine Editors—the top cops of magazine standards, with 867 members from 370 magazines—issued a statement expressing "deep concern" over the trend to give "advertisers advance notice about upcoming stories." Some advertisers, ASME said, "may mistake an early warning as an open invitation to pressure the publisher to alter, or even kill, the article in question. We believe publishers should—and will—refuse to bow to such pressure. Furthermore, we believe editors should—and will—follow ASME's explicit principle of editorial independence, which at its core states: 'The chief editor of any magazine must have final authority over the editorial content, words, and pictures that appear in the publication.' "

On July 24, after meeting with the ASME board, the marketing committee of the Magazine Publishers of America —which has 200 member companies that print more than 800 magazines— gathered to discuss this issue, and agreed to work against prior review of story lists or summaries by advertisers. "The magazine industry is united in this," says ASME's president, Frank Lalli, managing editor of *Money*. "There is no debate within the industry."

How many magazines will reject Chrysler's new road map? Unclear. Lalli says he has not found any publisher or editor who signed and returned the Chrysler letter as demanded. "I've talked to a lot of publishers," he says, "and I don't know of any who will bow to it. The great weight of opinion among publishers and editors is that this is a road we can't go down."

Yet Mike Aberlich, Chrysler's manager of consumer media relations, claims that "Every single one has been signed." Aberlich says that in some cases, individual magazines agreed; in others a parent company signed for all its publications.

CJR did turn up several magazines, mostly in jam-packed demographic niches, whose executives concede they have no problem with the Chrysler letter. One is *Maxim*, a new book aimed at the young-men-with-bucks market put out by the British-based Dennis Publishing. "We're going to play ball," says *Maxim*'s sales manager, Jamie Hooper. The startup, which launched earlier this year, signed and returned the Chrysler letter. "We're complying. We definitely have to."

At *P.O.V.*, a two-and-a-half-year-old magazine backed largely by Freedom Communications, Inc. (owners of *The Orange County Register*) and aimed at a similar audience, publisher Drew Massey says he remembers a Chrysler letter, can't remember signing it, but would have no problem providing advance notice. "We do provide PentaCom with a courtesy call, but we absolutely never change an article." Chrysler, alerted to *P.O.V.*'s August "Vice" issue, decided to stay in. Massey argues that the real issue is not about edgy magazines like *P.O.V.*, but about larger and tamer magazines that feel constrained by advertisers from being adventurous.

Hachette Filipacchi, French-owned publisher of twenty-nine U.S. titles, from *Elle* to *George*, offered Chrysler's plan for a safe editorial environment partial support. Says John Fennell, chief operating officer: "We did respond to the letter, saying we were aware of their concern about controversial material and that we would continue—as we have in the past —to monitor it very closely and to make sure that their advertising did not appear near controversial things. However, we refused to turn over or show or discuss the editorial direction of articles with them."

* * *

It has long been a widely accepted practice in the magazine industry to provide "heads-up"—warnings to advertisers about copy that might embarrass them—say, to the friendly skies folks about a scheduled article on an Everglades plane crash, or to Johnnie Walker about a feature on the death of a hard-drinking rock star. In some instances, advertisers are simply moved as far as possible from the potentially disconcerting material. In others, they are offered a chance to opt out of the issue altogether, ideally to be rescheduled for a later edition.

In the 1980s, Japanese car makers got bent out of shape about news articles they saw as Japan-bashing, says *Business Week*'s editor-in-chief, Stephen B. Shepard, a past ASME president. Anything about closed markets or the trade imbalance might be seen as requiring a polite switch to the next issue.

Chrysler, some magazine people argue, is simply formalizing this long-standing advertiser policy of getting magazine executives to consider their special sensitivities while assembling each issue. But Chrysler's letter clearly went beyond that. PentaCom's president and c.e.o., David Martin, was surprisingly blunt when he explained to *The Wall Street Journal* the automaker's rationale: "Our whole contention is that when you are looking at a product that costs $22,000, you want the product to be surrounded by positive things. There's nothing positive about an article about child pornography."

Chrysler spokesman Aberlich insists the brouhaha is no big deal: "Of the thousands of magazine ads we've placed in a year, we've moved an ad out of one issue into the next issue about ten times a year. We haven't stopped dealing with any magazine." He compares placing an ad to buying a house: "You decide the neighborhood you want to be in." That interesting metaphor, owning valuable real estate, leads to other metaphors— advertisers as editorial NIMBYs (Not In My Back Yard) trying to keep out anybody or anything they don't want around.

As for the current contretemps, Aberlich says it's nothing new, that Chrysler has been requesting advance notice since 1993. "We sent an initial letter to magazines asking them to notify us of upcoming controversial stuff—graphic sex, graphic violence, glorification of drug use." But what about the updated and especially chilling language in the 1996 letter, the one asking to look over editors' shoulders at future articles, particularly *political, social* material and *editorial that might be construed as provocative*? Aberlich declines to discuss it, bristling, "We didn't give you that letter."

* * *

How did we get to the point where a sophisticated advertiser dared send such a letter? In these corporate-friendly times, the sweep and powers of advertisers are frenetically expanded everywhere. Formerly pure public television and public radio now run almost-ads. Schools bombard children with cereal commercials in return for the monitors on which the ads appear. Parks blossom with yogurt- and sneaker-sponsored events.

Meanwhile, a growing number of publications compete for ad dollars—not just against each other but against the rest of the media, including news media. Those ads are bought by ever-larger companies and placed by a shrinking number of merger-minded ad agencies.

Are magazines in a position where they cannot afford to alienate any advertiser? No, as a group, magazines have done very well lately, thank you. With only minor dips, ad pages and total advertising dollars have grown impressively for a number of years. General-interest magazines sold $5.3 billion worth of advertising in 1987. By 1996 that figure had more than doubled, to $11.2 billion.

Prosperity can enhance independence. The magazines least susceptible to advertiser pressures are often the most ad-laden books. Under its new editor-in-chief, David Granger, the anemic *Esquire* seems to be getting a lift, but *GQ* had supplanted it in circulation and in the serious-article business, earning many National Magazine Awards. This is in part because it first used advertiser-safe service pieces and celebrity profiles to build ad pages, then had more space to experiment and take risks.

Catherine Viscardi Johnston, senior vice president for group sales and marketing at *GQ*'s parent company, the financially flush Condé Nast, says that in her career as a publisher she rarely was asked to reschedule an ad—perhaps once a year. Meddling has not been a problem, she says: "Never was a page lost, or an account lost. Never, never did an advertiser try to have a story changed or eliminated."

At the other extreme, *Maxim*, which signed the Chrysler letter, does face grueling ad-buck competition. The number of new magazine startups in 1997 may well exceed 1,000, says Samir Husni, the University of Mississippi journalism professor who tracks launches. And *Maxim*'s demographic—21- to 24-year-old males —is jam-packed with titles.

This is not to say that prosperity and virtue go hand in hand. Witness Condé Nast's ad-fat *Architectural Digest*, where editor-in-chief Paige Rense freely admits that only advertisers are mentioned in picture captions. The range of standards among magazines is wide.

And that range can be confusing. "Some advertisers don't understand on a fundamental level the difference between magazines that have a serious set of rules and codes and serious ambitions, and those that don't," says Kurt Andersen. "The same guy at Chrysler is buying ads in *YM* and *The New Yorker*."

If it is up to editors to draw the line, they will have to buck the industry's impulse to draw them even deeper into their magazines' business issues. Hachette Filipacchi's U.S. president and c.e.o., David Pecker, is one who would lower the traditional ad-edit wall. "I actually know editors who met with advertisers and lived to tell about it," he said in a recent speech. Some editors at Hachette—and other news organizations —share in increased profits at their magazines. Thus, to offend an advertiser, it might be argued, would be like volunteering for a pay cut. So be it; intrepid editors must be prepared to take that.

* * *

Ironically, in fretting over public sensibilities, advertisers may not be catering to their consumers at all. In a recent study of public opinion regarding television—which is even more dogged by content controversies than magazines—

87 percent of respondents said it is appropriate for network programs to deal with sensitive issues and social problems. (The poll was done for ABC, NBC, and CBS by the Roper Starch Worldwide market research firm.) Asked who should "have the most to say about what people see and hear on television," 82 percent replied that it ought to be "individual viewers themselves, by deciding what they will and will not watch." Almost no one—just 9 percent—thought advertisers should be able to shape content by granting or withholding sponsorship. Even PentaCom admitted to the *Journal* that its own focus groups show that Chrysler owners are not bothered by Chrysler ads near controversial articles.

So what's eating these folks? Partially, it may be a cultural phenomenon. Ever since magazines began to attract mass audiences and subsidize subscription rates with advertising, many magazines have chased readers—just as networks chase viewers now—with ever more salacious fare. But corporate executives have often remained among the most conservative of Americans. Nowhere is this truer than in heartland locations like Chrysler's Detroit or Procter & Gamble's Cincinnati.

Ad executives say one factor in the mix is sponsors' fear of activist groups, which campaign against graphic or gay or other kinds of editorial material perceived as "anti-family." Boycotts like the current Southern Baptist campaign against Disney for "anti-family values" may be on the rise, precisely because advertisers do take them seriously. This, despite a lack of evidence that such boycotts do much damage. "Boycotts have no discernible impact on sales. Usually, the public's awareness is so quickly dissipated that it has no impact at all," says

Elliot Mincberg, vice-president and general counsel of People For the American Way, a liberal organization that tracks the impact of pressure groups. Why, then, would advertisers bother setting guidelines that satisfy these groups at all? "They're trying to minimize their risk to *zero*," says an incredulous Will Blythe, *Esquire*'s former literary editor.

Yet not every advertiser pines for the bland old days. The hotter the product, it seems, the cooler the heads. The "vice" peddlers (booze & cigarettes), along with some apparel and consumer electronics products, actually like being surrounded by edgy editorial copy—unless their own product is zapped. Party *on!*

Even Chrysler's sensitivities appear to be selective. *Maxim*'s premier issue featured six women chatting provocatively about their sex lives, plus several photos of women in scanty come-hither attire, but Chrysler had no grievances.

* * *

The real danger here is not censorship by advertisers. It is self-censorship by editors. On one level, self-censorship results in omissions, small and large, that delight big advertisers.

Cigarettes are a clear and familiar example. The tobacco companies' hefty advertising in many a magazine seems in inverse proportion to the publication's willingness to criticize it. Over at the American Cancer Society, media director Susan Islam says that women's magazines tend to cover some concerns adequately, but not lung cancer: "Many more women die of lung cancer, yet there have hardly been any articles on it."

To her credit, *Glamour*'s editor-in-chief, Ruth Whitney, is one who has run tobacco stories. She says that her magazine, which carries a lot of tobacco advertising,

publishes the results of every major smoking study. But Whitney concedes they are mostly short pieces. "Part of the problem with cigarettes was—we did do features, but there's nobody in this country who doesn't know cigarettes kill." Still, everybody also knows that getting slimmer requires exercise and eating right, which has not prevented women's magazines from running that story in endless permutations. Tobacco is in the news, and magazines have the unique job of deepening and humanizing such stories.

Specific editorial omissions are easier to measure than how a magazine's world view is altered when advertisers' preferences and sensitivities seep into the editing. When editors act like publishers, and vice versa, the reader is out the door.

Can ASME, appreciated among editors for its intentions, fire up the troops? The organization has been effective on another front—against abuses of special advertising sections, when advertisements try to adapt the look and feel of editorial matter. ASME has distributed a set of guidelines about just what constitutes such abuse.

To enforce those guidelines, ASME executive director Marlene Kahan says the organization sends a couple of letters each month to violators. "Most magazines say they will comply," she reports. "If anybody is really egregiously violating the guidelines on a consistent basis, we'd probably sit down and have a meeting with them." ASME can ban a magazine from participating in the National Magazine Awards, but Kahan says the organization has not yet had to do that. In addition, ASME occasionally asks the organization that officially counts magazine ad pages, the Publishers Information Bureau, not to count advertising sections that break the rules as ad pages—a tactic that ASME president Lalli says tends to get publishers' attention.

Not everyone in the industry thinks ASME throws much of a shadow. "ASME can't bite the hand that feeds them," says John Masterton of *Media Industry Newsletter*, which covers the magazine business. During Robert Sam Anson's brief tenure as editor of *Los Angeles* magazine, the business side committed to a fifteen-page supplement, to be written by the editorial side and called "The Mercedes Golf Special." Mercedes didn't promise to take any ads, but it was hoped that the carmaker would think kindly of the magazine for future issues. The section would appear as editorial, listed as such in the table of contents. Anson warned the business side that, in his opinion, the section would contravene ASME guidelines, since it was in effect an ad masquerading as edit. A senior executive told him not to worry—that at the most they'd get a "slap on the wrist." The section did not run in the end, Anson says, because of "deadline production problems."

* * *

The Chrysler model, however—with its demand for early warnings, and its insistence on playing editor—is tougher for ASME to police. Special advertising sections are visible. Killed or altered articles are not. And unless it surfaces, as in the *Esquire* case, self-censorhip is invisible.

One well-known editor, who asks not to be identified, thinks the problem will eventually go away. "It's a self-regulating thing," he says. "At some point, the negative publicity to the advertisers will cause them to back off."

Of course, there is nothing particularly automatic about that. It takes an outspoken journalistic community to generate heat. And such attention could backfire. The *Journal*'s Knecht told the audience of public radio's *On the Media* that his reporting might actually have aggravated the problem: "One of the negative effects is that more advertisers who weren't aware of this system have gone to their advertising agencies and said, 'Hey, why not me too! This sounds like a pretty good deal!'"

Except, of course, that it really isn't. In the long run everybody involved is diminished when editors feel advertisers' breath on their necks. Hovering there, advertisers help create content that eventually bores the customers they seek. Then the editors of those magazines tend to join the ranks of the unemployed. That's just one of the many reasons that editors simply cannot bend to the new pressure. They have to draw the line—subtly or overtly, quietly or loudly, in meetings and in private, and in their own minds.

POSTSCRIPT

Is Advertising Ethical?

Since a number of media technologies have become vehicles for advertising (such as the Internet and even broadcast/cable infomercials), questions about the ethics of advertising have taken yet another turn. In some ways, the current presence of advertising raises questions that are very basic to the phenomenon of advertising. Do the ads we see register on our conscious or subconscious minds? Do ads really make us buy things or think of things in a certain way? Do we perceptually "screen" unwanted information?

In recent years some of the basic questions about ads have shifted because our "use patterns" of media have changed. Today a prime-time network television program has more ad time than ever before. Remote controls allow viewers to "zap" through commercials on tape or change channels when commercials appear. Ads in the form of company logos are displayed on clothing and other personal items, which have, in turn, emphasized brand affiliation and status.

Since the development of the advertising industry, the question of advertising ethics has periodically resurfaced. *The Journal of Advertising Ethics* is a good source to begin investigating what leaders in the industry themselves say about ethical practices, but articles are often tied to specific products or issues. There have been some defenses of the ad industry, such as Yale Brozen's *Advertising and Society* (New York University Press, 1974) and Theodore Levitt's article "The Morality(?) of Advertising," *Harvard Business Review* (July/August 1970).

Stuart Ewen and Elizabeth Ewen's *Channels of Desire: Mass Images and the Shaping of American Consciousness* (McGraw-Hill, 1982) offers the idea that advertising in Western society has had a major influence on public consciousness. Stuart Ewen's more recent book *PR! A Social History of Spin* (Basic Books, 1996) also investigates the origin, effect, and impact of the public relations industry in America.

ISSUE 11

Do Paparazzi Threaten Privacy and First Amendment Rights?

YES: Jacqueline Sharkey, from "The Diana Aftermath," *American Journalism Review* (November 1997)

NO: Philip Jones Griffiths, from "No Di, No Pix," *Index on Censorship* (June 1997)

ISSUE SUMMARY

YES: Investigative reporter Jacqueline Sharkey argues that public outrage over the death of England's Princess Diana may fuel attempts to legally restrict the actions of paparazzi in order to protect individual privacy. Although such restrictions would almost certainly be deemed unconstitutional, she contends that the larger issue is the public's sense of betrayal and declining support for the First Amendment rights of journalists.

NO: Photographer Philip Jones Griffiths illuminates the symbiotic relationship between public personalities and their paparazzi: they feed off each other. But invoking privacy rights in public places, argues Griffiths, only scapegoats photographers, harms working journalists, and allows true invaders of privacy such as multinational corporations to persist.

The tragic death of Princess Diana unleashed a storm of protest over the actions of news photographers who chased her car through the streets of Paris. Accusations that aid was delayed while photographers took pictures, invading her privacy even as she died, sickened readers and viewers worldwide. Along with the outpouring of grief came an outpouring of anger, which ultimately touched the mainstream press as well as the tabloids. In many parts of the United States, tabloids were removed from grocery aisles, photojournalists were assailed on the street, and both electronic and print outlets publicly debated the hot issues.

Are media overzealous? Many Hollywood celebrities have spoken out about their own run-ins with photographers. Hastily called congressional hearings heard from celebrities about the need to control the actions of paparazzi. Yet many publishers point to celebrity cooperation and note that it sours when the celebrities cannot control the process. Should all this anger be directed at the paparazzi? Philip Jones Griffiths, in the second selection of this issue, argues that the relationship between paparazzi and celebrities is a symbiotic one. Paparazzi help to create the publicity that keeps celebrities in the public eye and fosters positive public impressions of their fame. It has been said that even Diana would frequently leak information about her schedule in order to obtain favorable mentions. Griffiths also decries the suggestions of Lord Wakeham, a British critic of photojournalist excess, to restrict the paparazzi.

The ethics of photojournalism are deceptively simple: anyone in a public place can be photographed. Photographs can be taken of events on private property that can be seen with the unaided eye from the street. Snooping with a telephoto lens is an invasion of privacy if it intrudes into a private space. Valuing people over photographs is the ethical golden rule: first, give aid; then and only then, photograph. Many photographs are never used because either the photographer or the editor decides it is inappropriate. Newsworthiness is supposed to be the criteria for decisions to "shoot" or "run the shot." Ellen Hume, executive director of PBS's Democracy Project, says, "It is honorable, within the limits of safety and the law, for a reporter or photographer to chase down real news. If they have to circle their quarry to expose public evil-doing, or simply to document the realities of governance, they should do so. But the chase is appropriate only if the news is truly of importance to the public."

Are such actions unacceptable? Should restrictions be imposed? Would such restrictions protect the privacy of personalities? At what cost? Would such restrictions threaten freedom of the press? We must remember that this issue is not limited to still photography. Any restrictions of "shooting" would also apply to electronic media.

YES
Jacqueline Sharkey

THE DIANA AFTERMATH

The Earl of Spencer's voice trembled slightly as he read a statement the day his sister, Princess Diana, died in an automobile accident. Initial press reports said the accident occurred as news photographers chased the car through the streets of Paris after midnight on August 31.

"I always believed the press would kill her in the end. But not even I could imagine that they would take such a direct hand in her death as seems to be the case," Spencer said.

"It would appear that every proprietor and editor of every publication that has paid for intrusive and exploitative photographs of her, encouraging greedy and ruthless individuals to risk everything in pursuit of Diana's image, has blood on his hands today."

New York Times columnist A. M. Rosenthal agreed. "Someday," Rosenthal wrote, "I believe, the words of Earl Spencer will hang in the private offices of publishers, network chiefs, and print and electronic editors worthy of any respect or trust."

The public, and some members of the press, denounced the photographers —and journalists in general—as "barracuda," "jackals," "piranha" and "vultures" feeding off celebrities.

Barbara Cochran, president of the Radio-Television News Directors Association, says it was impossible to "ignore how angry the public was" immediately after Diana's death.

"Numerous news directors have said to me that their photographers would be yelled at on the street," she says. Some passers-by accused photojournalists of "being responsible for killing Diana."

Following Diana's death, other issues involving the press emerged because of the public's lingering anger toward the news media. This hostility symbolizes what Nieman Foundation Curator Bill Kovach calls "an enormous disconnect" between the American people and the press that has "profound implications" for journalists' legal protections and privileges.

In addition, economic and technological developments made Diana's image such a marketing force that broadcast network news operations devoted more time in one week to her fatal accident than to any news event since the

1991 coup attempt against Soviet leader Mikhail Gorbachev, according to The Tyndall Weekly, a newsletter that monitors broadcast network news.

In the weeks since Diana's death, this confluence of controversies has led the American media to reexamine fundamental questions about their role, responsibilities and relationship to the American people.

It is ironic that this soul-searching began as U.S. journalism organizations were already launching initiatives to explore what Sandra Mims Rowe, president of the American Society of Newspaper Editors, calls "the damaging erosion of our credibility with the public."

One impetus for these initiatives has been a series of public opinion polls during the last 10 years that indicates many Americans have doubts about the news media's priorities and the ways in which they exercise their First Amendment rights.

A 1996 poll by the Center for Media and Public Affairs found that 80 percent of those surveyed thought the press ignored people's privacy; 52 percent thought the news media abused their press freedoms. More than 95 percent of respondents to an informal USA Today online survey thought the princess had been unfairly hounded by the news media, which confounded some journalists, given Diana's skill at using the press.

The day after the princess died, University of Southern California law professor and CNBC legal analyst Erwin Chemerinsky predicted that public outrage "will lead to attempts to restrict paparazzi in the United States and elsewhere."

During the next two weeks, French and British officials called for such laws, and

a U.S. congressman introduced a bill to make some invasions of privacy a federal crime. California state lawmakers drafted legislation to create a "zone of privacy" in public places, change state defamation law and establish a commission to examine paparazzi behavior.

These initial reactions could have troubling long term ramifications for the U.S. press:

- Technology and corporate values are increasingly influencing the priorities of U.S. news media, which are competing in a global information marketplace, say some media analysts. The fact that Diana's death received more network news coverage than the landing of U.S. troops in Somalia is a clear sign of this.

- Proposed federal and state laws indicate that privacy rights are becoming more important than press rights to legislatures and the public. These measures are part of a growing movement by legislators and courts to control newsgathering practices in the name of privacy.

- The increasing intrusiveness of some photographers has led to renewed debate about licensing journalists.

- Reaction to the press—and calls for additional regulations in the wake of Diana's death—shows that public support for the First Amendment can be very fragile. This support for limiting press freedom makes it imperative that journalists understand the dynamic that exists between the American people and the press, and reevaluate their responsibilities to the public.

* * *

Some journalists and press analysts believe coverage of Diana's life and death reflect how entertainment values have replaced traditional news values in many U.S. newsrooms.

Print media found coverage of Diana so profitable, both before and after her death, that Newsweek media critic Jonathan Alter wrote, "Lady Di launched at least a thousand covers, and hundreds of millions of newspaper and magazine sales."

When Diana died, magazines such as Time and Newsweek scrambled to redo their covers and devote dozens of pages to stories about the princess. As reporters started to question what Time contributor Martha Smilgis called the "media gush" about Diana, Time, Newsweek, People and TV Guide all published special commemorative editions.

Time's first issue about Diana's death had newsstand sales of about 850,000—650,000 more than normal. The commemorative edition sold about 1.2 million copies. They are the two largest sellers in the history of the magazine, according to Managing Editor Walter Isaacson.

Newspaper sales also rose. USA Today's total circulation for the week after Diana's death was several hundred thousand above normal. The Washington Post sold more than 20,000 additional copies of its Sunday editions the day Diana died and the day after her funeral.

Television news ratings also increased. CNN reported "a dramatic surge in viewership," and the highest ratings ever for its Sunday night newsmagazine, "Impact," which aired the night Diana died. More than 15 million people watched the August 31 "60 Minutes"

devoted to the princess, according to Nielsen Media Research.

Television coverage of Diana's funeral was watched in more than 26 million households, Nielsen estimates. The week of September 15—two weeks after Diana died—broadcast networks devoted more time to the princess and the British monarchy than any other story, according to The Tyndall Weekly.

"We overdosed on Diana," says Steve Geimann, immediate past president of the Society of Professional Journalists.

Jeff Cohen, an attorney who is executive director of Fairness & Accuracy In Reporting (FAIR), agrees. He notes with irony that in a country that revolted against the British crown to form a democratic union, many people "can give you chapter and verse now on the in-fighting amongst British royalty," but "can't identify their representative to the U.S. Congress.

"They're getting facts that are utterly meaningless to them acting as informed citizens in a participatory democracy," Cohen says.

Some journalists, however, think the coverage was appropriate. Jeff Fager, executive producer of the "CBS Evening News," says Diana's death had "huge political overtones," revealing the British people's animosity toward the monarchy, and involving top British and French officials in discussions of the accident investigation.

Maxwell E. P. King, editor and executive vice president of the Philadelphia Inquirer, who is stepping down in January, says the coverage "represented an important public catharsis about all sorts of different issues—about women and their

ALL DIANA, ALL THE TIME

STORIES OF THE WEEK

The amount of time the three major networks devoted to major stories in a week:

255 minutes: *Coup against Gorbachev*
197 minutes: *Princess Diana*
182 minutes: *U.S. Marines arrive in Somalia*
167 minutes: *Mississippi River floods*
151 minutes: *Hurricane Andrew*

BIG NIGHTS

The amount of time the three major networks devoted to major news stories:

60 minutes: *Los Angeles riots*
59 minutes: *O.J. Simpson verdict*
57 minutes: *Israeli-PLO handshake*
56 minutes: *Oklahoma City bombing*
55 minutes: *Princess Diana (Monday after her death)*
53 minutes: *TWA Flight 800 crash*

THE TOP TEN

The amount of time the three major networks devoted to stories on their evening newscasts the week of September 1:

197 minutes: *Princess Diana*
16 minutes: *Jerusalem suicide bombs kill seven*
16 minutes: *Mother Teresa dies*
13 minutes: *Campaign fund abuses*
6 minutes: *Bounty hunters kill two by mistake*
4 minutes: *NYSE-NASDAQ closing prices*
3 minutes: *Alternative medicine used by terminally ill*
3 minutes: *Ford stalling defect*

(Continued)

2 minutes: *IRS abuses to be exposed at Senate hearings*
2 minutes: *Teenage smoking ban*

DIANA DAY BY DAY

The amount of time the three major networks devoted to Princess Diana stories on their evening newscasts the week of September 1:

55 minutes: *Monday—Limousine driver was drunk*
40 minutes: *Tuesday—Criminal probe of paparazzi*
41 minutes: *Wednesday—Resentment of royals*
27 minutes: *Thursday—Royals bow to pressure*
33 minutes: *Friday—Queen Elizabeth's TV address*

SOURCE: THE TYNDALL WEEKLY

place in society, about how the famous and their fans interact."

CNN Editor-at Large Ed Turner points out that Diana's funeral enabled millions of Americans to share their grief, and "there aren't that many shared experiences that occur these days."

In the early days of TV, "the nation sort of went through the same news stories together," Turner says, but technology has been "fracturing the viewing audience" by providing "a diversity of not only sources, but alternatives to news."

Critics, he says, don't take this diversity into account. Turner points out that CNN, unlike the broadcast networks, provides news 24 hours a day and has given the public extensive coverage of events in Russia, the Middle East and Bosnia. "You think that's numbers? Wrong! It's a killer" for ratings, says Turner. "If at times we are excessive, in other ways, well, we paid our dues.... We're not tabloid all the time."

But several incidents during the coverage of Diana's death show how difficult it can sometimes be to distinguish between the so-called tabloid and mainstream media.

Newsweek, Time and other publications used photographs of Diana that some readers and journalists found intrusive, while captions talked about the pictures capturing intimate moments. Isaacson defends his magazine, saying Time used valid news photographs taken in public places, and rejected pictures by "stalking paparazzi invading people's privacy."

In the meantime, National Enquirer Editor Steve Coz made a televised plea for news organizations to refuse to publish pictures of the injured princess and her dead companion. "We have refused to buy these pictures," Coz said, "and we're asking that the rest of the world press join us in shunning these photos."

Dana Kennedy, an Entertainment Weekly reporter, called Coz's comments "the worst hypocrisy," especially since the National Enquirer's cover the previous week had a headline that said, "Di Goes Sex-Mad—'I Can't Get Enough!'"

However, journalists thought other news media also were hypocritical. Time columnist Margaret Carlson decried the practice of "tabloid-laundering, which is we take what the tabloids do and write about it, and that way get what we wouldn't write about originally into the magazine. And then we run pictures of the pictures to show how terrible the pictures are."

Newsweek seemed to do just that with two Alter stories. On September 8, his full page spread about the media's celebrity obsession included a color picture of one cover of the British tabloid The Sun, published before Diana's death. The cover included a now famous photo of Diana, her swimsuit straps slipped down her arms, on a boat with her companion, Emad Mohamed "Dodi" al-Fayed. The headline: "Dodi's to Di For, World Picture Exclusive."

The next week, his article about Diana and the news media—in which the princess is quoted as calling paparazzi photography "face rape"—was accompanied by a blurry full page picture of the princess, visibly upset, putting her hand in front of a camera lens.

Newsweek Managing Editor Mark Whitaker defends the pictures, saying, "You have to look at the context in which photographs are being used. When the subject of a legitimate news story is the paparazzi phenomenon, and you're running these pictures in a way that's used to illustrate ... that news story, and not just to titillate people with exclusive photographs that have never been seen that you pay a lot of money for, then I think that that is still a defensible and legitimate use of the photographs."

Alter believes the photos "are not a good example of tabloid laundering," because the motivation is to "illustrate a serious article," not a gossip-oriented feature.

But some readers were irate about the use of pictures they considered invasive. "I would never have expected to find such photos in your publication," wrote Allison Seale of Los Angeles to Newsweek. "Shame on you and shame on us all."

One reason the line between tabloid and mainstream media is fading is that the press is under mounting pressure to provide entertainment-oriented news, says longtime journalist Ben Bagdikian, author of "The Media Monopoly."

Stockholders in major media corporations expect high profits, and entertainment products deliver them, he says. This puts news subsidiaries "under terrible pressure" to deliver reports that will boost the bottom line.

"The value system of commercial television and of entertainment companies has made dangerous intrusions into the integrity of real news," says Bagdikian.

King says this has not happened with Knight-Ridder, which he says has "a very, very good level of awareness of news values." But he acknowledges that "some so-called news companies," which he declined to name, "don't reflect the most serious values."

U.S. News & World Report Editor James Fallows believes corporate pressures are forcing more news organizations to produce entertainment-oriented reports, and says this is a "Faustian bargain."

"In the short run it raises your audience," Fallows says, but "in the long run it threatens to destroy your business, because if the only way you make journalism interesting is by making it entertainment, in the long run people will just go to entertainment, pure and simple, and skip the journalistic overlay."

Meanwhile, despite the high ratings and circulation figures for stories about Diana, a Wall Street Journal/NBC News poll of more than 2,000 people in mid-September showed 56 percent of respondents thought there had been too much coverage of Princess Diana's death.

Some news executives say such polls reveal a paradox about the public's relationship with the press. People respond to certain types of coverage, then criticize the press for providing it. However, other polls show the American people want the news media to provide them with information that is not only interesting, but important to their lives, regardless of ratings.

So does one lawmaker who proposed legislation to restrict the press following Diana's death. If journalism is simply a "profit-seeking, market-oriented enterprise," then the controversy about the news media's involvement with Diana "becomes a much bigger issue than who chased who into a tunnel," says California State Sen. Tom Hayden. It's about whether entertainment has "taken root in the very heart of journalism" and become a "substitute for information."

The public's reaction to coverage of Diana's life and death, Hayden says, is "one of those moments along the way when we need to take an accounting."

* * *

Hayden is one of several lawmakers who, in the weeks after Diana died, drafted laws to limit access to public figures. On Capitol Hill, Rep. Sonny Bono (R-Calif.) introduced a bill that could result in jail sentences and fines for anyone who "persistently" follows a person who "has a reasonable expectation of privacy and has taken reasonable steps to insure that privacy," for the purpose of obtaining "a visual image, sound recording, or other physical impression of the victim for profit in or affecting interstate or foreign commerce."

In California, State Senate Majority Leader Charles Calderon has prepared draft legislation for a "Personal Privacy Act" that provides broad definitions for terms such as "intrusion" and would change the civil defamation law.

Hayden is drafting a "Paparazzi Harassment Act" that would enable courts to fine journalists engaging in behavior that was "threatening, intimidating, harassing, or causes alarm, harm or the potential of harm to any person who is the subject of media interest." Such behavior could be penalized even if it is unintentional.

Publishers who know or have reason to know of such behavior also would be liable. Pursuit of a story "of meaningful public interest" would be a recognized legal defense, says Hayden.

The draft legislation also calls for creating a Commission of Inquiry into Paparazzi Behavior to evaluate the impact of new technology, such as long-range telephoto lenses, on privacy and trespass laws; to study "the growth, behavior, structure, funding and ethics of the paparazzi and tabloid journalism"; and to explore ways to "preserve and enhance freedom of the press while curbing abusive practices that threaten legitimate privacy and safety rights."

Miami Herald Executive Editor Douglas C. Clifton thinks these laws could be passed, "given the state everyone seems to be in" following Diana's death. He is concerned that "political figures will use this as an opportunity to further restrict press coverage of public events."

Some journalists and attorneys are optimistic that such legislation won't be enacted because it is unconstitutional and unnecessary.

"There are enough laws on the books already to protect the privacy of public figures," says Cohen of FAIR. These include criminal laws dealing with assault, stalking and trespass, and civil remedies.

Hayden believes such laws are "insufficient." He compares these arguments to those used by opponents of sexual harassment laws, which he helped draft in California. "We heard all these same arguments—that women didn't need a specific sexual harassment statute, there was existing law," he says. But specific legislation was needed to deal with the unique circumstances surrounding date rape and domestic violence. Now, Hayden believes, special laws also need to be written to address the paparazzi's invasion of privacy.

Attorney Martin London disagrees. He argued in a New York Times op-ed piece that in 1973 he and other attorneys helped Jacqueline Kennedy Onassis get an injunction preventing photographer Ron Galella from approaching her or her children by asking a judge to apply principles in existing law "to the singular phenomenon of paparazzi." The injunction was tailored specifically to Onassis' situation. London urged other public figures to look to the court rather than the legislature for relief.

Some journalists believe the proposed laws would not stop the paparazzi. "Extremist photographers," says David R. Lutman, president of the National Press Photographers Association, believe "chancing arrest for breaking a minor law" is worth the risk, because they can make hundreds of thousands of dollars for a single picture. Lutman worries that the law will be used to stop other news photographers from pursuing legitimate stories.

Media analysts and attorneys also are concerned that the bills being considered by Congress and California lawmakers are the latest indication that privacy rights are superseding press rights.

"It seems more and more in our society that we want the right to be left alone to trump the right to know," says Paul McMasters, The Freedom Forum's First Amendment ombudsman. "If that happens, democracy is in real danger."

The proposed laws are the latest in a series of moves by legislatures and the courts to cite privacy as a reason for restricting newsgathering techniques. Some states restricted access to drivers' license information after a stalker obtained actress Rebecca Schaeffer's address from the California motor vehicle department and killed her in 1989. The federal government passed a similar law in 1994.

Some news outlets originally supported the drivers' license laws, not realizing these measures don't protect people from stalkers, says Jane Kirtley, executive director of the Reporters Committee for Freedom of the Press, but do provide governments with a rationale for declaring public records off-limits.

The courts also have moved to limit newsgathering. A federal judge in Pennsylvania granted an injunction last year prohibiting an "Inside Edition" team from following executives of a large health maintenance organization. The team was preparing a story on the large compensation packages paid to HMO executives.

The judge ruled that "the right to gather the news is not absolute," and that a jury would probably agree the team was not trying to obtain information for journalistic purposes, but for "entertaining background for their TV exposé."

Although "Inside Edition" frequently is referred to as a "tabloid" television show, it has won several journalism awards from groups such as Investigative Reporters & Editors.

The Freedom Forum's McMasters is "very troubled" by the "trend for the public to want judges and now legislatures to take on a new job of being editors and reporters." If the trend continues, he says, "it will be a travesty for the public" because "when you put shackles on news-gathering operations, it's across the board. It doesn't just apply in one place. Because a law that perhaps is meant to help a future Princess Diana will be used and abused by an elected official to restrict the kind of coverage that might expose corruption or malfeasance."

Some media analysts worry that these initiatives could erode journalists' privileges as well as protections.

Kovach of the Nieman Foundation expects that "rules and regulations that keep the press out, that restrict the press access both to institutions and to people in certain circumstances, are going to get a hell of a lot tighter."

Another development that jolted news organizations and their attorneys was the serious discussion of whether journalists —especially photographers—should be licensed.

Security consultant Gavin de Becker wrote in USA Today that "a person who chooses to earn money as a paparazzo should be required to obtain a permit, just like any street vendor. Permits could then be revoked for violations of the law.

Paparazzi want to call this a profession, so let's regulate it."

According to California State Sen. Diane Watson, the legislature is "looking at" licensing professional photographers.

"That is completely out of bounds in a country that values a free press," says RTNDA President Cochran. She points out that the licensing system used by the British crown to stifle the press in the 1700s was one reason the First Amendment was written.

But some mainstream journalists have unwittingly helped fuel the licensing debate by struggling to distinguish themselves from colleagues who work for the so-called "tabloid" press. USA Today White House Bureau Chief Susan Page told CNN's Frank Sesno that she didn't think "the paparazzi who pursued this car are part of the press, frankly."

Katharine Graham of the Washington Post Co. wrote in an essay published in the Post and Newsweek, "One point we all have to keep clear is that the paparazzi are different from the news media. The problem the paparazzi present will not be solved by abridging press freedom."

But pushing the distinction too hard is not without peril, says CNN executive Ed Turner. "This characterizing as 'legitimate' or 'not legitimate' seems to me to be a dangerous sort of road to travel" because such statements imply that restrictions on "irresponsible" journalists might be acceptable.

* * *

Many members of the public already believe restrictions on the press are acceptable. A survey last year by the Center for Media and Public Affairs showed 53 percent of the 3,000 respondents support licensing, and 70 percent favored court-imposed fines for inaccurate or biased reporting.

Some of these attitudes might result from ignorance. A 1997 Freedom Forum poll showed that 85 percent of respondents could not name press freedom as one of the five First Amendment freedoms.

But others arise from anger and resentment. That poll, and others during the past five years, show that a majority of Americans believe that special interests, such as corporate media owners and advertisers, as well as pressures for profits, improperly influence the way news is gathered and presented.

People's perception that the news media don't "seem to be serving their needs very well" is often correct, says Washington Post Ombudsman Geneva Overholser. "The trouble is that newspapers have become so profitable—profitable beyond any normal retailers' dreams—that the pressure on corporate executives to run them with an emphasis on the short term as opposed to the long term is just enormous."

This means "the debate is between enormous profit expectations... and the community's need to know, which requires real investment."

Advertisers contribute to the problem. They used to be interested in newspapers' mass market appeal, but now "think it's altruistic to service a wide readership," says Overholser. Advertisers want to attract wealthy, well-educated readers, so they want to place ads in sections where subjects aren't too controversial and have strong human interest components, she says.

Broadcast, cable and satellite media face similar pressures, which increase as they become subsidiaries in multinational conglomerates, some media analysts say. These corporations believe that "the marketplace sets the standard" for what is important, Kovach says.

Executives look at a picture of Princess Diana and ask, " 'What's the picture worth to us economically?' " says Kovach. "That has nothing to do with the journalistic value of it. It has to do with the uses they can put it to.

"All of those trends take journalism closer to entertainment values and further away from what I think are the values that justify the protection the First Amendment offers a free press."

Some news executives say not all corporations view information this way. Time magazine Managing Editor Isaacson says there "absolutely" is a wall between Time Warner's news and entertainment divisions. In the two years since he has been in his job, the magazine has done "fewer pure entertainment covers than were done in the '70s," Isaacson says.

The press has a moral obligation to balance profits and public benefits, because it is the only business given explicit constitutional protection, says Lutman of the National Press Photographers Association. "It isn't necessarily our responsibility to give people what they want, it's to give them what they need." Those who put profitability ahead of public service, he says, "are betraying our profession."

When the public senses this betrayal, its support for the media's First Amendment protections and privileges begins to decline, SPJ's Geimann points out. This sets up a climate in which legislatures, judges and juries feel justified in placing limits on the press.

"We the press depend on the public support for all the rights and liberties that are built into the Constitution and the Bill of Rights," he says. "When the public support disappears, our rights and liberties disappear."

McMasters believes journalists must address the situation quickly, because "the global nature of news today presents some unique challenges to the First Amendment."

As the American people gain access to news around the world via satellite television feeds and the Internet, they are questioning whether the restrictive laws of countries such as France and England do in fact lead to a more responsible press, he says.

This is why "freedom of the press in the United States depends as much on how we fulfill our responsibilities as they do on how we exercise our rights," says McMasters.

* * *

Journalism organizations initiated several projects during the past year to focus attention on the media's responsibilities and to look for ways to restore public confidence in the press.

The American Society of Newspaper Editors recently began a three-year project to examine how to increase the print media's credibility. The Society of Professional Journalists updated its code of ethics, adding a section on accountability, and is sponsoring ethics workshops at news organizations and professional conferences. The National Press Photographers Association plans to emphasize privacy issues during workshops and seminars.

CBS newsman Mike Wallace is leading a drive to establish a national news council that would consider complaints about the media. The Freedom Forum recently announced a major initiative to improve press fairness and freedom. The Nieman Foundation and the Project for Excellence in Journalism, funded by the Pew Charitable Trusts, have helped organize the Committee of Concerned Journalists, which hopes to clarify the purposes and principles that should guide the news media.

Several new programs involve public participation. The ASNE Journalism Credibility Project includes research partnerships with eight newspapers that will study creditability issues in their communities and implement solutions. The Freedom Forum's Free Press/Fair Press project will include town meetings and discussions with business leaders and minority groups.

The Committee of Concerned Journalists will hold public meetings as part of a "period of national reflection about journalism," says Nieman Curator Kovach, the committee chairman. The meetings will deal with issues such as "the meaning of news" at a time "when serious journalistic organizations drift toward opinion, infotainment and sensation," according to the committee's Statement of Concern. Any journalist can join the committee by signing its statement.

Doug Clifton of the Miami Herald believes that during such a period of reflection, a journalist should think about the First Amendment in terms of what it means to the American people. "They don't see us as defenders of their First Amendment freedom; they see us as protectors of a special legislation that permits us to make a profit," Clifton says.

McMasters has been surprised at how many journalists have "a real ignorance of what the First Amendment stands for," and how many do not understand the ethical responsibilities that come with the rights the press enjoys.

"Journalists," he says, "sometimes are the First Amendment's worst enemy."

NO

Philip Jones Griffiths

NO DI, NO PIX

In the delirium over Di's death it may seem unwise to reveal that photographing people without asking their permission is what I do for a living.

Of course, I do my best to be low-key, unthreatening and sensitive to people's feelings. This means I've sometimes lost a picture by not lifting the camera, but it also means I've never been abused by a subject and never ever been sued over a published photograph. Generally, the only annoyance I've received from a subject is when I've either not taken a picture or not taken enough. This is fairly normal—people love being photographed.

I think of myself as a privileged observer wandering the world recording what people do, documenting social behaviour, political shenanigans and the occasional war. I strive to be as compassionate as possible and humble enough to learn. As I cannot be invisible, I try to be unthreatening and sympathetic. If I had to ask the subject every time before pointing the lens, then the person would either do something different or appear self-conscious enough to sow doubt in the mind of the viewer that the subject was somehow 'performing', making any picture worthless.

Photography is a meaningless endeavour, without veracity. People believe photographs: they regard them as true and hence their power. It's a photograph we have in our passport, not a drawing—as George Bernard Shaw once declared: 'I would willingly exchange every painting of Christ for one snapshot!' The ability of, say Henri Cartier-Bresson's photographs to captivate, enlighten and inform relies on the fact that he photographs a 'real life' that the viewer can relate to, and not some models 'pretending'.

Picturing society, warts and all, quickly relegates the photographer to the unpopular role of critic. Unpopular, that is, with those responsible for the warts, popular with those concerned about them. The Lord Wakehams

From Philip Jones Griffiths, "No Di, No Pix," *Index on Censorship* (June 1997). Copyright © 1997 by Writers and Scholars International. Reprinted by permission of Index on Censorship. For more information, contact: +44 (171) 278 2313 (Tel.), +44 (171) 278 1878 (Fax), contact@indexoncensorship.org (e-mail), or visit Index on the Web at http://www.oneworld.org/index_oc.

of Hogarth's day were, I'm sure, anxiously looking for ways to prevent him from exposing the plight of the dispossessed although, as far as I know, no one invoked invasion of their privacy!

Nowadays, the dominant 'potent' media are firmly in the hands of multinational corporations, which control what we see and hear. Because democracies have enshrined the concept of the 'freedom of the press' in their constitutions, it is too embarrassing to be seen censoring news-gathering. By actually owning the media—and, as they say, the freedom of the press belongs to those that own one —corporate giants can regularly distort and censor news presentation to serve their requirements. As our minds are increasingly manipulated by imagery intended to subjugate us, the need for independent observers/critics is more compelling than ever.

The media moguls slipped up over Diana and they naturally want to appear eager to accept the restraints proposed by Wakeham. Restraints they will never observe, because they interfere with profits. Since when did respecting the royal family enhance Murdoch's wealth? In the meantime, the Wakeham proposals will act to restrict the independent observer with a camera—all in the name of protecting people's privacy.

The real invaders of privacy are big business and government. The supercomputers at Visa and American Express will have known in advance what purchases Di and Dodi would have made, had they lived. And they sell this information to anyone who can pay. For every person hounded by a paparazzo, a million are photographed in their cars by police and 10 million are videotaped in banks and public buildings. And none of those recorded want to be recorded, whereas most people pursued by paparazzi do. They employ public relations personnel to ensure that the photographers turn up at the right place at the right time.

A symbiotic relationship has always existed between personalities and their paparazzi. In today's world the famous would not be famous without exposure. For them, the more pictures, the greater the fame and power. No one should forget that there exists a direct relationship between each cubic metre of flowers placed before the palace and every square meter of photographs printed of the princess. The media inveigled the public with a torrent of hype about her, producing an appetite satiated only by ever more daring paparazzi production, which increased circulation, which in turn swelled the coffers of the proprietor. It was a closed loop in which everyone was a winner.

Diana's death requires a scapegoat. Although the verdict is not in, the photographers are considered guilty until proven innocent. One, ironically, is a colleague who risked legs, if not life, photographing victims in the minefields of Cambodia. Lord Wakeham has wacky proposals to protect privacy, proposals that include defining beaches as 'private places'! This should certainly liven them up when consenting adults with an exhibitionist streak get going.

It seems obvious to me that his proposals are the wrong answer to the wrong question. The issue of privacy is straightforward. Privacy is what you get when you are in a private place. Privacy is what you do not get in a public place. British law (up to now, at least) recognises this in as much as there is no specific offence known as 'invasion of privacy', only trespass.

For the photographer, anything seen in 'public' can be recorded but, in 'private' the subject's permission is needed.

The logic is impeccable: if you have sex with the curtains open, you lose your right to privacy and there is no hope of successfully suing a passing photographer. But, if a photographer broke into the house to get the picture, he would be punished for trespassing and we would all cheer.

POSTSCRIPT

Do Paparazzi Threaten Privacy and First Amendment Rights?

Many feel that neither the media industries nor the consuming public can escape blame in the case of Princess Diana's death. As Jerry Nachman, former editor in chief at the *New York Post* and former vice president for news at WCBS-TV, notes that the so-called elite press is also guilty. "Yet which of us has not published those now-cursed photographs? Our network news divisions and wire service news photo arms have aired and transmitted them all.... Our crime is not intrusiveness but hypocrisy. And the public has caught us."

However, to some extent, the debate concerning media excess is irrelevant to the inciting event, in this case, the death of Princess Diana and her companions. As Louis Boccardi, president and CEO of the Associated Press commented, "No, there should not be new laws governing coverage of public figures. No, nobody has a right to endanger human life to get a picture. If a crime was committed, the law should deal with it. Yes, the driver should not have been behind the wheel. We have much to deal with: public discourse has become coarser, tabloid influences make themselves felt more widely and more strongly, we operate in a culture of celebrity and glitz, mistrust has developed between us and some of the audience.... This tragedy will lead— it has already led—to worthwhile discussion of what we do and how we do it. I think, in the end, it will curb at least some of the worst excesses." (See *Columbia Journalism Review,* November 1997.)

Although press rights and responsibilities vary from country to country, a larger issue in the United States seems to be the public perception of abuses by the press of their First Amendment freedoms. From a journalistic perspective, the chilling insight is that the public seems quite willing to discuss limitations on the press that would limit press performance. Although there is a belief that the courts would not allow these regulations to stand, Steve Geimann, past president of the Society of Professional Journalists, warns, "We the press depend on the public support for all the rights and liberties that are built into the Constitution and the Bill of Rights. When the public support disappears, our rights and liberties disappear."

For more information on these complex issues of ethics, rights, and responsibilities, see *Media Ethics: Cases and Moral Reasoning,* 4th ed., by Clifford Christians, Mark Fackler, and Kim Rotzoll (Longman, 1995); *Media Ethics* by Conrad Fink (Prentice Hall, 1995); and *Electronic Media Ethics* by Val Limberg (Butterworth-Heinemann, 1994). Journals such as *Columbia Journalism Review* and *American Journalism Review* are excellent sources for articles on recent issues.

On the Internet . . .

http://www.dushkin.com

The Federal Communications Commission
This official site of the Federal Communications Commission (FCC) provides comprehensive information about U.S. federal media rules and guidelines.
http://www.fcc.gov/

Federal Communications Law Journal
This site is an online communications journal maintained by the Indiana University School of Law–Bloomington.
http://www.law.indiana.edu/fclj/pubs/pubs.html

Law Journal Extra! Media Law
This site features abundant resources in media law, including the most recent developments on this subject.
http://www.ljx.com/practice/media/index.html

PART 3

Regulation

For the media, the First Amendment entails both rights and responsibilities. How to ensure that these responsibilities will be met is the subject of much of communications law and legislative action. What are the valid limits of the rights of free speech and the press? How should society respond when First Amendment rights are in conflict with other individual rights? We interpret policies and laws by reflecting on specific precedents and by considering the implications of protectionist policies for long-term social change. The issues in this section deal with who should be responsible for media content and with the rights of groups who find this media content offensive.

■ Should Children Be Protected from Internet Pornography?

■ Are V-Chips and Content Ratings Necessary?

ISSUE 12

Should Children Be Protected from Internet Pornography?

YES: Philip Elmer-Dewitt, from "On a Screen Near You: Cyberporn," *Time* (July 3, 1995)

NO: Julia Wilkins, from "Protecting Our Children from Internet Smut: Moral Duty or Moral Panic?" *The Humanist* (September/October 1997)

ISSUE SUMMARY

YES: Philip Elmer-Dewitt, a technical issues writer, discusses a Carnegie-Mellon study indicating that the Internet has pornographic pictures and materials that are easily accessible to anyone. He describes efforts to control access to pornography and identifies how and why the issue is of such concern for parents of young children.

NO: Author Julia Wilkins refutes studies that purport to demonstrate children's easy access to Internet pornography, and she maintains that such studies contribute to an unwarranted moral panic about pornography.

In this issue we can see not only the problem of pornography on the Internet but the problems inherent in reporting a story when facts are misrepresented. As you read the following selections, think critically about the issue of pornography, Internet access, and the way certain terms and definitions can be used to influence the messages we see and hear. Consider this issue with regard to both regulation and the social impact of the framing of stories.

The Internet, or World Wide Web, has challenged traditional forms of communication media by the nature of the immediacy of the communicated message, the simultaneous participation of private communicators (like individuals) and commercial enterprises, practically unrestricted access to information sources stored on the service, and the availability of content to anonymous users. These factors have challenged the traditional regulatory system because they transcend many of the laws and standards of decency that have been debated with regard to other forms of communication media.

The availability of pornography on the Internet is an example of the type of content that has tested traditional legal boundaries. Without even attempting to define what pornography is, issues of traditional freedom of speech are inevitably called into question. The following selection by Philip Elmer-Dewitt calls attention to the Communications Decency Act (passed in 1996 and rescinded shortly thereafter). This act was a serious attempt to curb pornographic images on the Internet but was later deemed unconstitutional by the U.S. Supreme Court, largely because its scope was so broad that it limited freedom of speech.

In the second selection, Julia Wilkins explains why the Communications Decency Act was rescinded, but she also discusses why she feels the original report cited by Elmer-Dewitt inaccurately portrayed the problem of pornography and access by children. She goes on to explain other safeguards that are available to combat specific problems, but she emphasizes that panic can occur from misleading reports in the media.

Both authors raise questions of whether or not pornography is easily accessible and whether or not it should be controlled on the Internet. But both also demonstrate that journalists have a huge responsibility to carefully report stories and that we, as consumers of media, should question what we see and hear.

YES   Philip Elmer-Dewitt

ON A SCREEN NEAR YOU: CYBERPORN

Sex is everywhere these days—in books, magazines, films, television, music videos and bus-stop perfume ads. It is printed on dial-a-porn business cards and slipped under windshield wipers. It is acted out by balloon-breasted models and actors with unflagging erections, then rented for $4 a night at the corner video store. Most Americans have become so inured to the open display of eroticism—and the arguments for why it enjoys special status under the First Amendment—thay they hardly notice it's there.

Something about the combination of sex and computers, however, seems to make otherwise worldly-wise adults a little crazy. How else to explain the uproar surrounding the discovery by a U.S. Senator—Nebraska Democrat James Exon—that pornographic pictures can be downloaded from the Internet and displayed on a home computer? This, as any computer-savvy undergrad can testify, is old news. Yet suddenly the press is on alert, parents and teachers are up in arms, and lawmakers in Washington are rushing to ban the smut from cyberspace with new legislation—sometimes with little regard to either its effectiveness or its constitutionality.

If you think things are crazy now, though, wait until the politicians get hold of a report coming out this week. A research team at Carnegie Mellon University in Pittsburgh, Pennsylvania, has conducted an exhaustive study of online porn—what's available, who is downloading it, what turns them on—and the findings (to be published in the *Georgetown Law Journal*) are sure to pour fuel on an already explosive debate.

The study, titled *Marketing Pornography on the Information Superhighway*, is significant not only for what it tells us about what's happening on the computer networks but also for what it tells us about ourselves. Pornography's appeal is surprisingly elusive. It plays as much on fear, anxiety, curiosity and taboo as on genuine eroticism. The Carnegie Mellon study, drawing on elaborate computer records of online activity, was able to measure for the first time what people actually download, rather than what they say they want to see. "We now know what the consumers of computer pornography really look at in the privacy of their own homes," says Marty Rimm, the study's principal investigator. "And we're finding a fundamental shift in the kinds of images they demand."

What the Carnegie Mellon researchers discovered was:

There's an awful lot of porn online. In an 18-month study, the team surveyed 917,410 sexually explicit pictures, descriptions, short stories and film clips. On those Usenet newsgroups where digitized images are stored, 83.5% of the pictures were pornographic.

It is immensely popular. Trading in sexually explicit imagery, according to the report, is now "one of the largest (if not the largest) recreational applications of users of computer networks." At one U.S. university, 13 of the 40 most frequently visited newsgroups had names like *alt.sex.stories, rec.arts.erotica* and *alt.sex.bondage.*

It is a big moneymaker. The great majority (71%) of the sexual images on the newsgroups surveyed originate from adult-oriented computer bulletin-board systems (BBS) whose operators are trying to lure customers to their private collections of X-rated material. There are thousands of these BBS services, which charge fees (typically $10 to $30 a month) and take credit cards; the five largest have annual revenues in excess of $1 million.

It is ubiquitous. Using data obtained with permission from BBS operators, the Carnegie Mellon team identified (but did not publish the names of) individual consumers in more than 2,000 cities in all 50 states and 40 countries, territories and provinces around the world—including some countries like China, where possession of pornography can be a capital offense.

It is a guy thing. According to the BBS operators, 98.9% of the consumers of online porn are men. And there is some evidence that many of the remaining 1.1% are women paid to hang out on the "chat" rooms and bulletin boards to make the patrons feel more comfortable.

It is not just naked women. Perhaps because hard-core sex pictures are so widely available elsewhere, the adult BBS market seems to be driven largely by a demand for images that can't be found in the average magazine rack: pedophilia (nude photos of children), hebephilia (youths) and what the researchers call paraphilia—a grab bag of "deviant" material that includes images of bondage, sadomasochism, urination, defecation, and sex acts with a barnyard full of animals.

The appearance of material like this on a public network accessible to men, women and children around the world raises issues too important to ignore—or to oversimplify. Parents have legitimate concerns about what their kids are being exposed to and, conversely, what those children might miss if their access to the Internet were cut off. Lawmakers must balance public safety with their obligation to preserve essential civil liberties. Men and women have to come to terms with what draws them to such images. And computer programmers have to come up with more enlightened ways to give users control over a network that is, by design, largely out of control.

The Internet, of course, is more than a place to find pictures of people having sex with dogs. It's a vast marketplace of ideas and information of all sorts—on politics, religion, science and technology. If the fast-growing World Wide Web fulfills its early promise, the network could be a powerful engine of economic growth in the 21st century. And as the Carnegie Mellon study is careful to point out, pornographic image files, despite their evident popularity, represent only about 3% of all the messages on the Usenet newsgroups, while the Usenet itself represents only 11.5% of the traffic on the Internet.

As shocking and, indeed, legally obscene as some of the online porn may be, the researchers found nothing that can't be found in specialty magazines or adult bookstores. Most of the material offered by the private BBS services, in fact, is simply scanned from existing print publications.

But pornography is different on the computer networks. You can obtain it in the privacy of your home—without having to walk into a seedy bookstore or movie house. You can download only those things that turn you on, rather than buy an entire magazine or video. You can explore different aspects of your sexuality without exposing yourself to communicable diseases or public ridicule. (Unless, of course, someone gets hold of the computer files tracking your online activities, as happened earlier this year to a couple dozen crimson-faced Harvard students.)

The great fear of parents and teachers, of course, is not that college students will find this stuff but that it will fall into the hands of those much younger —including some, perhaps, who are not emotionally prepared to make sense of what they see.

Ten-year-old Anders Urmacher, a student at the Dalton School in New York City who likes to hang out with other kids in the Treehouse chat room on America Online, got E-mail from a stranger that contained a mysterious file with instructions for how to download it. He followed the instructions, and then he called his mom. When Linda Mann-Urmacher opened the file, the computer screen filled with 10 thumbnail-size pictures showing couples engaged in various acts of sodomy, heterosexual intercourse and lesbian sex. "I was not aware that this stuff was online," says a shocked Mann-Urmacher. "Children should not be subjected to these images."

This is the flip side of Vice President Al Gore's vision of an information superhighway linking every school and library in the land. When the kids are plugged in, will they be exposed to the seamiest sides of human sexuality? Will they fall prey to child molesters hanging out in electronic chat rooms?

It's precisely these fears that have stopped Bonnie Fell of Skokie, Illinois, from signing up for the Internet access her three boys say they desperately need. "They could get bombarded with X-rated porn, and I wouldn't have any idea," she says. Mary Veed, a mother of three from nearby Hinsdale, makes a point of trying to keep up with her computer-literate 12-year-old, but sometimes has to settle for monitoring his phone bill. "Once they get to be a certain age, boys don't always tell Mom what they do," she says.

"We face a unique, disturbing and urgent circumstance, because it is children who are the computer experts in our nation's families," said Republican Senator Dan Coats of Indiana during the debate over the controversial anti-cyberporn bill he co-sponsored with Senator Exon.

According to at least one of those experts—16-year-old David Slifka of Manhattan—the danger of being bombarded with unwanted pictures is greatly exaggerated. "If you don't want them you won't get them," says the veteran Internet surfer. Private adult BBSs require proof of age (usually a driver's license) and are off-limits to minors, and kids have to master some fairly daunting computer science before they can turn so-called binary files on the Usenet into high-resolution color pictures. "The chances of randomly coming across them are unbelievably slim," says Slifka.

While groups like the Family Research Council insist that online child molesters represent a clear and present danger, there is no evidence that it is any greater than the thousand other threats children face every day. Ernie Allen, executive director of the National Center for Missing and Exploited Children, acknowledges that there have been 10 to 12 "fairly high-profile cases" in the past year of children being seduced or lured online into situations where they are victimized. Kids who are not online are also at risk, however; more than 800,000 children are reported missing every year in the U.S.

Yet it is in the name of the children and their parents that lawmakers are racing to fight cyberporn. The first blow was struck by Senators Exon and Coats, who earlier this year introduced revisions to an existing law called the Communications Decency Act. The idea was to extend regulations written to govern the dial-a-porn industry into the computer networks. The bill proposed to outlaw obscene material and impose fines of up to $100,000 and prison terms of up to two years on anyone who knowingly makes "indecent" material available to children under 18.

The measure had problems from the start. In its original version it would have made online-service providers criminally liable for any obscene communications that passed through their systems—a provision that, given the way the networks operate, would have put the entire Internet at risk. Exon and Coats revised the bill but left in place the language about using "indecent" words online. "It's a frontal assault on the First Amendment," says Harvard law professor Laurence Tribe. Even veteran prosecutors ridicule it. "It won't pass scrutiny even in misdemeanor court," says one.

The Exon bill had been written off for dead only a few weeks ago. Republican Senator Larry Pressler of South Dakota, chairman of the Commerce committee, which has jurisdiction over the larger telecommunications-reform act to which it is attached, told TIME that he intended to move to table it.

That was before Exon showed up in the Senate with his "blue book." Exon had asked a friend to download some of the rawer images available online. "I knew it was bad," he says. "But then when I got on there, it made *Playboy* and *Hustler* look like Sunday-school stuff." He had the images printed out, stuffed them in a blue folder and invited his colleagues to stop by his desk on the Senate floor to view them. At the end of the debate—which was carried live on C-SPAN—few Senators wanted to cast a nationally televised vote that might later be characterized as pro-pornography. The bill passed 84 to 16.

Civil libertarians were outraged. Mike Godwin, staff counsel for the Electronic Frontier Foundation, complained that the indecency portion of the bill would transform the vast library of the Internet into a children's reading room, where only subjects suitable for kids could be discussed. "It's government censorship," said Marc Rotenberg of the Electronic Privacy Information Center. "The First Amendment shouldn't end where the Internet begins."

The key issue, according to legal scholars, is whether the Internet is a print medium (like a newspaper), which enjoys strong protection against government interference, or a broadcast medium (like television), which may be subject to all sorts of government control. Perhaps the most significant import of the Exon bill, according to EFF's Godwin, is that it would place the computer networks under the jurisdiction of the Federal Communications Commission, which enforces, among other rules, the injunction against using the famous seven dirty words on the radio. In a TIME/CNN poll of 1,000 Americans conducted last week sharply split on the issue: 42% were for FCC-like control over sexual content on the computer networks; 48% were against it.

By week's end the balance between protecting speech and curbing pornography seemed to be tipping back toward the libertarians. In a move that surprised conservative supporters, House Speaker Newt Gingrich denounced the Exon amendment. "It is clearly a violation of free speech, and it's a violation of the right of adults to communicate with each other," he told a caller on a cable-TV show. It was a key defection, because Gingrich will preside over the computer-decency debate when it moves to the House in July. Meanwhile, two U.S. Representatives, Republican Christopher Cox of California and Democrat Ron Wyden of Oregon, were putting together an anti-Exon amendment that would bar federal regulation of the Internet and help parents find ways to block material they found objectionable.

Coincidentally, in the closely watched case of a University of Michigan student who published a violent sex fantasy on the Internet and was charged with transmitting a threat to injure or kidnap across state lines, a federal judge in Detroit last week dismissed the charges. The judge ruled that while Jake Baker's story might be deeply offensive, it was not a crime.

How the Carnegie Mellon report will affect the delicate political balance on the cyberporn debate is anybody's guess. Conservatives thumbing through it for rhetorical ammunition will find plenty. Appendix B lists the most frequently downloaded files from a popular adult BBS, providing both the download count and the two-line descriptions posted by the board's operator. Suffice it to say that they all end in exclamation points, many include such phrases as "nailed to a table!" and none can be printed in TIME.

How accurately these images reflect America's sexual interests, however, is a matter of some dispute. University of Chicago sociologist Edward Laumann, whose 1994 *Sex in America* survey painted a far more humdrum picture of America's sex life, says the Carnegie Mellon study may have captured what he calls the "gaper phenomenon." "There is a curiosity for things that are extraordinary and way out," he says. "It's like driving by a horrible accident. No one wants to be in it, but we all slow down to watch."

Other sociologists point out that the difference between the Chicago and Carnegie Mellon reports may be more apparent than real. Those 1 million or 2 million people who download pictures from the Internet represent a self-selected group with an interest in erotica. The

Sex in America respondents, by contrast, were a few thousand people selected to represent a cross section of all America.

Still, the new research is a gold mine for psychologists, social scientists, computer marketers and anybody with an interest in human sexual behavior. Every time computer users logged on to one of these bulletin boards, they left a digital trail of their transactions, allowing the pornographers to compile data bases about their buying habits and sexual tastes. The more sophisticated operators were able to adjust their inventory and their descriptions to match consumer demand.

Nobody did this more effectively than Robert Thomas, owner of the Amateur Action BBS in Milpitas, California, and a kind of modern-day Marquis de Sade, according to the Carnegie Mellon report. He is currently serving time in an obscenity case that may be headed for the Supreme Court.

Thomas, whose BBS is the online-porn market leader, discovered that he could boost sales by trimming soft- and hard-core images from his data base while front-loading his files with pictures of sex acts with animals (852) and nude prepubescent children (more than 5,000), his two most popular categories of porn. He also used copywriting tricks to better serve his customers' fantasies. For example, he described more than 1,200 of his pictures as depicting sex scenes between family members (father and daughter, mother and son), even though there was no evidence that any of the participants were actually related. These "incest" images were among his biggest sellers, accounting for 10% of downloads.

The words that worked were sometimes quite revealing. Straightforward oral sex, for example, generally got a lukewarm response. But when Thomas described the same images using words like choke or choking, consumer demand doubled.

Such findings may cheer antipornography activists; as feminist writer Andrea Dworkin puts it, "the whole purpose of pornography is to hurt women." Catherine MacKinnon, a professor of law at the University of Michigan, goes further. Women are doubly violated by pornography, she writes in *Vindication and Resistance*, one of three essays in the forthcoming *Georgetown Law Journal* that offer differing views on the Carnegie Mellon report. They are violated when it is made and exposed to further violence again and again every time it is consumed. "The question pornography poses in cyberspace," she writes, "is the same one it poses everywhere else: whether anything will be done about it."

But not everyone agrees with Dworkin and MacKinnon, by any means; even some feminists think there is a place in life—and the Internet—for erotica. In her new book, *Defending Pornography,* Nadine Strossen argues that censoring sexual expression would do women more harm than good, undermining their equality, their autonomy and their freedom.

The Justice Department, for its part, has not asked for new antiporn legislation. Distributing obscene material across state lines is already illegal under federal law, and child pornography in particular is vigorously prosecuted. Some 40 people in 14 states were arrested two years ago in Operation Longarm for exchanging kiddie porn online. And one of the leading characters in the Carnegie Mellon study—a former Rand McNally executive named Robert Copella, who left book publishing to make his fortune selling pedophilia on the networks—was extradited from Tijuana, and is now awaiting sentencing in a New Jersey jail.

* * *

For technical reasons, it is extremely difficult to stamp out anything on the Internet—particularly images stored on the Usenet newsgroups. As Internet pioneer John Gilmore famously put it, "The Net interprets censorship as damage and routes around it." There are border issues as well. Other countries on the Internet—France, for instance—are probably no more interested in having their messages screened by U.S. censors than Americans would be in having theirs screened by, say, the government of Saudi Arabia.

Historians say it should come as no surprise that the Internet—the most democratic of media—would lead to new calls for censorship. The history of pornography and efforts to suppress it are inextricably bound up with the rise of new media and the emergence of democracy. According to Walter Kendrick, author of *The Secret Museum: Pornography in Modern Culture,* the modern concept of pornography was invented in the 19th century by European gentlemen whose main concern was to keep obscene material away from women and the lower classes. Things got out of hand with the spread of literacy and education, which made pornography available to anybody who could read. Now, on the computer networks, anybody with a computer and a modem can not only consume pornography but distribute it as well. On the Internet, anybody can be Bob Guccione.

That might not be a bad idea, says Carlin Meyer, a professor at New York Law School whose *Georgetown* essay takes a far less apocalyptic view than MacKinnon's. She argues that if you don't like the images of sex the pornographers offer, the appropriate response is not to suppress them but to overwhelm them with healthier, more realistic ones. Sex on the Internet, she maintains, might actually be good for young people. "[Cyberspace] is a safe space in which to explore the forbidden and the taboo," she writes. "It offers the possibility for genuine, unembarrassed conversations about *accurate* as well as fantasy images of sex."

That sounds easier than it probably is. Pornography is powerful stuff, and as long as there is demand for it, there will always be a supply. Better software tools may help check the worst abuses, but there will never be a switch that will cut it off entirely—not without destroying the unbridled expression that is the source of the Internet's (and democracy's) greatest strength. The hard truth, says John Perry Barlow, cofounder of the EFF and father of three young daughters, is that the burden ultimately falls where it always has: on the parents. "If you don't want your children fixating on filth," he says, "better step up to the tough task of raising them to find it as distasteful as you do yourself."

NO

Julia Wilkins

PROTECTING OUR CHILDREN FROM INTERNET SMUT: MORAL DUTY OR MORAL PANIC?

The term *moral panic* is one of the more useful concepts to have emerged from sociology in recent years. A moral panic is characterized by a wave of public concern, anxiety, and fervor about something, usually perceived as a threat to society. The distinguishing factors are a level of interest totally out of proportion to the real importance of the subject, some individuals building personal careers from the pursuit and magnification of the issue, and the replacement of reasoned debate with witchhunts and hysteria.

Moral panics of recent memory include the Joseph McCarthy anti-communist witchhunts of the 1950s and the satanic ritual abuse allegations of the 1980s. And, more recently, we have witnessed a full-blown moral panic about pornography on the Internet. Sparked by the July 3, 1995, *Time* cover article "On a Screen Near You: Cyberporn," this moral panic has been perpetuated and intensified by a raft of subsequent media reports. As a result, there is now a widely held belief that pornography is easily accessible to all children using the Internet. This was also the judgment of Congress, which, proclaiming to be "protecting the children," voted overwhelmingly in 1996 for legislation to make it a criminal offense to send "indecent" material over the Internet into people's computers.

The original *Time* article was based on its exclusive access to Marty Rimm's *Georgetown University Law Journal* paper, "Marketing Pornography on the Information Superhighway." Although published, the article had not received peer review and was based on an undergraduate research project concerning descriptions of images on adult bulletin board systems in the United States. Using the information in this paper, *Time* discussed the type of pornography available online, such as "pedophilia (nude pictures of children), hebephelia (youths) and ... images of bondage, sadomasochism, urination, defecation, and sex acts with a barnyard full of animals." The article proposed that pornography of this nature is readily available to anyone who is even remotely computer literate and raised the stakes by offering quotes from worried parents who feared for their children's safety. It also presented the possibility that pornographic material could be mailed to children without their

From Julia Wilkins, "Protecting Our Children from Internet Smut: Moral Duty or Moral Panic?" *The Humanist* (September/October 1997). Copyright © 1997 by Julia Wilkins. Reprinted by permission of the author.

parents' knowledge. *Time*'s example was of a ten-year-old boy who supposedly received pornographic images in his e-mail showing "10 thumbnail size pictures showing couples engaged in various acts of sodomy, heterosexual intercourse and lesbian sex." Naturally, the boy's mother was shocked and concerned, saying, "Children should not be subject to these images." *Time* also quoted another mother who said that she wanted her children to benefit from the vast amount of knowledge available on the Internet but was inclined not to allow access, fearing that her children could be "bombarded with X-rated pornography and [she] would know nothing about it."

From the outset, Rimm's report generated a lot of excitement—not only because it was reportedly the first published study of online pornography but also because of the secrecy involved in the research and publication of the article. In fact, the *New York Times* reported on July 24, 1995, that Marty Rimm was being investigated by his university, Carnegie Mellon, for unethical research and, as a result, would not be giving testimony to a Senate hearing on Internet pornography. Two experts from *Time* reportedly discovered serious flaws in Rimm's study involving gross misrepresentation and erroneous methodology. His work was soon deemed flawed and inaccurate, and *Time* recanted in public. With Rimm's claims now apologetically retracted, his original suggestion that 83.5 percent of Internet graphics are pornographic was quietly withdrawn in favor of a figure less than 1 percent.

Time admitted that grievous errors had slipped past their editorial staff, as their normally thorough research succumbed to a combination of deadline pressure and exclusivity agreements that barred them from showing the unpublished study to possible critics. But, by then, the damage had been done: the study had found its way to the Senate.

GOVERNMENT INTERVENTION

Senator Charles Grassley (Republican–Iowa) jumped on the pornography bandwagon by proposing a bill that would make it a criminal offense to supply or permit the supply of "indecent" material to minors over the Internet. Grassley introduced the entire *Time* article into the congressional record, despite the fact that the conceptual, logical, and methodological flaws in the report had already been acknowledged by the magazine.

On the Senate floor, Grassley referred to Marty Rimm's undergraduate research as "a remarkable study conducted by researchers at Carnegie Mellon University" and went on to say:

> The university surveyed 900,000 computer images. Of these 900,000 images, 83.5 percent of all computerized photographs available on the Internet are pornographic.... With so many graphic images available on computer networks, I believe Congress must act and do so in a constitutional manner to help parents who are under assault in this day and age.

Under the Grassley bill, later known as the Protection of Children from Pornography Act of 1995, it would have been illegal for anyone to knowingly or recklessly transmit indecent material to minors. This bill marked the beginning of a stream of Internet censorship legislation at various levels of government in the United States and abroad.

The most extreme and fiercely opposed of these was the Communications Decency Act, sponsored by former Senator James Exon (Democrat–Nebraska) and Senator Dan Coats (Republican–Indiana). The CDA labeled the transmission of "obscene, lewd, lascivious, filthy, indecent, or patently offensive" pornography over the Internet a crime. It was attached to the Telecommunications Reform Act of 1996, which was then passed by Congress on February 1, 1996. One week later, it was signed into law by President Clinton. On the same day, the American Civil Liberties Union filed suit in Philadelphia against the U.S. Department of Justice and Attorney General Janet Reno, arguing that the statute would ban free speech protected by the First Amendment and subject Internet users to far greater restrictions than exist in any other medium. Later that month, the Citizens Internet Empowerment Coalition initiated a second legal challenge to the CDA, which formally consolidated with *ACLU v. Reno.* Government lawyers agreed not to prosecute "indecent" or "patently offensive" material until the three-judge court in Philadelphia ruled on the case.

Although the purpose of the CDA was to protect young children from accessing and viewing material of sexually explicit content on the Internet, the wording of the act was so broad and poorly defined that it could have deprived many adults of information they needed in the areas of health, art, news, and literature —information that is legal in print form. Specifically, certain medical information available on the Internet includes descriptions of sexual organs and activities which might have been considered "indecent" or "patently offensive" under the act—for example, information on breastfeeding, birth control, AIDS, and gynecological and urinological information. Also, many museums and art galleries

now have websites. Under the act, displaying art like the Sistine Chapel nudes could be cause for criminal prosecution. Online newspapers would not be permitted to report the same information as is available in the print media. Reports on combatants in war, at the scenes of crime, in the political arena, and outside abortion clinics often provoke images or language that could be constituted "offensive" and therefore illegal on the net. Furthermore, the CDA provided a legal basis for banning books which had been ruled unconstitutional to ban from school libraries. These include many of the classics as well as modern literature containing words that may be considered "indecent."

The act also expanded potential liability for employers, service providers, and carriers that transmit or otherwise make available restricted communications. According to the CDA, "knowingly" allowing obscene material to pass through one's computer system was a criminal offense. Given the nature of the Internet, however, making service providers responsible for the content of the traffic they pass on to other Internet nodes is equivalent to holding a telephone carrier responsible for the content of the conversations going over that carrier's lines. So, under the terms of the act, if someone sent an indecent electronic comment from a workstation, the employer, the e-mail service provider, and the carrier all could be potentially held liable and subject to up to $100,000 in fines or two years in prison.

On June 12, 1996, after experiencing live tours of the Internet and hearing arguments about the technical and economical infeasibility of complying with the censorship law, the three federal judges in Philadelphia granted the request for a preliminary injunction against the CDA.

The court determined that "there is no evidence that sexually oriented material is the primary type of content on this new medium" and proposed that "communications over the Internet do not 'invade' an individual's home or appear on one's computer screen unbidden. Users seldom encounter content 'by accident.'" In a unanimous decision, the judges ruled that the Communications Decency Act would unconstitutionally restrict free speech on the Internet.

The government appealed the judges' decision and, on March 19, 1997, the U.S. Supreme Court heard oral arguments in the legal challenge to the CDA, now known as *Reno v. ACLU.* Finally, on June 26, the decision came down. The Court voted unanimously that the act violated the First Amendment guarantee of freedom of speech and would have threatened "to torch a large segment of the Internet community."

Is the panic therefore over? Far from it. The July 7, 1997, *Newsweek,* picking up the frenzy where *Time* left off, reported the Supreme Court decision in a provocatively illustrated article featuring a color photo of a woman licking her lips and a warning message taken from the website of the House of Sin. Entitled "On the Net, Anything Goes," the opening words by Steven Levy read, "Born of a hysteria triggered by a genuine problem—the ease with which wired-up teenagers can get hold of nasty pictures on the Internet—the Communications Decency Act (CDA) was never really destined to be a companion piece to the Bill of Rights." At the announcement of the Court's decision, anti-porn protesters were on the street outside brandishing signs which read, "Child Molesters Are Looking for Victims on the Internet."

Meanwhile, government talk has shifted to the development of a universal Internet rating system and widespread hardware and software filtering. Referring to the latter, White House Senior Adviser Rahm Emanuel declared, "We're going to get the V-chip for the Internet. Same goal, different means."

But it is important to bear in mind that children are still a minority of Internet users. A contract with an Internet service provider typically needs to be paid for by credit card or direct debit, therefore requiring the intervention of an adult. Children are also unlikely to be able to view any kind of porn online without a credit card.

In addition to this, there have been a variety of measures developed to protect children on the Internet. The National Center for Missing and Exploited Children has outlined protective guidelines for parents and children in its pamphlet, *Child Safety on the Information Superhighway.* A number of companies now sell Internet newsfeeds and web proxy accesses that are vetted in accordance with a list of forbidden topics. And, of course, there remain those blunt software instruments that block access to sexually oriented sites by looking for keywords such as *sex, erotic,* and *X-rated.* But one of the easiest solutions is to keep the family computer in a well-traveled space, like a living room, so that parents can monitor what their children download.

FACT OR MEDIA FICTION?

In her 1995 *CMC* magazine article, "Journey to the Centre of Cybersmut," Lisa Schmeiser discusses her research into online pornography. After an exhaustive search, she was unable to find any pornography, apart from the occasional commercial site (requiring a credit card for access), and concluded that one would have to undertake extensive searching to find quantities of explicit pornography. She suggested that, if children were accessing pornography online, they would not have been doing it by accident. Schmeiser writes: "There will be children who circumvent passwords, Surfwatch software, and seemingly innocuous links to find the 'adult' material. But these are the same kids who would visit every convenience store in a five-mile radius to find the one stocking *Playboy*." Her argument is simply that, while there is a certain amount of pornography online, it is not freely and readily available. Contrary to what the media often report, pornography is not that easy to find.

There *is* pornography in cyberspace (including images, pictures, movies, sounds, and sex discussions) and several ways of receiving pornographic material on the Internet (such as through private bulletin board systems, the World Wide Web, newsgroups, and e-mail). However, many sites just contain reproduced images from hardcore magazines and videos available from other outlets, and registration fee restrictions make them inaccessible to children. And for the more contentious issue of pedophilia, a recent investigation by the *Guardian* newspaper in Britain revealed that the majority of pedophilic images distributed on the Internet are simply electronic reproductions of the small output of legitimate pedophile magazines, such as *Lolita*, published in the 1970s.

Clearly the issue of pornography on the Internet is a moral panic—an issue perpetuated by a sensationalistic style of reporting and misleading content in newspaper and magazine articles. And

probably the text from which to base any examination of the possible link between media reporting and moral panics is Stanley Cohen's 1972 book, *Folk Devils and Moral Panic*, in which he proposes that the mass media are ultimately responsible for the creation of such panics. Cohen describes a moral panic as occurring when "a condition, episode, person or group of persons emerges to become a threat to societal values and interests;... the moral barricades are manned by editors... politicians and other 'right thinking' people." He feels that, while problematical elements of society can pose a threat to others, this threat is realistically far less than the perceived image generated by mass media reporting.

Cohen describes how the news we read is not necessarily the truth; editors have papers to sell, targets to meet, and competition from other publishers. It is in their interest to make the story "a good read"—the sensationalist approach sells newspapers. The average person is likely to be drawn in with the promise of scandal and intrigue. This can be seen in the reporting of the *National Enquirer* and *People*, with their splashy pictures and sensationalistic headlines, helping them become two of the largest circulation magazines in the United States.

Cohen discusses the "inventory" as the set of criteria inherent in any reporting that may be deemed as fueling a moral panic. This inventory consists of the following:

Exaggeration in reporting. Facts are often overblown to give the story a greater edge. Figures that are not necessarily incorrect but have been quoted out of context, or have been used incorrectly to shock, are two forms of this exaggeration.

Looking back at the original *Time* cover article, "On a Screen Near You: Cyberporn," this type of exaggeration is apparent. Headlines such as "The Carnegie Mellon researches found 917,410 sexually explicit pictures, short stories and film clips online" make the reader think that there really is a problem with the quantity of pornography in cyberspace. It takes the reader a great deal of further exploration to find out how this figure was calculated. Also, standing alone and out of context, the oft-quoted figure that 83.5 percent of images found on Usenet Newsgroups are pornographic could be seen as cause for concern. However, if one looks at the math associated with this figure, one would find that this is a sampled percentage with a research leaning toward known areas of pornography.

The repetition of fallacies. This occurs when a writer reports information that seems perfectly believable to the general public, even though those who know the subject are aware it is wildly incorrect. In the case of pornography, the common fallacy is that the Internet is awash with nothing but pornography and that all you need to obtain it is a computer and a modem. Such misinformation is integral to the fueling of moral panics.

Take, for example, the October 18, 1995, *Scotland on Sunday,* which reports that, to obtain pornographic material, "all you need is a personal computer, a phone line with a modem attached and a connection via a specialist provider to the Internet." What the article fails to mention is that the majority of pornography is found on specific Usenet sites not readily available from the major Internet providers, such as America Online and Compuserve. It also fails to mention that this pornography needs to be downloaded and converted into a viewable form, which requires certain skills and can take considerable time.

Misleading pictures and snappy titles. Media representation often exaggerates a story through provocative titles and flashy pictorials—all in the name of drawing in the reader. The titles set the tone for the rest of the article; the headline is the most noticeable and important part of any news item, attracting the reader's initial attention. The recent *Newsweek* article is a perfect example. Even if the headline has little relevance to the article, it sways the reader's perception of the topic. The symbolization of images further increases the impact of the story. *Time*'s own images in its original coverage—showing a shocked little boy on the cover and, inside, a naked man hunched over a computer monitor—added to the article's ability to shock and to draw the reader into the story.

Through sensationalized reporting, certain forms of behavior become classified as *deviant.* Specifically, those who put pornography online or those who download it are seen as being deviant in nature. This style of reporting benefits the publication or broadcast by giving it the aura of "moral guardian" to the rest of society. It also increases revenue.

In exposing deviant behavior, newspapers and magazines have the ability to push for reform. So, by classifying a subject and its relevant activities as deviant, they can stand as crusaders for moral decency, championing the cause of "normal" people. They can report the subject and call for something to be done about it, but this power is easily abused. The *Time* cyberporn article called for reform on the basis of Rimm's findings, proclaiming, "A new study shows us how pervasive and wild [pornography on the Internet] really is. Can we protect our kids —and free speech?" These cries to protect our children affected the likes of Senators James Exon and Robert Dole, who took the *Time* article with its "shocking" revelations (as well as a sample of pornographic images) to the Senate floor, appealing for changes to the law. From this response it is clear how powerful a magazine article can be, regardless of the integrity and accuracy of its reporting.

The *Time* article had all of Cohen's elements relating to the fueling of a moral panic: exaggeration, fallacies, and misleading pictures and titles. Because certain publications are highly regarded and enjoy an important role in society, anything printed in their pages is consumed and believed by a large audience. People accept what they read because, to the best of their knowledge, it is the truth. So, even though the *Time* article was based on a report by an undergraduate student passing as "a research team from Carnegie Mellon," the status of the magazine was great enough to launch a panic that continues unabated—from the halls of Congress to the pulpits of churches, from public schools to the offices of software developers, from local communities to the global village.

POSTSCRIPT

Should Children Be Protected from Internet Pornography?

There will probably be many attempts to create some type of control over content on the Internet in the near future, but these decisions will undoubtedly be difficult and controversial. Many decisions may be made at the international level with regard to intercountry flow of information and through privacy legislation. Parents can purchase software "locks" to protect children from accessing some types of content, but even these are not effective all of the time.

While there is much social debate about questionable content on the Internet, there are also many "tests" of content, which may result in additional forms of regulation or control. Purchasing goods over the Internet has recently spawned a number of initiatives in controlling credit card numbers, access to purchasing records, and other issues that have not been presented through other communication forms. As the number of questions, possible answers, and perspectives increases, it will become even more difficult to enact controls that do not affect other uses.

There are many public debates on these issues presented in the media today. *Wired* magazine is an excellent resource for a number of perspectives on issues dealing with computers and the Internet. Kevin Kelly, executive editor of *Wired*, has collected a number of good essays in a book entitled *Out of Control* (Addison-Wesley, 1992). A different perspective is offered by Brian Kahin and James Keller, who have edited *Public Access to the Internet* (MIT Press, 1995), which features articles that focus on the benefits of Internet use.

Pornography also presents an important topic for thought. Deciding exactly *what* is pornographic forces us to make some moral choices. Some recent publications dealing with this subject include Nicholas Wolfson's *Hate Speech, Sex Speech, Free Speech* (Praeger, 1997) and Jane M. Ussher's *Fantasies of Femininity: Reframing the Boundaries of Sex* (Rutgers University Press, 1997).

ISSUE 13

Are V-Chips and Content Ratings Necessary?

YES: Joseph Lieberman, from "Why Parents Hate TV," *Policy Review* (May/June 1996)

NO: Jon Katz, from *Virtuous Reality* (Random House, 1997)

ISSUE SUMMARY

YES: Senator Joseph Lieberman (D-Connecticut), coauthor of the Parental Empowerment Act, outlines the history of arrogance and unconcern on the part of network and program executives when faced by parents and policy-makers. He argues that this history makes legislation necessary in order to bring about responsible reaction to valid social concerns.

NO: Media critic Jon Katz rails against the blindness of those who would control children's viewing but will not tackle the real problems of poverty, the breakdown of family structure, and the culture of helplessness. He maintains that the media are not the cause, just the messenger, and that America's real problems lie elsewhere.

Politicians and the public worried about the effects of media on children long before television. Novels, movies, music, radio, and comic books came under scrutiny for their potential negative consequences on the behaviors and attitudes of the young. But in the 1950s the spotlight turned to television, when reports began circulating that children were jumping off roofs in emulation of Superman. Decades of intermittent hearings and high-profile research reports linked television and aggression. However, for many years the networks successfully argued that the linkage was not proven and that First Amendment concerns precluded any control of media content.

The 1990s brought in a new era of social action. The 1990 Children's Television Act was the first congressional act that specifically regulated children's television. In order to codify the requirements of the act, the Federal Communications Commission (FCC) implemented a three-hour rule in 1997, requiring broadcasters to schedule at least three hours of educational and informational (E/I) programming for children per week. Concerns about children also emerged in the final version of the 1996 Telecommunications Act. The law forced the industry to implement a ratings system, and it required the installation of a V-chip in television sets, which would "read" violence ratings so families could block violent programming.

Now a rating system is in effect. After much controversy over whether ratings should be age or content based, most networks are using a combination of age and content systems. Yet the controversy over the involvement of the government in programming for children remains. Is this an infringement on the free speech rights of broadcasters? Should government get involved in order to protect a vulnerable group, such as children? If ratings are used for movies, television, and music releases, should they also be used for books, magazines, and other fare for children? Is it right to require broadcasters to provide three hours of E/I programming weekly based on the premise that they are licensed to operate in the public interest?

The Telecommunications Act raises a number of questions. At one level, it indicates a willingness of Congress to become involved in the control of media content. It is argued that parents now have a tool for concerned individuals who would be otherwise unable to evaluate all the available programs. Hollywood has accommodated the movie rating system; will the television rating system be much more difficult? Yet when do regulators cross the line into censorship and face the legitimate obstacles of the First Amendment? If Congress is allowed to regulate what we watch on television, some argue, where will it stop? And what are the consequences for the creative process when television violence is required to be rated? Are there nuances of violence portrayed within creative media? Who can decide when violence is artful and when it is gratuitous? What about news and documentary programs? What about offensive material other than violence, particularly sexual material? These and other questions are explored in the following selections by Joseph Lieberman and Jon Katz.

YES   Joseph Lieberman

WHY PARENTS HATE TV

Over the past few months, the V-chip has quickly become the most cele-brated piece of computer circuitry in America. In swift succession, President Clinton championed this little byte of technology in his State of the Union address, Congress passed legislation mandating its use, and the major net-works grumbled loudly about challenging the law in court. The drama finally culminated in February [1996] at a summit at the White House, where the TV industry's chieftains grudgingly accepted the president's challenge to do more for America's parents and create a ratings system compatible with the V-chip.

The story of the V-chip unfolded so fast, and its potential impact is so great, that the media has spent most of its time struggling to answer a host of basic questions: How does this signal-blocking technology work? When will it be available? How much will it cost? Will it live up to its billing? Some are still not even sure what the "V" actually stands for. (It originally stood for "violence," but it seems everyone has their own interpretation. I hope it comes to mean "values.")

As a Senate cosponsor of the V-chip bill along with Democrat Kent Conrad, I know these details matter, but I also believe the media's focus on them has obscured a larger point. Far more important than what the "V" stands for is what the coming of the V-chip tells us about the public's plummeting regard for the product that television delivers to our homes. Although this invention may merely be an irritant to those in the television business, to millions of Americans the V-chip is a surrogate for their anger at the entertainment industry for degrading our culture and our society.

That anger is clearly reflected in any number of public opinion polls, which uniformly show that the public is fed up with the rising tide of sex, violence, and vulgarity in the entertainment media. These surveys are useful, but based on my conversations with people in diners, schools, and small businesses back in Connecticut, I believe they barely begin to measure the public's intense feelings toward television.

My experience tells me that beneath the surface of the Telecommunications Revolution bubbles a revolution of another kind—a "Revolt of the Revolted," as William Bennett and I have taken to calling it. It is being fueled by a growing sense that our culture is not only out of touch with the values of mainstream America, but out of control as well. Many people believe that there are no standards that television will not violate, no lines television will not cross. Broadcasters may see the V-chip as a threat to their independence and financial well-being, but many average citizens see television as a threat to their children and their country. In the V-chip, they perceive a modicum of protection for their families.

Why are people afraid of television? Much of the news media has focused on the violence, but that is only part of the problem. Millions of Americans are fed up with explicit sex scenes and crude language during prime time and with the pornographic content of those abysmal talk shows and soap operas during the day. They feel television is not only offensive, but on the offensive, assaulting the values they and most of their neighbors share.

People are angry because they cannot sit down to watch TV with their children without fearing they will be embarrassed or demeaned. And they are angry because they feel our culture has been hijacked and replaced with something alien to their lives, something that openly rejects rather than reflects the values they try to instill in their families. In the world they see on TV, sex is a recreational pastime, indecency is a cause for laughter, and humans are killed as casually and senselessly as bugs. It is a coarse caricature of the America they love.

David Levy, the executive producer of the Caucus for Producers, Writers, and Directors, aptly describes this situation as "television without representation."

Some critics tell me that, in the zealous pursuit of the prized demographic cohort of young adults, the industry has shut out the rest of the public, and let the tastes of a few dictate the menu for all.

Average viewers may not be aware of market dynamics at work, but they certainly understand the consequences. They have a growing sense that anything-goes mentality permeating our electronic culture contributes to the moral crisis facing America. I believe this notion —that the contemporary entertainment culture is affecting our values in a deeply troubling way—is at the core of the brewing cultural rebellion.

This is a very anxious time in our history. The bonds of trust that people once took for granted in their neighborhoods and schools and workplaces are withering, and the social order that once anchored their lives and their communities is breaking apart. Stability is giving way to an increasingly chaotic and threatening world in which a snowball fight can quickly escalate into fatal shotgun blasts, as happened recently on a major thoroughfare in the city of Hartford.

The source of this social breakdown, many people believe, is the collapse of fundamental values. A critical connection exists between the erosion of morals and the explosion of social pathologies around us—brutal violence committed more and more often by strangers, the disintegration of the family, the epidemic of illegitimacy. In much the same way, many of us see a critical link between the erosion of values and the plummeting standards of decency on television and in our culture.

Some in the entertainment industry continue to argue that they are merely holding up a mirror to our culture, and scoff at the notion that the entertainment culture is responsible for all our social ills. The time has come to take a torch to this straw man. Neither President Clinton nor William Bennett nor I nor anyone I know is suggesting that any individual entertainment product, or even the whole of the entertainment industry, has single-handedly caused the rise in juvenile violence or illegitimacy. We are saying that the entertainment culture is immensely powerful, more powerful than any lawmaker in Washington, and that this power is wielded in ways that make our country's problems worse, not better.

Consider a few facts. There are 95 million households in America with televisions, which means more households own TV sets than telephones. Sixty-five percent of those homes have at least two TVs, which on average are turned on seven hours a day. The typical child watches 25 hours of television every week. That is more time than most of them spend attending religious services, talking to their parents, reading books, or even listening to their teachers. Many kids spend more time watching television than any other activity except sleeping.

No one can seriously deny the potential influence that kind of constant exposure carries with it. And because of that power, those responsible for television programming do not just mirror, but also mold, attitudes and behaviors. Whether they want the responsibility or not, they are influencing our values. And whenever they air degrading programs, they contribute to—not cause, but contribute to—the moral and social breakdown we are suffering.

So many studies have documented the threat posed by steady exposure to violence on television that the point should not even be subject to debate. But to add yet another voice to the mix,

consider this passage from a stunning article Adam Walinsky wrote last year in the *Atlantic Monthly*, in which he warned of a coming generation of "superfelons" who when they mature will likely make the cities of today look peaceful:

"These young people have been raised in the glare of ceaseless media violence and incitement to every depravity of act and spirit. Movies may feature scores of killings in two hours time, vying to show methods ever more horrific.... Major corporations make and sell records exhorting their listeners to brutalize Koreans, rob store owners, rape women, kill police.... These lessons are being taught to millions of children as I write and you read."

The media's messages are not transforming these young people into killers, Walinsky says, but they are feeding into a cycle of violence that is getting harder and harder to break and that has dire repercussions for our country. Much the same could be said about the effect of sexual messages sent to our children. No single show is corrupting America's youth, or creating the epidemic of teen pregnancy or sexually transmitted diseases. But television as a whole says over and over to our children that sex is as devoid of consequences as a game of charades, and they are missing out on something great if they don't have sex right away. It is hardly surprising, then, that a recent poll of kids aged 10 to 16 found that nearly two-thirds believe TV encourages them to become sexually active too soon.

If you still doubt the influence that television wields, just listen to America's parents. I cannot tell you how many times I've heard mothers and fathers say that they feel locked in a struggle with the powerful forces of the electronic culture to shape their children's values

—and that they're losing. They feel that television and the culture undermine their fundamental duty as a parent —teaching right and wrong, instilling a sense of discipline—and that their kids' lives are increasingly controlled by careless strangers a world away.

This is why the concept of the V-chip is so appealing to parents. It offers them a silicon hard hat to protect their kids from television's falling standards. The implications of the V-chip's popularity are remarkable. The public feels so strongly that their children need to be shielded from words and images in the entertainment media that they are turning to the government for help— not censorship, but help. Considering the low esteem with which Americans today regard Washington, this should tell us something about the public's faith and trust in the TV industry.

The public's fear and anger is understandable when you consider the industry's thoughtless response to its concerns. For instance, after hearing a growing chorus of complaints last year about the quality of prime-time programming, capped by last summer's debate in Congress over the V-chip, the major networks reacted by unleashing what critics widely assailed as the crudest, rudest new fall season in history. All too typical were scenes like the one from *Bless This House* on CBS, broadcast during the old Family Hour, when a female character said she was so sex-starved that she wanted to "do it on the coffee table." To that another character responded, "Don't you ever get your period?"

This rash of vulgarity is only the latest step down in an ongoing trend. A study done by a research team at Southern Illinois University recently found that the frequency of indecent and profane language during prime time had increased 45 percent from 1990 to 1994.

But the most disturbing thing about this fall's "slow slide into the gutter," as the *Hartford Courant*'s TV critic called it, was that much of it was happening in the 8 P.M. time slot when millions of children are watching. As the Media Research Center documented in a recent report, this crossover marked the death knell of the traditional Family Hour. Among other things, this study found that in 117 hours of programming reviewed over a recent four-week period, 72 curse words were used, including 29 uses of the word "ass," 13 uses of "bitch" and 10 uses of "bastard."

If these developments are not enough to drive parents to embrace the V-chip, then consider how several network executives responded recently to criticism of the decline in prime-time standards. One top official's justification was that "sexual innuendoes are part of life." Another said, "Society has become crasser, and we move with that." And yet another said, "It is not the role of network TV to program for the children of America."

After hearing these comments, I can't help but ask how these industry leaders would feel if I came into their home and used some of this kind of foul language in front of their children. I doubt they would stand for it. But why then do they feel it is perfectly acceptable and appropriate to use that kind of language in my home, in front of my child? That is essentially what is happening when they decide to send these shows into my living room—they are speaking to me and my family, which includes my eight-year-old daughter.

The same question could be asked of the major syndicators who produce and distribute the daytime "trash TV" talk shows. I recently joined William

Bennett and Sam Nunn in a public campaign to focus attention on these degrading, offensive, and exploitative programs. The point we are trying to make is there are some things that are so morally repugnant that they should not be broadcast for mass consumption, least of all by the eight million children who watch these shows regularly. The examples we cite [see box], such as the teenage girl who slept with more than a hundred men, or women who marry their rapists, were unequivocally beyond the pale.

Yet, although we have received comprehensive public support for our efforts, not one of the major communications companies that own the shows we raised concerns about—such as Gannett, Tribune, Sony, Time Warner, Viacom—would publicly acknowledge that their products were problematic in any way. Nor, to our disappointment, has the leadership of the broadcasting industry stepped forward to talk about this genre's excesses.

Those same corporate leaders tried to kill the V-chip in its legislative crib, and for a long time they seemed prepared to pursue a court challenge at all costs. But to their credit, the networks and the National Association of Broadcasters dropped their opposition following the president's appeal in his State of the Union address and agreed (albeit reluctantly) to create a comprehensive, self-enforced rating system. Regardless of how it came to pass, this was a historic breakthrough. The tools offered by the V-chip and a ratings system will go a long way toward empowering parents to keep overly violent and offensive programs out of their homes and out of reach of their children.

But the industry must realize that these tools will not eliminate the fundamental problem that is fueling the deep-seated anger felt by so many Americans: the deterioration of the industry's programming standards. The V-chip is no panacea; the harmful messages abounding on television are still going to reach many young kids. Moreover, the V-chip is no substitute for network responsibility, for recognizing that the programming they send into our homes carries with it enormous influence. Simply put, the American public wants more from television than just good warnings on bad programming.

There is some reason for hope. A growing chorus of voices within the industry is calling for fundamental changes in the way television does business. For instance, in a recent high-profile speech, Richard Frank, the president of the Academy of Television Arts and Sciences, recently said, "Why do you think people such as C. Delores Tucker, William Bennett, Tipper Gore, Reed Hundt and many others are attacking music and the media? Because *the reality is frightening*" (emphasis added). Frank went on to urge the industry to use the enormous power at its disposal to take some risks and set higher standards. "We cannot and will not ignore the important issues facing television," he said. "We must deal with them responsibly."

One of the most important steps the industry can take now to address the concerns we have raised, and to begin to restore public confidence in its programming, would be to adopt once again a voluntary code of conduct. I know that some in the creative community will charge that such a code is an attempt to chill their free speech, but the truth is

TALKIN' TRASH

Democratic Senators Joseph Lieberman of Connecticut and Sam Nunn of Georgia have joined Heritage Foundation fellow William J. Bennett in urging producers, broadcasters, and advertisers to scale back their support of talk-show sleaze. *Policy Review* offers these descriptions of actual topics discussed on daytime television talk shows.

Jenny Jones (**Warner Bros. Television**).   Guests have included: a woman who said she got pregnant while making a pornographic movie; a husband who had been seeing a prostitute for two years and whose wife confronted him on the show. *Selected show titles:* "A Mother Who Ran off with Her Daughter's Fiancé," "Women Discuss Their Sex Lives with Their Mothers."

Sally Jessy Raphael (**Multimedia Entertainment**).   Guests have included: a 13-year-old girl who was urged to share her sexual experiences, beginning at age 10; a person who claimed to have slept with over 200 sexual partners; a man who appeared on stage with roses for the daughter he had sexually molested, and revealed that he had been molested when he was five. *Selected show titles:* "Sex Caught on Tape," "My Daughter is Living as a Boy," "Wives of Rapists," "I'm Marrying a 14-year-old Boy."

Jerry Springer (**Multimedia Entertainment**).   Guests have included: a man who admitted to sleeping with his girlfriend's mother; a 16-year-old girl (wearing sunglasses to disguise her identity) who said she buried her newborn baby alive in her backyard; a 17-year-old who had married her 71-year-old foster father (with whom she first had sex when she was 14) and had borne four children by him; a husband who revealed to his wife on the show that he was having an affair, after which the mistress emerged, kissed the husband, and told the wife that she loved them both.

Montel Williams (**Paramount**).   Guests have included: a pregnant woman who boasted of having eight sexual partners during her first two trimesters; a 17-year-old girl who boasted of having slept with more than a hundred men; a man claiming to be an HIV-positive serial rapist of prostitutes. *Selected show titles:* "Married Men Who Have Relationships with the Next-Door Neighbor," "Promiscuous Teenage Girls."

Maury Povich (**Paramount**).   Guests have included: a young mother who had no qualms about leaving her sons in the care of her father, a convicted child molester, because the father had only molested girls.

(Continued)

Geraldo **(Tribune Entertainment).**   Guests have included: a gold-chained pimp who threatened to "leave my [expletive] ring print" on the forehead of an audience member, while scantily clad prostitutes sat next to him. *Selected show titles:* "Men Who Sell Themselves to Women for a Living," "Mothers Try to Save Their Daughters from Teenage Prostitution," "Women Who Marry Their Rapist."

Richard Bey **(All American Television).**   Guests have included: a woman who said her 16-year-old sister had slept with 15 men; two sisters who hate each other and who mudwrestled while the show played pig noises; a man who wanted to have sex with his girlfriend's sister before he and his girlfriend got married. *Selected show title:* "Housewives vs. Strippers."

Ricki Lake **(Columbia Tri-star Television).**   Guests have included: a woman who boasted she once pulled a gun on her boyfriend's wife; a man who explained to his surprised roommate that he had revealed the roommate's homosexuality to the roommate's mother. *Selected show titles:* "Women Confront Exes Who Cheated and Then Warn New Girlfriends," "Now That I've Slept with Him, He Treats Me Like Dirt!"

Rolanda **(King World).**   Guests have included: a woman who revealed her love for her female roommate, whose response was, "Now I know why she comes in the bathroom every time I take a shower"; a woman serving as maid of honor to her best friend who alleged that she had slept with the groom a week before the wedding. *Selected show titles:* "I Use Sex to Get What I Want," "Get Bigger Breasts or Else."

Sources: Compiled by Empower America from *Electronic Media, Portland Oregonian, American Prospect,* Media Research Center, *Talk Soup,* and *Tuning In Trouble: Talk TV's Destructive Impact on Mental Health,* by Jeanne Albronda Heaton and Nona Leigh Wilson (Jossey-Bass Publishers).

that self-regulation is common sense, not censorship.

The time has come to recognize that not every aberrant behavior or hostile voice has the right to be featured on television on a daily basis, especially at times when large numbers of children are watching. That means asking the industry to draw some lines which programmers cannot and will not cross, something Court TV has already done by adopting a code of ethics for its own programming.

I hope that the industry will include in any voluntary code they develop a commitment to bring back the Family Hour and to recreate a safe haven for children during prime time. The major broadcast networks would not only be helping parents by taking this step, they would also be helping themselves.

There clearly is a market for high-quality, family-friendly material, as evidenced by the fact that Nickelodeon was the top-rated cable network in the nation last year. This channel has viewers that ABC, NBC, CBS, and Fox could win back.

Lastly, we must not just focus on what is bad about television, we must also talk about what could be good and even great about television. One of the most revealing studies I've come across recently showed that at-risk children who watch *Sesame Street* score significantly higher on math and verbal tests than peers who do not. Just imagine what we could do for the nation's children if there were 20 variations of *Sesame Street* to choose from after school instead of 20 *Jerry Springers*. While that is not likely to happen any time soon, it's a safe bet that the president and many others will continue to push the industry to increase the amount of quality educational programming for kids.

These are just a few suggestions. The devil here is not in the details but in the big picture—or rather, in all the troubling pictures and words the TV industry is pumping into our homes, and in the damage that the sum of those messages inflicts upon our society. The people who run television have a choice before them: Respond to this Revolt of the Revolted, or face the Sentinels of Censorship. The last thing I want is the government setting standards, but I fear the public will soon turn again to Congress to take stronger actions if the TV industry continues on its path downward.

We must avoid that outcome at all costs. To do so, the TV industry must see the V-chip for the powerful symbol of discontent it is, and treat it as a beginning and not an end. More and more these days television is becoming a pariah in America's living rooms, and no slice of silicon can block out that reality.

NO

Jon Katz

... AND ABOUT VIOLENCE

A central tenet of the Mediaphobe is that guns don't kill people; unwholesome movies, tabloid telecasts, video games and rap music do. That new media are not only corrosive and decivilizing but literally dangerous.

Consider Beavis and Butt-head, MTV's pair of repulsive animated geeks. In 1993, an Ohio woman blamed a *Beavis & Butt-head* episode after her five-year-old son set fire to their trailer home, killing her two-year-old daughter. The following year a watchdog group called Morality in Media said *Beavis & Butt-head* might be responsible for the death of an eight-month-old girl, killed when a bowling ball was thrown from an overpass onto a New Jersey highway and struck her family's car. The group cited an episode of the show in which Beavis and Butt-head loaded a bowling ball with explosives and dropped it from a rooftop. "We're not saying there is a connection," said a spokeswoman for the group, saying there was a connection. "But certainly the coincidence is difficult to ignore."

As a result of these and other widespread attacks in the press, MTV canceled the early evening showing of *Beavis & Butt-head* so that young children wouldn't see it. And the program's scripts have been supervised and sanitized ever since to remove controversial segments that might be blamed for inducing violence. The *Beavis & Butt-head* syndrome has come to typify the ways in which opportunistic politicians and eager journalists convince millions that culture, not social trauma, causes violence.

The 1995 firebombing of a New York City subway station was a classic example. Several would-be thieves squirted flammable liquid into a Queens token booth, causing it to explode. The clerk inside later died from his burns. The attack followed by two weeks the release of the movie *Money Train*, including a scene in which a pyromaniac squirts flammable liquid into token booths (though the celluloid clerks escape injury). *The New York Times* said the movie joined a "long list of films and television shows blamed for prompting acts of violence." It included the Martin Scorsese film *Taxi Driver*, cited by prosecutors as the inspiration for the attempted assassination of President Reagan by John W. Hinckley, Jr., in 1981; Oliver Stone's *Natural Born Killers*, said by the Utah police to have prompted a teenager to kill his stepmother and half sister; and *The Program*, blamed for the deaths of two teenagers because this 1993 movie showed drunken football players lying down in traffic.

Critics, reporters and politicians jumped on the *Money Train* parallels, with Bob Dole one of the first out of the gate. "The American people have a right to voice their outrage," he told reporters. "For those in the entertainment industry who too often engage in a pornography of violence as a way to sell movie tickets, it is time for some serious soul-searching." Dole, an opponent of gun control, did not comment on the M-1 carbine, with a clip holding seventeen cartridges, that was found at the scene of the fire-bombing. Nor did he have much to say when a couple of weeks later, the district attorney and the police said the attack had not been inspired by the film at all.

This distraction is not just a matter of journalistic harrumphing. It is a significant distortion of a major, American social problem, with enormous impact on the way our society does—or doesn't —react to violence. "Americans have a starkly negative view of popular culture," *The New York Times* found in a survey taken in August 1995, "and blame television more than any other single factor for teenage sex and violence."

Twenty-one percent said television was most responsible for teenage violence, compared with only 13 percent who blamed lack of supervision, 8 percent who blamed the breakdown of family, and 7 percent who blamed drugs. In all, a third put the primary blame on some aspect of popular culture.

WHO'S GETTING HURT BY WHAT

As it happened, weeks before the subway attack, the Justice Department re-leased a crucial report on juvenile crime. Nearly one in four people arrested for weapons crimes in America were juveniles (23 percent), the report said, compared with 16 percent in 1974. Such juvenile arrests more than doubled, from fewer than 30,000 to more than 61,000 between 1985 and 1993, while adult arrests for the same crimes grew by only one-third. Weapons offenses include the illegal use, possession, trafficking, carrying, manufacturing, importing and exporting of guns, ammunition, silencers, explosives and some types of knives. The statistics closely mirrored the surge in violent youth crimes, reported the federal officials. Teenage violence, particularly with guns, has been rising steadily since 1985, even as the number of teenagers nationwide has been declining.

But the Justice Department report got little attention in the media, compared with the furor over *Money Train*. It was the *Beavis & Butt-head* syndrome repeated, another purported link—advanced by politicians and the eager news media —between culture and danger. Even a meticulous newspaper reader or television watcher would naturally conclude that movies have more to do with violence than guns, poverty or drugs—and that without such graphic portrayals, the kids with the M-1 wouldn't have torched a token booth.

The fact is that during the past couple of years, as mediaphobes have decried the supposedly pernicious effects of pop culture, violent crime has decreased, not grown, in most of America. Homicides showed the largest drop in thirty-five years—12 percent—during the first six months of 1995, continuing the decline seen in 1994. In both cities and suburbs, there were double-digit decreases in the murder rate. New York City, which has logged five successive years of declining crime, has returned to levels of homicide not seen since 1971.

If it weren't so pervasive an idea, the suggestion that those who watch MTV and talk shows or buy rap CDS are primed to commit mayhem would seem idiotic. Clearly, crime rises and falls for other reasons.

Yet violence among the young—who are presumed by mediaphobes to be particularly vulnerable to forces like lyrics and action movies—has been, sadly, on the rise. The urban underclass in particular—mostly black and Latino—has been engulfed in a wave of escalating violence. A slight dip (of less than 3 percent) in the juvenile violent crime rate in 1995, the first in a decade, shouldn't obscure that fact.

According to the National Criminal Justice Reference Service, homicide is now the second leading cause of death among young Americans. But it's hardly uniformly distributed. From 1986 to 1989, for example, the homicide rate for white twenty-to-twenty-four-year-olds was 12 deaths per 100,000. Among blacks, it was 72 per 100,000. Though black males age twelve to twenty-four represent 1.3 percent of the population, the FBI's Uniform Crime Reports for 1992 show that they experienced 17.2 percent of single-victim homicides. That translates into a homicide rate of 114.9 killings per 100,000 black males of that age, more than ten times the rate for their white male counterparts.

Scholars like Andrew Hacker, Christopher Jencks, Elijah Anderson and Cornel West have meticulously documented the origins of this tragedy—racism, disintegrating family structures, the rise of births among single teenage mothers, lack of job training and economic oppor-

tunity, deteriorating schools, the proliferation of weapons, the drug epidemic. Among the white suburban middle class, by contrast, violence remains relatively rare. And it is the affluent middle class, of course, that is targeted by marketers of CDS (including rap), cable and computer technology. Underclass kids can't afford computers or piles of CDS.

We know what's killing young people, and it isn't lyrics, cartoons or computers.

According to the Justice Department, 57 percent of young homicide victims are killed with firearms. In fact, between 1979 and 1989, the *non*-firearm homicide rate decreased 29 percent. Once again, the phenomenon is selective: In 1989 the firearm homicide rate among black males age fifteen to nineteen in metropolitan counties was 6.5 times the rate in suburban and rural counties.

In the debate over violence and culture, the White Rabbit seems to have become the moderator. Much of what we hear is the opposite of what our common sense and individual experience tell us. Violence among the young has escalated among underclass minorities. Violence among the more affluent young, the kids who use computers, watch a lot of MTV and are the primary purchasers of CDS, is rare, was never pervasive and has, in fact, decreased. The suburban middle class, of all ethnicities and races, is one of the safer groups on the planet.

Journalists understand the meaning of the chilling statistics as well as, or better than, the rest of us: Danger to the young is greatest among young urban black males, for whom the leading cause of death has been, for years, a bullet. This did not merit a *Time* cover in 1995, while Internet pornography did. The truth about violence in America receives only a fraction of the coverage given to "violence-inducing" new media. The media tell us more about violent pop culture—Snoop Doggy Dogg, say—than about the people who sell guns and drugs to children.

The history of crime and violence in America is little understood, rarely placed in context. But in *Crime and Punishment in American History*, criminologist Lawrence Friedman exhaustively traces crime and violence all the way back to Colonial America. More than two hundred years ago, Friedman writes, the criminals were primarily "men at the bottom of the heap." Recent studies by urban scholars like Hacker and Jencks have found similar patterns—that violent crimes are overwhelmingly committed by underclass men, with drug use, inadequate law enforcement, the disintegration of family structures, an epidemic of single young women having children and the availability of firearms all major factors.

Friedman concludes that the level of violence has stayed roughly the same and that the country has always refused to come to terms with it, preferring to sermonize rather than actually try measures that might work, from the Draconian (cutting off the hands of thieves) to the innovative (controlling guns, reshaping the police, legalizing drugs).

It's true: Americans would rather denounce representations of violence than attack the real thing. Yet, although conservative gurus like Dole and Bennett rail about the destructive effects of new media and culture, even conservative think tanks like the Heritage Foundation don't uphold their conclusions.

"Over the past thirty years," the Heritage Foundation reported in a March 1995 study, "the rise in violent crime parallels the rise in families abandoned by fathers." Foundation researchers concluded after a state-by-state analysis that a 10 percent increase in the percentage of children living in single-parent homes leads typically to a 17 percent increase in juvenile crime.

"Even in high-crime, inner-city neighborhoods," the report noted, "well over 90 percent of children from safe, stable homes do not become delinquents. By contrast only 10 percent of children from unsafe, unstable homes in these neighborhoods avoid crime."

The Heritage Foundation report never mentions TV violence, rap lyrics or other forms of pop culture as factors in the rise of violence in urban neighborhoods. What scholarly evidence suggests, the study concluded, was that "at the heart of the explosion of crime in America is the loss of the capacity of fathers and mothers to be responsible in caring for the children they bring into the world."

In fact, this very theme was sounded again and again at the Million Man March on Washington in October of 1995. "There's plenty of racism to fight," one black father told CNN, "but what we're talking about down here on the mall is that we are responsible for keeping our families together and saving our children from danger."

A Justice Department study called *Juvenile Offenders and Victims: A Focus on Violence*, released last year, also refuted misplaced boomer phobias and ignorant representations by critics of popular culture, offering a chillingly detailed portrait of violence among the young.

It is not a comforting report. While murder rates declined by substantial amounts in most age groups between 1983 and 1992, murder arrest rates for juveniles and young adults soared. And the report confirms again the disparity between white and black arrest rates among juveniles arrested for murder. Between 1983 and 1992, the black rate increased by 166 percent, in comparison with the white rate increase of 94 percent. Black youths—specifically black males age fourteen to seventeen—are far more likely than other juveniles to also be homicide *victims*. Young black males have the highest homicide-victimization rate of any racial/sexual category: twice the murder rate of black females, five times that of white males, and nine times that of white females.

Furthermore, in murder cases where the assailant is known, most juveniles (76 percent) were killed by adults, not other children, and 40 percent were killed by family members, most by parents. The Justice Department study also made clear, as have many others, the correlation between rising juvenile violence and firearms.

What's missing from this very comprehensive document? Any suggestion of a link between the violence it describes and pop culture—which indicates that journalistic coverage of youth violence has been consistently confused, incomplete or misleading.

The coverage of the *Money Train* incident was typical: Numerous therapists and psychologists decried the screen violence that "led to" real violence. In an audience of about a million, said one psychologist, perhaps fifty people will act violently who otherwise would not have done so, and the more exciting and graphic the violence portrayed, the more likely it will be to have an effect. It seems logical that some already disturbed people can be influenced by depictions of violence, but that is hardly what most parents or pols are worrying about.

"Beneath the huffy sound bites," reported *Newsweek* in an unusually nuanced story at the time, "lie nearly 40 years of extremely murky scientific research on the subject." Thousands of studies are cited by researchers. Really, there are closer to two hundred; the rest are rehashes of data. The press in turn reports the research uncritically, repeating, for instance, figures about how many acts of violence kids see each year without noting that the figures are derived from nature shows, cartoon violence and slapstick, along with grislier fare. A closer look at the actual research literature reveals that what we don't know about the effects of the media is often as dramatic as what we do.

The real outrage is that the more the media focus on pop culture, the less they—and we—grasp the real causes of violence. This kind of bad reporting permits people to be killed or maimed, a far more offensive consequence than anything Beavis, Howard Stern or Tupac Shakur could say or do.

TIPTOEING AROUND THE TRUTH

Why then, is this astonishing lie, this persistent effort to link culture with violence, presented to Americans day after day?

The most-prized consumers of media live in middle-class suburbs. They may watch in horror the bodies shown nightly in their urban-based TV newscasts, but most of the kids they're watching don't live nearby.

Although the media are frequently accused of racism in the way they cover blacks and whites, the truth is that modern media have no ideology. Almost everything they do is rooted in marketing and economics. Newspapers and TV stations rarely focus on inner-city issues and problems simply because there's no money in it; most people who live in the inner city don't spend enough money to attract advertisers. Journalism doesn't see any viable economic future in Watts or the South Bronx—the very neighborhoods where explorations of the real causes of violence would take place. The 1995 death of *New York Newsday* ended print journalism's most ambitious modern experiment to remain viable in central urban areas.

Because journalism does care deeply, as most profit-making commercial enterprises do, about the suburban middle class, it provides what it sees as a valuable consumer service by warning about new media, in the same way it would sound the alert about onrushing hurricanes, defective playpens or the latest cholesterol findings.

To be fair, journalists also receive confusing messages and pressures from African-Americans, many of whom argue that too much coverage of violence among young blacks creates unhealthy stereotypes. Far more whites commit crimes than blacks, they contend, but black crime is disproportionately covered. Blacks are also frustrated because their fastest-growing socioeconomic group—the middle class—rarely shows up on the news.

Such issues are volatile, often linked with other dangerous topics like race, the underclass, and immigration. The culture of political correctness has damaged journalism in visible ways. Reporters approach charged issues like race and gender only gingerly.

Journalism doesn't distinguish between middle-class and underclass crises because reporters don't like being accused of stereotyping minorities or the poor, as they have often been in the past. It's easier and more prudent to generalize about social problems, to present them as universal dangers, rather than sort through them and isolate the real sources and causes. Thus affluent suburban children are lectured endlessly about social problems that are far less likely to affect them directly than to harm their counterparts in poverty-stricken minority neighborhoods—illegitimate-birth rates, for example, and AIDS.

A number of affluent private schools participate in national ban-TV-for-a-week campaigns, distributing literature that claims American children watch an "average of seven hours of TV a day." Underclass children, whose (frequently single) parents can't afford day care or other supervised activities, are at greater risk of ODing on TV; few private-school children could survive for long in their schools if they watched that much television. But since journalism makes no class distinction concerning the victims of social plagues like violence, neither do we. So boomer parents whose children are safe and well educated panic at persistent reports of pornography online or violence on television, while the children who truly suffer are ignored by government and society.

As a profoundly middle-class medium, mainstream journalism lacks any economic incentive to cover the underclass thoroughly; in fact, news media that pay too much attention risk losing or alienating prized upper-middle-class consumers.

Finally, journalism has become addicted to studies, surveys, polls, spokespeople and lobbyists. Reporters have become fat and lazy relying on other people to do their talking and reporting for them. Issues like violence, race and crime are relayed almost entirely in terms of what proponents of specific points of view say about them. Our civic consciousness is paralyzed by checkmating arguments. How could we possibly reach anything like consensus when our primary information media don't permit their own reporters to reach conclusions, only to quote from spokespeople whose livelihood literally depends on never changing their minds?

Covering the true causes of urban violence would mean taking on some of the most difficult and sensitive issues in American life—race, poverty, welfare systems, law enforcement. Many journalists, like academics, have come to fear such issues; probing them inevitably brings accusations of racism or some other form of bigotry. Blaming violence on media and culture is easier and safer, both for journalists and for opportunistic politicians.

Besides, the structure, power and function of mainstream journalism are deeply threatened by new media, which are siphoning off viewers, readers, and ad revenue. By portraying new media as dangerous and decivilizing, the press appears responsible and safe in contrast. If nothing else, it feels virtuous. Maybe it thinks it will eventually convince others of that, too. So far, its prospects are dim; more and more, the young are abandoning what we used to call "the press."

PARENTS, PROBLEMS AND THE PRESS

One of the mainstream journalism's modern tragedies, in fact, is the way it attacks new forms of media and culture, alienating their users rather than serving them and retaining them by covering their world well. Thus *TV Guide* —little more than page after page of small print of the kind newspapers have provided for decades—becomes one of the largest-circulation magazines in the world, while newspapers that preferred to sneer at television and declined to cover it now hemorrhage circulation and income. Although individual journalists are pouring online, especially on increasingly fashionable conferencing systems like the WELL, journalistic institutions remain hostile to new media. Few editors watch *Jenny Jones*, or much television at all; even fewer understand the digital culture and its many offshoots. When someone offers a study purporting to show that the online culture is riddled with pornography and is dangerous to children, they are as happy to believe it and spread the message as they were to report that comic books threatened decency (in the forties), that rock and roll was dangerous (in the fifties), that video games turned kids violent (in the eighties).

Well-to-do boomers are profoundly anxious parents, and mediaphobic reporting plays into their deepest fears. Attentive to each new spate of warnings, they use them as rationales for further encircling their children in protective cocoons. Thus, cable and computers are not liberating, empowering, or community-building new media but menaces to be warded off by V-chips, blocking software and anti-porn legislation.

The conversations about the degradation and dangers of modern culture have become universal. I've had variations of this discussion hundreds of times in recent years with friends, neighbors, other parents and journalists:

The Conversation

Don't you think that rap and sleazy talk shows and *Beavis & Butt-head* are disgusting? I don't want my kids anywhere near that garbage. No wonder there's so much violence!

But do you know who the kids are who buy rap CDS and listen to MTV?

Who?

They're white middle-class suburban kids—overwhelmingly.

But you're not denying that the stuff is disgusting.

Maybe it is. But that doesn't mean it's responsible for violence. The rise in violence in recent years has to do primarily with underclass kids. The common threads are they have no fathers, they go to lousy schools, they have easy access to guns and they've grown up amid a drug epidemic. But they aren't the viewers that racy talk shows or *Beavis & Butt-head* want to reach, and they can't afford all those CDs.

But have you listened to this stuff? It's sexist. It's awful.

Maybe. But it has little to do with violence. Since you're so concerned about violence, tell me if you know how many kids were killed by guns in America last year?

I have no idea.

Look, I'll agree that some of this stuff is vulgar and offensive. Will you agree that it's astonishing to know so much about scary rap and talk shows but almost nothing about how many kids get killed each year and why? Or how they get the guns?

The conversation usually ends there.

Popular culture, using its many new means of transmission, has exploded. Some of the art, information and drama it creates—*NYPD Blue, The Larry Sanders Show, Law and Order*; CDS from R.E.M. and the London Symphony; CD-ROMs from artists like Pedro Meyer; museum Web pages; religious and political conferences online—is classy, even fascinating. Some of it—the nastiest rap lyrics, the dumbest talk shows, certain karate-kicking video games—is mind-numbing and offensive to adult sensibilities.

But grown-ups all seem to lose the neurological chip that enables them to call up their own youth. The point of much of adolescent culture is to be offensive, to individuate kids from their parents, to help define their own ideas and values. Popular culture has been helping them to do that for a good half-century now.

Adult America—astonishingly, including the very boomers who helped mid-wife rock and roll—takes pop culture literally, which is the worst and most useless way to approach it. Beavis and Butt-head are not advocates of stupidity but ironic commentators on it. The rhetorical styles of many rap artists are absorbed by listeners not as literal advisories but as more complex expressions of attitude, values and group identity. Oliver Stone's *JFK* was never meant to depict historical truth; it was a prescient reflection of the angry paranoia which subsequently became unmistakable in American politics. And Spike Lee's relentless poking is intended as provocation, a challenge to both whites' and blacks' views on race.

The problem isn't that popular culture is eroding our civic and moral fabric, but that we take it far more seriously than its creators or consumers do; we give it more weight than it deserves. There is no more evidence that teenagers who cheer on the riotous discussions of sexual betrayal on *Ricki Lake* then go out and sleep with their best friends' friends than there is that kids who listen to Ice-T go out and murder cops.

Concerns about how much time children spend unattended in front of screens, or locked in their bedrooms with computers, are perfectly valid. Good parents always curb their children's unhealthy excesses, from overindulging in Chee-tos to joining a pack of neighborhood vandals. But the notion that exposure to pop culture is inherently dangerous is unsupported by research, statistics or common sense. We lose credibility with kids by giving it such weight. Most MTV watchers are safe, law-abiding, middle-class children; they know quite well that exposure to vulgar videos won't send them out into the streets packing guns or into their bedrooms wearing leather bustiers.

Years of battles over comics, rock and other forms of youth culture seem to have left us none the wiser. We take the bait every time. Rather than engage our children in intelligent dialogue, we simply come across as the pompous out-to-lunch windbags many of us have become.

For black artists and audiences, the cultural issues are more complex. Expressions of anti-establishment anger and provocative lyrics about sex and violence are jarringly offensive to many adults, white and black, but seem an almost inevitable reflection of the anger, disconnection and violence in many minority communities. When thousands of kids are injured or die violently every year, how could the music their peers create be uplifting and "moral" in the tradition of William Bennett and parents whose experiences are so strikingly different?

One of the reasons we have so much trouble understanding complicated issues like purported connections between culture and violence—and why people like William Bennett can exploit them so profitably—is that so many "experts" are thrown at us, often peddling contradictory conclusions.

But some experts have better credentials than others.

Harvard psychiatrist Robert Coles, no fan of TV violence, has been studying and writing about the moral, spiritual and developmental lives of children for much of his life. His works have been widely praised and circulated as ground-breaking, insightful looks at kids' complex inner lives. Parents worried about the impact culture has on their kids should ignore the headlines and read *The Moral Life of Children*. They would know more and feel better.

A young moviegoer, Coles writes, can repeatedly be exposed to the "excesses of a Hollywood genre"—sentimentality, violence, the misrepresentation of history, racial stereotypes, pure simplemindedness—and emerge unscathed intellectually as well as morally. In fact, sometimes these images help the child to "sort matters out, stop and think about what is true and what is not by any means true—in the past, in the present." The child, says Coles, "doesn't forget what he's learned in school, learned at home, from hearing people talk in his family and his neighborhood."

Culture offers important moments for moral reflection, and it ought not to be used as an occasion for "overwrought psychiatric comment," Coles warns, or for making banal connections between films and "the collective American conscience."

But is it. All the time.

This discussion—of culture, morality and violence—is made more difficult because of not irrational fears on the part of minorities that their children will be demonized and stereotyped as lawless and dangerous, when only a small percentage are involved in crime or violence. Understandably, black leaders want to project more positive images of African-American life than the young black men so often seen in handcuffs on the local news.

But black political leaders who insist that violence is a universal American problem equally affecting blacks and whites, or who point to media and popular culture as its primary causes, are hardly advancing any racial goals or staving off prejudice. They simply make it easier for the majority of Americans to ignore poverty, bad schools and guns— since those problems are purportedly less to blame than *Money Train*. Unwittingly, this particular brand of mediaphobe conspires to keep Americans ignorant about what really causes violence and what can be done to prevent it. . . .

THE V-CHIP, DIGITAL PLACEBO

A group calling itself the National Television Violence Study issued yet another "definitive" report in 1996 that concluded that "violence predominates on television, often including large numbers of violent interactions per program." This study, like previous and similar ones, generated substantial publicity and was invoked by members of Congress to justify passage of legislation requiring the V-chip.

Groups of coders, selected from undergraduate volunteers at two participating universities, were asked to watch shows and tabulate violent acts based on the following definition: "any overt depiction of the use of physical force or the credible threat of such force intended to physically harm an animate being or group of beings."

The group conceded that Wile E. Coyote's being pushed off a cliff would probably count as violence in their survey, because "there was intent to commit harm." Presumably, then, millions of parents will use the V-chip to protect their offspring from *Road Runner* cartoons.

At about the same time, *Newsweek* ran a story called "Parental Control Ware," a cheerful consumer guide to blocking software, "the alternative to censoring the Internet." *Newsweek* recommended four programs—Cybersitter, Surfwatch, Net Nanny and Cyber Patrol. The very names are patronizing and demeaning.

One program would automatically block children from a Web site on the poet Anne Sexton because her name includes those three scary letters *s-e-x*.

This approach is the antithesis of trust and national discourse between adults and children, and more evidence of the growing need to protect children from adult abuses of power.

Blocking software is noxious and potentially unlimited. Once applied, the censoring and restrictions will spread inevitably beyond violence into other areas adults want to place off-limits: political topics that differ from their own values, music and movie forums that don't conform to their adult tastes, online friends they don't approve of.

Although it's being introduced in America as a means of protecting children, this technology, as it evolves, . . . could easily become the tyrant's best technopal, offering ever more ingenious ways to control speech and thought. Some children reared on this stuff will inevitably grow up thinking the solution to topics we don't like is to remove them from our vision and consciousness. In any other context, defenders of freedom and free speech would be bouncing off walls.

Like the movie industry's silly ratings codes, blocking software gives the illusion of control. It doesn't ensure safety, since sophisticated evildoers will circumvent it even more quickly than kids will. And it doesn't teach citizenship in the digital world.

As parents withdraw, secure in the conviction that their Net Nanny will do the work they should be doing, count on this: Children, many of whom helped build the digital culture, will circumvent this software, and quickly. They would be much better off if their parents accompanied them when they first set out online, showing them what is inappropriate or dangerous.

Blocking deprives children of the opportunity to confront the realities of new culture. Some of it is pornographic, violent, even dangerous. They need to encounter those situations in a rational, supervised way in order to learn how to truly protect themselves.

WHAT CHILDREN NEED IN THE DIGITAL AGE

Children need to get their hands on the new machines. They need equal access to the technology of culture, research and education. Poor and working-class families have few computers compared with the educated, affluent middle class. And we are learning that some minority children are resisting computers as the toys of the white nerd.

But if new technology can create a gap between haves and have-nots, it can also narrow it. Cheap, portable PCTVs with computers and cable modems would equalize access to the digital revolution in a hurry. Making that happen should be the first and most pressing moral issue of the digital generation.

Children also need to learn to use the machinery of culture safely and responsibly. That means grasping the new rules of community in the online world, acquiring digital manners and courtesy, transcending the often abrasive, pointlessly combative, disjointed tone that permeates many online discussions. They need to learn how to research ideas, history and culture as well as to chat and mouth off.

They need to understand from an early age that their culture poses challenges and responsibilities, even some dangers. That time with TV or computers needs to be managed, considered, kept in proportion. That they need to get help if they can't do this themselves. New technology can enhance social skills and broaden experience, but it also raises all sorts of unexplored political and civic issues for the young—how ideas travel and are debated, how the like-minded can link up, how to sort through the growing options.

Children need help in becoming civic-minded citizens of the digital age, figuring out how to use the machinery in the service of some broader social purpose than simply entertainment or technology for its own sake; how to avoid the dangers of elitism and arrogance; how to manage their new ability to connect instantly with other cultures.

But more than anything else, children need to have their culture affirmed. They need their parents, teachers, guardians and leaders to accept that there is a new political reality for children, and the constructs that governed their own lives and culture are no longer the only relevant or useful ones.

They are never going back.

POSTSCRIPT

Are V-Chips and Content Ratings Necessary?

A common theme of arguments for and against ratings has to do with the responsibility of parents. To monitor your children's viewing you have to be a full-time television watchdog, says George Gerber, head of the Violence Index projects. Monitoring children's viewing is exactly what parents should be doing. Television should not be used as a babysitter. These are the claims of those who argue that ratings systems invade First Amendment rights. Selectivity is a responsibility within the home. Individuals who take this perspective frequently worry that concern over ratings will produce homogenous, uninteresting entertainment fare.

A sobering look at the attitudes of media executives can be found in Ken Auletta's article "What Won't They Do?" *The New Yorker* (May 17, 1993). *The National Television Violence Study*, 3 vols. (Sage Publications, 1996–1998), conducted by a consortium of professors from several universities, offers a commentary on the state of violence on American television for viewers, policymakers, industry leaders, and scholars.

The Annenberg Public Policy Center (APPC) has been studying the state of children's television for the last three years. The aims of this research have been to determine whether or not there are enough high-quality choices available to children of different age groups with different resources, to identify the high-quality programs that exist on broadcast and cable, and to track the impact of government regulation of children's television programs. The 1998 State of Children's Television report came to some interesting conclusions. The researchers found that, as in previous years, nearly two-thirds of all programs for children address 5- to 11-year-olds, yet many of these programs are not enriching. The long-ignored teen audience received more programming, but the overall quality dropped. PBS is the most consistent provider of quality programming. The study does note, however, that parents most often agree that "educational" shows are of high quality but frequently fail to assign a quality rating to shows that provide more of a "social learning" perspective, such as *Doug*. Also, despite regulation, many programs do not contain appropriate labels previewing violent content. The APPC makes the following recommendations: routinize the use of the "FV" (fantasy violence) rating for children's programs with heavy violence, rather than the less-informative TV-Y7 that is more commonly used; all parties must place a greater emphasis on informing parents about the meaning of the violence ratings and the E/I designation; and newspapers and other outlets need to do a better job of providing parents and children with the ratings and with critiques of shows.

On the Internet . . .

http://www.dushkin.com

National Association of Broadcasters

The National Association of Broadcasters (NAB) is dedicated to promoting the interests of broadcasters. Some of the pages found at this site include information on television parental guidelines, laws and regulations, and research on current issues. *http://www.nab.org/*

The National Cable Television Association

The National Cable Television Association (NCTA) is dedicated to promoting the interests of the cable television industry. *http://www.ncta.com*

Telecom Information Resources

This site has over 7,000 links to telecommunication resources throughout the world. At this site you will find information on service providers, government agencies, government policies, economic policies, and much more. *http://china.si.umich.edu/telecom/telecom-info.html*

PART 4

Media Business

Freedom of speech and the press makes producing news and entertainment content somewhat different from manufacturing widgets. It is important to realize that media industries are businesses and that they must be profitable to be able to continue. However, are there special standards to which we should hold media industries? Are the structures of media industries responsive to the public's interest? How do monopolies affect media content? What is the primary function of advertising, and to what extent does it influence our behavior? Will current media businesses be able to survive as newer forms of media and alternative modes of delivery become available?

■ Media Monopolies: Does Concentration of Ownership Jeopardize Media Content?

■ Will Traditional Advertising Survive the New Technology Revolution?

ISSUE 14

Media Monopolies: Does Concentration of Ownership Jeopardize Media Content?

YES: Ben H. Bagdikian, from "The Media Monopoly," *Television Quarterly* (vol. 29, no. 1, 1997)

NO: Eli M. Noam and Robert N. Freeman, from "The Media Monopoly and Other Myths," *Television Quarterly* (vol. 29, no. 1, 1997)

ISSUE SUMMARY

YES: Ben H. Bagdikian, a Pulitzer Prize–winning journalist, contends that only 10 corporations control American mass media, with sobering consequences for control of news and loss of citizen access. He argues that the 1996 Telecommunications Act has fostered even more concentration and has aided companies that are intent upon diversifying into every aspect of the media industries.

NO: Professors Eli M. Noam and Robert N. Freeman contend there will be more competition among U.S. media markets, not less. Using U.S. Department of Justice procedures for identifying overly concentrated markets, they demonstrate that media industries are only moderately concentrated and advise that such concern should focus on local, not national, media.

The Telecommunications Act of 1996 was designed to increase telecommunications industry competition, primarily by removing barriers between what are now distinct industries and by reducing restrictions on ownership of multiple stations, sometimes in the same market. Yet the media industry has a special function defined by its journalistic endeavors and protected by the Constitution as freedom of the press. Can this restructuring of the American media industry threaten the ability of that industry to fulfill its surveillance function?

The long tradition of private, rather than governmental, ownership of media in the United States stems from the legacy of libertarian philosophy, which argued that truth would emerge from a diversity of voices in the communication marketplace. These diverse voices, says this traditional philosophy, can best provide the public with information on which to base its decisions. Another important legal foundation for broadcast outlets has been the requirement that broadcast stations "operate in the public interest," which was imposed upon them due to their use of a scarce spectrum—the public airwaves.

According to Ben H. Bagdikian in the following selection, large corporations are gaining control of the media at an alarming rate. Control of media by a few giant corporations is tighter than it was when the first edition of his book *The Media Monopoly* (now in its fifth edition) came out in 1983. These dominant corporations, through their control of news and other public information, can censor public awareness of the dangers of information control by the corporate elite. When the central interests of controlling corporations are at stake, Bagdikian further argues, news becomes weighted toward what serves the economic and political interests of the corporations that own the media, not the public interest. The concept of media as public trust seems to be lost in the new era of corporate restructuring.

In the second selection, Eli M. Noam and Robert N. Freeman question the basic premise of whether or not media are becoming more concentrated. Despite some concerns about concentration with the local media and with companies such as Microsoft, Noam and Freeman maintain that once the initial spate of mergers has been accomplished, the barriers that have reduced competition will foster a new competitive environment.

Note that several issues are intertwined. Is media concentration increasing? If so, is it necessarily a problem? We may not think so if economies of scale reduce the prices we pay for our media. We may, however, have problems if most of the media outlets in our community are owned by the same corporation. What implication does concentration have for news coverage? For example, is a chain owner more likely to impose a one-size-fits-all perspective on its coverage of local events, thus reducing diversity? Is a local or a national corporation more likely to stand up to attempts to control editorial content by advertisers or other powerful people? The Telecommunications Act of 1996 has unleashed a torrent of mergers and acquisitions. Is the promise of erasing traditional monopolies, which will reduce prices for services, being realized? Or has the law opened the door for new forms of monopoly?

YES

Ben H. Bagdikian

THE MEDIA MONOPOLY

In the last five years, a small number of the country's largest industrial corporations has acquired more public communications power, including ownership of the news, than any private businesses have ever before possessed in world history.

Nothing in earlier history matches this corporate group's power to penetrate the social landscape. Using both old and new technology, by owning each other's shares, engaging in joint ventures as partners, and other forms of cooperation, this handful of giants has created what is, in effect, a new communications cartel within the United States.

At issue is not just a financial statistic, like production numbers or ordinary industrial products like refrigerators or clothing. At issue is the possession of power to surround almost every man, woman, and child in the country with controlled images and words, to socialize each new generation of Americans, to alter the political agenda of the country. And with that power comes the ability to exert influence that in many ways is greater than that of schools, religion, parents and even government itself.

Aided by the digital revolution and the acquisition of subsidiaries that operate at every step in the mass communications process, from the creation of content to its delivery into the home, the communications cartel has exercised stunning influence over national legislation and government agencies, an influence whose scope and power would have been considered scandalous or illegal twenty years ago.

The new communications cartel has been made possible by the withdrawal of earlier government intervention that once aspired to protect consumers and move toward the ideal of diversity of content and ownership in the mass media. Government's passivity has emboldened the new giants to boast openly of monopoly and their ability to project news, commercial messages, and graphic images into the consciousness and subconscious of almost every American.

Strict control of public information is not new in the world, but historical dictatorships lacked the late twentieth century's digital multimedia and distribution technology. As the country approaches the millennium, the new cartel exercises a more complex and subtle kind of control.

Michael Eisner, chairman and chief executive officer of the second largest media firm in the world, Disney/ABC/Cap Cities, put it succinctly:

"It doesn't matter whether it comes in by cable, telephone lines, computer, or satellite. Everyone's going to have to deal with Disney."

In his imperial euphoria, Eisner neglected to mention what for centuries used to be the only mass medium, words printed on paper, as in newspapers, books and magazines, though these, too, are an important part of the Disney empire.

Even though the new interlocked system of giants is entirely private, it promotes itself as a triumph of patriotic national power. The editor of *Vanity Fair*, a magazine owned by one of the large media corporations (Advance), wrote with evident pride:

"The power center of America... has moved from its role as military-industrial giant to a new supremacy as the world's entertainment-information superpower."

* * *

It is not an idle boast. By almost every measure of public reach—financial power, political influence, and multiple techniques—the new conglomerates have more influence over what Americans see and hear than private firms have ever before possessed.

Because each of the dominant firms has adopted a strategy of creating its own closed system of control over every step in the national media process, from creation of content to its delivery, no content —news, entertainment, or other public messages—will reach the public unless a handful of corporate decision-makers decide that it will. Smaller independents have always helped provide an alternative and still do, but they have become ever more vulnerable to the power of the super-giants. As the size and financial power of the new dominant firms has escalated, so has their coercive power to offer a bothersome smaller competitor a choice of either selling out at once or slowly facing ruin as the larger firm uses its greater financial resources to undercut the independent competitor on price and promotion. In the process, consumers have become less influential than ever.

Financial news still is full of the sounds of clashes between giants. But the new media leaders compete only over marginal matters: their imperial borders, their courtship of new allies, and their acquisitions of smaller firms. Underneath these skirmishes, they are interlocked in shared financial ownership and a complex of joint ventures. With minor exceptions, they share highly conservative political and economic values. Most also own interests in other industries—defense, consumer products and services; firms like General Electric, Westinghouse, and the country's cash-rich telephone companies—and have shown little hesitation in using their control of the news to support the fortunes of their other subsidiaries.

The new cyberspace revolution typified by the Internet and the World Wide Web has been held out as offering the promise of altering our definition of "mass" in the phrase "mass media." Individuals operating from their own home computers connected to telephone lines can communicate with other individual computers. But by the mid-1990s fewer than 15 percent of American households were equipped with modems that connect computers to phone lines. That number will undoubtedly grow, but even now, in the Internet's infancy, concerted corporate efforts are turning the Internet into the most direct mass merchandising vehicle ever invented, with much of the sales promotion directed at children. An IBM executive in charge of computer networking has said that by the year 2000 he expects that the Internet will be "the world's largest, deepest, fastest and most secure marketplace... worth $1 trillion annually."

Perhaps the most troubling power of the new cartel is its control of the main body of news and public affairs information. The reporting of news has always been a commercial enterprise and this has always created conflicts of interest. But the behavior of the new corporate controllers of public information has produced a higher level of manipulation of news to pursue the owners' other financial and political goals. In the process, there has been a parallel shrinkage of any sense of obligation to serve the noncommercial information needs of public citizenship.

The idea of government interceding to protect consumers is contrary to the ideology of most of the media cartel's leaders, who, with few exceptions, pursue the conservative political and economic notion of an uninhibited free market that operates without social or moral obligations.

But today some of the leading members of the media cartel openly order their journalists to report news with an eye to helping advertisers and promoting their owners' other nonjournalistic goals. In a speech at the 1995 convention of the Newspaper Association of America, the publishers invited a major advertiser to make a speech criticizing the country's reporters for being reluctant to redefine news as part entertainment and an aid to advertisers.

* * *

Emergence of the new cartel does not change the basic impact of media conglomeration on society.... Earlier, it was possible to describe the dominant firms in each separate medium—daily newspapers, magazines, radio, television, books and movies. With each passing year,... the number of controlling firms in all these media has shrunk: from fifty corporations in 1984 to twenty-six in 1987, followed by twenty-three in 1990, and then, as the borders between the different media began to blur, to less than twenty in 1993. In 1996 the number of media corporations with dominant power in society is closer to ten. In terms of media possessions and resources, the newest dominant ten are Time Warner, Disney, Viacom, News Corporation Limited (Murdoch), Sony, Tele-Communications, Inc. Seagram (TV, movies, cable, books, music), Westinghouse, Gannett, and General Electric.

Ironically, some of the American media giants that have cowed our own government are restrained in their foreign operations by the governments of other democratic nations more serious than the United States about preventing monopolies.

Some of the firms powerful within the United States are based outside the country, like Murdoch's News Corporation (Australia), Thomson (Canada), and Bertelsmann (Germany). Some must meet more stringent rules against monopoly in their own countries than those imposed upon their United States operations.

The warning expressed in the first edition of *The Media Monopoly*—"media power is political power"—has come to pass to a degree once considered unthinkable.

* * *

The magnitude of the new media cartel's power is reflected in the simple dollar size of recent transactions that produced it.

In 1983, the biggest media merger in history was a $340-million matter, when the Gannett Company, a newspaper chain, bought Combined Communications Corporation, an owner of billboards, newspapers, and broadcast stations. In 1996, when Disney merged with ABC/Cap Cities, it was a $19-billion deal —fifty-six times larger. This union produced a conglomerate that is powerful in every major mass medium: newspapers, magazines, books, radio, broadcast television, cable systems and programming, movies, recordings, video cassettes, and, through alliances and joint ventures, growing control of the golden wires into the American home—telephone and cable.

But the quantity of money involved is the least disturbing measure of events. More ominous is how this degree of concentrated control translates into the power to shape the country's political and economic agendas, to create models of behavior for each generation, and to achieve ever more aggressive, self-serving access to every level of government.

A prime exhibit of the cartel's new political power is the Telecommunications Act of 1996. This act was billed as a transformation of sixty-two years of federal communications law for the pur-

pose of "increasing competition." It was, with some exceptions, largely described as much by most of the major news media. But its most dramatic immediate result has been to reduce competition and open the path to cooperation among the giants.

The new law opened the media field to new competitors, like the large regional telephone companies, on the theory that cable and telephone companies would compete for customers within the same community. In practice, the power of one company in television was enlarged to permit a single firm to reach 35 percent of all American households. The act made it possible, for the first time, for a single company to own more than one radio station in the same market. A single owner was not permitted to own both TV stations and cable systems in the same market. License periods for broadcasters were expanded.

The Telecommunications Act of 1996 swept away even the minimal consumer and diversity protections of the 1934 act that preceded it. Though this was an intricate bill of 280 pages that would transform the American media landscape, its preparation and passage did not meet the standards of study and public participation that ordinarily would precede an historic transformation of a major influence on society.

While most of the media, especially broadcasters, gave the public little useful information on the depth of the change involved, a few newspapers tried.

The *Wall Street Journal* reported very early on how directly the 1994 Congress had become a partner with the media industry: "House Republicans are planning a closed-door meeting this week with top communications executives to learn how Congress can help their companies become more 'successful' as legislators overhaul laws regulating the industry." The paper also reported that Donald Jones, a cable operator, was a volunteer in House Speaker Newt Gingrich's office and attended meetings as an "advisor" while the bill was being written.

The *New York Times* editorialized, "Forty million dollars' worth of lobbying bought telecommunications companies a piece of Senate legislation they could relish."

After late filings of campaign contributions became available, *Common Cause Magazine* reported that major media companies had given political candidates and lawmakers more than $4 million in contributions in the years leading up to passage of the new act. The Consumer Federation of America said, "If you look at the legislation, there is something for absolutely everyone—except the consumer." Jeff Chester and Kathryn Montgomery of the Center for Media Education warned that American culture for the twenty-first century was at stake. But these were not warnings that most Americans saw.

The new law permitted some of the country's largest industries, previously not active in creating content, like telephone companies, to enter the fields of television, radio, and cable. The official rationale was that this would offer consumers new choices because the new entries into the mass media industry would compete independently and thereby force down prices and increase the quality of services. In most instances, the opposite has happened. The new industries entering the media field quickly joined the older ones in shared stock, joint ventures, and the creation of closed systems to produce interlocks that make them partners in

the cartel rather than independent and serious competitors.

Even the meaning of the word "competition" has become blurred by reality. Of the 1,500 daily newspapers in the country, 99 percent are the only daily in their cities. Of the 11,800 cable systems, all but a handful are monopolies in their cities. Of the 11,000 commercial radio stations, six or eight formats (all-talk, all-news, variations of rock music, rap, adult contemporary, etc.), with an all but uniform content within each format, dominate programming in every city. The four commercial television networks and their local affiliates carry programs of essentially the same type, with only the meagerly financed public stations offering a genuine alternative. Thus, most of the media meet the tongue-twisting argot of Wall Street in being oligopolies that are collections of local monopolies. This means few choices for citizens looking for genuine differences.

In 1994, a member of the media consulting firm Kagan Associates, commenting on cable companies, told the *New York Times*, "The top twenty are merging themselves, and will turn into five companies." At the time, the two largest cable firms already had 40 percent of all cable subscribers.

Upon passage of the Telecommunications Act of 1996, the presumed new "competitors" (cable and telephone) quickly became partners or merged into even larger firms. These were predictable marriages. It costs an average of $200,000 a mile to lay down fiber optic telecommunications channels in city streets. It did not take an angel from heaven to whisper to the cable and phone companies planning to dig side by side at $200,000-a-mile that they could join forces and make more money at less expense without competing. And that is what happened.

Given their local monopolies, cable companies should have been common carriers, like electronic companies, providing the wires and making money by leasing space on their lines to the creators of programs, subject to proving in public that their rates are not exorbitant. The new act has produced a very different result.

Though "competitors" greeted the Telecommunications Act of 1996 by joining hands, telephone carriers continued to compete, launching noisy advertising promotions. But is was far from clear that the result would mean ultimate savings or conveniences for average telephone users.

Almost all of the media leaders, possibly excepting Ted Turner of Turner Broadcasting, are political conservatives, a factor in the drastic shift in the entire spectrum of national politics to a brand of conservatism once thought as an "extreme." ...

* * *

Advertisers continue to enjoy privileged access to the news. Both the ABC and CBS news staffs were forced by their managements to apologize or censor stories on deceptions and possible perjury by tobacco industry leaders. (Tobacco is no longer advertised on television, but tobacco companies now own major food and other firms that do advertise heavily on television, a connection not lost on broadcast executives.) A Marquette University poll of newspaper editors in 1992 found that 93 percent of them said advertisers tried to influence their news, a majority said their own management condoned the pressure, and 37 percent of the editors polled admitted that they had suc-

cumbed. A recent Nielson survey showed that 80 percent of television news directors said they broadcast corporate public relations films as news "several times a month."

In the reign of the new media cartel, the integrity of much of the country's professional news has become more ambiguous than ever. The role of journalists within news companies has always been an inherent dilemma for reporters and editors. Reporters are expected by the public and by reportorial standards to act like independent, fair-minded professionals. But reporters are also employees of corporations that control their hiring, firing, and daily management—what stories they will cover and what part of their coverage will be used or discarded. It is a harsh newsroom reality that never seems to cause conservative critics to speculate why their corporate colleagues who own the news and have total control over both their reporters' careers and the news that gets into their papers would somehow delight in producing "liberal bias."

The new media conglomerates have exacerbated the traditional problems of professional news. The cartel includes some industries that have never before owned important news outlets. Some of the new owners find it bizarre that anyone would question the propriety of ordering their employee-journalists to produce news coverage designed to promote the owner's corporation.

Seeing their journalists as obedient workers on an assembly line has produced a growing incidence of news corporations demanding unethical acts. There are more instances than ever of management contempt and cruelty toward their journalists.

Letting advertisers influence the news is no novelty but in the past it was usually done by innuendo, or quiet editing reassignment or firing. It has seldom before been so boldly stated and practiced, in ways that typify the new contempt that some news companies feel for the professional independence of their journalists—and for the news audience. The trend typifies a growing attitude that reporting the news is just another business....

* * *

Only fifteen years ago, it was possible to cite specific corporations dominant in one communications medium, with only a minority of those corporations similarly dominant in a second medium. Today, as noted, the largest media firms have an aggressive strategy of acquiring dominant positions across every medium of any current or expected future consequence. Known and admired on Wall Street as "synergy," the policy calls for one company subsidiary to be used to complement and promote another. The process has helped produce a quantum leap in the power of a dominant media corporation to create and manipulate popular culture and models of behavior (or misbehavior) —and to use this power for narrow commercial and political purposes.

Opportunities for this kind of information "synergy" have become rampant. The country's second-largest cable company, Time Warner, is a leader in the ownership of magazines, books, and movies, which originate news and entertainment. But the firm also owns video production operations, the leading pay cable network, Home Box Office (HBO), and it has merged with Turner Broadcasting, which in turn owns several popular cable networks, including CNN and TNT.

The most spectacular example of unified multimedia ownership is also the leading example of acquiring control of every step in the mass-media process, from creation of content to its delivery into the home.

The Disney empire includes—in addition to non-media interests in oil and insurance—interests in interactive TV and the America Online computer network, Buena Vista home video, Hyperion and Chilton book publishing, four movie and TV production studios and a national distribution system for them, four magazine publishing groups (including *Women's Wear Daily* and other garment-trade newspapers), 429 retail stores for selling Disney products, television and cable networks (including part ownership of A&E, Lifetime, and ESPN), a major league baseball team and a National Hockey League team, three record companies, eleven newspapers (including the *Fort Worth Star-Telegram* and the *Kansas City Star*), and nine theme parks in the United States and other countries.

A major addition to the Disney empire is its ownership of ABC, which owns twenty-one local radio stations, the largest radio network reaching a quarter of all U.S. radio homes, ABC video, and ABC Network News, whose programs include *Prime Time Live, Good Morning America, World News Tonight with Peter Jennings*, and *20/20.*

Rupert Murdoch's entry into national network broadcasting, the FOX network, did little to introduce new or different choices for the public. It followed the Murdochian doctrine of increasing sex and violence while using his ownership of *TV Guide* to cover stories and other feature articles in that publication in an attempt to increase ratings of his weather TV and cable shows.

contract w/ America originally here

* * *

What emerged by the late 1990s was an intertwining of partners in a variety of joint ventures that controlled a rearrangement of the country's media landscape. Missing was a partner that would protect consumer needs in that landscape.

Interactive television and high-definition digital television raised visions of a bonanza of future profits among big cable and telephone companies, but they found themselves confronted with the digital revolution's "500-pound gorilla" —Bill Gate's Microsoft.

Gates, with seemingly endless quantities of money and ambition, could add even greater liquid cash to the interlocked complexes. Not only was he the richest man in America and the manufacturer of the operating systems in 80 percent of personal computers, he also announced plans to decide what the public's standards would be for use of the Internet, World Wide Web, and the coming era of digital interactive television.

Gates has even included still photographs in his empire. His Microsoft bought control of the Bettmann Archives, the most important collection of historic photographs in the world, and has moved to acquire other photo archives worldwide. As a source of images, still photographs continue to be a major product in commercial and editorial illustration in both printed and electronic media.

The Internet and the World Wide Web had been hailed as providing the ultimate freedom of the individual from mass media control. Individuals could use their phone-connected computers to talk to other computers without corporate or governmental intercession. On the Web they could express their opinions on anything—and "anything" was literally interpreted—and establish groups and bulletin boards for digital conversations with like-minded computer users.

However, the supposedly free-form Internet and World Wide Web were quickly exploited as an even more powerful tool of mass merchandising than television. The Internet and Web can generate millions of impulse purchases made by those "surfing the net" and encountering moving, four-color advertisements for products that can be ordered instantly by a keystroke.

Local newspapers and broadcast stations continued to shrink their news of local civic and community groups, a loss with special meaning in the United States as compared to other developed democracies. Control of political and social institutions in this country—schools, police, land use policy, etc.—is extraordinarily local. That is why, unlike in other countries, every holder of an American broadcast license must own a local studio. Yet, increasingly over the years, broadcasters have been permitted to abandon access to air time by serious local civic groups. In their place, broadcasters have substituted happy-talk, gossipy features. The result is locally broadcast programs that are in fact standardized national ones with no relationship of local civic needs.

In 1987, cancellation of the Fairness Doctrine made another new antidemocratic phenomenon almost predictable. Talk radio has become an overwhelming ultra-conservative political propaganda machine. The most influential propagandist, Rush Limbaugh, has nineteen million listeners, and there is no right of reply to his extraordinary record of lies, libels, and damaging fantasies. (When the extremely conservative new Republicans took control of the House of Representatives in 1994, the keynote speaker for their first private meeting was Limbaugh.) . . .

The growth of corporate control and loss of citizen access reflects the fading of a crucial reality about broadcasting that the standard news outlets seldom mention.

Almost from the start, national communications law has been based on the concept that the public owns the airwaves. For their part, broadcasters insist on government policing and penalties to prevent unlicensed operators from wittingly or unwittingly jamming the frequencies of established stations: otherwise there would be a chaos of static on radio and screens full of "snow" on television. But federal law also mandates that those who hold licenses must maintain local studios and operate "in the public interest," which, given the local nature of studios, has meant significant access to the airwaves by community groups. Holders of broadcast licenses have no right to licenses beyond their term limits and presumably may renew them only if they have fulfilled their community obligations.

Despite the law, in recent years both the major media operators and the Congress have acted as though its "public ownership" phrases are not there or can be safely ignored. The Congress, the White House, and the Federal Communications Commission have steadily relaxed standards to permit the growing exclusion of community voices on the country's

11,000 local commercial radio stations, 1,500 television stations, and 11,800 local cable systems.

Meanwhile, the familiar broadcast twins, sex and violence, have maintained their apparently unchangeable hold on American commercial television, notwithstanding decades of complaints by parents, educators, and the Surgeon General of the United States, who has shown that TV violence increases real violence in society. Ironically, the increasing number of broadcast channels has lead to even more aggressive sex and violence programming as more channels compete for fixing viewers' attention by using the same formula endlessly replicated without the need for talent or creativity. . . .

* * *

The domination of private money in public politics, which has subverted so much public policy, also prevents legal solutions to problems in the mass media. Most media proprietors show little or no evidence in their programming of any sense of obligation to treat the American audience as citizens of a democracy. Campaign finance reform and media reform are directed at the same societal sickness—the influence of private money that improperly negates civic need and public choice. Linked to the same problem, they have become linked in the ultimate remedy. At stake is the accountability of politics and with it the media's socialization of American children and the nation's culture.

NO

Eli M. Noam and
Robert N. Freeman

THE MEDIA MONOPOLY
AND OTHER MYTHS

It's been said that generals always fight the last war, not the new one. And the question is whether media critics sometimes do that, too. For many years, we were worried about the concentration of private power over the media. The fear was a media mogul with a political agenda: a William Randolph Hearst, who started a war and ran himself for Mayor, Governor, and President. And that was just using newspapers. Later, when television was controlled by three networks, all within ten blocks of each other in Manhattan, the fear of control over hearts, minds, pocketbooks, and voting booths was amplified from the left and right. And today, with electronic media becoming smart, powerful, and pervasive, and with media mergers reported every week, the same fear is around more than ever, that in the end there will be only four media companies left in the world, and running the world, half of them owned by a guy named Rupert.

Ben Bagdikian expresses this fear in his article *The Media Monopoly*, published in *Television Quarterly* (Volume 28, Number 4). He pointed to the growing size of media mergers, the shrinking number of major media corporations, and their increasing diversification into multiple branches of media. He discounted the relevance of the diverse and publicly accessible Internet by pointing to the small share of Americans that have the equipment to get online. He also expressed frustration that the Telecommunications Act of 1996 has so far led to more cooperation than competition.

To evaluate all this, it is important to understand how the media world has evolved through stages. In the past of electronic media, twenty years ago, we had *limited* media, with only three networks, one phone company, and one computer company. Today, we are in the stage of multi-channel media, with many dozens of TV channels and with multiple phone networks. But this is still not the end of the story. The third stage, and the one we are entering now, is *cyber-media*. Cyber-text is already established. Cyber-audio is here. And

From Eli M. Noam and Robert N. Freeman, "The Media Monopoly and Other Myths," *Television Quarterly*, vol. 29, no. 1 (1997). Copyright © 1997 by The National Academy of Television Arts and Sciences. Reprinted by permission.

cyber-telephony and cyber-video are emerging. In time, this will led us to an entirely different system of mass media. Yet governments, media companies, and media critics are still looking backward to the good old days of scarcity.

The discussion over media concentration often has that anachronistic flavor. So let's first look at the facts. Yes, there have been lots of mergers. Some are troubling, some are not. Going beyond the specific deal, the more important question is, in the aggregate, have American media become more concentrated?

Despite the conventional wisdom, the answer is not an obvious "yes." First, while the fish in the pond have grown in size, the pond did grow, too, and faster. The growth of the information industry has been 8% faster than inflation since 1987. Second, all these separate ponds are becoming more of a large lake, as the technological and regulatory dikes between them fall.

The combined share of the top 10 companies in the US information industry declined from 59% in 1987 to 39% today. This is a totally different conclusion from those who claim that US media are now controlled by ten firms. In 1979, AT&T alone accounted for a full quarter of the entire media and information industry (*Table 1*). Today, even with two divestitures, AT&T is larger in dollar terms, but now commands only 7% of the total industry. IBM tripled in the past 15 years, but its share in the media and information industry dropped by one third, to less than 10%. CBS used to have 2%.

A decade later, even after mergers with Westinghouse and Infinity, the new company has only 1%. Bell Atlantic and Nynex both used to have about 3.5% each. A decade later, after their merger, their combined share is barely

Table 1

Share of Information Industry

	1979	1987	1997
AT&T	24%	16%	7%
IBM	14%	17%	9%
CBS/ Westinghouse	2%	1%	1%
Bell Atlantic		3.2% ↘	
			→ 4%
Nynex		3.7% ↗	
Disney	0.5%	1% ↘	
			→ 2%
ABC	0.2%	1% ↗	
Microsoft	0.0%	0.1%	0.7%
TCI	0.0%	0.5%	0.7%

higher, at 4%. The major exception was Disney/CapCities/ABC, with a share that is now twice the combined share of these firms in 1979. But it's still only 2%. Also, both Microsoft and TCI grew from nothing to each capture 1% of the industry. But little of that growth was due to mergers.

When it comes to concentration, views are strong, talk is cheap, but numbers are scarce. Therefore, we have gotten our hands dirty by collecting the actual market share numbers, industry by industry, company by company, for 60 subindustries from book publishing to film production to microprocessors, in order to trace the concentration trends over the past 15 years. We then aggregated these data into broader sectors such as telecommunications, video distribution, etc. And we aggregated those sectoral figures again into an overall industry concentration trend. This is probably the most detailed study ever of media concentration in America.

What did we find? Surprisingly, the overall concentration of the information industry did not increase, but declined somewhat in the past decade (*Table 2*).

Table 2
**Total Information Sector
Concentration (weighted aggregates)**

	1986	1990	1995
Top 4 Firms	52%	49%	50%
HH Index	1839	1347	1262

Table 3
**Mass Media Sector Concentration
(weighted aggregates)**

	1986	1990	1995
Top 4 Firms	33%	27.5%	40%
HH Index	514	491	574

To confirm this result, we used two separate measures of concentration: the combined share of the top four firms in each sector, and the Justice Department's HHI index, a more sensitive but less intuitive measure. An HHI under 1,000 means a market is unconcentrated, an HHI over 1,800 means a market is highly concentrated, between 1,000 and 1,800, a market is moderately concentrated.

If one looks at the classic mass media industries alone (excluding telecommunications, computers, software, and equipment) they did increase in concentration (*Table 3*), but remained unconcentrated by Justice Department standards. The main factors increasing these concentration figures were cable television systems (accounting for half) and home video (accounting for 20%).

The greatest drops occurred in telecommunications services, computers, TV programming, and music (*Table 4*). In long distance, AT&T's shares dropped from 80% to just over half. Soon, new entrants into mobile and local telephony will gradually further that trend. In computers, the market shifted away from mainframes to micro computers, where no top firm controls much more than 10%. This shift also lowered entry barriers in the software market, which used to be vertically integrated with hardware, reducing the share of the top four firms to about one third. Concentration in TV programing dropped with the launch of new broad-

cast and cable networks. The share of the top four cable channel firms dropped from two thirds to about 40%. In pay cable, the share of Time Warner shrank slightly, but it still controls half the market. In music, the share of the top four labels dropped from 80% to 60%.

On the other hand, concentration *increased* in other industries (*Table 5*). Microsoft controls 90% of the microcomputer operating system market, for all the talk about platform independent Java. This is the Bill Gates problem.

* * *

There is also a cable issue. The share of the top four cable firms grew from one-fourth in 1979 to nearly two-thirds today. That's a lot of gatekeeping power, though they now must contend with satellite TV firms. Concentration also increased in TV station ownership and retail bookstores, and more than doubled in radio station ownership and book publishing. But the top four firms still have only about a quarter of these markets, as measured by revenue. In terms of stations, the largest radio firm has 102 stations, which sounds like a lot, but there are over 12,000 stations nationwide.

In other industries, concentration held relatively steady (*Table 6*). Film production remained fairly concentrated, with the top four firms controlling 60%. The movie theater, newspaper and magazine markets remained relatively unconcen-

Table 4
**Declining Concentration
(4 firm shares)**

	1986	1990	1995
Telecom. Services	77%	76%	73%
Computer Hardware	56%	45%	45%
Computer Software	42%	39%	35%
3 Major TV Networks	70%	63%	53%
Basic Cable Channel Firms	67%	53%	39%
Pay Cable (Time Warner)	57%	57%	51%

trated, with the top four firms accounting for a quarter of sales.

Therefore, it cannot simply be said that US media have become, in general, more concentrated. Still, the next question then must be raised: even if a firm does not dominate any specific market, could it not be overpowering by being a medium sized firm in every market? The fear is that vertically integrated firms will dominate by having their tentacles in each pie. But in economic terms, this can only happen if a firm has real market power in at least one market, which it then extends and leverages into other markets. And such single-firm dominance of a market is becoming rare, as we have seen.

One exception is cable TV, where TCI and Time Warner can still favor their own channels over those of competitors. In New York, Time Warner could have shut out Murdoch's Fox News Channel, as a rival to its own CNN. This problem may disappear with satellite TV. The second important exception is Microsoft, which could extend its market power from computer operating systems to become the gatekeeper of other cyber-media. If this control persists with no competitive relief, Microsoft will become the major media policy headache of the 21st century.

But where markets are competitive, vertical integration makes little sense. Disney should not earmark its best programs for ABC if other networks offer more money. Conversely, for Disney to force its lemons on the ABC television network would only hurt the company. This creates major centrifugal forces inside the organization which in a competitive environment will lead to a breakup of the company. In a competitive environment, media firms must divest and focus for optimal efficiency. To attract viewers, content production will separate from distribution, and news writing will separate from political lobbying.

And what about all those famous synergies? These have been more asserted than shown. In announcing its mega-merger, Disney CEO Michael Eisner invoked the word not less than five times in four consecutive sentences, like a mantra. But most of those cross-promotional benefits—film, books, toys, etc.—could be established by simple contracts. You don't need $15 billion mergers to create them.

Twenty years ago, CBS bought the New York Yankees baseball team and the big publisher Simon & Schuster, all to achieve those same vaunted synergies. Nothing came of it. Sony bought Columbia Pictures and Records, to merge film and music with consumer electronics, and lost billions on movies. Its share in music fell from one-fourth to one-sixth. In Time Warner's case, the synergies became negative as the rap music business dragged down the respectability of the news magazines; today, the company is a collection of feuding fiefdoms. Disney, Viacom, and News Corp. will get there too, after their empire-building leaders have left the scene.

Although media companies have become more diversified, they can only

Table 5

Rising Concentration (4 firm shares)

	1986*	1990	1995
Microcomputer			
Operating Systems	55%	85%	90%
Cable TV Distribution	37%	46%	60%
TV Stations	15%	16%	26%
Radio Stations	8%	9%	20%
Book Publishing	15%	30%	33%
Book Stores	20%	23%	26%

*The 1986 column actually contains Microsoft's 1984 market share.

Table 6

Stable Concentration (4 firm shares)

	1986	1990	1995
Film Production	62%	62%	61%
Cinemas	29%	29%	29%
Newspapers	25%	25%	26%
Magazines	23%	22%	22%

exploit cross-ownership for so long as they retain market power in distribution. While the Telecommunications Act of 1996 led to an immediate spurt of media mergers, it also opened the door to competition between cable, wired, and both satellite-based and terrestrial wireless distribution systems. Such developments will not be as instantaneous as the media deals. But in time they will undermine the economic power and rationale for diversified media corporations.

* * *

Does this mean there is no concentration problem? No. But the real problems in media concentration are not national, but local. 98.5% of American cities have only one newspaper. They rarely editoralize about that. 98% of American homes have no choice in their cable provider. Alternative local residential phone service may be coming, but is not here yet. Local radio concentration has increased considerably since the Telecommunications Act of 1996 relaxed local ownership ceilings, and is more of a problem than national radio concentration.

None of this is surprising. Local media are the weak link in the media revolution. Competing national media lead

to narrow-casing. Programs are expensive, and must be produced for the world, not just for a town, in order to make money. Media companies must aggregate increasingly scarce eyeballs nationally and internationally. That's also true for cyber-media, which have been worldwide from the beginning. And local media are even more in trouble in the future. In cyber-television, advertising can be customized and targeted, and advertisers will migrate away from local newspapers as advertising vehicles.

But on the national level, to repeat, there will be more competition, more conduits, more content. With the number of channels increasing, smaller firms can enter. The Internet is rapidly becoming an important media outlet. In 1996, somewhere between 9 million and 42 million US residents used the Internet, depending on whose estimate you believe. These estimates have been doubling annually. The current Internet is primarily a medium for text, graphics, and audio information. In the future, small firms will connect their video servers to such cyber-networks, and users will come to them. It will be more like in book publishing today, some big players and many small ones.

Does this solve all of our concerns? Not all of them. Diversity still does not assure openness. Competition can lead to exclusion of unpopular voices in order not to offend. Advertisers have more power. Content becomes more sensationalized. In the past, common carriage was the bedrock of free speech in an environment of private carriers because it prevented a carrier from discriminating against any speaker or lawful speech. But now, the days of common carriage are numbered. Most importantly, the regulatory status of the Internet is up for grabs. And those are the issues we should focus on.

POSTSCRIPT

Media Monopolies: Does Concentration of Ownership Jeopardize Media Content?

Media mergers are the topic of a special issue of the *Media Studies Journal* (Spring/Summer 1996). Todd Gitlin argues in that special issue that today's deals may weigh on the culture for decades. The potential for harm, he suggests, is as great as the potential for good. In a counterpoint, Steven Rattner predicts benefits for consumers. He foresees the consequences of technology development and corporations that are large enough to fund expensive new undertakings as producing exciting new options for the public. Both agree that attention must be paid to traditional expectations of freedom of expression. They diverge considerably on whether or not large corporations can accomplish that end.

This counterpoint was represented in the debate over the Telecommunications Act. *Congressional Digest* (January 1996) reports the divergent opinions of a number of representatives, including Thomas Bliley, Jr. (R-Virginia), who says, "For the first time, communications policy will be based on competition rather than arbitrary regulation"; John Conyers, Jr. (D-Michigan), who contends, "For American consumers, this is one big sucker punch"; and William Coyne (D-Pennsylvania), who argues, "The rush to deregulate opens the floodgates for companies which already enjoy a monopoly position in one market to expand their dominance to other segments."

A number of authors have examined the issue of concentration of ownership in the media industries. Mark Crispin Miller offers what he calls a guide to our contracting media cosmos in his article "Free the Media," *The Nation* (June 3, 1996). A number of people from the media, the academic world, and public interest groups offer responses to his work. The Center for Media Education's 12-step program for media democracy is presented at the end of the article. A *Columbia Journalism Review* forum on the dangers of corporate control (March 1997) is a nicely balanced representation of varying opinions.

Whatever their persuasion, observers seem to share a concern about the impact of Bill Gates and Microsoft as it enters the media industries. This is reflected in "Will Gates Crush Newspapers?" *Columbia Journalism Review* (November 1997). Some other recent volumes include *Triumph and Erosion in the American Media and Entertainment Industries* by Dan Steinbock (Quorum Books, 1995), *Commercial Culture: The Media System and the Public Interest* by Leo Bogart (Oxford University Press, 1995), and *Conglomerates and the Media* edited by Patricia Aufderheide (New Press, 1997).

ISSUE 15

Will Traditional Advertising Survive the New Technology Revolution?

YES: Amy Waldman, from "Lonely Hearts, Classy Dreams, Empty Wallets: How Home Shopping Channels Prey on the Hunger for Class and Companionship," *The Washington Monthly* (June 1995)

NO: Roland T. Rust and Richard W. Oliver, from "The Death of Advertising," *Journal of Advertising* (December 1994)

ISSUE SUMMARY

YES: Media commentator Amy Waldman asserts that home shopping channels deliver enormous markets for companies selling products and that the isolating features of the television medium make traditional sales tactics such as promising happiness through goods effective.

NO: Professor of marketing Roland T. Rust and professor of management Richard W. Oliver argue that traditional advertising agencies are no longer powerful mediators of products in an environment in which companies find more customized ways to reach their potential audiences.

Each of the following selections acknowledges that a variety of media technologies has influenced how advertising works in our society. Amy Waldman does not question the role of advertising industries per se, but she does discuss the enormous power of television as a sales medium. She considers the Home Shopping Network to be one long, uninterrupted commercial for selling goods. She discusses the role of testimonials, the values of consumerism, and individuals' needs to connect with others in some form of community. She paints a picture of lonely people who, for whatever reason, seek a sense of "belonging" through the purchase of goods that promise to make them feel better.

Roland T. Rust and Richard W. Oliver claim that there has been a recent decline in the profits of the advertising industry because it has not kept pace as America has moved from a "product-oriented economy toward a services-oriented economy." They see the loss of mass audiences as a challenge to develop a new system of marketing called "adaptive" marketing. Their scenario for the advertising industry is that the challenges of new ways of doing things will undoubtedly influence the number of jobs and the skills necessary for a career in marketing and/or advertising. The future, they write, may bring a new role called "customer communications," which will be responsive to forms of media in the same way that the advertising industry responded to social needs up until the middle of the nineteenth century.

Although neither Waldman nor Rust/Oliver takes the perspective that advertising will become obsolete in the future, both present different scenarios for how the traditional advertising industry will change in response to more segmented audiences and different formats for selling goods. In many ways, the effect of the home shopping channels discussed by Waldman is an example of adaptive marketing, which Rust and Oliver say is necessary for advertising industry change. The important difference, however, is that Waldman focuses on the effect on consumers, while Rust and Oliver present the issue from the perspective of the advertising industry. These two approaches outline the importance of specificity in understanding how new directions in media industries can be thought of in light of the inevitability of market change.

YES

Amy Waldman

LONELY HEARTS, CLASSY DREAMS, EMPTY WALLETS: HOW HOME SHOPPING CHANNELS PREY ON THE HUNGER FOR CLASS AND COMPANIONSHIP

After a man died several months ago at the Virginian Retirement Community in Fairfax, his family went to collect his worldly goods. They found more than they bargained for: His home was crammed, floor to ceiling, with possessions they never knew he had. There were kitchen gadgets, costume jewelry, bed linens, and cleansers, all by the dozens.

He had bought it all from the world's most accessible stores: the home shopping networks that came through his television into his living room 24 hours a day, seven days a week. This man, whose name the retirement home withheld for privacy, ordered a package from QVC or Home Shopping Network (HSN), the two leading home shopping channels, almost every day. Some of what came he gave away. Most of it simply piled up, unused.

What had brought him to line his walls with the fruits of home shopping? In a word, companionship. Home shopping hosts didn't just sell to him—they spoke to him. An employee at the Virginian recalls that the man spent a lot of time by himself. He did not make friends easily and he spoke of being lonely. But when he bought, he said he could keep operators chatting to him for half an hour. He had found a way to fill his days and sleepless nights.

He was not alone in his discovery. As the hours cycle past on home shopping channels, the disembodied voices of buyers, calling in to offer "testimonials" on their purchases, float above the sparkling descriptions of cubic zirconium jewelry. Most are female—Dorothy from Daytona, Betty from Fresno, Helen from Mexico City, Indiana. Many of the voices are beginning to crack with age. And their extraordinary enthusiasm for the products—and the hosts, and the show itself—masks something else: a deep, abiding need for human contact. "I live alone," says a woman named Erma who calls in on a Monday morning. "All I've got to do is watch QVC."

To Erma, the man from Virginia, and many others like them, home shopping channels sold more than $3 billion of goods [in 1994]. QVC, which stands for

Quality Value Control, alone sold $1.4 billion worth of goods in 1994, logging 55 million phone calls. The channel is the world's largest purveyor of gold jewelry. It once sold $1.4 million worth of Kodak products in 70 minutes and $1.9 million of Mighty Morphin Power Rangers paraphernalia in two hours. In a record day, it took $18 million in orders. The second-place Home Shopping Network, or "Club" (as it's known on the air), nearly matches that pace.

That the two channels, and a host of smaller rivals, could do so well runs counter to conventional wisdom, for in an age of ironic, sophisticated advertising, the home shopping pitch seems amateurish. The camera zooms in on an item, which rocks back and forth, back and forth on a pedestal; the hosts, in living-room sets, praise each bauble in a frenzy of superlatives. A clock counts down to whip up a sense of urgency as the number sold mounts on the screen. The suggested retail price hovers above the low, low home shopping price.

Many of the goods—imitation jewelry, collectibles, gadgets, polyester pantsuits —are junk, often selling at more-than-junk prices. And while "convenience" is a favorite home shopping buzzword, the description could not be less apt: It might take hours, even days, of home shopping viewing to come upon something you need.

Spend some time in front of the television, though, and you sense that while the pitch is predictable, it is anything but amateurish. As low-tech as they are, the home shopping networks understand that the real work of advertising is not to publicize bargains—it is to appeal to deeper needs. They turn their constant, mesmerizing presence and viewer participation into a mock community, a "universe," as QVC calls it, that seems to break the isolation television perpetuates. And even for those who are not lonely, home shopping promises something else: the lives of the rich, the famous, the glamorous—on the cheap, and just a phone call away.

SOMEPLACE VERY SPECIAL

Home shopping is just one more chapter in the evolution of marketing to a consumer culture—a process that began in earnest in the twenties and accelerated with the post–World War II economic expansion that established America's middle class as a potent consumer force. In response, advertisers went to work creating what one General Motors executive called the "organized culture of dissatisfaction"—bringing out new, "better" models each year so previous models seemed inadequate, or offering consumers a choice of, say, 15 shoe colors so one no longer seemed enough.

Advertisers were so successful in unleashing desire that a traditionally frugal nation began to redefine "need" as whatever ads told them they had to have. It was the creation and fulfillment of these needs that John Kenneth Galbraith probed in his 1958 classic, *The Affluent Society*. Ad men, he wrote, "are effective only with those who do not know what they want. In this state alone, men are open to persuasion."

In such a culture, home shopping, with its introduction of newer, better items every 10 minutes, finds fertile ground. The channels target the credit-card carrying working and middle-class consumers who may have enough but can be persuaded they need more. "It's things you need, but you don't realize you need," one regular home shopper tells me. "But then you see it and it looks so good."

Between midnight and 1 a.m. one night, QVC sells 8,400 terrycloth robes ($24.95 apiece—the day's "special value"), an item the host also pushes as "a beach cover-up." Nancy calls from Middletown, Ohio. "What did you like about the robe?" the host asks. "Well, I thought it would make a nice beach cover-up," Nancy says. "Do you live near a beach?" asks the host. "No," admits Nancy, "No, I don't."

In their effort to cultivate such needs, the effervescent female home shopping hosts and their unctuous male counterparts know their audience well: more than 80 percent female, mainly middle-aged or older. Occasionally, they fall back on the tactics glossy women's magazines have used for decades to target younger women in the prime of their insecurity. "Summer's coming up," says the no-nonsense marketer of a nail buffing kit. "That means beach weather, that means sandals, ladies. Do you want to show your toenails the way they look right now?... If you're not picking up our kit today, you're a loser."

But most often, the hosts head straight for the class-anxiety jugular. They play to a modern-day version of Gustave Flaubert's Emma Bovary, the woman who drives her family into debt because of her conviction that material things will bring some sort of transcendence from her bourgeois existence. "In Rouen she saw ladies with charms dangling from their watch fobs; she bought some charms.... Though she had no one to write to, she had bought herself a blotter, a writing case, a pen, and envelopes."

In America after the twenties, the rich held their edge over the Bovarys not by the gaudiness of their wealth but by their elite tastes—knowing the right vintages or the right vacation spots, which meant shunning Cancun once the Smiths from Des Moines could afford it.

In the eighties, arguably for the first time since the twenties, conspicuous consumption came back into style. Television programs like "Dallas" and "Dynasty" ogled the lifestyles of the rich and famous, and the media elevated money-makers like Donald Trump to celebrity status. Taste was suddenly very, very expensive. For those on the outside looking in, the problem was, as home shopping hosts put it, how to get gemstones at costume jewelry prices.

Into this anxious void rushed HSN, which went on the air in 1985, and QVC, which followed a year later. Both began offering truckloads of low-quality "luxury" items, most of it costume jewelry and imitation gemstones—merchandise that caters to the need to look like you have more than you do.

Home shopping pretends to offer the requisite knowledge to establish good taste. For several hundred dollars, the host sells a rug and the conversation to go with it: "Well, it's an Aubusson rug, it goes back to the time of Louis XV, Marie Antoinette and so on.... It's made from long-haired sheep in Northern China. They have long hair because it gets very cold up near Siberia and Mongolia...."

Halfway into the downscaled nineties, though, what home shopping really pushes are the values of the eighties. "This bracelet says money, money, money, money," QVC's Gwen Owen gushes over a fake diamond bracelet, which sells for $80. The home shopping hosts are marketing the pearly gates of upper-class heaven. They just happen to be *faux* pearl.

That this market is a gold mine is apparent in the cadre of celebrities —from Pete Rose to Joan Rivers to John Tesh—who now peddle on home shopping channels. Since home shopping is about making excess affordable, it's no surprise that among the most popular celebrity-salespeople are the icons of the eighties. A decade ago, on "Dallas," Victoria Principal embodied everything out of reach. Today, on QVC, dressed down, with minimal make-up, she's in middle-America's living room, eager to talk and take calls. Her presence seems to represent a leveling, an accessibility unprecedented in American culture.

The idea is tantalizing, but deceptive. The celebrities foment status anxiety as successfully from a living room like yours and mine as they did from the pages of glossy magazines a decade ago. HSN showcases Vanna White, the "Wheel of Fortune" letter-turner who rocketed to fame in the eighties by wearing a different designer dress every night, and who now, stripped of her gowns, sells her own label clothes and shoes on Home Shopping Club. A woman calls in to tell Vanna she has 20 pairs of Vanna White shoes, and begins listing the colors: red, white, gold, silver.... "I'm so happy to hear that," White interrupts, "but do you have this one?" She is holding up a shoe described as "halfway between gold and silver."

And then there is Ivana Trump, perhaps the ultimate emblem of eighties excess-as-success, a woman, her co-host Bobbi reminds us, "who knows what it is to roll down Rodeo Drive and go shopping." In her pink silk "House of Ivana" outfit, girlish blond curls, and what looks like tens of thousands of dollars of plastic surgery, she comes on HSN to share her designs and her secrets (and plug her new book). She is holding out a hand from the Beautiful People to the Little People.

"You have the opportunity to have in your wardrobe items that Ivana has in her collection," co-host Bobbi observes, "and that takes you someplace very special." You can, Ivana explains, wear an outfit "to drop your kids off in the morning, go to the doctor, go shopping, put some earrings on and go to a lovely lunch. It's perfect for a cruise."

That women are unnervingly grateful for these nuggets from Park Avenue, Palm Beach, and Hollywood lives is a poignant reminder of just how central an issue class continues to be in American life. "You can afford anything, Ivana," one caller says, "and due to you, people like me—I'm a nurse—can too. We live vicariously through you."

But even as Ivana seems to forsake her class advantage, she leverages it. Her perfume must be good because "I could purchase any perfume in the world," she boasts. "Silver is in this year," she proclaims. "I already knew that last year, because I go to parties...I'm always dead ahead." And then comes the tease: "But now everyone's going to catch up to me."

Truth is, Ivana has no intention of letting everyone catch up to her. "I have a suggestion," a caller named Anne says to Ivana. "Everyone is crazy about your engagement ring. You should do it in imitation stones and put it in the collection." Ivana giggles: "I have to discuss it with my fiancé. I don't think he will like it. He'll say, 'I spent millions on it and now you share it with the ladies?'"

In the end, home shopping channels peddle only the illusion that you can fake your way into the upper class, that snobbery can come cheap. They are less interested in democratizing status than preserving the status quo. Like all home shopping hosts, HSN's Alan Skanz regularly plugs cubic zirconium by asking: Why pay for diamonds when you can get Como Diamante (as they call the imitation gems) for so much less? "You are going to walk into a room," he says, "and people are going to think you spent $15,000 for these earrings." So it seems a cruel joke when one afternoon he sells a diamond ring by mocking its cheap cousin: "Enjoy your cubic zirconium," he says sarcastically. "I have a *real* diamond."

24 HOURS OF SUNSHINE

In their possession of an audience's hopes and fears, home shopping hosts are like no one so much as the fictional advice columnist in Nathaniel West's 1933 novella *Miss Lonelyhearts*. A young reporter takes the job as a joke, but then realizes that the letters to him are genuine expressions of suffering. Even worse, their writers take him seriously.

"Dear Miss Lonelyhearts. . . ." begin the letters from "Desperate," "Disillusioned-with-tubercular-husband," "Sick-of-it-All." "On most days," West wrote, "he received more than 30 letters, all of them alike, stamped from the dough of human suffering with a heart-shaped cookie knife."

The pain in his correspondents' lives, and his own powerlessness to help them, eats away at Miss Lonelyhearts. For each letter, he searches for a sincere reply, and always, he comes up empty. Finally, unable to bear the pathos of human existence, he is driven to self-destruction.

Today, the lonely and desperate turn to home shopping hosts who seem to have no such interest in acknowledging the limits of their powers. They appear perfectly comfortable marketing miracles.

"It's raining," says one caller with a hint of sadness. "We'll keep the sunshine going," Bobbi replies.

Another host reads a written testimonial from Bethlehem, Pennsylvania. The letter begins like any to Miss Lonelyhearts could: "I was really at a low point. I needed something." But then comes a distinctly un-Westian salvation: "Then someone turned me onto Destiny Perfume. It smells so good that it has really given me strength to go on for me and my family."

When real pain and loneliness do seep through, the home shopping solution is to studiously ignore it. Alan and Wendi are plugging a diamond ring. Edna from Ohio calls in. "If you think your life is going pretty good right now, wait until you buy this ring," says Alan. "Well actually," Edna responds. "It's going pretty bad." Her words vanish, unacknowledged, beneath the chatter of the hosts.

Sally from Chicago has bought some perfume, and she calls in to talk about it: "I'm lying in bed, this is my day off, I'm being a princess." Her voice is raspy with age and cigarettes. She works in a store, and says men tell her how good she smells. "That's wonderful," the host asks, and then asks, suggestively, "Did you put some on before you went to bed last night?" "No," says Sally. "I'm a widow."

When women describe their bouts with cancer or their hospital stays, as many do, the testimonials become farcical struggles between hosts trying to truncate the calls or push them toward the product-driven point, and callers hanging on for dear life, trying to prolong the conversation.

The question is why anyone would turn for comfort to talking heads out to make a sale. The answer lies partly in the same post–World War II social transformation that gave more Americans spending power. With increased income, Americans moved into dispersed suburbs. As women moved into the workforce, neighborhood networks and social clubs shrunk, isolating the women left behind. Driven to spend more, men and women worked more. Families broke more easily, and even those that held together felt the pressures of work and mobility. And television pulled us off streets and front porches and into living rooms.

As political scientist Robert Putnam writes in "Bowling Alone, Revisited," affiliation to organized religion, parental involvement in schools, participation in voluntary associations have all declined over the past two decades. Our community participation now takes the form of writing checks to organizations.

So it's not all that surprising that people have figured out how to line their pockets by bleeding our unhappiness. Harder to come by naturally in our social environment, connection has become a commodity. Well before home shopping offered purchasing as a path to salvation, televangelists were offering prayer, usually for profit. Pat Robertson's 700 Club, for example, markets itself as "Friends you can turn to!" and tells viewers, "You're like a part of the family!" The Club's prayer counselors, on call seven days a week, 24 hours a day (1-800-Help-4-Me) took 1,785,000 calls last year. Most callers ended up paying to join the Club.

To belong to the home shopping "club," you have to buy. If you don't, you can't go on-air to talk to your friends, and you can't win their approval. And that is how home shopping channels prey on the lonely, the alienated: by offering a haven, then charging admission.

Despite the cynical sell, it's not hard to understand the appeal of home shopping's soothing, ever-positive hosts, who respond to their devoted customers with matching enthusiasm: "Thank you so, so, so much for calling in today.... We took a risk and brought some new items. You responded with an outpouring of support—and we love you for it."

The format plays on our nostalgia for a simpler, friendlier time. The cheery home shopping pitch—"Get some coffee and OJ and come right back!"—is a far cry from the bleak, unsmiling Calvin Klein ads that characterize the cutting edge of advertising today. The home shopping hosts exclaim "Nice to meet you!" and "Thanks for stopping by tonight!"—as if the caller had ambled into the corner store in a small town for an evening's gossip.

In its evocation of Tupperware parties, the kaffeeklatsch, Mary Kay cosmetics saleswomen stopping by your home— all traditions that have fallen, or are falling, by the wayside—home shopping hearkens back to the past in another way: It speaks to women as they were before women's liberation. Callers are "honey" and "dear." "That executive look" is just another fashion statement. Women lunch, they shop, they entertain, they go on cruises, they have craft parties. Femininity sells. Dolls, cooed over by hosts as if they were children, are very popular.

Watching this throwback to another era, it's easy to forget that for many women, the underbelly of that era was a gnawing sense of dissatisfaction. But that's the idea: to banish both the dark side of history and the bright side of real life from living rooms. For a woman like Dorothy from North Carolina, who says, "I watch home shopping from the time I get up until my husband comes home from work," home shopping channels affirm, indeed encourage, her choice to wile away her days with them. "I hope you're going to stay with us for the whole show," hosts implore callers.

The community that home shopping offers is made even more enticing by something no real community can offer: anonymity—the freedom to dream without being judged. The flip side of that, though, is the absence of any of the complex, enriching interactions, images, or conversations of daily life. There is no such thing as neighborliness or charity or civic virtue in this universe, no relationship that extends beyond the purchase.

TELEFRIEND

In fact, home shopping is the latest advancement in business's quest to make spending money as painless as possible, an effort that picked up steam with layaways and installment plans in the twenties and made a quantum leap with credit cards in the fifties. Academics have proven what common sense suggests: We spend more with credit cards because it feels like we're spending nothing. That's one reason that debt, once a social embarrassment, has become socially acceptable, and why consumer debt in the United States today is close to $1 trillion.

Before, advertisers had to make their message powerful enough to motivate shoppers to go to a store. Now it just has to be good enough to get you to pick up the phone. After your first purchase, your credit card number is in the computer. You can punch your "membership" number and the item number into an automated voice system, or feed it to a friendly operator. That's not what spending money feels like.

And so women call to confess they have "maxed out" on their credit cards, or to offer thanks for "flex" and "easy pay" plans that enable them to keep buying while putting off the paymaster. "I've got about two-thirds of your things," Vada Sue from Winston-Salem, North Carolina, tells Home Shopping Club when she calls in to make yet another purchase, "and you all have about two-thirds of my money."

The marriage of technology and commerce will make consuming ever more convenient: Our homes can become retail outlets, we can visit virtual shopping malls from our couches, shop for new homes on CD-ROM. We will, in other words, never have to leave home to fill the needs that marketing creates.

The potential is enormous, but so are the implications. One virtue of the postwar consumer binge in America was the number of jobs it created in manufacturing and retail. But over the last decade, automation of industry eliminated many manufacturing jobs, and now retailing is automating too.

"We don't need bricks and mortar," QVC president Douglas Briggs boasted to *USA Today*. "We can cover the whole nation with twenty salespeople." QVC racked up $1.4 billion in sales last year with a mere 6,100 employees, and that's only the beginning. Shopping services are going on-line; stores are experimenting with robots in place of human salespeople. Since 1989, more than 411,000 retail jobs have been eliminated. The reduction of labor, and costs, is great news for corporations like QVC; it's lousy news for Americans who at least could count on a consumer culture to provide jobs.

And then there is the human cost, the deepening of isolation, the erosion of live—in the human, not television, sense

—communities. If the success of home shopping portends the future, marketing will turn to ever more sophisticated attempts to play on our nostalgia for what we've lost, to peddle connections to other people via commerce. Take First National Bank in Chicago, which now charges $3 for the use of a human teller rather than an automated one: Getting some warmth requires cold cash.

Home shopping foreshadows what's so insidious about that prospect: Even as QVC and HSN try to mimic the feeling of community, they draw us, as television always has, even further away from the real thing. At 6 a.m., a woman named Doris phones HSN to purchase a portable copier for $229. "How are you?" the host asks. "Fair," Doris replies, her voice shaking slightly. She explains that she orders things from home shopping and mail order catalogues, forgets what she orders, and then orders them again. She wants the copier to keep track of her purchases.

"Good idea," the host says, smothering her pathos with his enthusiasm. "And running down to the corner copier is *so* inconvenient." Doris will have her copier. And she will be yoked even more tightly to an isolation that only her television—and another purchase—can penetrate.

NO

Roland T. Rust and
Richard W. Oliver

THE DEATH OF ADVERTISING

ADVERTISING ON ITS DEATHBED

Never has advertising appeared so pale and lifeless. Advertising expenditures as a percentage of personal consumption expenditures peaked in 1984, and have been trending down ever since. Advertising agencies are in a state of siege, as billings shrink, layoffs abound, and accounts are lost to nontraditional players. Media fragmentation reduces the potential to reach large numbers of consumers. The dramatic shift away from a product-oriented economy toward a services-oriented economy reduces the effectiveness of traditional advertising approaches. Even in the product sector, mass customization and flexible manufacturing subsume the concept of mass production and mass advertising.

These dramatic changes caught ad agencies unaware. As the *Wall Street Journal* points out: "the $138 billion advertising industry seems unprepared for an interactive future." What's more, the agencies seem incapable of sustaining the sort of investment required to become more relevant, because "layoffs and other cutbacks have left ad agencies without the resources to reinvent themselves." Industry commentators worry that the big advertising agencies may not survive. For example, *Advertising Age's* Joe Cappo predicts that "By the year 2000, the advertising business we know so well will have transformed into something new."

The prognosticators' pessimism is supported by statistical trends from the advertising business. In spite of a dramatically growing economy over the same period of time, ad agency gross income, adjusted for inflation, has flattened since 1985. The stagnation of earnings, threats to the traditional 15% commission rate, and increasing cost pressures forced massive layoffs in the advertising industry. Declines in employment were reported for each year from 1991 to 1993.

Meanwhile, non-advertising marketing communication expenditures are both larger than media expenditures and are growing much faster. Where is the money going if not to advertising? For one thing, nontraditional "ad-

From Roland T. Rust and Richard W. Oliver, "The Death of Advertising," *Journal of Advertising*, vol. 23, no. 4 (December 1994). Copyright © 1994 by The American Academy of Advertising. Reprinted by permission. References omitted.

vertising" companies are beginning to make inroads with large clients. For example, the Coca-Cola Company has engaged Creative Artists Agency to handle much of the creativity of its Coke account. Moreover, the largest portion of marketing communications dollars formerly designated for mass media now go to non-advertising communications programs such as public relations, sales promotion, sponsorships, and special events. *"Advertising Age* estimates that 65% of all marketing expenditures in the U.S. now go to these non-media sectors."

The rise of Integrated Marketing Communications (IMC) is a result of this changing marketing environment. Advertisers require greater efficiency and coordination in reaching their target audiences through a variety of communication approaches and the large ad agencies have shown themselves to be incapable of this sort of integration.

The integration of marketing communication approaches gains importance with increased media fragmentation. The more fragmented media become, the more integration is required, and the less the task resembles that of a traditional advertising agency.

In fact, the major media show significant fragmentation over the last 40 years and the trend threatens to accelerate in the coming decade. Forty years ago, the three major TV networks had 100% share of the viewing audience. It was easy to obtain wide reach by sponsoring a popular program. By 1980, the three major networks still owned 87% of the viewing audience, but by 1990 that percentage was reduced to 62%. The cause of the decline was the penetration of cable TV. Needless to say, the projected 500-channel TV environment will greatly accelerate the trend.

Likewise, magazine readership has become increasingly fragmented over the years. Forty years ago, big national publications such as *Life, Look,* and the *Saturday Evening Post* (many of which are now defunct) dominated the magazine industry. By 1963, there were still only 445 consumer titles. That number tripled to 1,275 titles in 1988. Similarly, the number of business publications has grown dramatically, from 2,255 in 1972 to 3,676 in 1991....

Because most services, and especially the new information services, must be marketed in ways which are quite different from marketing a product, the traditional consumer goods mass marketing approach has become increasingly irrelevant. The value-added of many traditional products today is their information content. Again, the traditional advertising approach is inadequate for today's intelligent products and informationally-empowered consumer.

Finally, the development of flexible manufacturing, using robotics, transformed the old industrial paradigm of mass production (which also created mass media, mass audiences, and mass advertising) to one of mass customization, allowing "manufacturers" of both products and services to produce for market segments of one. This type of marketing calls for a radically new form of detailed, information-oriented communications, as opposed to the image-oriented 15- or 30-second spot.

HOW TECHNOLOGY HAS SHAPED ADVERTISING

The above trends illustrate the effect of technology upon advertising. It is our contention that technology has always been the skeleton around which advertising was formed. If this is true, then the increasing rate at which technology is currently changing promises a radical transformation of advertising. To understand how advertising is shaped by technology, it is useful to consider how and why advertising has evolved.

Viewing branding as a primitive form, advertising can be traced back to the ancient Egyptian's bricklayers who branded their bricks. As an advertising medium, however, bricks were rather limited. We characterize this period through the middle of the 19th century as the birth of advertising.

The rise of advertising was made possible by the advent of new printing technologies, the rise of literacy rates and consumer affluence, and other factors, which made possible mass circulation newspapers and magazines and mass audience radio programs. Not coincidentally this period coincided with the founding of J. Walter Thompson, the first modern advertising agency in the U.S. At first the new agency served only as a media buying service, but customer demand dictated expansion into a full line of advertising services.

Advertising reached its prime in the 1950s, sparked by the popularity of a small number of major networks which made delivery of a mass audience relatively easy. Mass media created a mass audience for mass-produced products. Popular culture celebrated the advertising executive as the epitome of the post-war marketing executive. However, by the mid-1980s, the first signs of terminal illness were evident.

Since 1985, the signs of advertising decline have been inescapable. Again, the reason is technology. The mass media could no longer deliver a mass audience. At the same time, consumers demanded more customization in their products (of which "service" was a major component) or flexibly manufactured hard goods.

THE RISE OF THE NEW MEDIA

The New Technology

Earlier, we discussed the fragmentation of media (created by technological change) and its impact on advertising. Underlying this fragmentation, paradoxically, is the convergence of a number of industries and technologies: computers (both hardware and software), telecommunications, information services, CATV, consumer electronics, and content providers such as entertainment, news, and educational services. This convergence has created a new media market estimated at one trillion dollars.

Most importantly in the present context, however, are the new media's rich interactive communications channels, offering consumers virtually unlimited control and a vast new array of services. One of the most exciting new services is Video Dial Tone (VDT), "the instantaneous transmission of a full range of interactive voice, data, and full-motion video services." VDT will provide new dimensions to the rapidly growing direct marketing and home shopping services.

Together, the new media represent a vast "network of networks," now often referred to as the information superhighway. A technical reality (if not completely commercialized yet), major parts of the information superhighway are under construction all over the U.S. For example, tests of interactive TV are already being undertaken by GTE (Cerritos, California), and U.S. West, TCI, and AT&T (Denver). Tests (or partial rollouts) are being readied by Time Warner (Orlando), U.S. West (Omaha), Bell Atlantic (Virginia), Viacom and AT&T (Castro Valley, California), and BellSouth (Nashville).

The information superhighway will become the global electronic supermarket of the 90s, uniting producers and consumers directly, instantly, and interactively. Advertising will be transformed from *involuntary* (and necessarily intrusive) to *voluntary* (and sought out). It expands consumer access to information and offers options which provide layers of additional information.

Likewise, the new media will provide more information about customers (privacy laws permitting). Rather than being a negative, as some have suggested, this will allow producers to customize both products and communications to customer needs, reducing much of the waste circulation and viewership of mass media, and lowering costs of market research, communications, and even distribution. In many ways, the new media puts the customer in control.

Mass agencies work best for mass products aimed at mass audiences. On the information superhighway, direct links between customers and producers, providing in-depth information in an interactive form, signal the death knell of traditional advertising.

The Economics of the New Media

The economics of the new media environment is likely to be unfamiliar. For example, we are accustomed to advertisers "bribing" television viewers to sit through their ads. The bribe is the program. The implicit assumption is that advertising is something unwanted by the viewer. That is generally true in the traditional mass media environment. If there is no mass market, however, the traditional economics break down.

The effectiveness of traditional mass advertising declines with the reduction of audience levels. The inevitable reaction is the transfer of resources away from traditional advertising and toward nontraditional marketing communication activities. We have already experienced a significant shift in this direction.

As the ability of receivers of mass advertising to profitably support the media declines, the financial support of the media increasingly shifts to the consumer, resulting in more pay TV and user-supported media. Meanwhile advertising-supported mass media must lower quality standards and are targets for the have-nots of the information superhighway: those who cannot afford pay programming. Clearly these trends are well underway, as we see more premium programming appearing on a pay basis, and network programming consciously targeting the economically disadvantaged (e.g., "Roseanne").

Interactive media offer the consumer a wider range of choices and, simultaneously, greater individualization. Thus it is possible to provide product and service information for the consumer, which is sufficiently well-targeted to be actually welcome. For example, a consumer who is looking for a new car may select from a wide variety of automobile information sources *voluntarily*, without any programming bribe whatsoever. The consumer may even be willing to pay for advertising under some circumstances. A precedent can be seen in the popularity of *Consumer Reports* which is essentially product information that people pay for. It is not much different in content from information-oriented advertising, such as infomercials.

THE POST-ADVERTISING WORLD

The post-advertising world will be characterized by both empowerment of the consumer and new methods of marketing appropriate to the interactive environment, which we refer to collectively as "21st Century Marketing."

The Empowered Consumer

In advertising's prime, producers held virtually all of the power in the marketplace. This was true in part because their agents, the advertising agencies, controlled the then very powerful mass media. Producers controlled the products, terms and conditions of sale, and the communications environment. Power has been steadily shifting toward the consumer since the advent of television. In the late 1950s, networks took power from the ad agencies as television shows were no longer backed by single sponsors. Instead, the networks controlled all the time and sold it off in little pieces. In the 1990s, the powershift continues as the networks lose power to the consumer.

With the changes in technology described earlier (and others such as bar coding, real time inventory control, and improved logistics), consumers became informationally-empowered and the muscle in the marketplace shifted dramatically in their favor. Closest to the consumer in the distribution channel, retailers became more important and powerful in comparison to manufacturers. Big retailers like Wal-Mart now dictate distribution patterns and even control the inventories of producers. Today the retailer has become the marketplace agent of the consumer and not that of the producer.

21st Century Marketing

Changes in the marketing environment to date have resulted in two marketing techniques which exploit the technology now available. These two techniques are *relationship marketing* (a broad term that can refer to alliances and relationships between channel members, but which we use here in a more restricted sense to mean the growing "relations" between the producer and consumer), which takes advantage of computer data bases to provide targeted services and product offerings (most often by direct mail) based on the customer's history of transactions with the company, and *mass customization*, which takes advantage of flexible manufacturing to make individualized products.

The technology of the information superhighway will allow these techniques to merge, providing a new marketing technique which has been referred to as "adaptive marketing." Adaptive marketing means continually revising the product offering, on an individual basis, to satisfy customer demands. Adaptive marketing is made possible in the new multi-media environment by intelligent agents known in their primitive form as personal digital assistants (PDA's) or what will become "knowbots" (knowledge robots), computerized helpers that look out for their human "masters." The knowbot searches through the vast amount of information available to find the information that will most likely interest the consumer. The knowbot can also help design the product or service that the customer receives. Information services, easily customized, will be common on the information superhighway. For example, the MIT Media lab has an experimental electronic newspaper called the "Daily Me," which is customized for the individual reader.

Because the knowbot will be housed with the consumer, the key to success for the marketer will be getting past the knowbot. This means that 21st Century Marketing is likely to be preoccupied with two things: 1) making the service (remember that services will dominate the economy) easy for the consumer to customize, and 2) making information appealing to the knowbots.

THE DEATH OF ADVERTISING

The future of 21st Century Marketing is exciting and will reach its maturity much faster than did traditional advertising and marketing. The birth or inception stage, which we are just entering, will be characterized by the provisioning of the information infrastructure and experimentation, by both producers and users, with new information services. On-line services such as Prodigy and CompuServe already have a total of over two million users. The creation of new media has been accelerated by the mergers which began in the mid 1970s and grew in the 1980s and 1990s (e.g., Sony and Columbia, AT&T and NCR). This trend will continue in the future despite the recent setbacks in the proposed mergers of TCI-Bell Atlantic and others. Small and local at first, the information superhighway will, by the turn of the century, encompass the entire U.S. The fiber optic backbone will carry a vast amount of information instantaneously from coast to coast. During this period, traditional mass media advertising will begin to diminish, while the new intelligent and individualized advertising will gain prominence.

By the year 2010, new media and the new marketing we have described will be the dominant paradigm. In a commercial context, for instance, consider the following: "a financial services salesman in New Jersey has a face-to-face meeting via computer with a client in California. While on the line, the customer tries the product. She likes it, downloads it into her computer, and the salesman bills her right then. Nobody left their office or home, and it all gets done in a nanosecond." Further, industrial buyers will be linked with suppliers in sophisticated Electronic Data Interconnection (EDI) networks that will allow industrial transactions to occur at amazing quality and efficiency levels and at ever decreasing prices. Such EDI networks are already in evidence in health care, automotive production, and several other industries.

In consumer markets, 21st Century Marketing, via the new media, will have radically transformed retailing as well as advertising. While some limited number of hard goods will still require in-person shopping (due to consumer preference, sizing, and the need for tactile evaluation), most goods, and virtually all services, will be bought and sold on the network. As with industrial and commercial markets, consumer information commerce will not only be technologically feasible but economically compelling (increasing speed and variety and reducing price) and ecologically imperative. The ecological tradeoff between shopping by car and shopping on the network is enormous. For example, if 100% substitution of communications for transportation could be accomplished, this would result in a savings of $123 billion annually.... [E]ven a 10-20% substitution would eliminate 1.8 million tons of pollutants, save 3.5 billion gallons of gasoline, and replace three billion shopping trips annually. Obviously, shopping on the network will not replace all retail shopping as there will be a need to shop in person for some goods and the social aspects of shopping will continue to be important for some.

During this period, the last vestiges of traditional mass advertising will disappear, as the logic of the new media advertising approach begins to dominate. This period will last well into the middle of the 21st century, as the only real value of products, services and communications becomes their information content. The information content of products and services themselves will be transformed during this period into what we call "wisdom products." Such "wisdom products" will provide customers not only data and information, but knowledge and wisdom for decision making and action. Today's embryonic artificial intelligence software is an early indicator of such capabilities. Further, the information superhighway will extend to the rest of the developed world and the electronic supermarket and the intelligent information-oriented marketing communications that supports it will be global in scope and multicultural and multilingual as well as multimedia. In such a marketplace, global success and effectiveness will be determined by the breadth and depth of both the product and communications architecture....

SUMMARY

Advertising is on its deathbed and it will not survive long, having contracted a fatal case of new technology. Advertising's heir will be customer communications, a broader and more flexible topic which will be able to incorporate the dramatic changes introduced by the information superhighway.

POSTSCRIPT

Will Traditional Advertising Survive the New Technology Revolution?

In the course of pursuing a career within a media industry, it can be disheartening when changes in the industry make the career less appealing. Changes in a media industry may result in fewer job opportunities or necessitate reevaluation of one's current skills. It is therefore a good idea for media job seekers to become familiar with industry trade magazines, in which new trends are often first discussed.

Advertising Age, Electronic News, Broadcasting, Variety, and *Broadcasting and Cable* are all periodicals in which changes in the markets as well as different perspectives on issues within each field are discussed. Many of these publications also include available job postings too. Industry professionals say that it is critical to keep up with the changes in each field and that research and learning are important tools for continued adaptability to changing market conditions.

Regardless of whatever changes to media industries come about, what role and what form do you think advertising will take? Will traditional forms of salesmanship survive, as Waldman says? Or has the advent of new technologies displaced the need for traditional advertising?

On the Internet . . .

Copyright Crash Course

Developed at the University of Texas, this site offers
background information and legal summaries concerning
copyright law and fair use guidelines.
http://www.utsystem.edu/ogc/intellectualproperty/cprtindx.htm

The Electronic Frontier Foundation

The Electronic Frontier Foundation (EFF) is a nonprofit
civil liberties organization working to protect free expression and access to public resources and information online and to promote responsibility in this new media.
http://www.eff.org/

The Journal of Computer-Mediated
Communication

This electronic journal, maintained by the Annenberg
School of the University of Southern California, addresses
the issues surrounding electronic media. Such issues as electronic commerce, law and the electronic frontier, Netplay,
and designing virtual environments are discussed.
http://www.ascusc.org/jcmc/

Yahoo! Countries

At this site, you can find information about the media
systems found throughout the world.
http://www.yahoo.com/regional/countries/

PART 5

The Information Society

Predictions of a world that is increasingly reliant upon media and communication technologies have generally provided either utopian or dystopian visions about what our lives will be like in the future. But now, the ability to communicate instantly around the world has become a reality.

New media distribution technologies present new options for traditional ways of doing things. Not too many years ago, people were talking about the potential of an information superhighway. Today, surfing the World Wide Web is common. Although we are still learning how electronic communication may change our lives and the ways we work and communicate, many questions have not changed. Will new ways of communication change the way individuals interact? Will citizen decision making change? Will everyone have access to the services and technologies that enable more immediate information exchange? And what will new technologies do to us as individuals as we enter the information age?

■ Do Media Technologies Increase Citizen Participation?

■ Does the Globalization of Media Industries "Homogenize" Media Content?

■ Do New Media Have an Immediate Effect on Our Behaviors and Attitudes?

ISSUE 16

Do Media Technologies Increase Citizen Participation?

YES: Ted Becker, from "Teledemocracy: Gathering Momentum in State and Local Governance," *Spectrum: The Journal of State Governments* (Spring 1993)

NO: Christopher Georges, from "Perot and Con," *The Washington Monthly* (June 1993)

ISSUE SUMMARY

YES: Ted Becker, a writer who specializes in telecommunication issues and who is interested in the success of teledemocratic systems, asserts that online information and communication systems may be very effective for political purposes. Additionally, greater use of the media for democratic purposes ensures greater interest on the part of citizens and more activism.

NO: Christopher Georges, who writes frequently on politics and government, looks specifically at "teledemocracy" as practiced and promoted by Ross Perot. Following Perot's use of the media for creating opportunities for dialogue among citizens, Georges warns that even though the process may be popular, it does not necessarily mean that the best candidates are chosen for the job.

Teledemocracy may actually use online systems such as cable, telephone, television, and computer to allow people to register their opinions in a quantitative manner. The term is also used to describe public forums where more discussion among a broader range of individuals can take place. Generally, teledemocracy uses some forms of telecommunication to increase the opportunities of citizens to make their views publicly and widely known. By increasing citizen involvement in the creation and discussion of the issues, some social scientists believe that government can better act in the true interests of the people represented.

As interactive technologies and services increase, they may bring new ways of doing things to society. Using online systems for voting or for registering opinions in some form could be a rapid way to "take America's pulse" and better understand the interests of individuals. Ted Becker argues in the following selection that these systems will increase politicians' accountability to citizens. In the second selection, Christopher Georges warns that rather than opening discussion to a greater number of people, the money invested in teledemocracy activities restricts the outcome to those who have money to pay for the services.

The two authors address the issue of motivating people to influence the actions of government. Government has been criticized for inaction and grid-lock; teledemocracy may promise greater input by citizens, but it does not necessarily ensure that government action will be taken in response to that input. Regardless of whether or not citizens could effectively hold national referenda on important issues, it might be difficult to know who is registering an opinion at any given moment, or why.

The new interest in teledemocracy merges issues such as the increasing discontent with the way politics has been conducted in the past, the potential of new technology to be used in innovative ways, and attempts to make government more representative of and responsive to the public's will. In combining these issues, technology is viewed as a catalyst for change. If these changes are satisfactory, technology will be heralded for all the good it does. If the changes are not appropriate or create more problems, technology will probably be blamed for causing the further breakdown of social institutions.

This issue makes clear that although new forms of technology may be used for new purposes, the outcomes of those uses may not be fully understood when change is implemented. New technologies and services promise much, but questions remain about what they can realistically deliver.

YES

Ted Becker

TELEDEMOCRACY: GATHERING MOMENTUM IN STATE AND LOCAL GOVERNANCE

In 1981, I defined "teledemocracy" to mean "democratically aided, rapid, two-way political communication" and said it would "offer the means to help educate voters on issues, to facilitate discussion of important decisions, to register instantaneous polls and even to allow people to vote directly on public policy" (Becker 1981, 6). My prediction was that advances in interactive electronic communication technologies would empower the American citizenry and lead to a much stronger democracy at the national, regional, state and local levels.

Since then, there has been a cornucopia of American innovation, experiments, analyses and critiques—all of which have reinforced my belief that electronic communications are strengthening the American political system at all levels of governance. Some recent experimentation has been designed to help the representative system function more effectively. In addition, methods were tested that were predicted to enlighten and empower citizens so as to prepare them for the responsibilities of direct democracy, such as the power to discuss and decide public priorities, agendas, directions and policies (Barber 1984, 9).

Since the American political system is a complex mixture of indirect and direct democracy, teledemocratic developments in one area are readily adaptable to the other. Moreover, although these projects in teledemocracy were either at the local, regional or state governmental level, there is no reason to believe that success at one level is not readily transferrable to the other.

The key hardware and software components to this nascent teledemocratic revolution are television; telephones; radio; personal computers; satellites; video, telephone and computer conferencing; and the increasing use of "common ground" facilitation techniques. In the last decade there have been teledemocratic innovations that are sufficient evidence to support my view that teledemocracy is rapidly gaining momentum—particularly in state and local governments.

From Ted Becker, "Teledemocracy: Gathering Momentum in State and Local Governance," *Spectrum: The Journal of State Governments* (Spring 1993). Copyright © 1993 by The Council of State Governments. Reprinted by permission of *Spectrum: The Journal of State Governments*.

The Electronic Town Meeting Format

Each of the projects discussed here used an Electronic Town Meeting (ETM) format as a principal feature of its design or tested a feature that will be indispensable to future ETMs that make laws or elect officials. ETM, however, means different things to different people.

In recent years, the label electronic town hall or electronic town meeting has been used for events where political leaders have met with citizens to hear complaints and answer questions. When these events have been televised, and particularly when the viewing audience is invited to pose questions by telephone, they are invariably called ETMs by the media and politicians. What they are, however, is more accurately defined as electronic forums (EFs) or electronic hearings (EHs) because they are simply the televised exchange of ideas, sentiments, facts and opinions between the public and officialdom.

Those who experiment with genuine ETMs emulate the New England town meeting—an entirely different breed of cat. In the New England town meeting, political leaders are rarely the center of attention and only part of the locus of power. The citizens who participate are the decision-makers. The citizens debate among themselves. The person leading the meeting serves merely as a moderator. These town meetings conclude with a citizen vote and the majority vote becomes the law of the town. Thus, those who have been testing electronic versions of traditional town meetings in the past decade agree that the generic ETM format needs to include an opinion tally following sufficient time for discussion, vigorous debate and deliberation.

This is not meant to deny the political utility in the explosive growth of electronic forums, particularly at the national level. Clearly, forums starring luminaries such as George Bush, Bill Clinton and Ross Perot helped immeasurably in clarifying the issues and candidates' positions in the 1992 presidential campaign. Furthermore, the forums were partly responsible for increased voter interest and turnout.

ETM formats can clarify issues and candidate positions. They add an extra, extremely useful element: the responsibility and power of the vote.

Some Remarkable ETMs: Local, Regional, State

One hypothesized use for ETMs is to increase citizen input and influence in legislative hearings. This important governmental function is about as popular with the American public as a cricket match (with the exception of government soap operas such as the U.S. Senate confirmation of Justice Clarence Thomas). Indeed, the smattering of people who attend public hearings are the regulars: professional lobbyists, special interests and political junkies. A number of teledemocratic projects have tried to improve public knowledge and support of this critical part of the representative system with some success. The QUBE project of Columbus, Ohio, and the Berks County, Pa., interactive TV hearings are among the most well-known (Becker and Scarce 1986).

The Honolulu Interactive CATV City Council Project (1987): Improving Public Participation at Hearings

The Honolulu City Council began a Cable Television project in the late 1980s, broadcasting hearings during evenings. The impression was that more people tuned in than were physically present.

But how many more? How involved were they? And how could they influence the process?

The director of this project, Henry Freund, and I agreed upon a novel ETM format designed to stoke meaningful public participation. At issue that evening was renovating the Waikiki Shell, a beautiful but overused public amphitheater.

The hearing was broadcast live over CATV which, at that time, penetrated into 70 percent of the homes in Hawaii. The citizenry of Honolulu could testify by calling one of three telephone numbers displayed on the tube. By using a system called Symetrix Telephone Interface, a random sampling of telephone calls were channeled into the City Council's audio system. This allowed callers at home to be heard in the hearing room and simultaneously on TV. The callers could converse with council members, lobbyists and citizens in the hearing room.

Citizens watching the hearing also were welcome to use two telephone numbers on the screen to voice their opinion on the issue. One number was for "yes" (pro-renovation) while the other registered "no" votes (anti-renovation).

The room was packed with about 100 people. We do not know how many people watched the hearing over CATV that evening. But we do know that more than 7,000 ballots were cast by telephone in six hours. In addition, our system doubled the number of witnesses who testified that night. What is more, the telephone testimony was different from the hearing room testimony. Most of the witnesses in the room were friendly to either the contractors or the labor unions, both of whom favored renovation. On the other hand, the overwhelming majority of the CATV witnesses were negative to the proposal. Likewise, the home vote was 75 percent opposed to renovation.

Those who stood in our telephonic queue waited to speak their mind and they listened closely to both what was said in the City Council chambers and by other telephone witnesses. Some read their testimony and others made mention of previous statements at the hearing. Thus, a whole new form of lateral communication and community discussions was facilitated by this ETM format.

Postscript: a few months later, the Honolulu City Council voted 6–2 against refurbishing the Waikiki Shell.

Vision 20/20 and the Savannah/ Chatham County ETM (1990): Democratizing the Long-Range Planning Process

Another hypothesized function of ETMs is that they are capable of helping facilitate a consensus on future objectives upon which a polity should set its sights —particularly when more conventional methods (electoral campaigns, the legislative process) have produced endless battling, backbiting and bickering.

"The Coastal Empire" region of Georgia (The City of Savannah and Chatham County included) was mired in just such a morass. The situation was analogized to: "A bushel of crabs that reaches up and pulls any one of our own that tries to crawl over the edge back into our clawing, pinching mess" (Thomas 1992). A fresh approach was needed and Vision 20/20 was created.

This was a multimonth, open planning process designed to hew a broad-based regional agreement on priorities and direction for the city and county including education, economic development, environmental protection, social equity and, of course, how to raise public funds in the face of strong public resistance to increased taxation.

Ronald Thomas, a nationally regarded community and city planner, designed the process which employed a complex and sophisticated ETM at an early, strategic point. The second phase of the project, it generated widespread publicity and attracted extensive participation. The object of the ETM was to stimulate involvement from a diverse citizen-base. It achieved that in the following manner:

The top-rated television station in the Savannah market, a CBS affiliate, launched the ETM with a half-hour prime-time show, part minidocumentary and part expert panel, on the nature of the problem and the Vision 20/20 process. Citizens were urged to call during the TV show and to join one of 24 neighborhood assemblies throughout the region at the end of the TV show. They also were asked to mail in a survey printed in a major local newspaper afterwards.

Each of the public community meetings was facilitated by trained volunteer discussion leaders. The results from these meetings were broadcast after the late news. Different values were immediately visible between communities but there were also surprising similarities—especially regarding the rank order of issues to be addressed. Each neighborhood assembly elected a representative to attend subsequent Vision 20/20 gatherings. The process eventually produced a broad plan of action that community leaders and government officials still rely on for guidance.

A Conversation with Oregon (1991): Public Budget Input

Involving the ordinary citizen in setting agendas, solving problems and participating in state politics is a daunting task.

ETMs, however, have proved equal to this challenge.

The granddaddy of these, Alternatives for Washington, met with mixed results (Stilger 1978). Even so, tens of thousands of Washingtonians participated in this nonbinding state planning exercise and produced a coherent plan. But the mother of statewide ETMs was the Alaska Television Town Meeting (1980) which sought to determine, among other things, how Alaskans wanted to spend transportation funds. Ultimately 100,000 or so Alaskans, from all nooks, crannies and demographic groups in the state, participated through interactive TV methods that were tested in this state-of-the-art-and-science experiment (Becker and Scarce 1986; Slaton 1992).

Most recently, Oregon Gov. Barbara Roberts used ETM to get a fix on how Oregonians felt about "some unpleasant choices like fewer services, higher taxes and other forms of political suicide" (Hanson 1992). Roberts presided over 500 meetings around the state with a total of 10,000 randomly selected constituents. The one-way video by which Roberts addressed the citizens was supplemented by two-way audio that allowed citizens to speak to the governor. A state educational telecommunications network connected meeting sites.

A nagging design flaw in this ETM was its voting methodology. Instead of using an instantaneous electronic tabulation system, informal exit polls were taken after the meetings concluded. Never-the-less, the governor was able to get some kind of vote count on how to proceed on budget priorities. Moreover, this project won a first place award in 1992 from the National Association of Information Resource Executives.

Nova Scotia and New Mexico's Televoting (1992–94): Making the Electoral Process Convenient

An accurate, reliable and secure form of an electronic registration and voting system is the business end of any ETM—particularly when the ETM process is eventually plugged into real-life, real-time elections for office holders or referenda and initiatives. Several ETM experiments registered phone voters with great success (Slaton 1992), but it was not until 1992 that an actual election was conducted via telephone voting.

The first to accomplish this feat was the Liberal Party of Nova Scotia, Canada. During its party convention in Halifax in June 1992, the Liberal Party allowed every registered member to get a Personal Identification Number (PIN) to vote by phone for party leader. Although a software glitch by Maritime Telephone and Telegraph stymied the process in its opening run, two weeks later it worked like a charm and the party leader was elected by telephone. More than 7,000 Nova Scotians balloted this way and most called the new system a success.

New Mexico experimented later in 1992 with a similar system and intends to permit absentee voters to elect office holders by telephone during 1994 primary elections. The 1992 experiment allowed televoters to cast their choice for president via their phones. Who won? According to *The Albuquerque Tribune:* "The real winner of last week's experiment was the proof that voting by phone works." This system, developed by Sandia National Laboratories, was used by high school students who reported no trouble in understanding the instructions and no difficulties in using the phone-in voting system. Those working on this system are convinced it is tamper proof and protects voter privacy from government "snooping."

Conclusion

Teledemocracy and ETMs continue advances and improvements in technologies, techniques and applications at all levels of government. Despite occasional lapses, mistakes and problems, the level of citizen satisfaction with each experiment has been high, the amount of citizen participation has far exceeded that in conventional processes, and the quality of citizen input has been impressive. It is only a matter of time until this momentum reaches the point of critical mass and starts a chain reaction. At that point, teledemocracy and ETMs will spread rapidly and become a normal feature of 21st century governance.

REFERENCES

Barber, Benjamin. *Strong Democracy.* Berkeley: University of California Press, 1984.

Becker, Ted. "Teledemocracy." *The Futurist.* December 1981, pp. 6–9.

— and Richard Scarce. "Teledemocracy Emergent," Brenda Dervin and Melvin J. Voight, eds. *Progress in Communications Science.* Norwood, NJ: Ablex Publishing, 1986.

Hanson, Wayne. "Oregon's Electronic Town Hall," *Government Technology.* October, 1992.

Slaton, Christa. *Televote.* New York: Praeger, 1992.

Stilger, Robert. "Alternatives for Washington," Clement Bezold, ed. *Anticipatory Democracy.* New York: Random House, 1978.

Thomas, Ronald. "An Electronic Town Meeting in the Old South," *Futures Forum: Working Papers.* National League of Cities, 1992.

NO

Christopher Georges

PEROT AND CON

By the time of the Major League All Star game last July, Edgar Martinez was near the top of virtually every stack of numbers in the big leagues: third in the league in hitting (.319 average), 46 runs-batted-in, 14 home runs—and a standout third baseman. But come the big game, starting at third was not Martinez, but struggling Boston Red Sox Wade Boggs, whose ho-hum .268 average was 64th in the league, and who had 25 runs-batted-in and 6 home runs. So why did Boggs get the nod over Martinez? All Star starters aren't selected by experts, but by the fans in a popular vote. So while Seattle Mariner Martinez garnered 500,000 votes from the bleacher set—finishing *fifth* in the third base plebiscite—he wasn't even close to Boggs's 1.2 million. Were the fans duped—fooled perhaps by the cachet of the Boggs name? Or did they know Martinez was the best man, but still wanted to see the hobbling Fenway legend in one more All Star go-round?

Whatever the reason, Boggs's selection raises a broader question: The All Star selection process appeals to the fans, but does it produce the best team? The answer is relevant to more than just readers of *Baseball Digest*, because in a very different realm—the political one—we are creeping ever closer towards the kind of system that put Boggs in the All Star lineup: a direct, let-the-majority-decide democracy. That drift towards direct democracy, while certainly part of a larger movement, is currently led by Ross Perot. Problem is, the Prince of Populism's vaunted teledemocracy will not only give us more Boggs's and fewer Martinez's, but rather than, as advertised, "taking America back," it may well hand it over to the special interests.

Of course, populist yearnings among the American people—from Thomas Jefferson to Robert LaFollette to Bill Clinton—have been as common as House scandals. But today, three forces have converged to make direct democracy a viable, even appealing, option. For one, the public's frustration with government—and with Congress in particular—has reached new heights: Eighty percent of those surveyed earlier this year in a *Washington Post*/ABC News poll, for example, said that the "country needs to make major changes in the way government works." At the same time, the public is more eager than ever to give the government a piece of its mind. You don't have to be a talk

From Christopher Georges, "Perot and Con," *The Washington Monthly*, vol. 25, no. 6 (June 1993). Copyright © 1993 by The Washington Monthly Company, 1611 Connecticut Avenue, NW, Washington, DC 20009. (202) 462-0128. Reprinted by permission of *The Washington Monthly*.

show junkie to spot this trend; just ask the White House operators, who on a busy day during the Reagan years might have fielded 5,000 calls, but in 1993 are busy with 40,000 *a day*. Finally, factor in the most recent and significant development: the flourishing of technological tools that will allow anyone with a TV, a phone line, and a few minutes to spare to vote on any issue, any time.

This technology is expected to be on line by the time we elect our next president, and the public apparently has few reservations about using it. More than two thirds of all Americans favor national binding referenda on major issues, according to a 1993 survey by the Americans Talk Issues Foundation. Gallup surveys have put the figure at nearly 70 percent. All of which helps explain the rise of a populist like Perot, who can preach with complete credibility, as he did during the campaign, that "we can show everybody in Congress what the voters want, and we'll be programming [Congress]. That's the way it's supposed to be."

What Perot's getting at—and what most advocates of teledemocracy preach —is that empowering the people with a direct vote in policy-making is the surest cure for the two great plagues of our representative system: It is strangled by special interests, and it moves at a glacial pace. Teledemocrats figure that if only we turned the levers of power over to the people, well, we'd fix all that. For one, the people, by going over the heads of Congress, could quickly eliminate the tiresome, time-consuming political haggling and, say, decide to outlaw fat cat political contributions tonight at 10, and, if we felt so inclined, approve stricter gun laws tomorrow at noon. And at the same time, in a single stroke, we'd wipe out the

clout of the nasty special interests. That's because the people cannot be bought, making all the lobbying by the monied interests as relevant as eight-track tapes. "It's the best way I know," says Mike McManus, organizer of USA Vote, a Maryland-based group attempting to organize national televotes, "to empower the people against the special interests."

Or is it? As we take our first timid steps towards Perot's push-button utopia, it's worth pausing to consider what we might forfeit in the process. Despite the rhetoric of populists like McManus, the evidence is that the closer we get to direct democracy, the more we *disempower* the common man, and at the same time enhance—or at the very least keep intact —the muscle of the monied interests. And while teledemocracy, no doubt, can short-circuit the haggling that throttles Congress and jump start our chronically gridlocked process, that much maligned horse trading may, in fact, be more valuable than any legislation it holds up.

So what will it be? No doubt, James Madison and bookish fellow Framers were bright guys, but they weren't seers: Let's face it, America's no longer a nation of yeomen. Perhaps technology has made their experiment in government obsolete. Perhaps it's time to deposit those interminable *Federalist Papers* in the recycling bin and move our system of government into this century. Should we, in short, stick with representarian Madison or turn to majoritarian Perot?

MASS APPEALS

That question has been developing steam longer than Con Edison. Back when Madison and company ruled America, the nation was governed by the elite, thanks to devices such as the election of senators by state legislatures and property qualifications for voting. Andrew Jackson gave the masses a louder voice a few decades later with universal white male suffrage. Gradually, political parties, replete with blustery conventions, opened the door a crack wider, and in 1968, the grassroots were further empowered through nominating primaries. By the eighties, TV had further eroded the filter between the governors and the governed, and, as the most recent election showed, even the Dan Rathers are being brushed aside. These days, if you're unsure whether to vote for a candidate, you can call him up on "Larry King" and interview him yourself.

In the meantime, while the U.S. has never held a national referendum, 26 states now permit citizens to put measures on the ballot for a public vote. And while initiatives have been possible in many states since the early 1900s, only in the last 20 years have they grown truly popular. From 1950–69, for example, only 19 state ballots were held in the entire nation. In 1988 alone, 50 were conducted. And if those referenda don't occur quite quickly enough for you, move to Colorado, where Gov. Roy Roemer has installed unofficial voting computers in shopping malls and public buildings to let citizens register how they'd like their tax dollars spent (more—or less—money for a. schools b. prisons c. voting kiosks, etc.).

Roemer, however, is no match for Referendum Ross. "We go to the people on television," Perot told the nation during the campaign, "and explain an issue in great detail, and say: 'Here are the alternatives that we face. As owners of the country, what do you feel is best for the country?' The American people react... and we know what the people want." Just to make sure we knew he wasn't bluffing, citizen Perot gave his televote a dry run not long after his 19 percent Election Day showing, holding a "national referendum" on 16 issues which, although statistically dubious, was a referendum nonetheless. If you're un-American enough to believe Perot's gone a bit far, you're decisively in the minority; while Clinton's favorability ratings have deflated since Election Day, recent polls show that if the election had been reheld in May, Perot and Clinton would have finished dead even.

While Perot is out in front on the referendum bandwagon, other high profile politicians such as Jack Kemp, Pat Buchanan, Richard Gephardt, and Phil Gramm have all supported the idea. And, in 1977, the last time the notion of a national referendum was raised in Congress, more than 50 Members supported the measure. (The bill would have permitted any initiative backed by 3 million signatures to be voted on by the public; if a majority of Americans approved, the initiative would have become law.)

Not to be left behind, the Clinton administration has hooked up a White House phone line to record public sentiment ("for the budget plan, touch one if you support the program"); holds conference calls run by the president to families around the nation; has signed on to a $5 billion plan to support the design of a fiber optics "data superhighway"; and has linked the White House to computer bulletin boards. It even plans to create BC-TV, the political equivalent of MTV, so that Americans craving a presidential fix can tune in to the Bill, Hillary, Al, and Tipper show 24 hours a day. And if you're not inclined to turn on BC-TV, the administration's got an answer for that, too: Clinton advisers Doug Ross and David Osborne are reportedly developing a communications strategy that would be based on sending —just after Clinton unveils any new initiative (through a public meeting, of course)—video and audio cassettes as well as quick response questionnaires to millions of Americans.

But with or without Clinton, or even Perot, most Americans will soon be hooked into our leadership through the already-under-construction data super-highway. In April, the nation's largest cable company, Tele-Communications, Inc., sharply accelerated the race to link the nation by unveiling a $2 billion plan to lay fiber optic cable throughout 400 communities by 1996. One hundred and fifty cities, the company said, will be on the interstate network by 1993. Tele-Communications is not alone; the more than 60 firms scrambling to get a toehold in the interactive market come straight from the Fortune 500: Intel, Time Warner, Microsoft, General Instruments, NBC.

The cyberprize they're chasing is the edge in the two-way fiber optic cable communications market, which will not only allow users, through their TV sets, to respond instantly to commercials, order food, conduct bank transactions, play along with live sporting events, pay bills, or guess the outcome of "Murder She Wrote" (for cheesy prizes), but vote—or at least instantaneously voice an opinion. So when, say, President Perot gives us his pie chart lecture on the Social Security crisis, and then asks us for some insta-policy, you need only pick up your book-sized interactive box and let your fingers do the voting.

That's no hype dream. In fact, such a system is already in place in several cities and has been used for just that purpose. Interactive Network in Mountainview, California, for example, which has linked

more than 3,000 homes, held instant votes immediately after both Clinton's State of the Union address (four minutes after the speech was completed, 71 percent of the viewers punched in that they supported the Clinton plan), as well as Perot's most recent 30-minute infomercial. Perot was so enamored of the results that he contacted Interactive regarding a more formal link between the two organizations, Interactive officials said.

And while televoting is just one of several two-way TV applications companies are pursuing, more than a half dozen for- and not-for-profit organizations are aiming to put the new fiber optic technology to use for national on-line voting. USA Vote, for example, plans to launch an interactive TV show later this year that will feature 30 minutes of debate followed by an instant call-in vote on a major issue. Bruce Jaynes, president of Ohio-based Voter Systems Inc., who has spent eight years designing a system that will allow instant voting, is already attempting to negotiate a contract with a TV network to make his plan fly. And not-for-profits like the Markel Foundation and the Aspen Institute, as well as independent academics such as Amitai Etzioni and the University of Texas's James Fishkin, are examining ways to put the new technology to work. "The weird thing about all this," explains Gary Arlen, president of Arlen Communications Inc., a Bethesda research firm specializing in interactive media, "is that if you don't pay attention, you'll look up one day and it will all be here."

GREECED WHEELS

What's not weird, however, is the larger question that the push-button technology brings: whether to push. If, as teledemocrats claim, majoritarian government is the magic bullet that will at long last make our government the true servant of the common man, why not?

Several decades of experience in direct democracy at the state level—namely state initiatives and referenda—provide a clue. California in particular offers a useful model, where citizens have voted on more ballot initiatives—more than 200 since 1912—than anywhere in the nation. In fact, no society since ancient Greece has sustained such a long history of direct democracy. But not even Homer could mythologize the success of majoritarian government in California and other states, especially with regard to the clout of the monied interests. Of course, there have been some notable reforms passed directly by the people over the years, such as campaign finance reforms, bottle bills, tobacco tax hikes, and term limits for state legislators. Even so, even Hill and Knowlton couldn't put a happy face on the larger referendum picture:

More, not less, money is spent in direct democracy politics than in representative politics.

In California, in both 1988 and 1990, more money (about $125 million each year) was spent—through ad campaigns, ballot signing drives, and get-out-the-vote efforts—to influence California voters on initiative measures than was spent by all special interests to lobby California legislators on all other legislation (more than 1,000 bills). Spending on single initiatives there and in other states can run as high as tens of millions of dollars. The alcohol industry, for example, spent $38 million defeating a proposed alcohol tax in 1990. The truly bad news, however, is not so much that the people eventually end up paying for these massive industry-run campaigns in higher prices, but that to battle the well-oiled industries, the goo-goos have to raise equally huge sums. Alcohol tax proponents in California, for example, wasted $1.3 million on their losing effort and environmentalists there squandered more than $1 million in 1990 on a campaign to save the trees. Not only is coming up with that kind of cash a task in itself, but it saps valuable time and resources from other areas of the cause, such as, say, funding anti-drunk driving campaigns.

Not only is more money spent, but direct democracy does not diminish—and can even enhance—the wealthy interests' ability to affect legislation.

"Money is, all things being equal, the single most important factor determining direct legislation outcomes," concludes Colorado College political scientist Thomas Cronin, who authored perhaps the most comprehensive examination of direct democracy in the U.S. "Even proponents of direct democracy campaign reforms are pessimistic about solving the money problem." Study after study backs Cronin's claim: The Council on Economic Priorities found that in state initiatives the corporate-backed side almost always outspends its opponents, and wins about 80 percent of the time. And another recent examination that charted 72 ballot questions from 1976–82 similarly found that nearly 80 percent of the time the higher spending side won.

And who has the most money to spend? Certainly not tree huggers nor mothers against drunk driving. Businesses in California kicked in more than 80 percent of the money for the 18 highest-spending initiatives since 1956, while grassroots organizations were able to raise just 3 percent of all funds spent. It's not unusual for monied interests to outspend their opponents by factors of 20-to-1. In 1980, for example, Chevron, Shell, ARCO and Mobil and friends made a more than $5 million investment, outspending their opponents by 100-to-1, to ensure the failure of a proposed California oil surtax. Not even OPEC could buy this kind of clout: Five months prior to the vote, 66 percent of the people favored the tax, but after the industry bludgeoned the public with TV ads and other propaganda, only 44 percent of the voters stuck with the humbled reformers. In 1990, a Los Angeles initiative to ban the use of a highly toxic chemical at a Torrance, California, refinery lost, thanks to Mobil Oil's $750,000 effort—a campaign that cost the company $53 per vote, or nearly 12 times what the ballot's proponents could muster. A few of the measures that big money helped defeat in recent years included bills that would have raised the alcohol tax, required greater oil and gas conservation, brought tougher insurance regulation, created smoking regulations, required stricter handgun control, promoted forest conservation, placed a surtax on oil profits, and limited state salaries.

Voters are just as likely—and perhaps more likely—to be conned by special interests as representatives are to be bought by them.

Look at it this way: If you are a salesman trying to sell a car to an 80-year-old woman, would you rather deal with her, or her representative—her son the lawyer? For the monied interests, that's a no-brainer. One clever technique concocted by industry groups is wait to see what do-gooder initiatives qualify for the ballot, and then quickly draft counter measures—measures which have no hope of passing a plebiscite, but are intended instead merely to confuse voters; the monied interests are well aware of studies showing that voters are easily confused by conflicting initiatives and as a result tend to simply vote "no" on both of them. A 1990 California environmental reform package, for example, known as "Big Green," was matched by two corporate-backed initiatives, one of which was billed as a "pesticide safety policy," funded by Atlantic Richfield ($950,000), Chevron ($800,000), Shell ($600,000), and Phillip Morris ($125,000), among others. All three were voted down. Also in 1990, part of the $38 million outlay by the alcohol industry to kill a proposed liquor tax was spent pushing two counter measures: a bill proposing the industry's own version of a liquor alcohol tax as well as an anti-tax measure.

If the special interests don't baffle you with their counter measures, they'll probably get you with their deceptive advertising. One recent study of 25 initiatives concluded that the most successful initiative opposition campaigns have won in large part based on airing confusing messages through paid advertising. In fact, dubious initiative ad campaigns are more likely to confuse voters than negative or false advertising in candidate campaigns simply because issue initiatives fail to provide voters with the traditional political cues, such as party affiliation, to help voters decide. And while representatives are not immune to lies and deception, it's a lot easier, not to mention cheaper, for an environmental advocate to counter a dubious claim if he's only got to convince a few congressmen—as opposed to a few million otherwise-distracted citizens—that Exxon's pulling a con.

Consider, for example, an ad run as part of a $6 million effort by Californians for Sensible Laws, an industry group led by beverage firms such as Budweiser, Coke, and Pepsi, opposing a 1982 container recycling initiative. The spot falsely claimed the bill would cripple the state's voluntary recycling program, making life especially tough for Boy and Girl Scouts: The ad featured a uniformed Boy Scout asking his father why "the grown-ups" were trying to close down "Mr. Erikson's recycling center and put us Scouts out of business?" Another beverage industry ad presented five Oregonians who claimed a similar law was unpopular in their state, even though polls showed Oregonians overwhelmingly favored the measure. It was revealed later that the "citizens" in the ad were four Oregon beer distributor employees and one supermarket employee. Sure enough, the sponsors of the initiative could not afford a response, and although the bottle bill had 2–1 support in early polls, it failed by 44–56 percent.

What's also failed is direct democracy's ability to work in favor of racial and ethnic minorities. A few of the numerous examples where voters ganged up on those groups over the years include a 1964 California referendum in which citizens overturned by a 2-to-1 margin a law passed by the state legislature that prohibited racial discrimination by realtors. (In fact, of five referenda ever held in states to prohibit racial discrimination, not one has passed.) Last year, voters in Colorado passed an anti-gay measure voiding any existing gay rights laws in Denver, Aspen, and Boulder. And if you think majority tyranny is limited just to ethnics, racial groups, and gays, talk to the children of Kalkaska, Michigan, where citizens earlier this year voted to close down the school system three months early instead of paying an extra $200–$400 each in taxes.

POPULAR DEMANDS

Despite the evidence, let's assume the teledemocrats are *right:* Suppose that the people will take the time to be educated, and that the special interests will be persuaded or forced to refrain from false advertising and other deceptions. Suppose, in short, we *can* create a utopian system of majoritarian rule.

The good news for the Majoritarian Majority is that in some cases direct democracy will probably produce better results than representative government —say, in gun control laws. Which is precisely why the notion of push-button democracy plays so well in Perotville: It would be a wonderful world, indeed, if we could get the people together to vote on just those issues where we think the special interests are oppressing the rest of us.

But what about the rest of the issues, and especially those issues of belief, where fundamental rights come into play —issues such as the death penalty or gay rights? Do you want the majority deciding for you in those cases? One way to find out is by examining some examples of what the majority does believe. The majority of Americans would:

- sentence anyone who commits a murder to death
- send all occasional drug users to military style boot camps
- not allow any group to use a public building to hold a meeting denouncing the government
- ban movies with foul language or nudity

- ban from libraries books that preach the overthrow of the U.S. government
- make it illegal to publish materials the government classifies as secret
- outlaw the use of obscene gestures towards public officials
- favor the government keeping lists of people who partake in protest demonstrations
- keep in custody, when the nation is at war, people suspected of disloyalty
- require the reading of the Lord's Prayer in schools
- make homosexual relations between consenting adults illegal
- have rejected the Marshall Plan, and every year since 1950 voted to have spent less on foreign aid, and currently oppose aid to Russia

Of course, it is possible that the polls that produce such results were flawed; opinion can be distorted, after all, by the way questions are phrased. This is, in fact, the heart of the problem with majority rule through referendum. When the wording of an issue is frozen, and printed on the ballot, or even worse, flashed on the TV screen, there is no opportunity to do anything but take one side or the other—no chance, in other words, to see enough wisdom in the other person's arguments, or for him to see the point in yours, and for the wording to be amended accordingly.

In a representative government, legislators can, and do, deliberate and amend. These discussions can, of course, lead to imperfect compromise. But accommodation, however imperfect, may be essential to preserving the very fabric of democracy, especially when issues of morality and belief threaten to tear the nation apart. And the accommodation does not have to be imperfect. With deliberation, there is at least a chance that not only a better, but even the *right* law will result. Teledemocracy will deprive us of that chance. And, if you're not convinced, we can always vote on it.

POSTSCRIPT

Do Media Technologies Increase Citizen Participation?

In addition to the benefits cited by the authors, teledemocracy offers many prospects for increasing participation of the disabled, the isolated, and the individual who has little time away from work or family. Today, people are becoming increasingly reliant upon technology to reduce problems of time, space, and access to specific environments. Likewise, teledemocracy (as a social action) requires new principles for understanding citizen involvement and opinion formation.

There have been several attempts to apply teledemocratic processes to specific situations. The subject is still so new that many books on the subject are in press. The first full-length treatment of teledemocracy was F. Christopher Arterton's *Teledemocracy: Can Technology Protect Democracy?* (Sage Publications, 1987). Some of the earlier critiques of technology's relationship to democratic procedures include Benjamin Barber's article "Voting Is Not Enough," *The Atlantic Monthly* (June 1984) and Jean Bethke Elshtain's "Democracy and the Qube Tube," *The Nation* (August 7–14, 1982).

More recent explorations into case studies can be found in "Electronic Democracy: The Great Equalizer," by Howard Rheingold, *The Whole Earth Review* (Summer 1991) and "Conscious Democracy Through Electronic Town Meetings," by Duane Elgin, *Whole Earth Review* (Summer 1991). Tom Dworetzky has written "Electronic Democracy" for the February 1992 edition of *Omni*.

In recent years there have been several excellent approaches to the study of increased technology as presenting a new form of community. *CyberSociety* edited by Steven G. Jones (Sage Publications, 1995) is a good example of contemporary thought toward creating communities in cyberspace.

ISSUE 17

Does the Globalization of Media Industries "Homogenize" Media Content?

YES: Robert W. McChesney, from *Corporate Media and the Threat to Democracy* (Seven Stories Press, 1997)

NO: Georgette Wang, from "Beyond Media Globalization: A Look at Cultural Integrity from a Policy Perspective," *Telematics and Informatics* (November 1997)

ISSUE SUMMARY

YES: Robert W. McChesney, an associate professor of journalism and mass communication, discusses the wave of mergers and acquisitions among media companies in the 1990s and addresses the way content is modified to be palatable to the widest possible audience. He contends that because many of the corporations controlling the media are international, they also seek to develop content for an international market.

NO: Georgette Wang, director of the Graduate Institute of Telecommunications at National Chung Cheng University in Taiwan, acknowledges that communication technologies and international media content have changed the amount of information available to other countries, but she asserts that countries have maintained their own cultural integrity in addition to accepting other media fare.

Long before the wave of corporate mergers and acquisitions throughout the 1990s, the question of whether or not "smaller" or less-powerful countries could maintain indigenous programming in the shadow of powerful media companies was an important issue. From the days of early radio, when emerging companies in the United States and Europe sought to expand markets, or merely serve nationals in colonies with radio programming from the home country, the influence of foreign media in a country has raised the question of whether or not any nation can maintain its own values and culture when subject to new ideas from elsewhere.

In the following selection, Robert W. McChesney takes the perspective that corporate media have, by their nature, a need to expand and globalize. The result, he feels, is the development of media content that is most suited to the largest possible audience. Joint ventures and direct overlapping ownership of firms may then result in trivialization of media content, so as to capitalize on large market profits. Content that deals with relevant social topics, for example, is less likely to be produced than trivial, noncontroversial media product. McChesney agrees that some of what the big media producers present can be good but that, in general, the content may tend to homogenize cultures, values, and ideals.

In the second selection, Georgette Wang states that predictions of a "global village" have been with us for some time but that, despite a growth in technologies capable of globalization (like satellites), predictions about transnational broadcasting have not come true. She discusses the type of "ethno-nationalist revival" that she sees in Asia as an alternative to large-scale media content produced for a global audience. While Wang agrees that ownership of media corporations has indeed been centered in the United States and Europe, she focuses on what people choose to watch; and in many cases, even the content produced for a global market may be "read" differently by individuals in different cultures.

The selections in this issue demonstrate that there is no one correct answer to the question of global media. Media businesses operate according to a set of rules or guidelines, but the businesses, though powerful in themselves, are also consumed differently in the process of reaching audiences. No one specific model can be applied to all situations—and both McChesney and Wang would very likely agree with this concept. Still, each presents an excellent perspective from which to consider contemporary global media and information flow.

YES

Robert W. McChesney

CORPORATE MEDIA AND THE THREAT TO DEMOCRACY

CORPORATE MEDIA CONSOLIDATION

The journalism that emerged in the 20th century is a product well suited to the needs of the dominant media firms and advertisers that profited from the status quo. Yet the system was far from stable. On the one hand, new technologies like radio and television emerged and changed many aspects of media and journalism. On the other hand, the market moved inexorably toward becoming an integrated oligopoly, with a handful of firms dominating all forms of U.S. media, from radio, television, music and film to newspapers, magazines, and book publishing. In the early 1980s, Ben Bagdikian's *The Media Monopoly* concluded that less than 50 firms had come to dominate the entirety of the U.S. media, with the result that journalism was increasingly losing its ability to address the role and nature of corporate power in the U.S. political economy. As Bagdikian put it, the range of debate in U.S. journalism concerning capitalism and corporate power was roughly equivalent to the range of debate in the Soviet media concerning the nature of communism and the activities of the Communist Party. In the decade following the publication of *The Media Monopoly,* as traditional ownership regulations were relaxed, the market continued to consolidate at an even faster rate. By the time of the fourth edition of *The Media Monopoly,* in 1992, Bagdikian calculated that mergers and acquisitions had reduced the number of dominant media firms to two dozen.

Since 1992 there has been an unprecedented wave of mergers and acquisitions among media giants, highlighted by the Time Warner purchase of Turner and the Disney acquisition of Cap Cities/ABC. Fewer than ten colossal vertically integrated media conglomerates now dominate U.S. media. The five largest firms—with annual sales in the $10–25 billion range—are News Corporation, Time Warner, Disney, Viacom, and TCI. These firms are major producers of entertainment and media software and have distribution networks like television networks, cable channels and retail stores. Time Warner, for example, owns music recording studios, film and television production studios, several cable television channels, cable broadcasting systems, amusement parks, the WB television network, book publishing houses, magazine publishing interests, retail stores, motion picture theaters, and much else. In most of the above categories, Time Warner ranks among the top five firms in the world. The next three media firms include NBC (owned by General Electric), Universal (formerly MCA, owned by Seagram), and Sony. All three of these firms are conglomerates with non-media interests, with Sony and GE being huge electronics concerns that at least double the annual sales of any other media firm.

Below this first group there are another dozen or so quite large media firms —usually conglomerates—with annual sales generally in the $2–5 billion range. This list includes Westinghouse (owner of CBS), Gannett, Cox Enterprises, The New York Times, Advance Communications, Comcast, Hearst, Tribune Co., The Washington Post Co., Knight-Ridder, Times-Mirror, DirecTV (owned by General Motors and AT&T), Dow Jones, Reader's Digest, and McGraw-Hill. By the year 2000 it is probable that some of these firms will make deals to get larger or be acquired by other firms seeking to get larger.

The most striking development in the 1990s has been the emergence of a global commercial media market, utilizing new technologies and the global trend toward de-regulation. A global oligopolistic market that covers the spectrum of media is now crystallizing with very high barriers to entry. National markets remain, and they are indispensable for understanding any particular national situation, but they are becoming secondary in importance. The U.S. based firms just named dominate the global media market along with a handful of European-based firms and a few Latin American and Asian operations. By all accounts they will do so for a long time to come. Firms like Disney and Time Warner have seen their non-U.S. revenues climb from around 15 percent in 1990 to 30 percent in 1996. Sometime in the next decade both firms expect to earn a majority of their income outside of the United States. What stimulates much of the creation of a global media market is the growth in commercial advertising worldwide, especially by transnational firms. Advertising tends to be conducted by large firms operating in oligopolistic markets. With the increasing globalization of the world economy, advertising has come to play a crucial role for the few hundred firms that dominate it. From this vantage point it becomes clear, also, how closely linked the U.S. and global media systems are to the market economy.

Media firms have great incentive to merge, acquire, and globalize. It is when the effects of sheer size, conglomeration, and globalization are combined that a sense of the profit potential emerges. When Disney produces a film, for example, it can also guarantee the film showings on pay cable television and commercial network television, it can produce and sell soundtracks based on the film, it can create spin-off television series, it can produce related amusement park rides, CD-roms, books, comics, and merchandise to be sold in Disney retail stores. Moreover, Disney can promote the film and related material incessantly across all its media properties. In this climate, even films that do poorly at the box office can become profitable. Disney's *Hunchback of Notre Dame* (1996) generated a disappointing $99 million at the North American box office. However, according to *Adweek* magazine, it is expected to generate $500 million in profit (not just revenues), after the other revenue streams are taken into account. And films that are hits can become spectacularly successful. Disney's *The Lion King* (1994) earned several hundred million at the box office, yet generated over $1 billion in profit for Disney. Moreover, media conglomerates can and do use the full force of their various media holdings to promote their other holdings. They do so incessantly. In sum, the profit whole for the vertically integrated firm can be significantly greater than the profit potential of the individual parts in isolation. Firms without this cross-selling and cross-promotional potential are simply incapable of competing in the global marketplace.

In establishing new ventures, media firms are likely to participate in joint ventures, whereby they link up—usually through shared ownership—with one or more other media firms on specific media projects. Joint ventures are attractive because they reduce the capital requirements and risk on individual firms and permit the firms to spread their resources more widely. Each of the eight largest U.S. media firms has, on average, joint ventures with four of the other seven giants. They each also have even more ventures with smaller media firms. Beyond joint ventures, there is also overlapping direct ownership of these firms. Seagram, owner of MCA, for example, owns 15 percent of Time Warner and has other media equity holdings. TCI is a major shareholder in Time Warner and has holdings in numerous other media firms. The Capital Group Companies mutual fund, valued at $250 billion, is among the very largest shareholders in TCI, News Corporation, Seagram, Time Warner, Viacom,

Disney, Westinghouse, and several other smaller media firms.

Even without joint ventures and cross-ownership, competition in oligopolistic media markets is hardly "competitive" in the economic sense of the term. Reigning oligopolistic markets are dominated by a handful of firms that compete—often quite ferociously within the oligopolistic framework—on a non-price basis and are protected by severe barriers to entry. The "synergies" of recent mergers rest on and enhance monopoly power. No start-up studio, for example, has successfully joined the Hollywood oligopoly in 60 years. Rupert Murdoch of News Corporation poses the rational issue for an oligopolistic firm when pondering how to proceed in the media market: "We can join forces now, or we can kill each other and then join forces."

When one lays the map of joint ventures over the global media marketplace, even the traditional levels of competition associated with oligopolistic markets may be exaggerated. "Nobody can really afford to get mad with their competitors," says TCI chairman John Malone, "because they are partners in one area and competitors in another." *The Wall Street Journal* observes that media "competitors wind up switching between the roles of adversaries, prized customers and key partners." In this sense the U.S. and global media and communication market exhibits tendencies not only of an oligopoly, but of a cartel or at least a "gentleman's club."

CORPORATE MEDIA CULTURE

The corporate media produce some excellent fare, and much that is good, especially in the production of entertainment material in commercially lucrative genres. But in view of the extraordinary resources the corporate media command, the quality is woeful. In the final analysis, this is a thoroughly commercial system with severe limitations for our politics and culture. As George Gerbner puts it, the media giants "have nothing to tell, but plenty to sell." The corporate media are carpet-bombing people with advertising and commercialism, whether they like it or not. Moreover, the present course is one where much of the world's entertainment and journalism will be provided by a handful of enormous firms, with invariably pro-profit and pro-global market political positions on the central issues of our times. The implications for political democracy, by any standard, are troubling.

One need only look at the United States to see where and how journalism factors into the operations of the media giants. By the end of the 1980s, the wheels had come off U.S. journalism. In the new world of conglomerate capitalism the goal of the entire media product was to have a direct positive effect on the firm's earnings statement. The press, and the broadcast media, too, increasingly use surveys to locate the news that would be enjoyed by the affluent market desired by advertisers. This, in itself, seriously compromises a major tenet of journalism: that the news should be determined by the public interest, not by the self-interest of owners or advertisers. It also meant that media firms effectively wrote off the bottom 15–50 percent of U.S. society, depending upon the medium. As newspapers, for example, have become increasingly dependent upon advertising revenues for support, they have become anti-democratic forces in society. When newspapers still received primary support from circulation income, they courted every citizen with the funds necessary to purchase the paper, often a pittance. But now they are reliant on advertisers whose sole concern is access to targeted markets. Hence media managers aggressively court the affluent while the balance of the population is pushed to the side. Indeed, the best journalism being done today is that directed to the business class by *The Wall Street Journal, Business Week,* and the like. We have quality journalism aimed at the affluent and directed to their needs and interests, and schlock journalism for the masses. As Walter Cronkite observes, intense commercial pressures have converted television journalism into "a stew of trivia, soft features and similar tripe."

To do effective journalism is expensive, and corporate managers realize that the surest way to fatten profits is to fire editors and reporters and fill the news hole with inexpensive syndicated material and fluff. The result has been a sharp polarization among journalists, with salaries and benefits climbing for celebrity and privileged journalists at the elite news media while conditions have deteriorated for the balance of the working press. Layoffs among news workers have been widespread in the past decade; one study reveals that there has been a marked decrease in the number of Washington network correspondents alone in that period. With all this unemployment, salaries for non-elite journalists have plummeted, and beginning salaries are so low that young journalists have a difficult time supporting themselves. These developments have contributed to a collapse in the morale of U.S. journalists, a real loss of faith in their enterprise. The past few years have seen several major editors and journalists leave the profession in anger over these trends. James Squires, former editor of the *Chicago Tribune*, argues that the corporate takeover of the media has led to the "death of journalism." And, aside from the pursuit of profit, even business commentators have been struck by how the media conglomerates are willing to censor and distort journalism to suit their corporate interests. Nowhere is this more evident than in the virtual blackout of critical coverage of the operations of the giant media and telecommunication firms, beyond what is produced in the business press and directed at investors.

What is tragic—or absurd—is that the dominant perception of the "free press" still regards the government as the sole possible foe of freedom. That this notion of press freedom has been and is aggressively promoted by the giant media corporations should be no surprise, though that is rarely noted. Imagine if the federal government demanded that newspaper and broadcast journalism staffs be cut in half, that foreign bureaus be closed, and that news be tailored to suit the government's self-interests. There would be an outcry that would make the Alien & Sedition Acts, the Red Scares and Watergate seem like child's play. Yet when corporate America aggressively pursues the exact same policies, scarcely a murmur of dissent can be detected in the political culture.

With fewer journalists, limited budgets, low salaries and lower morale, the balance of power has shifted dramatically to the public relations industry, which seeks to fill the news media with coverage sympathetic to its clients. In the United States today, one expert estimates that there are 20,000 more PR agents than there are journalists. Their job is to offer the news media sophisticated video press releases and press packets to fill the news

hole, or contribute to the story that does fill the news hole.

The effects of this PR blitz on journalism can be seen on the two most important issues in U.S. politics in the 1990s: foreign trade and health care. These two issues are unusual because they provided clear public policy debates on the types of all important long-term issues (globalization of the economy and collapse of living standards and economic security) that professional journalism usually avoids. In the case of GATT [General Agreements on Tariffs and Trade] and NAFTA [North American Free Trade Agreement], the large transnational corporations were almost unanimous and aggressive in their support of "free trade." While there was not the same unanimity in the business community regarding health care, the insurance industry had an enormous stake in maintaining control of the health sector. In both cases, these powerful interests were able to neutralize public opinion, even though, initially, based on personal experience, it was against GATT and NAFTA and for a single-payer health care system.

The demise of journalism was readily apparent in this process. In each of these issues, big business mounted sophisticated, multi-million-dollar PR campaigns to obfuscate the issues, confuse the public and, if not weaken the opposition to the business position, at least make it easier for powerful interests to ignore popular opinion. In effect, corporate America has been able to create its own "truth," and our news media seem unwilling or incapable of fulfilling the mission our society so desperately needs it to fill. And this is the likely pattern for the new global commercial journalism of the media giants.

Nor are newspaper and broadcast journalism the only casualties of a corporate-dominated, profit-motivated media system. The corporate takeover of much of U.S. magazine publishing has resulted in increased pressure upon editors to highlight editorial fare that pleases advertisers or that serves the political agenda of the corporate owners. By 1996 magazine editors were calling for a minimal standard to be voluntarily accepted by their corporate overlords that would respect some rudimentary notion of editorial integrity. A similar process is taking place with book publishing. After a wave of mergers and acquisitions, three of the world's four largest media giants now own the three largest global book publishers. At the retail end, U.S. bookselling is becoming highly concentrated into the hands of a few massive chains; nearly one-half of U.S. retail bookselling is accounted for by Barnes & Noble and Borders. This corporatization of publishing has led to a marked shift to the political right in what types of books clear the corporate hurdles, as well as a trend to make books look "like everything else the mass media turn out." Book publishing, which not too long ago played an important role in stimulating public culture and debate, has largely abandoned that function, except to push the ideas of the corporate owners' favored interests. "The drive for profit," writes former Random House book editor Andre Schiffrin, "fits like an iron mask on our cultural output." He concludes that we may well have corporate "purveyors of culture who feel that one idea can fit all."

Corporate concentration and profit-maximization have similarly disastrous effects upon music, radio, television and film. The stakes have been raised for commercial success. *Variety* concluded after a 1996 study of 164 films that "Films with budgets greater than $60 million are more likely to generate profit than cheaper pics." One Hollywood movie producer notes that media mergers accelerate the existing trend toward "greater emphasis on the bottom line, more homogenization of content and less risk taking." The one film genre that has proven least risky and has the greatest upside has been "action" fare. This is encouraged by the rapid rise in non-U.S. sales for Hollywood, such that they are now greater than domestic revenues. Violent fare, requiring less nuance than comedy or drama, is especially popular across markets. As one media executive said, "Kicking butt plays everywhere." The other route for the corporate media giants to lessen risk is to specifically produce films that lend themselves to complementary merchandising of products: The revenues and profits generated here can often be equal or superior to those generated by traditional box-office sales or video rentals. The ultimate result of this marriage of Hollywood and Madison Avenue came with the 1996 release of Time Warner's film *Space Jam*, based upon Nike shoe commercials, starring Bugs Bunny and Michael Jordan and directed by "the country's hottest director of commercials." As *Forbes* magazine puts it, "the real point of the movie is to sell, sell, sell." Time Warner "is looking to hawk up to $1 billion in toys, clothing, books, and sports gear based on the movie characters." The implications for the "art" of filmmaking are evident.

NO

Georgette Wang

BEYOND MEDIA GLOBALIZATION

INTRODUCTION

When Marshall McLuhan proposed the concept of "global village", it stirred a widespread sense of novelty; that was nearly 30 years ago. Today the idea is coming closer to our everyday reality than ever before; satellite television reaches the most remote corners of the world, and information flows across national borders at a speed and volume never seen in human history.

Yet despite all these developments, we have not seen the emergence of a unified, homogeneous global culture as some had anticipated; on the contrary, there seems to be a trend moving toward the opposite direction. In Europe, there are reports of an ethno-nationalist revival, and in Asia, "Asian values" are high on both the political and the cultural policy agenda.

Whether the current emphasis on cultural identity and values reflects a reaction to media's power in undermining information control and national sovereignty is open to discussion. But even if such reaction is short-term and rhetorical in nature, the fact that there are such developments shows that several questions are begging for answers: has media influence on cultural change been overestimated, and perhaps more precisely, how much do we understand the interactive relationship between media and culture? In addition, what is actually taking place in the process of media globalization, and what is its implication to the way we conceptualize cultural integration which has presumably preoccupied the mind of policy makers?

Obviously not all the questions can be answered at one time, but by examining audience responses to the advent of transnational broadcasting, business strategies adopted by media corporations and policy measures in response to the changes that are taking place, this [selection] seeks to analyze the influence of media in their globalization process. The analysis then formulates the basis for discussing the meaning of cultural integrity, and options for policy makers.

From Georgette Wang, "Beyond Media Globalization: A Look at Cultural Integrity from a Policy Perspective," *Telematics and Informatics*, vol. 14, no. 4 (November 1997). Copyright © 1997 by Elsevier Science. Reprinted by permission. Notes and references omitted.

MEDIA GLOBALIZATION

The term "globalization" is often used to denote the growing importance of the global community as an economic, political and cultural entity that forms the framework for individual activities and nation-state operations. It brings events and relationships "at distance" into local contextualities, and at the same time subjects nation-states to increasing external influences. It is conceived both as a journey and a destination—the arrival at the globalized state.

Despite its popularity in the 1990s, the concept is not without problems. As pointed out by Ferguson, first is the ambiguity in meaning. Some have attempted to interpret globalization by focusing on the forces that contribute to the structuration of the world as a whole: growing economic interdependence, expanding transnational business community, eroding national sovereignty, and homogenizing material and cultural consumption. Meanwhile, others, notably postmodernists, have placed the centre of attention on the emergence of a common culture of consumption and style.

Ferguson argued that in addition to the problem with meaning, there is also the problem of evaluation, namely confusing what "should be" and what "is", and the problem of evidence when the supposedly "global" linkages remain confined to one-third of the world population.

To avoid the problem of evaluation, . . . "globalization" will be discussed in light of what is, instead of what should be. The problem of evidence, however, is closely linked with the problem of meaning; obviously there is no telling what empirical evidence is called for if there is no consensus on what the term means. Like some other concepts in social sciences, there is not yet a set of accepted criteria on which we can determine whether, or to what extent "globalization" has been fulfilled, let alone media globalization.

While scientifically "measuring" media globalization may be difficult, it is possible to discuss it as a trend on the basis of empirical data which indicate a rapid growth of transnational media, most notably satellite broadcast industry because of its ability to reach vast audiences, and international trade of cultural products.

A look at the recent growth of satellite television shows both the scope and scale of globalization. In Asia, Star TV reached a penetration rate of 11.1 million households in 12 nations within 2 years of its inauguration. It is estimated that by the year 2000, there will be 900 satellite transponders serving the region. In Latin America, the number of satellite television viewers is expected to reach one million by the end of 1997. As a single medium, Cable News Networks (CNN), [which] was reaching audiences in over 150 nations and territories in the early 1990s, more than doubled the number in the late 1980s.

Faced with such a surge in satellite broadcast popularity, one immediate concern of many governments—especially those with tight rules on the diffusion of information—was their weakening control, a concern reflected in the initial attempts in restricting, or banning satellite dishes. After reviewing policy measures regarding satellite television in Asian nations, Chan discovered four major types of responses: virtual suppression as found in Singapore and Malaysia, where satellite television was banned; regulated openness as found in Hong

Kong and the Philippines, where direct reception of satellite television programs was allowed, but the government maintains control over redistribution of such programs over cable networks; illegal openness such as the case of India and Taiwan, where direct reception was legal, redistribution over cable networks was not—but was flourishing anyway; and suppressive openness as in China, where the execution of orders banning satellite dishes was ineffective.

Of the four types of responses Chan observed, three—including virtual suppression, illegal openness and suppressive openness—featured measures to restrict the expansion of satellite television. However, what took place in many of these countries, for example, Taiwan, Malaysia, China, Indonesia and Turkey only served to prove Jussawalla's point that "there is no way that governments can stop the flow of information from entering their countries because of the wide prevalence of satellite technology."

Faced with the challenge of deregulation and increasing popularity of transnational broadcasting, governments were left with little choice but to adopt a more liberalized policy strategy. In Taiwan, first satellite dishes, then cable television were legalized; the Malaysian government has softened its stance against the reception of satellite programs, and Singapore is on its way to a 100-channel cable system which will allow the government to retain some form of control.

What is worthy of our attention in this process, is why some governments looked the other way when restrictions on receiving satellite television programs were violated. As one may suspect, failure to stop the growth of satellite dishes may be the result of a shortage in government resources in carrying out or-

ders; but ironically, in other instances, orders were not effectively executed because government agencies were divided in regard to policy measures on satellite dishes, and it was they themselves who bent the rules—especially when personal or institutional interests are involved. In China, for example, the Ministry of Electronics sees the manufacture and sales of satellite dishes a major source of income, while in Turkey where satellite television was not allowed according to its constitution, many of the retransmitters that redistributed satellite television programs were installed by municipal governments.

Compromising with the presence of transnational broadcasting may be pragmatic, yet to many policy makers, it is not without worries, especially when the content of such broadcast is taken into consideration.

Along with the rapid growth of transnational media, empirical data also showed a high concentration of media power. For example, by the end of the 1980s, the most films traded internationally were made in the United States; US products accounted for 75% of broadcast and basic cable television revenues and 85% of pay-television revenues worldwide.

The dominance of American products is also highly visible when the situation in regions and individual nations is examined. In Asia, programs from transnational broadcasters, including CNN, HBO, ESPN, BBC and Australian Television International have flooded its airwaves. In Europe, the situation is not much different; according to President Mitterrand of France, European programmes accounted for only 20,000 hours of the 125,000 hours (16%) shown annually on European television. By 1992,

American films had a 95% share of the British market and a two-thirds share of the French. In Canada, 98% of the television entertainment programs were imported. Even when trade is taking place, the deficit may be enormous; the value of Australian cultural products exported to the States was not more than one-fifth of what US exported to Australia.

With a different set of figures, the picture depicted by such statistics is utterly similar to what we have witnessed since two decades ago, when communication scholars sounded alarms on an imbalanced flow of information across national borders, mainly that between North and South.

The gap between centre and periphery is still as alarming as ever. As pointed out by Hall, transnational media is first of all West-centered, and secondly, speaks English as an international language. In the eyes of many third world leaders, such development is both threatening and suspicious. Upon learning Murdoch's investment in Star TV, Malaysia's Prime Minister Mahathir was quoted as saying: "If he [Rupert Murdoch] is not going to control news that we are going to receive, then what is it?"

Meanwhile it is also worthy of notice that today the gap no longer exists between just the North and South. With production in the hands of a few media corporations which are predominantly American, some are concerned that the current trend of globalization may be American in nature, or is simply a symbiosis of Americanization.

Globalization as indicated by the growth of transnational broadcasting by satellite, therefore, not only implies the weakening power of the sovereign states to control information flow, but also the loss of cultural autonomy and integrity

to a more homogenized metaculture, perhaps with an American touch to it.

Concerns of this nature have stirred extensive debates within the communications research community. In Ferguson's words, disentangling the globalizing tendencies of technology and economy from the processes of national and local acculturation has produced some interesting "intellectual bedmates", those including the post modernists, media reductionists, neotechnological determinists, and corporate conspiracists.

Although to many the concern is a genuine one, validity of the theories, especially that of the cultural imperialism and postmodernism, has been a nagging problem, especially in the face of emerging empirical data which can be examined from two different perspectives: audience responses to foreign programs and business strategies of transnational media corporations.

Audience Responses

Since the days of the "bullet theory", communications research has been haunted by a tendency to overestimate the power of mass media in shaping the individual mind and bringing socio-cultural changes. Although the bullet theory is now part of the history and the dominant paradigm proclaimed fallen over 10 years ago, the role of the audience and the intricacies involved in media consumption is still consistently overlooked in the discussion of cultural imperialism and the global cultural homogeneity.

As a matter of fact, empirical evidence from audience research does not necessarily lend support to the imperialist, nor the postmodernist points of view. A study by Wang showed a decline of broadcast television prime time viewing rates as satellite television began to enter Taiwan and Hong Kong. However, audiences are by no means passive receivers of whatever is fed to them. According to American film distributors interviewed in a study, quality local programs almost always outperform even good imported programs. Statistics showed that in six of the seven Asian nations surveyed, 90% of the top 20 programs were locally made, a finding supported by Lee's study of audience preferences in Taiwan, and Karthigesu's observations that Chinese audiences in Malaysia were heavy consumers of Chinese television programs produced in Taiwan and Hong Kong. Sen made a similar observation that third world audiences, especially those living in rural areas, tended to cling to their own music, drama, dance, language and customs.

A better indicator of the influence of media globalization, therefore, is not just the value of cultural product traded or number of hours on air, but what is actually consumed by the audience.

In addition to what is told by statistics, one cannot overlook the way viewers interpret what they watch on television. A growing number of studies, especially ethnographic audience research, have found that audiences tend to rely on their personal experiences and sociocultural resources in interpreting the meaning of what they watch.

In a cross-cultural study of viewing Dallas—considered by many as a symbol of American cultural imperialism—Katz and Liebes found that the understanding of the story is influenced by the viewers' cultural background, and reinforced by interactions with other members of the same ethnic group. In one instance, a group of Arab viewers insisted that Sue Ellen ran away from JR and moved into the house of her own father, instead of the father of her lover as was told in the televised drama. In another study of American and Hong Kong viewers' response to Forrest Gump, American viewers were found to have picked up messages which were incomprehensible or completely missed out by the Hong Kong viewers. For example, few of the Hong Kong participants fully understood the statement: "life is like a box of chocolate, you never know what you will get", simply because in Hong Kong, chocolate candies usually come in bars or blocks without filling.

One may argue that differences as such are trivial; that few could escape from the dazzling scenes of decadent capitalist lifestyle or the messages conveyed by cold and calculating human relationships that make up the story. But the above finding shows that it would also be presumptuous to assume that everyone in the audience will always receive exactly the same message.

Business Strategies of Media Corporations

... There may be little agreement on the influence of imported programs or transnational media, recent developments showed a rallying of forces for "local" programs to "go global"; nations which have formerly played an insignificant role in the international trade of cultural products have taken up the opportunity offered by satellite technologies and made themselves known on the market....

Turkey, where audiences were quite content with terrestrial broadcasting, had its first encounter with Magic Box in 1990, a satellite television service with the then Turkish president's son as a shareholder. In a few months' time, satellite television was spreading "like wildfire", reaching

[a] large part of the country, bringing down the monopoly the state held over television broadcasting.

Broadcasting into Turkey from Germany to avoid legal entanglement, satellite television brought to the Turkish audience American series, sport matches, and also programs which were designed for the Turkish audiences, but may not be allowed to go on air on Turkey's broadcast television, for example, talk shows in which sensitive political and social issues were freely discussed.

Because of its wide coverage, satellite broadcasts targeted at the Turkish audiences were not only picked up by the nation's overseas community, [they were] reaching into the newly independent Muslim states of the former Soviet Union. In April 1992, Turkish Radio and Television Corporation (TRT) began broadcasting to these republics. By sharing airwaves with a Moscow television channel, it reached about 57 million viewers with signals covering Europe, North Africa, the Middle East, and Central Asia, becoming a *de facto* global medium itself.

What we have witnessed in Turkey is an example of how satellite broadcast may change the nature and structure of television industry in a nation. Originally set up as a way to privatize television without invoking constitutional debates, Magic Box suddenly became the pioneer of a new style of television programming in which uncensored foreign films were not the only attraction. News and talk show programs free of ideological controls also proved to be vastly popular for their provoking style. The popularity of these programs in turn stimulated the growth of the "local" industry which may in fact be located outside of Turkey to stay "untamed", until it was clear that the existing regulatory framework was no longer manageable....

At least three observations that are relevant to the concerns of media globalization and its cultural implications can be made from the above statistics and development:

1. The audience does have an active role to play in the selection of television programs and interpretation of text; an act which heavily draws upon each individual's sociocultural experiences and resources. Preferences of the audience in turn hold the key to the development of local cultural industries and the impact foreign programs may have on them.

2. Media globalization may have a homogenizing effect, yet this homogenizing effect is more limited than previously anticipated, and it often occurs with a particularizing effect —if the Turkish case can be used as an example. According to Sahin and Aksoy, global media have not Americanized the Turkish culture, but have instead homogenized Turkish communities across national borders by connecting these "small worlds" to create what Anderson described as "imagined communities". On the other hand, global media also particularized their audiences by embracing differences and giving minority or disadvantaged social groups their voices.

   In fact, if we look at the overall picture, transnational broadcasting is bringing a greater variety of cultural products to the international market, as indicated by the active participation of nation states, serving better-defined, and more heterogeneous audience populations.

3. In contrast to the defensive measures many policy makers adopted at the initial stage of transnational broadcasting, we have witnessed a change of attitude. As it is becoming clear that blocking out transnational broadcasting is nearly impossible and as more nations seek to export as well as import cultural products, there is a more pragmatic view of media effect on culture with less talk of passive "protection", but rather, active "promotion" of cultural values or exchange of messages.

CULTURAL INTEGRITY AND MEDIA GLOBALIZATION

According to the thesis of cultural imperialism, the dominance of cultural products will have an inevitable assimilation and acculturation effect on their audiences.

While postmodernists treated an interdependent communication system as one level—instead of the cause—of a global culture, this system is expected to form the material base for all other levels and components, including standardized commodities, denationalized ethnic or folk motifs, generalized "human values and interests", and a uniform "scientific" discourse of meaning. In other words, communication was regarded as a condition for the development of a global culture; it was not a sufficient, but might well be a necessary condition.

While it is trite to point out the significance of media globalization, there is little evidence showing either the emergence of a homogeneous, Americanized world culture. As Ferguson pointed out, the assumptions about an indifferentiated culture as a result of consuming the same cultural and material products are "reductionist and fail even on a continental basis". After a careful review of communication and identity in Canada, a nation which has long been a heavy consumer of American films and television programs, Ferguson came to the conclusion that while cultural identities are open to influences, electronic media are not the ones that drive the dynamics of collective redefinition.

To prove cultural imperialism, we need evidence showing overall changes in both the abstract (beliefs, values) and material (artifacts, customs and rituals) aspects of a culture resulted from an unlimited exposure to foreign media content. So far, such evidence has yet been found.

Cultural imperialism has been criticized for invoking a video-determinism by overlooking audiences who, as shown by numerous studies, were seldom "assimilated" because of their exposure to media. They not only exhibit preferences in what to watch, even when surrounded by symbolic representation of a foreign culture, they are capable of reconstructing meaning, and are not necessarily socially and culturally influenced. As indicated by Cantor and Cantor, single source hegemony is inaccurate and outdated.

Postmodernists, on the other hand, have stayed away from the idea of an upcoming single, integrated global culture and tended to look at it more in terms of processes. However, with transnational media flourishing and cross-border communication expanding, have we truly witnessed the arrival of a global culture —in the postmodern sense?

Perhaps yes, but only to a certain extent. The state's power in controlling information flow in and out of its territory has been eroded, the emerging format of satellite television programming features a liberalized style which is embedded in the idea of freedom of expression, and by linking ethnic groups with transnational broadcasting, one may claim the birth of denationalized ethnic communities. However, we cannot afford to overlook developments which were missing, or moving away, from the post-modernist prescription.

In Asia, regionalism is on the rise as a safety net for taboo-bashing and free flow of (Western) information across national borders. As Yeap put it, it is both urgent and necessary for Asians to have a choice of identity in the upcoming age of global culture-based politics and secular state. The emphasis on Asian values, a concept which suggests a common core of values as compared to the West, not only serves as a basis for cultural resistance, but also reflects the priorities of national governments.

While Asian values are enjoying an unprecedented popularity, in Europe the desire of formulating a common culture is waning, and the talk of "European values" strained due to a rise of xenophobia derived from fears of massive migration from North Africa and Eastern Europe. To Schlesinger, what was suggested by postmodernists has not been taking place:

> ... the nation-state form persists as the frame of reference for all types of nation- alist currents. Thus, the postmodernists, with their dreams of flexi-identities, have it wrong. The nation-states have not been superseded. To be a contemporary Euro- pean nationalist is either to support the old state or to advocate the creation of a new one.

What cultural imperialists and post- modernists fail to see, is the fact that as open systems, social and cultural changes are seldom determined by the workings of just a handful of—let alone one— factors, no matter how powerful they may seem to be. While change and con- tinuity are both implicit in the nature of culture, like all other living systems, such change usually takes place through a complex process of selecting, integrating and organizing input from both interac- tions among elements within the system and with the environment. It is through this process that a culture is able to bring into being its own output, and to act back on its environment.

Continuous exchanges among ele- ments within the system and with the environment, therefore, is the very way that cultures operate, function, and sur- vive. As indicated by Ellen, "Although human systems may sometimes be seen to maintain a degree of system integrity, they are almost invariably engaged, ... in transaction with an ambiguously demar- cated wider environment". In addition, as such transaction and exchange are tak- ing place on a continuing basis, cultures seldom stay unchanged; only the scope and the scale of change may differ.

While the role of media may be prominent for all the glamour and public attention that are involved in the trade, it is, none-the-less, only one of the many factors in the system that influence change, and perhaps not even a highly significant one. As Ferguson put it quite cogently,

> In late capitalist societies the media's role is integrated to cultural formation and its symbolic representation; but this fact does not diminish the significance of historical and contextual factors as other sources of acculturation.

It is perhaps not a pure coincidence that cultural imperialists and postmodernists, coming from a Marxist tradition, and modernization theorists, coming from a positive-empirical tradition, should both place more weight in media influence than they seem to deserve. This is, of course, not to say that there is little danger in undermining media power, but now is perhaps the time for communication researchers to say: will the real media power please stand up?

POLICY IMPLICATIONS AND OPTIONS

Culture, therefore, is not to be regarded as a static, integrated whole that will be chipped, damaged or destroyed when coming in contact with the outside world. From this perspective, media policies that are aimed at protecting the integrity of a culture are in actuality doing very little —either to slow down, or to enhance its development.

An examination of media policy in Asia shows the beginning of the end for protective measures has arrived, not because the concept of cultural integrity is untenable given the nature of culture itself, but largely because information technologies have rendered the task extremely difficult to carry out. In Asia, only a few governments, for example, Singapore, are still trying to keep [their] people from information that is deemed potentially harmful.

The question then becomes, what happens after the floodgate is open and media become global? From empirical data that we have examined, audiences that are overwhelmed by information will still be opting for something familiar which they can relate to their own experiences and background. As a response to such needs, the transnational media corporations will likely continue on with their strategies of "going local", but the strate-

gies would be driven by market incentives, not by their social or cultural responsibilities to the receiving nations.

As mentioned earlier in this [selection], exposure to imported programs does not necessarily do harm to a culture, however, this does not mean one can overlook the need for an independent, vibrant local programming industry. As one of the most important forms of cultural activities, the production of video materials is far from just being a business venture; it signifies the vitality of a culture's artistic expression and reflects the meaning of its very existence. Without the ability to put its own products in the global market, a culture runs the risk in losing its footing in the surging flood of information sweeping the world. In this information age of ours, it is only appropriate for us to conceptualize and define "cultural integrity" not in terms of a static whole, but a continuously evolving entity that closely interacts with its environment.

It is the recognition of the importance in generating cultural products that governments in countries such as Singapore, Australia and Canada have undertaken measures to create a favorable environment for local production to grow, either through subsidies, quotas of local production in broadcast and cable television, or direct investment in the industry.

What we see in the mid-1990s, is a change in the role of communications policy, especially in third world nations, from that of a protective guardian against "harmful, alien information" to one of a supportive sponsor for cultural production. Globalization, therefore, does not need to be threatening; it would be so only when we lose sight of the nature of culture and power of media.

POSTSCRIPT

Does the Globalization of Media Industries "Homogenize" Media Content?

McChesney and Wang focus on what, in the words of sociologist Wilbur Schramm, has traditionally been called "big media." Film, television, and radio are all media systems that often require large infrastructural development. As a result, it is difficult for many countries to compete with the large industries and corporate power brokers that often dominate this media landscape.

Another perspective to consider is what Schramm called "small media." These communications technologies might include audio tape, CD-ROM, camcorders, VCRs, and the increasing market in digital tape and disc. These smaller, more portable technologies and software offer an alternative to more expensive "big media," and they can be tremendously powerful as tools that put the power of creating content in the hands of many. Additionally, subsidized networks, such as the Internet and the World Wide Web, offer an alternative to connecting individuals for a variety of communication purposes. While access and ownership issues are still uneven throughout the nations of the world, some alternatives have the potential to counteract the dominance of the major corporate media owners.

Audiences, too, have been regarded in recent years as more discerning, active agents in the media experience. The growth in audience studies has suggested that audiences think about the content they see and make choices about the meanings that are inherent in the content.

Media power will undoubtedly remain a controversial issue, but as we learn more from scholars and writers in other countries, we begin to understand that there is no one explanation for the effect of media concentration or ownership. Journals with international audiences, such as *Telematics and Informatics,* publish media studies from scholars in various countries, which provides a variety of perspectives. The prominence of comparative international studies in journals published in the United States and currently online also provide different perspectives on matters of policy, ownership, content, and audience use.

ISSUE 18

Do New Media Have an Immediate Effect on Our Behaviors and Attitudes?

YES: Sherry Turkle, from "Session With the Cybershrink: An Interview With Sherry Turkle," *Technology Review* (February/March 1996)

NO: Douglas Rushkoff, from *Media Virus! Hidden Agendas in Popular Culture* (Ballantine Books, 1994)

ISSUE SUMMARY

YES: Psychologist Sherry Turkle argues that an individual's behavior changes when he or she interacts with computer networks. She examines how the anonymity of the Internet changes a user's concept of identity and how individuals separate the cybercommunity of online communication from real life.

NO: Author Douglas Rushkoff contends that participants in media-saturated environments have adopted the values and techniques necessary to live in what he calls the "datasphere," or "mediaspace." For Rushkoff, it is not the immediate effects that are important but the long-term impact of more media that has conditioned us to change our attitudes and behaviors.

One of the earliest assumptions about media was that they had immediate, or direct, effects upon their users. The "Magic-Bullet," "Hypodermic Needle," and "Stimulus-Response" models were all attempts to describe what people thought was the impact of media and their messages. Over time, however, competing ideas challenged the direct-effects models and suggested that there were a variety of ways in which the effects of the media could be measured and experienced by audiences. This issue recalls one of the earliest debates in media research but presents a context in which new media may offer solutions to old ways of thinking about the relationship between media and society.

One of the most significant changes in recent years has been the change in thinking about media as a "mass" phenomenon rather than as a conduit to individuals for a variety of messages. Cable television and videotape rentals have changed the way people use broadcast television. The film industry has had to adapt to smaller, more highly segmented audiences for releases in movie theaters as well as to develop home markets. Compact discs have revolutionized the recording industry, and portable disc and tape technology have challenged radio's prominence as the primary acoustic medium. Computer networks are now widely discussed alternatives to traditional ways in which people work, are educated, and communicate.

Many of the basic questions asked of earlier media forms are now the focus of computer interaction, but different conditions now make it possible to see how direct effects may indeed take place. As illustrated in the following interview with Sherry Turkle, the personal use of the computer creates a situation in which the traditional communication patterns are changed. Although computers hooked up to networks may function as forms of mass media, they do so only because they have the potential to reach "masses." According to Turkle, networked computers are highly personal forms of communication that challenge the notion of the traditional "mass *audience*." Instead, individuals work with the medium in highly selective ways, allowing for greater immediacy of expression, even though the messages may be stored in "cyberspace" until the recipients choose to receive them. Because of the immediate, personal nature of this type of computer use, the individual's own behaviors and attitudes can be more easily monitored and understood.

Douglas Rushkoff, on the other hand, argues that the prominence of media in our lives has already conditioned us to think and react in media terms. Elaborating on Marshall McLuhan's famous statement "The medium is the message," Rushkoff discusses how the intimate environment created by media has conditioned us to substitute what he calls "media viruses" for real content. For Rushkoff, any immediate effects are irrelevant. Instead, it is the cumulative effect of living with so many forms of media that have changed the way we perceive the world around us and how we decide what is important in that world.

Rushkoff emphasizes the importance of understanding how media works. By comparing media to an extension of a living organism, he is suggesting that events are not situation-specific but, rather, that they affect a host of contingent and corresponding issues. The real effect, he says, is that living in a media-saturated world ultimately influences how we perceive reality.

YES

Sherry Turkle

SESSION WITH THE CYBERSHRINK:
AN INTERVIEW WITH SHERRY TURKLE

Attempting to unlock her office door, Sherry Turkle fumbles with her keys. She tries one way, then another. After good-naturedly grousing about the recalcitrant lock—so much more troublesome than opening a fresh window on a computer screen—Turkle finally succeeds, and the door swings open to a most uncybernetic office: wicker furniture, riverside view of the Boston skyline, photo of her four-year-old daughter. Surely a computer lurks somewhere in this den of the reigning psycho-guru of cyberspace, but it is tastefully unobtrusive.

Turkle has established herself as the Margaret Mead of the computer culture. Her 1984 book *The Second Self: Computers and the Human Spirit* examined the way people interacted with personal computers, just then becoming a common appliance. The book catapulted her into the pantheon of academic superstars: *Ms.* magazine named her its woman of the year, and *Esquire* entered her in its "registry of America's new leadership class."

The Brooklyn-born Turkle, with a joint doctorate in sociology and psychology from Harvard University, is a professor in MIT's Program in Science, Technology, and Society. Her interest in concepts of identity predates her fascination with computers; she has written extensively about psychoanalysis, and rarely does she give an interview or lecture without referring in some way to Freud, whose division of human identity into id, ego, and superego presaged the infinitely more diverse personas that people voluntarily assume in their travels through cyberspace.

Her latest book—*Life on the Screen: Identity in the Age of the Internet*, published in November [1995] by Simon and Schuster—assesses the impact of computer networks on the way people think about themselves and their role in society. Turkle, who is a licensed clinical psychologist, lived among the Net natives in order to learn their ways. In the spirit of the new medium, she sometimes donned a disguise—such as a thin veil in the persona of "Doctor Sherry," or even assumed a male persona to experience for herself the Net's fabled gender-bending abilities.

From Sherry Turkle, "Session With the Cybershrink: An Interview With Sherry Turkle," *Technology Review*, vol. 99, no. 2 (February/March 1996). Copyright © 1996 by *Technology Review*. Reprinted by permission.

Turkle spoke with [*Technology Review*] senior editor Herb Brody not only about the potential of the Net to enhance human experience but about elements of the online phenomenon that disturb her—in particular the fear that young people will succumb to the temptation to leave "real life" behind for the ever-so-much more controllable realm of cyberspace.

TR: When people in real life exhibit multiple distinct personalities, we call them psychotic, or at least sinister: In Robert Louis Stevenson's story, Dr. Jekyll shed his "gentle doctor" identity to liberate the "beast" within him as Mr. Hyde. Why are multiple personas not only accepted on the Net but considered cool?

TURKLE: People who suffer from multiple personality disorder have fragmented selves where different pieces are walled off from the others—often in the service of protection from traumatic memories. People who suffer in this way can have the experience of opening their closet in the morning and not knowing who bought some of the suits inside it. By contrast, people who assume online personas are aware of the lives they have created on the screen. They are playing different aspects of themselves and move fluidly and knowledgeably among them. They are having an experience that encourages them to challenge traditional ways of thinking about healthy selves as single and unitary.

TR: How so?

TURKLE: We live an increasingly multi-roled existence. A woman may wake up as a lover, have breakfast as a mother, and drive to work as a lawyer. A man might be a manager at the office and a nurturer at home. So even without computer networks, people are cycling through different roles and are challenged to think about their identities in terms of multiplicity. The Internet makes this multiplicity more concrete and more urgent.

TR: But the multiple personas people assume online are of a different sort from the roles you've described. In cyberspace a person may be a man sometimes and a woman another, for example.

TURKLE: Yes, cyberspace takes the fluidity of identity that is called for in everyday life and raises it to a higher power: people come to see themselves as the sum of their distributed presence on all the windows they open on the screen. The technical metaphor of cycling through computer windows has become a metaphor for thinking about the relationship among aspects of the self.

TR: So cyberspace is kind of a fun house mirror of our society—essentially reflecting what goes on off-line, but with some exaggeration?

TURKLE: Yes. And in a way, because it does allow for an extravagance of experimentation—with gender switching, age-flexibility, and all the rest made so easy—experiences in cyberspace are challenging us to revisit the question of what we mean by identity.

TR: But in the frenzy of attaining multiple identities, some people seem to be losing the sense that their "real world" self is any more important than their menagerie of online personas. In your book you describe one young man who tells you that for him, real life—RL, as he calls it—doesn't have any special status. It's just another window, along with the ones where he plays roles in a number of virtual communities.

TURKLE: Right. And he said RL is usually not even his best window.

TR: That sounds obsessive. Do you encounter that attitude a lot?

TURKLE: It's not uncommon. But for me, his case is important because it demonstrates how a bright young man who is doing well in school and who has real-life friends can easily go through a period when things are more interesting on the Net than off. This is what leads him to see his online experiences as a "genuine" part of his life. He still had a life off-line, but at the time of our conversation, events there were not going so well. From this perspective, the comment about RL not being his best window seems a bit less sinister.

TR: So retreat into online community is just a phase?

TURKLE: It can be. And in some cases it is not so much a retreat as a first step in developing strengths that can be brought into "real" life. I met a student who had a very bad time in his freshman year in college. His father was an alcoholic, and he was dealing with his own sense of his vulnerability to alcoholism. He coped by taking a job of great responsibility in a virtual community. When I met him the following summer, he was interested in going back to try things out in RL. In the best of cases, positive online experiences leave their mark on both the virtual and the real. And they can change the way people see their possibilities; it can affect self-esteem.

TR: Are social skills acquired online applicable in RL?

TURKLE: They can be. Much of what it takes to get along socially are things like having enough self-esteem to be willing to take risks, to have somebody not like you and yet be able to move on, to be able to take no for an answer, to not see things in black and white. An absence of these skills can make life on the Net seem attractive as a place of escape. But they can be learned by interacting with people within virtual communities. That's why I don't get upset that people, even children, are spending a lot of time online. They may be working through important personal issues in the safety of life on the screen. They may come out the other side having had some experience they're able to use to make their lives more fulfilling.

TR: Can casual relationships formed online survive the transition to the real world, where it's not so easy to hide behind an invented identity?

TURKLE: Sometimes, online relationships do not survive the voyage to the real. But in other cases, they survive very well. I know of real-life marriages between people who met each other in cyberspace. The way such intimacies develop usually follows a rather unsurprising pattern. You're in an online discussion group and you "hear" one of the contributors to the group sound interesting and appealing over a three-month period. You're finally going to want to talk to him or her in person. People want that flesh-and-blood connection. Of course, this can lead to problems too. Someone may begin an online extramarital affair thinking of it as a form of interactive erotic literature, typing provocative sentences back and forth, and then discover that the involvement has become a lot more complicated—something that they want to bring into their real life.

TR: Parents I know are ambivalent about their kids' use of computers. It's wonderful that children have this other world that they can inhabit and master. On the other hand, there seems to be an element of compulsion that's not particularly attractive. There are only so many hours in the day, and time spent on a computer is time not spent with friends, family, playing sports, or just reading.

TURKLE: If the computer is replacing time with peers and parents, that's not good. But if the computer is replacing television, then that may well be an upgrade.

TR: Do you worry that some people—children in particular—might be becoming addicted to computers?

TURKLE: It's not an addiction like with cocaine, where everyone on it develops a physical dependency, which is never good. When people respond to the holding power of computers, the situation is far more complex. A person can use computers in different ways at different times, and for different developmental tasks. A six-year-old who uses a computer, for example, may be working on an issue of mastery. A year later he may have shifted his attention to baseball cards. Both are developmentally appropriate, and there's little reason to think that mastery of the online world is much different from mastery of box scores in baseball. This is especially true now that kids can share their experiences online in much the same way that they can share their interest in baseball cards. In the same sense, computer programming is not that much different from, say, chess.

PALLIATIVE FOR A VULNERABLE TIME

TR: Many of the people you study are students attending college—traditionally a time when people leap into political activity. Are these young adults using the Net to try to change the world?

TURKLE: As someone whose political sensibilities were developed in the 1960s, I'm sorry to say that I see some evidence that things are not going in that direction. I talked with one young man of 22 or 23, who told me how involved he is in political activity within one of the Internet's virtual worlds—a multi-user domain (or MUD) where people create characters and build their own virtual living and working spaces as a backdrop for their online social lives. He just loved the grassroots feel of the involvement. Since this was right before the last congressional elections, and some key seats in his home state were up for grabs, I said, well—what about real-life politics? He said no, that was of no interest to him: politicians were all cynics and liars. Part of me wanted to cry.

TR: Why do you find that so disturbing?

TURKLE: I hear many of the people I interview expressing a genuine confusion, a sense of impotence, about how to connect to the political system. In cyberspace, they feel they know how to connect, how to make things happen. This is disturbing because as of now, most of the community life in MUDs and other virtual places has little effect in the real world —these online societies essentially disappear when you turn off your computer. It would be exciting to see online communities used more to address real-world social crises such as those around the environment, health, drugs, and education. This is starting to happen; I would like to see more of it. Online activists are learning a great deal as they build virtual worlds—it's like thousands of social experiments being conducted simultaneously, all over the world. I would like to see some of the knowledge gained from these efforts used to improve our off-line communities.

TR: Why do you think some young people are withdrawing from real political involvement and jumping instead into cyberspace?

TURKLE: For some people I interviewed who are in their twenties, cyberspace offers them a status that RL does not. These people grew up in middle class families, went to college, and many feel that they are slipping out of the middle class. They work jobs in fast food or sales, most share apartments, some have moved back to live with parents. They're not living in the way they were brought up to think somebody with a college education would live.

TR: But in cyberspace, they have higher status?

TURKLE: Right. In cyberspace they feel that they have rejoined the middle class. They are spending time with people whose interests and cultural background they recognize. They feel at home and in a political environment where they can make a difference. As one person put it, "I have more stuff on the MUD than off it," meaning that in her virtual community, she was able to build and furnish her own "room." Meanwhile, the real-world culture is supporting this notion with the hype that computers are sexy, that cyberspace is where it's happening. But I think that some of this hype can encourage a notion that what we do to the physical environment, say, doesn't count because we're creating a new environment in cyberspace. You don't want to lose a sense of urgency about the state of your city because you feel you have this other ready alternative. Yet, this is what I pick up in the attitudes of many cyber-enthusiasts I speak to.

TR: That would seem to be a self-fulfilling prophecy—as people withdraw from the real world, their talents are not available to solve our real problems. But they are available in cyberspace, which then

becomes a more and more attractive option.

TURKLE: Yes. As a society, we are at a particularly vulnerable point. There is a tremendous amount of insecurity about what kinds of jobs we are going to have and where they will be. How are we going to address the serious problems facing our children: drugs, violence, deteriorating education? How are we going to address problems of the environment and of cities and of health care? Do we have the political will to attempt to do all of these things? The challenges seem overwhelming. So people are very susceptible now to the notion that there's a better place—somewhere over the rainbow, way up high, where there isn't any trouble. Of course, that place is the online world. In other words, our confusion and insecurity make us want to believe that there is a technological alternative.

HAVING IT ALL

TR: Why do you think there's been a recent backlash against the Internet, with the publication of critical books and articles?

TURKLE: There are several reasons. Partly it is opportunistic—after a lot of hype, people sense that it's the right time in the news cycle to present a contrary point of view. Also, the same frustrations and the same desire for an easy fix that lead people to the safety of the Internet lead people to complain about it rather than other things. We don't know what to do about violence or about the poor quality of education in many schools. We don't know how to bring families back together. It's easy to blame technology for our ills. So you see the widespread fantasy that what's causing moral decay in America is online pornography. People are spending a lot of political capital making waves about the urgency of cleaning up the Internet. I think that energy might be better spent elsewhere.

TR: Pornography on the Net doesn't overly concern you?

TURKLE: Do I want my four year old sitting there scrolling through filthy pictures? Of course not. But I would rather not interfere with free speech and I prefer to keep the monitoring of children as something that gets done by parents in the home rather than have government agencies policing cyberspace. Yes, there is pornography online. But we should be able to recognize that it is a displacement of our social anxieties to be focusing disproportionately on cyberporn as a pressing problem.

TR: Many critics seem turned off by how shallow the Internet is, both in its informational content and in the kind of relationships it fosters.

TURKLE: When a new technology is introduced, people respond by complaining that it's not as good as what we have had before. But it is hard to argue that online information doesn't compete favorably with what television offers. And online communication is in many ways a return to print—to reading and writing. In any case, it has usually worked out that the introduction of a new medium does not displace the old in any simple sense. Television didn't kill movies, and neither did video games.

TR: So instead we end up with everything.

TURKLE: Yes—that seems to be a general pattern. I do not believe that people are going to choose between relationships in cyberspace and face-to-face relationships. I think that people are going to

have all kinds. It's not going to be one or the other. What I'm interested in—psychologically, socially, and politically—is making real life more permeable to cyberspace and cyberspace more permeable to real life. We need to think of ways to make the resources that are online have a positive impact on real life.

TR: But such "permeability" could come at a cost. For instance, if kids pursue more education through the Net and less through schools with other kids, won't they miss much of the socialization that schools have traditionally provided?

TURKLE: Well, in that sense the advent of a new technology leads us to ask what it is we most value in our way of life. Do we care, for example, about public schools? Because if the schools continue to deteriorate, and pose physical dangers, and an online alternative arises, then who could blame parents for keeping their kids home and having them just log on instead? It's a rational choice. Now if you don't like that, if you think that kids ought to be getting an education with other children, then you have to be willing to pay for it. And that will mean investing public money to make the schools better and safer. Online possibilities are forcing us to examine what we really care about. They are serving as a kind of a wake-up call.

NOT ALL BOYS AND THEIR TOYS

TR: Has the rise of the Internet made the computer culture more female-friendly?

TURKLE: Definitely. Computer technology is moving in a direction that makes it easier for women to see it as something that is culturally theirs. We're hearing a lot less of that stuff about girls having "computer phobia," which I never thought was a good way to explain what was going on.

TR: You don't think girls have tended to be more apprehensive than boys about using computers?

TURKLE: Maybe they were at one time, but the label "phobia" does not correctly describe the phenomenon and does not help girls get over what some of them feel, which is much more like computer *reticence.* Girls weren't afraid of computers, but many felt that dealing with a computer was just not very girl-like. The computer was culturally constructed as male, just as much of technology was. When I was a girl, I once wanted to build a crystal radio. My mother, usually very encouraging, said no, don't touch it, you'll get a shock. It wasn't that I didn't want to build it— I wasn't phobic. But somehow, this just wasn't what girls did. I became reticent about such things.

Traditionally, the computer culture has carried many associations that tended to alienate girls—I mean, if you made a mistake, the computer asked you if you wanted to "abort" or "execute" or "kill." Those words convey images that just didn't appeal to a girl. Also, computers took you away from people.

TR: But the Internet is making the computer more of a social tool?

TURKLE: Yes—using computers today tends not to involve conquest metaphors or isolation from other human beings. Interfaces encourage you to manipulate them, to play with objects on the screen as though they were tangible entities, like elements of a collage. And the Net is all about chatting with people, being with people. Women who get onto the Net are often turned off by the flaming and the ad hominem rudeness they see. But they find places on the Net where

this is not the case, and when they don't find them, they can create them. The Net desperately needs more of the characteristics that in our culture have been associated with women—skills such as collaboration and diplomacy. And many online communities are not only civil but actively encourage friendships and networking—it's not all boys and their toys.

TR: Still, the Net remains mostly male, doesn't it?

TURKLE: Women are present on the Net in greater and greater numbers. But I am often struck by the preponderance of messages that seem to come from men, even in places where there are many women around. Women tend to be less visible than men because when confronted with a rowdy group-flame session, women will move their conversations to private e-mail.

TR: Is there some way that women are using the Net more than men are?

TURKLE: Many women are getting access to the Internet in order to keep in touch with their families. For example, a parent with kids at college can use the Net to communicate with them. Parents know that their kids are logging on every day to get their e-mail. They're not going to resent an e-mail message from mom the way they might resent a badly timed phone call. A channel of communication that wasn't there before is opening.

TR: Does this new channel lead to new kinds of interactions?

TURKLE: Yes. A parent can send e-mail to a child away at college, saying, you know, it's 3 o'clock in the morning, I couldn't sleep, I was watching an old movie, I just thought I'd send you a note. In one case when this happened, the child, a freshman at college, responded immediately to a note from his mother and told her that he was up too—studying for a chemistry exam. The mother wrote right back, I wish you luck. The son appreciated the nurturance, something that he would not have permitted himself if he had had to call home. So all of a sudden you have an interaction that gratifies both people that never would have happened.

TR: So for many women, the Internet is a way to strengthen family ties?

TURKLE: Yes. Of course, the appeal of cyberspace for communication with family also draws in many men as well. And once they're in touch with their kids, why shouldn't they join a newsgroup about investments?

THE PERIL OF THE BLACK BOX

TR: Time was, effective use of a computer required at least a basic understanding of how the machine worked. One benefit of more advanced computers is that this is no longer the case—people can now control a powerful technology without knowing much of anything about how it operates. What are the consequences of relying on a technology that is so opaque?

TURKLE: I'm very concerned that technology may be fostering a kind of intellectual passivity, feeding into a cultural acceptance of a lack of understanding of how a lot of things work. I'm troubled by people's sense that this is all basically magic. I don't think people should have no idea how computer technology works. And increasingly, people have no idea. I interviewed one man who said that when BMW started using microchips in its cars, he lost interest in them although he had been an avid enthusiast. For him, the cars had become opaque. He enjoyed transparent technology because it made him feel more empowered to understand other things in his world. I have a lot of sympathy for his perspective.

TR: Cars that use computer chips need less maintenance and run better. A Macintosh is usable by millions more people than a DOS or Unix computer. Aren't such benefits worth the loss of "transparency"?

TURKLE: But some undesirable things may go along with this movement. When people deal every day with objects that are powerful but impenetrably complex, it can lead to feelings of impotence. Or, alternatively, to feelings of unreasonable power and retreat to radical oversimplifications. We need to be attentive to the social and psychological impact of a technology that encourages you to think that all you need to do is click, click. Double click and make public education go away. Double click and make taxes go away. Double click—three strikes and you're out and solve the crime problem. As a society, we're doing a lot of double clicking. And I think it is not a bad thing for us to get a better understanding of how this mentality might be flowing out of the habits of thought encouraged by our technology.

TR: All in all, are you an optimist or pessimist about the effects of the computer on the human psyche?

TURKLE: I think that computers offer dramatic new possibilities for personal growth—for developing personal senses of mastery, for forming new kinds of relationships, and for communicating with friends and family all over the world in immediate, even intimate ways. But I don't like thinking of things in terms of optimism or pessimism because it makes it sound as though one gets to take bets on whether the technology is going to have one kind of effect or another. I think that a lot of the effect of computers and the Internet is going to depend on what people do with it. We have to see ourselves as in a position to profoundly affect the outcome of how things are going to go. Hyping or bashing technology puts the emphasis on the power of the technology. I'm trying to put the spotlight on people, and the many human choices we face as we try to assimilate this technology.

Ultimately, there is a limit to the sorts of satisfactions that people can have online. We live in our bodies. We are terrestrial. We are physical as well as mental beings—we are cerebral, cognitive, and emotional. My optimism comes from believing that people are going to find ways to use life on the screen to express all these sides of themselves.

NO

Douglas Rushkoff

MEDIA VIRUS!
HIDDEN AGENDAS IN
POPULAR CULTURE

The average American home has more media-gathering technology than a state-of-the-art newsroom did ten years ago. Satellite dishes spot the plains of Nebraska, personal computers equipped with modems are standard equipment in a teenager's bedroom, cable boxes linking families to seventy or more choices of programming are a suburban necessity, and camcorders, Xerox machines, and faxes have become as accessible and easy to operate as public pay phones. Household television-top interactive multimedia centers are already available, promising easy access to the coming "data superhighway." Like it or not, we have become an information-based society.

We live in an age when the value of data, images, and ideologies has surpassed that of material acquisitions and physical territory. Gone are the days when a person's social stature could be measured by the distance he had to walk to see smoke from his neighbor's campfire. We've finally reached the limits of our continental landmasses; we've viewed the earth from space over national broadcast television. The illusion of boundless territorial frontiers has been destroyed forever. There's simply no more room, nothing left to colonize. While this may keep real-estate prices high, it also demands that real growth—and the associated accumulation of wealth and power—occur on some other level.

The only place left for our civilization to expand—our only real frontier—is the ether itself: the media. As a result, power today has little to do with how much property a person owns or commands; it is instead determined by how many minutes of prime-time television or pages of news-media attention she can access or occupy. The ever-expanding media has become a true region—a place as real and seemingly open as the globe was five hundred years ago. This new space is called the datasphere.

The datasphere, or "mediaspace," is the new territory for human interaction, economic expansion, and especially social and political machination. It has become our electronic social hall: Issues that were formerly reserved for hushed conversations on walks home from church choir practice are now debated openly on afternoon talk shows, in front of live audiences composed of people "just like us." Good old-fashioned local gossip has been replaced by nationwide coverage of particularly resonant sex scandals. The mediaspace has also developed into our electronic town meeting (to use Ross Perot's expression). Traditional political debate and decisions have been absorbed by the ever-expanding forums of call-in radio and late-night variety shows. Today's most media-savvy politicians announce their candidacies on Larry King and explain their positions on Rush Limbaugh, or, better yet, primetime "infomercials."

... Having been raised on a diet of media manipulation, we are all becoming aware of the ingredients that go into these machinations. Children raised hearing and speaking a language always understand it better than adults who attempt to learn its rules. This is why, educators believe, our kids understand computers and their programming languages better than the people who designed them. Likewise, people weaned on media understand its set of symbols better than its creators and see through the carefully camouflaged attempts at mind control. And now Americans feel free to talk back to their TV sets with their mouths, their remote controls, their joysticks, their telephones, and even their dollars. Television has become an interactive experience.

The advent of do-it-yourself (DIY) technology makes direct feedback even more far-reaching. Today, homemade camcorder cassettes are as likely to find their way onto CNN as professionally produced segments. Tapes ranging from "America's Funniest Home Videos" to the world-famous Rodney King beating

are more widely distributed through the datasphere than syndicated reruns of "I Love Lucy." Alternative media channels like the computer networks or even telephone and fax "trees" (distribution lists) permit the dissemination of information unacceptable to or censored by mainstream channels and have been heralded as the new tools of revolution in countries as "un-American" as Romania and Communist China. Pirate media, like illegal radio broadcasts and cable or satellite jamming, are even more blatant assertions of the power of individuals to hack the data network. ...

The messages in our media come to us packaged as Trojan horses. They enter our homes in one form, but behave in a very different way than we expect once they are inside. This is not so much a conspiracy against the viewing public as it is a method for getting the mainstream media to unwittingly promote countercultural agendas that can actually empower the individuals who are exposed to them. The people who run network television or popular magazines, for example, are understandably unwilling to run stories or images that directly criticize the operating principles of the society that its sponsors are seeking to maintain. Clever young media strategists with new, usually threatening ideas need to invent new nonthreatening forms that are capable of safely housing these dangerous concepts until they have been successfully delivered to the American public as part of our daily diet of mainstream media.

... These media events are not *like* viruses. They *are* viruses. Most of us are familiar with biological viruses like the ones that cause the flu, the common cold, and perhaps even AIDS. As they are currently understood by the medical community, viruses are unlike bacteria or germs because they are not living things; they are simply protein shells containing genetic material. The attacking virus uses its protective and sticky protein casing to latch onto a healthy cell and then inject its own genetic code, essentially genes, inside. The virus code mixes and competes for control with the cell's own genes, and, if victorious, it permanently alters the way the cell functions and reproduces. A particularly virulent strain will transform the host cell into a factory that replicates the virus....

Media viruses spread through the datasphere the same way biological ones spread through the body or a community. But instead of traveling along an organic circulatory system, a media virus travels through the networks of the mediaspace. The "protein shell" of a media virus might be an event, invention, technology, system of thought, musical riff, visual image, scientific theory, sex scandal, clothing style or even a pop hero—as long as it can catch our attention. Any one of these media virus shells will search out the receptive nooks and crannies in popular culture and stick on anywhere it is noticed. Once attached, the virus injects its more hidden agendas into the datastream in the form of *ideological code* —not genes, but a conceptual equivalent we now call "memes."[1] Like real genetic material, these memes infiltrate the way we do business, educate ourselves, interact with one another—even the way we perceive reality....

Phil Donahue [did] a show ... on the computer interface called virtual reality. Or at least that's what the show [was] supposed to be about. His guests [were] not computer programmers, interface designers, or even authors and researchers on cyberspace, virtual communities, or future technology. No, Phil ... invited the inventor of a pornography computer program to be the center of attention.... In order to spice up a potentially technical or information-based show, the producers of "Donahue" [fell] back on the easiest method of netting channel surfers: talking about sex.

Virtual reality is a tremendously promising new tool for media. Wearing apparatus such as goggles, headphones, gloves, or even whole body suits, the user can experience a programmed or unfolding world in a fully sensory manner. He can walk through a three-dimensional representation of the Coliseum, swim through the cytoplasm of a red blood cell, or create, with others, an imaginary universe of sight, sound, and even touch. It is no wonder that the technology has sparked imaginations and research spending. And, as with any new technology, many creative people are hard at work applying virtual reality to sex....

Media always serves to promote intimacy. The more linked up we are, the more we know about one another and the more everyone else knows about us. Media not only create lines of communication between people, but it also fosters the chaotic systems devices of feedback, iteration, and phase-locking between members of the societal organism. A population that can communicate with itself is difficult to deceive or control. When push comes to shove, the ultimate form of intimacy for most people is sex. As soon as a new mediating technology emerges from the laboratory, somebody, somewhere, is figuring out how to apply it to sexual intimacy. But while sex provokes technicians to develop new media and people to purchase the technology, it also provides ammunition for those against the new devices and their ability to empower the masses. By equating the power of new media with dangerous or immoral sexual deviancy, forces against these technologies can succeed in stunting or at least suspending their development.

Meta-media activists are virologists whose chief concerns are to bring people toward a greater self-awareness about the power of media and to reawaken awareness of the ancient mediating technologies of spirituality, drugs, sex and magic. These activists are the most modern in their thinking and the most ancient in their belief systems. They are "techno-pagans," who see in this rebirth of nature through technology the best opportunity yet to reclaim the power of the individual. The memes they develop are all geared toward presenting technology as a kind of modern magic that grants access to sexual power, psychedelic vision, and spiritual enlightenment.

Many meta-media activists argue that sex (and, for that matter, spirituality, drugs, and healing arts) was co-opted centuries ago by people in power. Religion and morality were put into place to deprive people of their natural sexual self-expression. People have been made to believe that sex is somehow wrong or dirty and fear that if left to their own devices, they would become libidinous maniacs. Without social controls and safeguards, we would all be raping each other. This imposed sexual tyranny, according to some of these activists, gave lawmakers and moral authorities absolute domination over the people. In constant need of sex, the populace could be controlled by associating sexually provocative imagery with the Church (i.e., medieval Virgin Mary imagery), state, or today, corporate interests. Deprived of healthy sex, men will buy the beer associated with the prettiest models on television. By controlling sexual expression in the media, one can control—to some extent—the direction of cultural focus and societal desire.

Phil Donahue is engaged in the same process, but with an interesting twist. He has chosen to highlight the sexual potential of virtual reality in order to make the subject draw in an audience. But the axis around which he chooses to organize the debate of the show serves to marginalize the technology itself. He presents VR as a fun but potentially dangerous form of pornography and demonstrates the opening section of a sex program on a big screen for his studio audience, who "ooh" and "ahh" as they watch a computer-animated model begin to strip off her clothes.

Despite the protests of the one true virtual reality designer on the panel, who begs everyone to understand that the technology is not exclusively used for pornography, the audience quickly sides against VR on moral grounds. They worry, along with Phil, that once a technology like this can be hooked up to the genitals, people will plug themselves into virtual sex programs and interactive computer sex clubs and masturbate themselves in this way for the rest of their lives. Many people even demand that the technology be outlawed, lest society come apart altogether. The only human being in the room who seems to understand what is going on is R. U. Sirius, the founding editor in chief of the brilliantly provocative meme collection, *Mondo 2000*. Although he is only given two brief opportunities to speak, he calls attention to the fact that the same audience that was so titillated by the sex programs is now condemning them as dangerous. The point went over their heads and Phil cut to a commercial, but Sirius, a savvy media ringleader on the order of Tim Leary or Ken Kesey, had exposed what was really going on in the center ring of this media circus. The audience is not innately against the technology, but embarrassed and ashamed of its own repressed desires.

The lure of sex drew them into the show in the first place. This is how sex is used by what activists call the "state and corporate conglomerates" to direct the attention, spending, and sentiments of the masses. But at the same time, over the course of the show, deeper, even more disempowering social programming emerges, as the audience voluntarily rejects the technology being offered to it. VR becomes the forbidden fruit, and the developers play the role of the serpent offering evil knowledge. What easier tyranny to maintain than over a population actively rejecting the tools that promote the sharing of information? This is how God maintained Eden and how hierarchical systems prevent the natural forces of feedback and iteration from dismantling their top-heavy and inefficient structures.

Activists differ on how intentionally this tyranny is being perpetrated. Some believe it is a conspiratorial effort by a small group of powerful families dating back before ancient Egypt. Others see the situation as a more self-imposed societal restraint—the result of cultural fear and guilt; culture manifests this way because each of us fears his own inner nature. In either case or anywhere in between, the purpose of meta-media activists is the same: to help people reclaim their right to technologies ranging from magic to morphing.

Most media virus formulators are already engaged in this battle in one form or another. The AIDS and smart drugs underground, for example, promote as one of their key memes the right of individuals to determine their own medical needs and not allow medical doctors or a federal bureaucracy to stand in the way of patients and their treatment technologies, or even psychedelics users and their consciousness tools. The Jerry Brown campaign hoped to demonstrate that the telephone is a technology already in place capable of overthrowing an unresponsive political machine. Computer activists try to show that personal computers give us the ability to monitor or even shut down the agencies that work to contain us.

But meta-media activists deal less directly with specific issues and attempt instead to demonstrate the principles of repression and emancipation by making audiences aware of the nature of their relationship to mediation. They want us to see our place in the overall network of reality, whether it is defined technologically, biologically, or even metaphysically. Their model poses that the world we live in is a kind of broth. The soup touches everyone and everything, no matter how dry and separate we are made to feel. The broth can take the form of the physical gases we exchange with the plants in the rain forest, the bits of data we share over fax lines, or the memes we share through mainstream media.

NOTES

1. See Dawkins, Richard, "Universal parasitism and the co-evolution of extended phenotypes," *Whole Earth Review* 62:90, Spring 1989.

POSTSCRIPT

Do New Media Have an Immediate Effect on Our Behaviors and Attitudes?

The selections in this issue raise a number of questions for us to consider as computer-aided technologies and networked systems become a larger part of our lives. Most fundamentally, we need to keep in mind who has access to these technologies and for what purposes. While we can see evidence of computer use and networking in the United States, we need to be mindful of how broadly these technologies and services are distributed. Likewise, we need to remember that the technological "revolution" does not affect all peoples of the world at the same time or even in the same ways.

Technologies and available services can be questioned in terms of personal use, as Turkle does, or they may be considered as aggregate phenomena, as Rushkoff does. Other perspectives from which to consider the issues are with regard to power, access, political economy, and international trade issues.

The questions about personal use of media, however, can be the subject of much introspection. What are your attitudes about technology? Do you welcome it, fear it, or take an apathetic view toward the way technology offers alternative ways of doing things? Can you choose to ignore it?

Two books by Sherry Turkle—*The Second Self: Computers and the Human Spirit* (Simon & Schuster, 1984) and *Life on the Screen: Identity in the Age of the Internet* (Simon & Schuster, 1995)—are of particular importance for exploring questions of self and identity. Douglas Rushkoff's works, including *Cyberia: Life in the Trenches of Hyperspace* (Ballantine Books, 1994), continue the analysis that Rushkoff presents in his selection here.

Textbooks that incorporate issues of technology theory, distribution, and related issues include Jarice Hanson's *Connections: Technologies of Communication* (HarperCollins, 1994) and *Communications Media in the Information Society* by Joseph Straubhaar and Robert LaRose (Wadsworth, 1996).

CONTRIBUTORS
TO THIS VOLUME

EDITORS

ALISON ALEXANDER is a professor in and chair of the Department of Telecommunications in the Henry W. Grady College of Journalism and Mass Communication at the University of Georgia in Athens, Georgia. She received a B.A. in education from Marshall University in 1971, an M.A. in communication from the University of Kentucky in 1974, and a Ph.D. in communication from Ohio State University in 1979. Her areas of research and publication include television and the family and children's interpretation of media. She is coeditor of *Media Economics: Theory and Practice* (Lawrence Erlbaum, 1993) and former editor of *Journal of Broadcasting and Electronic Media*.

JARICE HANSON is a professor in the Department of Communication at the University of Massachusetts–Amherst, where she also heads the Public Information Project. She received a B.A. in speech and performing arts and a B.A. in English at Northeastern Illinois University in 1976, and she received an M.A. and a Ph.D. from the Department of Radio-Television-Film at Northwestern University in 1977 and 1979, respectively. She is the author of *Connections: Technologies of Communication* (HarperCollins, 1994) and coauthor, with Dr. Uma Narula, of *New Communication Technologies in Developing Countries* (Lawrence Erlbaum, 1990). She is also coeditor, with David J. Maxcy, of *Sources: Notable Selections in Mass Media*, 2d ed. (Dushkin/McGraw-Hill, 1999). Her research focuses on technology, policy, and media images.

STAFF

David Dean   List Manager
David Brackley   Senior Developmental Editor
Juliana Poggio   Associate Developmental Editor
Rose Gleich   Administrative Assistant
Brenda S. Filley   Production Manager
Juliana Arbo   Typesetting Supervisor
Diane Barker   Proofreader
Lara Johnson   Design/Advertising Coordinator
Richard Tietjen   Publishing Systems Manager

AUTHORS

GEORGE J. ANNAS is the Edward R. Utley Professor of Law and Medicine at Boston University's Schools of Medicine and Public Health in Boston, Massachusetts. He is also director of Boston University's Law, Medicine, and Ethics Program and chair of the Department of Health Law. His publications include *Judging Medicine* (Humana Press, 1988) and *Standard of Care: The Law of American Bioethics* (Oxford University Press, 1993).

BEN H. BAGDIKIAN, an award-winning journalist and educator, is a former dean of the Graduate School of Journalism at the University of California, Berkeley. He has also been assistant managing editor of network news for the *Washington Post* and a contributing editor of *The Saturday Evening Post*. His book *In the Midst of Plenty: The Poor in America* (Beacon Press, 1964) had a substantial impact on shaping the public's and the federal government's views on poverty.

RUSS BAKER is a freelance writer based in New York City who often writes on issues of media and press policy.

TED BECKER is an author who writes extensively on issues of citizen activism and teledemocracy. His articles have appeared in a variety of publications, including *American Political Science Review* and *The Futurist*. He has also written and reviewed several books about telecommunications.

JOHN E. CALFEE is a resident scholar at the American Enterprise Institute in Washington, D.C. He is a former Federal Trade Commission economist, and he is the author of *Fear of Persuasion: A New Perspective on Advertising and Regulation* (Agora, 1997).

MILTON CHEN is director of the Center for Education and Lifelong Learning at KQED-TV in San Francisco, California. He is the author of *The Smart Parent's Guide to Kids' TV* (KQED Books, 1994).

MICHELLE COTTLE is a staff editor for *The Washington Monthly,* for which she occasionally writes key features.

JOSEPH R. DiFRANZA is an M.D. in the Department of Family Practice at the University of Massachusetts Medical School in Fitchburg, Massachusetts. He and his colleagues have written several articles on the effects of tobacco advertising on children.

LEONARD DOWNIE, JR., is executive editor of the *Washington Post*.

ROBERT N. FREEMAN is a media concentration research project manager at the Columbia Institute for Tele-Information.

PHILIP ELMER-DEWITT is assistant managing editor of *Time* magazine. He has been writing about science and technology for *Time* since 1982 and has produced over 450 news and feature stories on subjects ranging from in-vitro fertilization to computer sex.

MICHAEL GARTNER, former president of NBC News, is editor of the *Ames Daily Tribune,* a daily newspaper near Des Moines, Iowa. His 36-year-long career in print journalism includes 14 years with the *Wall Street Journal.* He received a J.D. degree from New York University and is a member of the bar associations in New York and Iowa.

JAMES W. GENTRY is a professor in the Department of Marketing, College of Business Administration, at the University of Nebraska–Lincoln. He received his Ph.D. from Indiana University.

CHRISTOPHER GEORGES is editor of *The Washington Monthly*. He writes frequently on politics and government.

DONALD GRAHAM is the publisher of the *Washington Post*.

PHILIP JONES GRIFFITHS has been a photographer since 1961. A former president of Magnum Photos, he has covered the Algerian, Vietnamese, and Yom Kippur Wars, among others.

KATHLEEN HALL JAMIESON is dean of the Annenberg School of Communications at the University of Pennsylvania. Her publications include *The Interplay of Influence* (Wadsworth, 1988), coauthored with Karlyn Kohrs Campbell, and *Packaging the Presidency: A History and Criticism of Presidential Campaign Advertising*, 2d ed. (Oxford University Press, 1992).

JON KATZ is a media critic and novelist. He is a contributing editor of *Wired* magazine, and he has written for *GQ*, the *New York Times, Rolling Stone, New York*, and other magazines. He was listed as one of the country's most influential media critics in a survey conducted by the Gannett Center's Freedom Forum Foundation in 1995. He is the author of the "Media Rant" column on HotWired's The Netizen. He is also the author of *Media Rants: Postpolitics in the Digital Nation* (Hardwired, 1997) and *Sign Off* (Bantam Books, 1991).

S. ROBERT LICHTER is president of the Center for Media and Public Affairs and an adjunct professor of government at Georgetown University. He has written extensively for the *Washington Post*, the *Wall Street Journal*, the *Los Angeles Times*, and the *Christian Science Monitor*.

JOSEPH LIEBERMAN, senator (D) from Connecticut, is chairman of the Democratic Leadership Council.

MARY C. MARTIN is an assistant professor in the Department of Marketing, Belk College of Business Administration, at the University of North Carolina at Charlotte. She received her Ph.D. from the University of Nebraska–Lincoln.

ROBERT W. McCHESNEY is an associate professor in the School of Journalism and Mass Communication at the University of Wisconsin–Madison. He is the author of *Telecommunications, Mass Media, and Democracy: The Battle for Control of U.S. Broadcasting, 1928–1935* (Oxford University Press, 1994) and coauthor, with Edward S. Herman, of *The Global Media: The New Missionaries of Global Capitalism* (Cassell, 1997).

ELI M. NOAM is director of the Institute for Tele-Information and a professor of finance and economics at Columbia University's Graduate School of Business.

RICHARD E. NOYES is political studies director of the Center for Media and Public Affairs, where he has worked since 1987. His current project is directing the center's ElectionWatch project on media coverage of the 1996 presidential campaign. He holds an M.A. in government from Georgetown University and a B.A. in political science from George Washington University.

PATRICK O'HEFFERNAN is a senior fellow and assistant to the director at the Center for International Strategy, Technology, and Policy at the Georgia Institute of Technology.

RICHARD W. OLIVER is a professor of management at the Owen Graduate

School of Management at Vanderbilt University in Nashville, Tennessee. He received a Ph.D. from the State University of New York at Buffalo, and he has been vice president of marketing at Northern Telecom, Inc.

KATHA POLLITT, a poet and an essayist, is associate editor for *The Nation*. Best known for her book of poetry *Antarctic Traveller* (Alfred A. Knopf, 1982), she has also written about the legal and moral ramifications of important social practices and decisions.

NEIL POSTMAN, founder of New York University's Program in Media Ecology, is a professor of media ecology and chair of the Department of Communication Arts at New York University in New York City, where he has been teaching since 1962. He has published 18 books and over 100 articles for the scholarly and popular press on media, culture, and education, one of which, *Amusing Ourselves to Death* (Viking Penguin, 1985), has been translated into eight languages and has sold 200,000 copies worldwide. In 1986 he received the George Orwell Award for Clarity in Language from the National Council of Teachers of English.

DOUGLAS RUSHKOFF, an author, journalist, and programmer, contributes regularly to several magazines and newspapers, including *Esquire* and the *Wall Street Journal*. He is the editor of *GenX Reader* (Ballantine Books, 1994) and the author of *Cyberia: Life in the Trenches of Hyperspace* (Ballantine Books, 1994).

ROLAND T. RUST holds a Ph.D. from the University of North Carolina–Chapel Hill. A professor of marketing, he is area head of marketing and director of the Center for Services Marketing at the Owen Graduate School of Management at Vanderbilt University in Nashville, Tennessee.

BRUCE W. SANFORD is a partner in the law firm Baker and Hostetler in Washington, D.C. He is also general counsel to the Society of Professional Journalists.

BARRY SCHECK is a defense attorney and a law professor. In the Innocence Project at Cardozo Law School of Yeshiva University, he works on the viability of DNA as evidence in trials. He was also a member of the defense teams for O. J. Simpson and Louise Woodward.

RUTH SHALIT is associate editor of *The New Republic*. She specializes in media organizations and social issues.

JACQUELINE SHARKEY is an award-winning investigative reporter and a frequent contributor to *American Journalism Review* and *The Nation*. She also teaches journalism at the University of Arizona.

WARREN P. STROBEL is the White House correspondent for the *Washington Times*. He is the author of *Late-Breaking Foreign Policy: The News Media's Influence on Peace Operations* (Institute of Peace Press, 1997).

SHERRY TURKLE is a professor in the Massachusetts Institute of Technology's Program in Science, Technology, and Society. She received her doctorate in sociology and psychology from Harvard University. She is the author of *The Second Self: Computers and the Human Spirit* (Simon & Schuster, 1984) and *Life on the Screen: Identity in the Age of the Internet* (Simon & Schuster, 1995).

AMY WALDMAN writes regularly for *The Washington Monthly* on a variety of topics, especially on issues of media, advertising, and the impact of popular culture on society.

GEORGETTE WANG is a professor in and director of the Graduate Institute of Telecommunications at the National Chung Cheng University in Jiayee, Taiwan. Among her extensive publications on media in Asia is her edited book *Treading Different Paths: Informatization in Asian Nations* (Ablex, 1994).

JULIA WILKINS is a special education teacher in Buffalo, New York. She received her master's degree in social policy from the University of Bristol, England, and she is the author of two books and several articles.

MARIE WINN is an author who has written 12 books for parents and children, including *Children Without Childhood* (Pantheon Books, 1983).

INDEX

ABC (American Broadcasting Company), 295. *See also* Disney/ABC/Cap Cities

Aberlich, Mike, 182, 183

acetaminophen, 176–177

ACLU. *See* American Civil Liberties Union

ACLU v. Reno, 219, 220

addiction, television and, 27–28

adolescents, controversy over emphasis on body image as harmful to females only and, 58–66

advertising, 257–258; controversy over emphasis on body in, as harmful to females only, 59–61, 62; controversy over ethics of, 168–186; controversy over media coverage of political campaigns and, 146–164; controversy over restricting tobacco, 112–126; controversy over revolution in, 270–284; media sensationalism and, 199

Advil, 176–177

adwatches, media coverage of political campaigns and, 148, 157, 159, 161

affirmative action, controversy over newspapers as insensitive to minorities and, 78–84

African Americans. *See* blacks

Alaskan Television Town Meeting, 293

Alter, Jonathan, 164, 192, 195

Alternative for Washington, 293

America Online, 10, 13

American Civil Liberties Union (ACLU), 100, 219, 220

American Lawyer, 135

American Society of Magazine Editors (ASME), 181, 185–186

American Society of Newspaper Editors, 83–84, 200

Anderson, Daniel, 31

Anderson, Kurt, 179, 184

Annas, George J., on restricting tobacco advertising, 119–126

anonymity, controversy over naming of rape victims and, 96–107

Arnett, Peter, 46

Asia, controversy over globalization of media industries "homogenizing" media content and, 313–314, 315–316, 319, 320

Asian Americans, controversy over newspapers as insensitive to minorities and, 80

AT&T, 180, 262, 280, 281, 283

attention spans, influence of television on, of children, 31

Auletta, Ken, 180

Australia, 315, 320

baby boomers, aging of, and increased vanity in men, 68

Bacon, Kenneth, 46, 52

Bagdikian, Ben, H. 195, 261, 306; on effects of concentration of ownership in media industries on media content, 252–260

Baker, James A., III, 47

Baker, Russ, on ethics of advertising, 178–186

Barlow, John Perry, 216

Barnes and Noble, 311

Barone Center, 158

Barry, Marion, 78, 87, 89

Beavis and Butt-head, 236

Becker, Ted, on teledemocracy, 290–294

behavior, controversy over influence of new media on, 324–337

Bell Atlantic, 262, 281, 283

Bennett, William, 231–232, 233

Berri, Nabbih, 39

Bettmann Archives, 259

blacks: and controversy over newspapers as insensitive to minorities, 78–90; juvenile crime rate and, 238, 240–241, 245

Bless This House, 231

Blitzer, Wolf, 48

Blythin, Edward, 137

body image, controversy over emphasis on, as harmful to females only, 58–73

Bono, Sonny, 196

book publishing industry, 311

Borders, 311

Bosnia, controversy over influence of mass media on foreign policy and, 50, 51–52

Boucher, Richard, 49

Bowman, Patricia, controversy over naming rape victims and, 96–107

Boycott Anorexic Marketing (BAM), 59, 66

boycotts, advertisers and, 184–185

Bradlee, Ben, 86

brain development, influence of television on, 30–31

Brennan, William, Jr., 139–140

Brill, Steve, 135

Britain. *See* Great Britain

Broder, David, 158

Bronfenbrenner, Urie, 23

Brown, Helen Gurley, 179

bullet theory, 315

bulletin-board systems (BBSs), pornography and, 211, 213, 215

Burger, Warren, 136, 137–138, 139